National Identities and Post-Americanist Narratives

New Americanists   *A Series Edited by Donald E. Pease*

NATIONAL IDENTITIES AND

Donald E. Pease, Editor

POST-AMERICANIST NARRATIVES

DUKE UNIVERSITY PRESS   Durham and London 1994

© 1994 Duke University Press

All rights reserved

Printed in the United States of America on
acid-free paper ∞

Library of Congress Cataloging-in-Publication Data
appear on the last printed page of this book.

The text of this book originally was published
without the present preface, index, and essays by
Lindberg and Rowe as Vol. 19, No. 1 of *boundary 2*.
The essay by Lindberg originally was published in
Vol. 20, No. 2 of *boundary 2*.

Contents

Preface

The idea for this volume germinated in the wake of three events—the breakdown of the Cold War, the breakup of the Soviet Empire, and the "emergence of global democracy"—whose impact on global politics was registered in the collective recognition of a postnational world. In its making heterogeneous cultural histories available to public and scholarly debate, multiculturalism was representative of this new political formation. It no longer authorized belief in an Americanness that somehow contained a plurality that it also transcended. In place of the melting pot capable of assimilating immigrants, the United States was understood as but a single unit in a global network.

To facilitate the production of an alternative to the national narrative confirmative of the "melting pot," I have gathered essays in this volume that trace the grand narrative of U.S. nationalism from its inception in antebellum slave narratives to its dissolution in the aftermath of the Cold War. The contributors examine the various cultural, political, and historical sources—colonial literature, mass movements, health epidemics, mass spectacle, transnational corporations, super-weapons—out of which this narrative was constructed, and propose different understandings of nationality and identity following in its wake.

Except for the essays by Rowe and Lindberg, this volume first appeared as a special issue of *boundary 2* (vol. 19, no. 1). For their help with this volume, I extend my gratitude to the contributors as well as the entire editorial collective of *boundary 2*. I am particularly indebted to Paul Bové, its present editor, and Meg Sachse, its managing editor, for seeing this volume into print as a *boundary 2* volume, and to Reynolds Smith for his enthusiastic and loyal support for the New Americanists Series.

National Identities, Postmodern Artifacts, and Postnational Narratives

Donald E. Pease

In my introduction to the first volume on New Americanists,[1] I constructed an account of the phenomenon by way of an argument with Frederick Crews, who, in a critical review of New Americanists, identified himself as an established representative of the field of American Studies and denied New Americanists official recognition. I understood the precondition for a successful argument with Crews to be the conceptualization of an alternative disciplinary field, whose practitioners were constructed out of assumptions wholly different from Crews's. For the sake of this argument, I constructed a purely fictive theoretical scenario, assigning to Crews's field of American Studies a crisis in what I called its "field-Imaginary" (wherein abided the "field's fundamental syntax—its tacit assumptions, convictions, primal words, and the charged relations binding them together" [11]), which had *already* resulted in a dramatic transformation in the self-understanding of American Studies; that is, a complete overhauling of its ruling assump-

1. See "New Americanists: Revisionist Interventions into the Canon," a special issue of *boundary 2* 17, no. 1 (Spring 1990). All quotations from this issue are cited parenthetically by page number only.

tions, defining consensus, certified practitioners, as well as their interpellation, the complex process of ideological linkage, whereby they were constituted as New Americanists.

I intended by way of this scenario a model of American Studies able
to displace Crews as the field's official representative. But, as some critics of the volume and several members of the *boundary 2* collective have
observed, I also thereby confirmed one of Crews's central assumptions,
namely, that the field of American Studies was monolithic, unidimensional,
and monocultural. In proposing a national meta-narrative able to discrimi-
nate those who could be included along its chain of substitutions from those
who could not, I had reconstructed Crews after the image of the series of
figures—African Americanists, feminist Americanists, Chicano Americanists, Asian Americanists, gay Americanists—he had excluded from his field
of American Studies and thereby had implied that all of these "minority
figures" had been constructed out of commensurable assumptions.

In constructing a field whose practitioners were identified with the
assumptions of a meta-narrative, I had simply replaced one grand narrative
of American Studies with another. In an unintended reprise of his conceptual model, I had reconstructed Crews's American Studies as if it were a
minority discourse in need of the new field of American Studies to become a
recognizable object of knowledge. Following his banishment from the newly
nationalized narrative, I had redescribed Crews as a social materiality unrepresentable within the new field and had left unexamined the process
whereby that field was delimited from its environment. Although I had asserted the New Americanists' ability to transform literary masterworks into
social forces, I nevertheless associated Crews with a social context wholly
separable from the new academic field. In so doing, I had reaffirmed one of
Crews's fundamental tenets: the necessity of a national meta-narrative as
the paradigmatic dimension necessary for a recognizably New Americanist
subject/object of knowledge.

This oversight followed from the failure to explain this crucial passage
from the first introduction:

> In denying the separation constitutive of their field, however, New
> Americanists have changed the field-Imaginary of American Studies.
> The political unconscious of the primal scene of their New Historicist
> readings embodies *both* the *repressed relationship between* the lit-
> erary and the political and the *disenfranchised groups previously
> unrepresentable in this relationship*. And as conduits for the return
> of figures and materials repressed through the denial of the rela-

> tionship of the field to the public world, New Americanists occupy a
> double relation. For as *liaisons between* cultural and public realms,
> they are at once within the field yet external to it. (31)

An adequate understanding of the New Americanists' status as liaisons between academic disciplines and U.S. publics would require an account of
their emergence from and continued interconnection with different emancipatory social movements.

The essays I have gathered for the second volume on New Americanists initiate such an account. They configure individually and collectively
*post*national narratives as the surfaces on which New Americanists have
constructed their identities. The term *postnational* indicates New Americanists' multiple interpellations: their different identifications with the disciplinary apparatuses in the new American Studies, as well as with social
movements comprised of the "disenfranchised groups" already cited.

These social movements emerged with the collective recognition of
the marked disequilibrium in the allocation of social empowerments and resources in the national narrative. The national narrative produced national
identities by way of a social symbolic order that systematically separated
an abstract, disembodied subject from resistant materialities, such as race,
class, and gender. This universal body authorizes the discrimination of figures who can be integrated within the national symbolic order and matters (of race, gender, class) external to it. Because the coherence of the
national narrative depends upon the integrity of its universal subject, that
figure is transformed into a tacit assumption and descends into the social
unconscious. Instead of accepting this assumption as the basis for their
social identities, the socially disenfranchised figures within emancipatory
political movements understand that the universality of the national identity
depends on their externality for its integrity. In the wake of this recognition,
these movement figures offered themselves up not for integration within the
national narrative but, by way of what I am calling postnational narratives,
actively contested its social arrangements.

This contestation between social demands developed within political
movements and a nation-state's power to misrecognize them did not originate with New Americanists; rather, it originated from within the discourse
of the Enlightenment. The term *national narrative* itself refers to the process
whereby the discourse of the Enlightenment produced particulars—nation-
states—out of universal norms: Reason, Equality, Social Justice, Liberty.
Acting as agents of the state, these national narratives constructed imaginary relations to actual sociopolitical conditions to effect imagined commu-

nities called national peoples. The image repertoire productive of the U.S. national community can be ascertained through a recitation of the key terms in the national meta-narrative commonly understood to be descriptive of that community. Those images interconnect an exceptional national subject (American Adam) with a representative national scene (Virgin Land) and an exemplary national motive (errand into the wilderness). The composite result of the interaction of these images was the mythological entity—Nature's Nation—whose citizens believed, by way of the supreme fiction called natural law, that the ruling assumptions of their national compact (Liberty, Equality, Social Justice) could be understood as indistinguishable from the sovereign power creative of nature.

In its representation of the transition from a proto-national to a national community, the national narrative proposed a scene of emancipation, wherein a captive people liberated themselves from a tyrannical power. That scene resulted in an utterly equal (because universally abstract and disembodied) subject position devoid of any particularity whatsoever. But alongside the nexus of belongingness established for the national community, the national narrative represented other peoples (women, blacks, "foreigners," the homeless) from whom the property of nationness had been removed altogether and upon whose differences from them the national people depended for the construction of the universality of their norms. When understood from within the context of the construction of an imagined national community, the negative class, race, and gender categories of these subject peoples were not a historical aberration but a structural necessity for the construction of a national narrative whose coherence depended upon the internal opposition between Nature's Nation and peoples understood to be constructed of a "different nature."

Whereas the national narrative resulted in the assimilation of differences to the self-sameness of ruling assumptions, whose universality was predicated upon their inapplicability for peoples construed as of "another Nature," the postnational narratives dismantle this opposition. The agents for this dismantling were the national subject peoples, figures of race, class, and gender, who had been previously interpellated within the hegemonic category of disqualified social agency. As motives for changing existing social models, the figures of race, class, and gender moved from the status of objects of social regulation within the national narrative into performative powers, postnational forces able to change that narrative's assumptions.[2]

2. Throughout this discussion of nationalism and narration, I have depended on the work of Ernesto Laclau, Chantal Mouffe, Edward Said, Homi K. Bhabha, Doris Sommer,

Strictly speaking, these postnational forces for social change are neither wholly intrinsic to the previously subjugated social categories of race, class, and gender nor reducible to a capability external to them. Idealized stereotypes of race and gender were often reaction formations designed to combat negative stereotypes but which in fact corroborated the same impulse to universalize social norms. Postnational forces understand every social category as the ongoing antagonism between internalized models and external forces. As such, they are productive of an internal divide (the contamination of the excluded/external), whereby the structures underwriting the stability of the national narrative can undergo transformations. At this divide, the figures who had been reproduced as subordinated objects and denied identification with the meta-national person could engage in ongoing struggles over the cultural models upon which cultural agents and their actions could be based. As I have indicated, this internal division of fully integrated and external matters is a structural feature of the social symbolic system. The national narrative sustains its coherence by transforming internal divisions into the symbolic demand that the subjects conscripted within its narrativity misrecognize the figures it excludes as simulacra of themselves. But when these figures surge up at these internal divides, as unintegrated externalities, they expose national identity as an artifact rather than a tacit assumption, a purely contingent social construction rather than a meta-social universal.

As a universally believed assumption, the meta-social subject underwriting the national symbolic order subsisted within the social unconscious. There, it guaranteed the narrativity, the chain of substitutions underwriting the social symbolic order, by demanding that national citizens constitute themselves out of its assumptions wholly and without residue. At the internal divide, where every given is exposed as an antagonism between the power to integrate into self-sameness and different matters, this deeply held assumption was drawn up to the narrative surface by forces that refused to be beholden any longer. Consequently, the paradigmatic dimension of the social unconscious guaranteeing the hermeneutic depth of the national narrative was flattened into postnational surfaces. On these surfaces, the energies that previously had bound the national identities, which could never wholly embody them, to the national symbolic order were recathected at the divide, thereby activating intranational relations between previously subjected and national peoples. At this intranational boundary,

---

Jonathan Arac, Simon Durang, Timothy Brennan, Benedict Anderson, Tom Nairn, Paul Smith, Alain Touraine, Geoffrey Bennington, Sneja Gunew, and Fredric Jameson.

6

the national subjects, who had previously derived their sense of identity from incomplete identification with the meta-social subject of the national narrative, could become dislocated from this structure and could rediscover national identity itself as a permanent instability, an endless antagonism between figures integrated within ever changing social imaginaries and singularities forever external to them. As a result, the nationalist assumptions that had been understood as preconditions for the constitution of a coherent national identity became post*national*, provisional strategies, subject to the ongoing revisions of movement politics.

This revision in the genealogy of national identity rediscovers its source in social movements rather than national narratives and entails a different understanding of the complex process whereby the New Americanists within social movements became figures within a new field of American Studies. In the introduction to the first volume, I described New Historicism as the disciplinary agency that returns questions of class, race, and gender to the field of American Studies:

> When a New Historicist makes explicit the relationship between an emancipatory struggle taking place outside the academy and an argument she is conducting within the field, the relationship between instruction in the discipline's practices and participation in emancipatory political movements can no longer be described as imaginary. Such *realized* relations undermine the separation of the public world from the cultural sphere and join, as Jonathan Arac puts it "the nexus of classroom, discipline, and profession to such political areas as those of gender, race, and class as well as nation." (19)

But in joining the "political areas" of race and class to nation, the new discipline of American Studies also, I must now add, constructed a reproducible pedagogy grounded in the construction of a disciplinary doublet: the dominative/subjugative subject. The subjects of knowledge constructed out of disciplinary norms never completely work through the double bind interconnecting domination and subjection. When construed as an objectification of the disciplinary norms in the field's positive unconscious, a New Americanist subject can misrecognize his/her determination by those norms as the power to subjugate others to its determinations and can further misrecognize the power to discipline another as his/her own freedom from *external* determination. The rhetorical figure enabling a New Americanist's misrecognition of his/her determination as absolute freedom from social determinants is *canonicity*.

The subtitle of the earlier volume, "Revisionist Interventions into the Canon," proposed an understanding of social change as if it simply entailed a transformation of a disciplinary field, American Studies, whose coherence had been previously guaranteed by the canonical works Americanists had integrated. Referring to an aspect of the work unrepresentable either as a formal quality or a historical force, canonicity names the irreducibility of a literary work to either intrinsic aesthetic features or extrinsic social forces. As the presence/absence of what can neither be internalized nor stipulated as external, canonicity is productive of literary historicity. Literary history refers to a complex temporal process wherein the absolute singularity of pure canonicity takes place within a discourse that compels its reiterability as generic conventions and literary periods. Literary history sutures canonicity to the generic conventions productive of heterogeneous literary discourses, and it stages, at another level of analytic density, subreption of those rules as the instantiation of different literary periods.[3]

Understood from within the social (as contrasted with the disciplinary) logic of American Studies, canonicity enables a New Americanist to misrecognize the norms constitutive of field identity as the canonical value of a literary work. This misrecognition indirectly confirms the universal value of a New Americanist identity. Canonicity binds the New Americanist to the norms informing disciplinary practices by designating the historicity of canonical literary works as the only appropriate sociohistorical site for those practices. When so defined, however, canonicity also projects a New Americanist who is identified with the assumptions of a national metanarrative rather than, as I had previously argued, one who is disassociated. If literary canonicity seals the space distinguishing Americanist literary historicity from extrinsic contamination, how could the national narrative become *post*national?

An adequate response requires a reconsideration of the crucial difference between the national narrative and the postnational narrative surfaces. Earlier, I located that difference in contrastive attitudes toward the hegemonic categories of race, class, and gender. Within the national narrative, these categories are declared resolvable social problems and result in a social process whereby the subjects constructed out of these categories are identified as universal norms. In postnational narratives, that universalizing

3. For an extremely important reading of the figurality of canonicity that has profoundly influenced this discussion, see Bill Readings, "Canon and On: From Concept to Figure," *Journal of the American Academy of Religion* 57, no. 1 (1989): 149–72.

process was redescribed as dependent for its efficacy on an overcoming of surface differences between dominant and dominated social groups. But if a national identity recognizes the difference between the meta-social person with whom he had identified himself and what he discovers, in an intranational encounter with alternative social objectifications of national materials, he could have become, then this person—formerly gendered "male," now gendered "differently"—discovers s/he is dislocated from his/her national identity and, in this surplus historicity, discovers alternative constructions. In order to achieve this discovery, New Americanists must understand themselves as multiply interpellated—within social movements as well as academic fields. As the subject effects of social movements, New Americanists cannot be interpellated within a national narrative understood now as a reiterative identification with disqualified assumptions.

Primary identification with the sociopolitical strategies of social movements, rather than the academic discipline they practice, leads to a very different description of what it means to be constituted as a New Americanist than the one I advanced in the first volume. There, I proposed a field-Imaginary as a depth dimension housing the unquestioned norms authorizing these practices. The field-Imaginary, I had argued, was related to the field-Symbolic as paradigm is to syntagm; that is, the inability fully to reconstitute the field's delimiting assumptions in its disciplinary objects (re)activated the desire to effect this impossible union as the sensed incompleteness of the disciplinary task. As the *positive* unconscious for the discipline, these deeply held assumptions could not be realized as either an *intrinsic* literary value or an *extrinsic* historical achievement. But they could be misrecognized as the *canonicity* of a literary work. The canonical work, in turn, enabled the practitioner of American Studies to understand the incommensurability between the historicity of a canonical literary work and that of sociopolitical events as the boundary separating the two realms.

Stated as a disproportion, when national historical events were represented within an Americanist masterwork, they lost their historical specificity and became part of that incommensurate literary realm where national assumptions became canonical values. When, however, canonical literary objects became involved in social movements, their canonicity became differently historicized as their capacity to disengage national identities from already realized social and political norms and to indicate incommensurate social values. The national meta-narrative interpellated a subject within a self-referential social symbolic order, but emancipatory social movements exposed the national meta-narrative as an ideological construct productive of imaginary relations to social movements and subsequently reactivated the divide between a fully objectified national identity and performative capacities that emerged with the consciousness of its partiality.

Any "I" interpellated within the national meta-narrative depended for its integrity upon its capacity to exclude externals, as well as to integrate an identity. Unlike other American identities, New Americanists subsist at the intersection between interpellation and exclusion. At this divide, they are able to recognize as their disciplinary practice the sheer constructedness of every one of the givens of the national narrative.

Having described the origin of the New Americanists in social movements, I must redescribe the emergence of New Historicism within the New Americanists' field as an occasion to produce as strategic resources the regimes of truth with which they would have otherwise colonized the ongoing negotiations of social movements. At this intersection between ongoing social movements and the new field of American Studies, post-national surfaces are traversed by the power to produce, in the exchange between disciplinary canonicity and social historicity, as many different instantiations of national identity as ongoing social movements demand.

In gathering essays for this second volume on New Americanists, I have displaced these practices from the field of American Studies to the ongoing negotiations that take place at the boundaries connecting that field with different social movements. To indicate the differences between the figures interpellated within the social field, guaranteed by what I have called the national meta-narrative and figures interpellated within strictly provisional structures of ongoing social movements, I have described the latter interpellations as *postmodern artifacts*. In the terms of the preceding discussion, a postmodern artifact refers to the activity whereby the fundamental assumptions that guaranteed the givens within the grand narratives (no matter whether national, local, or modernist) are identified as contestations between the already constituted and social materials not necessarily reducible to, but nevertheless apparent in, the internally contested categories of class, race, and gender. The redefinition of fundamentals as the repression of external social matters draws these assumptions from out of the depths of the political unconscious to narrative surfaces whose intensities are derived from the reinvestment of the affects binding metonyms and synecdoches to the metaphoricity of their unrepresentable assumptions. Here the national identities, bound to repeat the impossible task of the complete realization of unrepresentable assumptions, become detached from the narrativity of the national meta-narrative and become reattached to the ongoing social movements enabling their disassociation.

In "Nationalism, Hypercanonization, and *Huckleberry Finn*," Jonathan Arac locates the emergence of the concept of "literature" in the nineteenth century from within a contested discursive field occupied by national and local, as well as personal, narratives. The elevation of literature into a relatively autonomous realm was partially the result of what he calls "hypercanonization," a process whereby the national meta-narrative saturates a literary work with allegorical force and thereby disassociates it from either specific readers or particular historical issues. By resituating this hypercanonized monument within the highly contested space it shares with these other narratives, Arac rehistoricizes *Huckleberry Finn*, returning it to the scene of historical accountability it shares with these other social discourses.

In newly historicizing this hypercanonized artifact, Arac removes it from the realm of the literarily self-referential, a milieu literary modernism would later provide with a social logic. Literary modernists explain literature's value in terms of its immunity to commodification, no matter whether economic or hermeneutic. In "*As I Lay Dying* in the Machine Age," John Matthews disconfirms this claim by arguing that literary modernism is in dialectical relationship with the logic of commodity exchange. He describes the historical by-products of these warring logics of production as the New South, the New Criticism, and Faulkner's novels. By way of a rigorous analysis of the social text sedimented within the literary artifact, Matthews finds traces of the empirical within Faulkner's thoroughly aestheticized social reality.

Matthews deploys Adorno's notion of negative dialectic against literary modernism's putative autonomy and thereby precipitates a residue of the commodification process Faulkner's modernism had resistively internalized. But in "The Politics of Nonidentity: A Genealogy," Ross Posnock deploys Adorno's negative dialectics to oppose the surplus cooptative power of a society of consumption. After locating correlative versions of this politics of nonidentification in the writings of Henry James, Randolph Bourne, and John Dewey, Posnock persuasively demonstrates the ways in which these literary antisystems at once prefigure and outdistance the neopragmatism in left and right New Historicism. In his account of its resistance to all efforts at totalization, Posnock directs the politics of nonidentity against all forms of neo-Hegelianism (whether Marxian or neo-Foucauldian) that are able to reduce objects to concepts without leaving a residue, and he resists, as well, the capitalist logic of fungibility, which erases all traces of social difference.

Arac, Matthews, and Posnock all refind a source of historical resistance in the canonicity that otherwise would have interpellated literary works within the historicity kept by high modernism. Robert Corber, Lauren Berlant, Elizabeth Freeman, Alan Nadel, Rob Wilson, and Patrick O'Donnell examine the different social logics that inhabit the national narrative in the epoch of the Cold War. As a restorative framing of the relations between national identities and historical events, the Cold War impersonates the social logic of an emancipatory social movement. Claiming the power to decolonize national peoples subjected to foreign imperialism, the Cold War narrative effectively masks its own totalizing powers by projecting them onto the imperial Soviets. By opportunistically recoding every social force understood as external to its powers of interpellation, the Cold War narrative redescribes the national subject peoples—Chicanos, blacks, women, gays—it utterly subordinates to its logic as un-American, imperialist forces. Because gay Americans remain to this day a social category denied citizenship, I have chosen in the essays by Robert Corber and Lauren Berlant and Elizabeth Freeman to develop the problematic of national identity intensively, rather than extensively.

In "Resisting History: *Rear Window* and the Limits of the Postwar Settlement," Robert Corber explains "the homosexual totalitarian" as a political fiction constructed during the postwar era and designed to suture a U.S. citizen's psychic impulses together with political norms. By assigning all forms of domination to the totalitarian and all forms of submission to the homosexual component of this composite scapegoat, the political fiction tries to allay the suspicion that an identity constructed out of U.S. psychosocial norms might entail submission to a dominant power. This fiction thereby constructs a hegemonic narrative that Corber calls "the postwar settlement," which purchases citizens' consent to social control.

In a nuanced analysis of *Rear Window*, Corber demonstrates how this political fiction redescribes U.S. citizens' historical relation to political reality as their implicit homosexualization (which is to say, their subordination to foreign control), with the consequence that U.S. political identity is understood in the postwar years as a complete separation from a political past. Through a rigorous interpretation of the ways in which the national security state reinterpellates both the liberal and the conservative subjects within narrative positions that appropriate their function as spectators into the surveillance needs of the national security, Corber concludes that the two positions differ only in the affect applied to the objects of the gaze. Conservatives continue to identify Communists and homosexuals as security risks, while liberals transform them into objects of spectatorial pleasure.

Whereas Corber argues that U.S. national security is sustained through a citizen's distance from the spectacle he surveys, in "Queer Nationality," Lauren Berlant and Elizabeth Freeman demonstrate the ways in which the totalizing logic of spectacle can reduce nationality itself into a spectacular commodity citizens consume as national pleasures. According to Berlant and Freeman, the logic of national spectacle depends upon figures most resistant to interpellation within the national narrative's power to replenish the production and consumption of pleasure. At a time in which every other cultural stereotype had already been naturalized, Berlant and Freeman explain that the national spectacle depends upon "queer nationality" to intensify the pleasure of nationness. The politics of homophobia surrounding the AIDS epidemic propose a different motive for the gay community's construction of nationality. After a series of accounts of the scenarios out of which gays construct their relationships to nationness, Berlant and Freeman conclude their essay with an analysis of a lesbian counterinterpellation of a national subject from out of the heterospectacle that otherwise would completely ingest the gay national body as a spectatorial pleasure.

While Berlant and Freeman discern the differences between national spectacles and national narratives, Alan Nadel, in "Failed Cultural Narratives: America in the Postwar Era and the Story of *Democracy*," proposes two different understandings of the Cold War epoch. In its cultural narratives, the Cold War opportunistically conscripts every other narrative form to the needs of its totalizing social allegory, reducing them to the status of empty signifiers. Through a careful reading of Joan Didion's novel *Democracy*, Nadel persuasively argues for that narrative's power to expose the devastating effects of the Cold War allegory on U.S. cultural life.

In "Techno-euphoria and the Discourse of the American Sublime," Rob Wilson reinterprets what Nadel describes as the Cold War's power to empty the national narrative of its democratic contents as a continuation of the discourse of the American Sublime, which originated in the nineteenth century. According to Wilson, the national narrative, as a sublime instrumentality, has always already evacuated its content. The high-tech weaponry of the military industrial complex, Wilson concludes, transforms the nostalgia for referentiality informing Nadel's analysis into "techno-euphoria" over the power to erase all traces of man and nature from the landscape.

Throughout "Engendering Paranoia in Contemporary Narrative,"

Patrick O'Donnell demonstrates the ways in which the contemporary narratives of Mailer, DeLillo, and Pynchon have internalized what Wilson calls
euphoria and what Nadel calls nostalgia to construct a hyperinterpellation—
the capacity to produce narrative connections between completely disconnected cultural materials. According to O'Donnell, paranoia refers to the
desire to be totally inscribed within the social imaginary of the national
narrative, even when all of the positions within that narrative have been dispersed. It functions as a meta-category, a will to position cultural materials
within preexisting categories no matter what the expense.

   Whereas O'Donnell, Nadel, and Wilson expose the collective bankruptcy of the national narratives constructed out of Cold War logic, Daniel
O'Hara finds in Frank Lentricchia's literary career a way of living the postnational narrative as a rediscovery of what O'Hara calls "oneself." Because
Lentricchia never identifies with any of the disciplinary practices—New Historicism, neopragmatism, New Criticism, neoformalism, professionalism—
developing within the field of Literary Studies, he can discern the historicity
of these developments as the basis for the discovery of his own imaginative agency. In "becoming himself," instead of these academic personae,
Lentricchia explains resistively the social imaginaries into which he otherwise would have been absorbed.

   In the final two essays, John Carlos Rowe and Kathryne Lindberg
propose alternative archaeologies and teleologies for post-national U.S. literature. John Carlos Rowe reads Herman Melville's *Typee and Omoo* as
narratives critical of the U.S. imperial enterprise, and argues that Melville
rendered legible a U.S. imperialist history linking the antebellum North's
growing demand for global markets with the southern slave trade. The critical value of these narratives is derivable, according to Rowe, from Melville's
association of these narratives with fugitive slave testimonials and Puritan
captivity tracts, as intertextual resources for growing political opposition to
slavery and colonialism.

   In a carefully argued analysis of the commerce—as it was differently negotiated between such mass circulation journals as the *Saturday
Evening Post* and *The Masses*—between poetics and politics, Kathryne
Lindberg draws significant distinctions between what she calls revisionary
and ideological identities. In her essay Lindberg deploys Derrida's "logic
of the supplement" to complicate the relationship between literature and
social formation that points to new avenues for research in the field of
past-national U.S. literature.

Nationalism, Hypercanonization, and *Huckleberry Finn*

Jonathan Arac

I am not an Americanist by professional formation, and as in the 1980s I came to focus my teaching and reading in American literature, I was struck by what seems to me, compared to other national literatures I know or have studied, a state of hypercanonization. By hypercanonization, I mean that a very few single works monopolize curricular and critical attention: in fiction, preeminently *The Scarlet Letter*, *Moby-Dick*, and *Huckleberry Finn*. These works organize most American literature courses in high school, college, and graduate school; they form the focus for many dissertations and books. I have found literary history the best means by which to engage critically with these works and with the institutional structures that produce their hypercanonicity, the best means to address the works while displacing

My thanks to the School of Criticism and Theory, Dartmouth College, and its director, Michael Riffaterre, for the opportunity to develop these arguments in a course on "Writing Literary History Now," July 1990. I benefited greatly from the stimulation of dialogue at the School. In its written form, this essay has received valuable responses from Donald Pease, Paul Bové, and Daniel O'Hara.

the terms of address. For literary history, as I try to practice it, these works are not the answers but the problems.[1]

Literary history does not express a positive totality; it does, however, activate a critical demand for totalization. Facing a project of literary history, one is always entitled to demand more to be taken into account. This demand for new contexts, new connections, may be linked to the debates in all forms of recent history writing concerning the place of groups, often defined by race, gender, class, or ethnicity, that had not previously played a major role in historiography. One name for this topic is "history from below"; I prefer as a slogan "history from athwart." By this, I mean a concern with what goes "against the grain" or might have seemed beside the point of canonical understanding.[2] Such juxtaposition from athwart may lead to connection, and new connections produce new perspectives, which refresh, transform, and even reverse what we had thought. Irony by reversal, metaphor by perspective, and metonymy by connection are no less figures of history than is synecdoche by totality.

I have completed a portion of the new *Cambridge History of American Literature*. Asked to write on mid-nineteenth-century American prose narrative, I set myself this problem: How do I account for the emergence, around 1850, of works that count as what readers nowadays recognize as *literature*? I mean here *The Scarlet Letter* and *Moby-Dick*. In contrast to them, other valuable written productions of the time, however much they prove of interest in other ways, do not now widely count as literature. This is not simply an abstract issue of terminology. The designation *literature* is heavy with value. It affects what is studied, taught, and read, and it also greatly determines the terms in which new writing is reviewed in the public press. Books published in 1992 are praised for resembling *Huckleberry Finn* but not, I believe, any other single work of the later nineteenth century. My historical exploration of this issue involves two areas: (1) the changing definition of literature,[3] and (2) its relation to differing kinds of writing, that

1. My more extensive arguments on literary history may be found in *Critical Genealogies: Historical Situations for Postmodern Literary Studies* (New York: Columbia University Press, 1987).
2. I quote here and in the preceding sentence, with a twist, from Walter Benjamin, "Theses on the Philosophy of History," in *Illuminations*, ed. Hannah Arendt, trans. Harry Zohn (New York: Schocken, 1969), 257.
3. A brief, essential starting point for this topic is the entry in Raymond Williams, *Keywords: A Vocabulary of Culture and Society* (New York: Oxford University Press, 1976), 150–54.

is, a problem of genre. My solution involves reconceptualizing the emerging literary narrative type as one among several different competing generic types. The major narrative form that preceded literary narrative in the United States, and also succeeded it, was what I call *national* narrative. At about the time of Andrew Jackson's presidency (1829–1837), the fiction of James Fenimore Cooper and the *History of the United States* by George Bancroft defined national narrative. Cooper died in 1851, but Bancroft's *History* was in progress from 1834 into the 1880s.

Both contesting and presupposing the articulation of national narrative, two important smaller types of narrative emerged. First, in the 1830s, what I call *local* narrative, the line of descent from Washington Irving that includes the so-called southwestern humorists of Georgia, Alabama, Mississippi, and Tennessee, as well as the northeastern moralist Hawthorne in his shorter works; and second, in the 1840s, *personal* narrative, which, contrary to Puritan tradition and twentieth-century expectation, proved to be rather extroverted, first-person reports from the margins of the dominant culture. Important examples of personal narrative include Richard Henry Dana's *Two Years before the Mast*, Francis Parkman's *Oregon Trail*, Frederick Douglass's *Narrative*, and Harriet Jacobs's *Incidents in the Life of a Slave Girl*.

In response to the political crisis of 1850, which produced a compromise intended to subdue controversy, Melville and Hawthorne consolidated elements from their own earlier work and that of Poe and set themselves apart from national narrative. "The Custom-House" introduction to *The Scarlet Letter* illustrates the point. Through literary narrative, they developed a freely imaginative space, on the model of what transatlantic romantic theory and practice had set forth in the previous two generations. Both local and personal narrative elements could be incorporated under this new principle of integration. The contrast of *Moby-Dick* with another great novel of 1851, *Uncle Tom's Cabin*, makes this clear. Stowe's novel is no less comprehensive than *Moby-Dick*, but it integrates local and personal narrative materials under the dominance of a narrative concerning the salvation of America, and in Augustine St. Clare it incorporates the figure of the sensitive spectator associated with literary narrative. St. Clare is presented sympathetically, but very critically, and occupies only the middle third of the novel. In contrast, the literary figure of Ishmael engrosses attention from the opening and survives Ahab's quest as witness.[4]

4. For my full argument on *Moby-Dick*, see "'A Romantic Book': *Moby-Dick* and Novel Agency," *boundary 2* 17, no. 2 (1990): 40–59.

I find that Americans in the twentieth century have adopted as national exemplars precisely those works that were written at a distance from national narrative, while great national writers, such as Bancroft, Cooper, and (until recently) Stowe, have been comparatively neglected. If we rest in this imbalance, we damage our understanding of the present no less than of the past. In Europe, as well as in the United States, the nineteenth century was marked by two great cultural transformations that still powerfully shape our lives: the emergence of nationality and the emergence of literature (in the specialized sense of imaginative belles lettres, not all culturally valued writing).[5] In our contemporary world of nations in the last years of the twentieth century, the renewed power of nationalisms throughout what had been contained as the Second World, no less than the intensified American patriotism spurred by desert stormers, require rethinking this relation. As I understand the last 150 years of American history, literary culture and national culture may be seriously at odds, and they harmonize only when the nation is given a meaning more psychological than religious or political. This psychological understanding of the nation, in turn, has granted America the spiritual legitimacy of literature, while subordinating literature to an America so conceived as to disarm political criticism.

Let me now extend my line of thought from the *Cambridge History* work to consider the later nineteenth century. After the reawakening of widespread political controversy over Kansas in 1854, the consensual distance from politics that had permitted literary narrative to emerge closed up. The most ambitious writings of the immediate post–Civil War years were the volumes of Francis Parkman's national narrative of the struggle for the American forest. The most captivating writings of the same period were the first books of Mark Twain. Twain came directly from the newspaper milieu of local narrative. In *Innocents Abroad* and *Roughing It*, he strung together bits any one of which might have been a newspaper sketch, integrating them through the resources of "personal narrative" (as he characterized *Roughing It*).[6] Meanwhile, a steady trickle of posthumous materials from Hawthorne's estate kept alive the idea of literary narrative until Henry

---

5. A remarkably suggestive argument on the genealogy of this conjunction is sketched by Wlad Godzich and Nicholas Spadaccini, "Popular Culture and Spanish Literary History," in their edited volume *Literature among Discourses: The Spanish Golden Age* (Minneapolis: University of Minnesota Press, 1986), 41–61. For the American nineteenth century, see Lauren Berlant, *The Anatomy of National Fantasy: Hawthorne, Utopia, and Everyday Life* (Chicago: University of Chicago Press, 1991).
6. Mark Twain, *The Innocents Abroad* and *Roughing It* (New York: Literary Classics of America, 1984), 527.

James's study of Hawthorne (1879) marked the moment when James chose to reproduce and occupy that space with *The Portrait of a Lady*.

In *The Ordeal of Mark Twain* (1920) and *The Pilgrimage of Henry James* (1925), Van Wyck Brooks set James and Twain as polar, contrasting cases of the artist's relation to America. What I would emphasize more than the contrast is precisely the sense of artistic exemplarity by which each may be distinguished from their friend, editor, and supporter, W. D. Howells.[7] A moment of American literary history that has still not been adequately thought through is the period of early 1885 when the *Century Magazine* published excerpts from *Huckleberry Finn*, while also serializing Howells's *Rise of Silas Lapham* and James's *Bostonians*.[8] Subsequent institutional forces have prevented us from seeing how limited an event nineteenth-century literary narrative was, and the same forces account for the peculiar twentieth-century status of *Huckleberry Finn*.

Huckleberry Finn is filled with the materials of local humor writing, and it draws for its fundamental mode of presentation on the conventions of personal narrative, but by cutting off the address to any concretely imagined, culturally central readers or to acknowledged national concerns, *Huckleberry Finn* offers the freely aesthetically shaped world of literary narrative. It is possible to link *Huckleberry Finn* to fundamental national historical experiences, but the link can be made only allegorically, that is, only through an aggressively active process of reader's interpretation, about which readers, in fact, differ very widely. My name for this interpretive process is the nationalizing of literary narrative, and it seems to me the means by which hypercanonical idolatry takes place. Let me offer a brief illustration of what I mean. It will also serve as a warning that not even brilliance, learning, and literary history can assure that a critic will not succumb to the prevailing idolatry of *Huckleberry Finn* by nationalizing its literary narrative.

In his remarkable chapter on Twain in the *Columbia Literary History of the United States*, Philip Fisher makes two striking claims about *Huckleberry Finn* that I can understand only as allusively depending on allegorical political readings. Early in the chapter, he establishes a pattern in Twain's writing in which what is given as a gift may turn out to be terrible trouble,

7. The most challenging location of Howells and "American literary realism" is Donald E. Pease's introduction to his edited collection on *The Rise of Silas Lapham* (New York: Cambridge University Press, 1991), 1–28.

8. For example, nothing significant is said in Arthur John, *The Best Years of the "Century": Richard Watson Gilder, "Scribner's Monthly," and the "Century Magazine," 1870–1909* (Urbana: University of Illinois Press, 1981).

and he applies this pattern to warn against the consequences of "Huck's gift to Jim of his freedom."[9] This warning I take to allude to the studies that have placed *Huckleberry Finn* in the context of Emancipation and Reconstruction, its pains and failures. My problem with it is that Huck never does make Jim a gift of his freedom. When Huck decides in chapter 31 that he would sooner go to hell than report Jim's whereabouts to his owner, Jim is already captured, and also already free: The owner to whom Huck has decided not to write is already dead and has already freed Jim. If anyone makes a gift of freedom, it is Jim, who sacrifices what he believes is his chance to escape in order to care for the wounded Tom.

Complications grow when we consider the beautiful sentence with which Fisher ends his chapter, achieving his closure by echoing Twain's closure: "*Tom Sawyer* ends with boys made rich; *Huckleberry Finn* with men made free."[10] Fisher's cadence is from "The Battle Hymn of the Republic," which invokes Jesus Christ: "As he died to make men holy, let us die to make men free." In Fisher's national allegory, *Huckleberry Finn*, through its rejection of the southern system of slavery, is connected to a heroic interpretation of the Civil War (as well as to an ironic interpretation of Reconstruction) but only at the cost of a bizarre interpretive move that pluralizes Jim's freedom. What other man than Jim has been made free at the end of *Huckleberry Finn*? Perhaps Fisher means Huck's "freedom" through Pap's death, but in an allegory of the Civil War, this would give Pap the structural role of a liberating martyr, like Lincoln.

I want to make trouble for the hypercanonical construction of *Huckleberry Finn*. I hope to say things about *Huckleberry Finn* that can be accepted as true and that, if accepted, make it harder for the book to be treated so readily as an idol in American culture. The nationalizing of literary narrative, and concomitant psychologizing of politics, produces and reinforces the belief that there is a true America made up by those who take their distance from actually existing America.[11] In this respect, one of the most provocative features of *Huckleberry Finn* is a heightened instance of what is also true of the other hypercanonized works: Its very canonical prestige is connected to the sense that it is *counter*cultural. For example, let me cite

9. Philip Fisher, "Mark Twain," in *Columbia Literary History of the United States*, ed. Emory Elliott (New York: Columbia University Press, 1988), 629.
10. Fisher, "Mark Twain," 644.
11. See Sacvan Bercovitch, "Afterword," in *Ideology and Classic American Literature*, ed. Bercovitch and Myra Jehlen (New York: Cambridge University Press, 1986), 428, for a condensed statement of this argument, which runs through much of Bercovitch's work.

what many scholars still consider to be the definitive chapter-length treatment of *Huckleberry Finn*, by Henry Nash Smith, one of the founders of American Studies and for a long time in charge of the Mark Twain Papers. As have many readers, at least since V. L. Parrington, Smith gives special attention to chapter 31. Here, Huck contemplates writing to Miss Watson so that she can recover her runaway slave, but even though this seems to him what religion teaches, he can't do it and decides instead, "All right, then, I'll *go* to hell." [12] Smith argued from this that the crux of meaning in the book is Huck's choice between "fidelity to the uncoerced self" and the negative results, the "blurring of attitudes," that are "caused by social conformity." [13] This "fidelity to the uncoerced self" is the psychological hinge on which *Huckleberry Finn* is turned for national meaning, as a token of an America beyond conformity.

Smith's critical position helps define the intellectual and institutional context for what I consider an extraordinary anomaly in the major new scholarly edition of *Huckleberry Finn*. For decades now, the Mark Twain Project has been conducted from the repository of the Mark Twain Papers, the Bancroft Library, at the University of California Berkeley campus, and its editions and scholarship have been invaluable. Yet the California editors have decided that Twain's intentions require the text of *Huckleberry Finn* to include a sixteen-page section that never appeared in the book during Twain's lifetime. (The discovery in February 1991 of the missing portion of the manuscript of *Huckleberry Finn* confirms the facts, but does not affect the logic, of the editorial argument.) [14] Twain published the "Raftmen Episode" in *Life on the Mississippi* (chapter 3), describing it as excerpted from a work in progress about Huckleberry Finn, but he then omitted it from *Huckleberry Finn* itself. The documents concerning his intentions are three letters: first, one from Twain insisting that no part of this section be used in publicity materials, since it had already been published and might lead readers to fear that the whole new book would be largely familiar (*HF*, 442); next, a letter from his publisher wondering if the section might not be omitted entirely. "I think it would improve" the book, the publisher wrote (*HF*,

12. *The Works of Mark Twain*, vol. 8, *The Adventures of Huckleberry Finn*, ed. Walter Blair and Victor Fischer (Berkeley and Los Angeles: University of California Press, 1988), 271; hereafter cited in my text as *HF*.

13. Henry Nash Smith, *Mark Twain: The Development of a Writer* (Cambridge: Harvard University Press, 1962), 122–23.

14. Rita Reif, "A Manuscript Solves Huck Finn Mysteries," *New York Times*, 26 Feb. 1991, sec. B, page 2, including interview material with Victor Fischer.

446). In the third letter, Twain replied, "Yes, I think the raft chapter can be left wholly out" (*HF*, 446). The California editors argue that Twain omitted the episode only to "accommodate his young publisher on a practical matter," and that, in editorial theory, such a decision is equivalent to "accepting the publisher's censorship."[15] It is a nagging embarrassment to the editors' scholarly scruple that even where he might have tried to bring the passage back, no evidence exists that Twain ever brought it up (*HF*, 476–77).

I have three points to make about this matter. First, I emphasize that this editorial interpretive attempt to define and magnify the individuality of Twain the author, possessor of intentions and victim of censorship, is perfectly coherent with Smith's critical position on *Huckleberry Finn*. In combating what they consider the publisher's censorship, the editors accrue to themselves the spiritual authority of Huck's decision to reject "social conformity": "All right, then, I'll *go* to hell." Yet the editors take a more complex and accommodating stance in the Acknowledgments, the first words of the volume after its dedication and table of contents. They begin, "Our first thanks go to the American taxpayer" (*HF*, xvii). Next, they thank "the scholars who recommended federal funding," and the climax comes in thanks to the National Endowment for the Humanities, the "independent federal agency" that granted the funds to make the edition possible (*HF*, xvii). (That phrase, "independent federal agency," is almost a perfect verbal formula for what I have described as the psychological hinge that joins the literary to the national.)

The rhetoric of acknowledgment is highly interesting. Note the mediating role of the scholarly community. The "scholars who recommended federal funding" stand in the unemphasized second position between the strong opening invocation of the citizenry ("American taxpayer") and the climactic summoning of the state ("National Endowment for the Humanities"). Yet only through the scholarly community can the people receive the benefits of their federated agency, and only the initiative of the scholarly editors opened this possibility. The independence of the NEH is clearly meant to set it apart from the dangers of conformity, and the taxpayers whose "support" (*HF*, xvii) made the work possible are vicariously co-agents in fighting censorship. So the logic of America as the nation defined by its opposi-

15. Robert H. Hirst, "A Note on the Text," in Mark Twain, *Adventures of Huckleberry Finn*, Mark Twain Library edition (Berkeley and Los Angeles: University of California Press, 1985), 450. Hirst is the general editor of the Mark Twain Project, here explaining in the inexpensive paperback edition the logic of Fischer's textual decision, which Fischer himself explains in the massive, costly scholarly edition to which I otherwise refer.

tion to itself underwrites this sequence. From economic individual to federal agency, all are free and fight for freedom. I do not think Mark Twain believed anything like this.

My second point is that in insisting on the unfettered individuality of Twain, the editors nonetheless effectively split him in two. If the editors draw glory from being like Twain, he must be protected from being like them, for their scholarly narration of *Huckleberry Finn*'s process of publication constructs quite a different image of Twain from the one they invoke to justify their editorial decision but more like the selves they acknowledge in giving thanks. Recall that the very name by which Samuel Clemens is known to history as an author, Mark Twain, is itself not just a pen name—it is a registered trademark. This economic fact has weighty consequences for the logic of editorial argument. The editors base their decision on a split between "Mark Twain's intentions for his text" and "his publisher's needs"; they find "no documentary evidence" that these intentions and needs "coincide."[16] I read their evidence to different effect, however, as showing that Twain's intentions concerning *Huckleberry Finn* were inseparable from its status as an economic object. The California edition shows that Clemens himself was deeply involved in the whole process by which the book moved from his manuscript to its readers.

The publisher whom the editors believe censored Twain was Charles L. Webster. Webster was a young nephew of Samuel Clemens, and the publishing concern of Charles L. Webster & Co. was set up by Clemens, according to the California editors, so that the author "could have complete charge of issuing and selling the book" (*HF*, xlvii). As Webster wrote early in the process, "The Co. . . . is S. L. C." [Samuel Langhorne Clemens] (*HF*, xlvii). The correspondence between the two shows, according to the California editors, that "Clemens was indefatigable in directing every step" (*HF*, xlvii). There is a contradiction, then: on the one side, the scholarly characterization of the actual working relation between Clemens and Webster, in which Clemens was not only active but the senior, dominant figure for whom Webster was basically an agent; on the other side, the claim that there was no authorial intention in the omission of the passage. The myth of Frankenstein and the theory of alienation were invented to deal with such situations, but the editors do not invoke them; they simply make of Webster the representation of an alienating, conformist commercial culture, set against the freedom of the author's creative intentions. As a result of this defense of

16. Hirst, "Note," 450–51.

Twain's autonomy, the standard MLA-certified text of *Huckleberry Finn* is now nearly 5 percent longer than any edition published during Twain's life-time, by virtue of including a passage of some five thousand words that is identically available in another of his major works.

Here, I briefly note the third point. The "Raftmen Episode" involves Huck's witnessing a series of boasts and stories that brilliantly encapsulate Twain's mastery of the local narrative materials from which his art began. The logic of hypercanonization dictates that Twain's single greatest book must include as much as possible of his greatest writing. If some of the most wonderful pages from *Life on the Mississippi* are now also to be found in *Huckleberry Finn*, there will be that much less reason for anyone to read *Life on the Mississippi*, and the dominance of literary narrative over local and personal narratives will be further confirmed.

In principle, one might expect so substantial a change in the canoni-cal text of *Huckleberry Finn* to have drastic consequences for our critical understanding; in fact, it seems that critical argument has at least a 5 per-cent margin of error. There is no sign that this addition is having anything like the impact recent arguments on the text of *King Lear* have had. Despite *Huckleberry Finn*'s hypercanonicity, there is continuing variance in the fun-damental terms by which its place in American literary history has been understood, that is, in the question that I consider the essential inquiry of literary history, what kind of work it is. It is now usual to read *Huckleberry Finn* in relation to our contemporary concerns with problems of race and the history of slavery in the United States, and it is hard to doubt that these issues are at least intensely relevant to any apt response to the work.

Yet among the documents relating to the distribution of *Huckleberry Finn* is one that I find astonishing precisely because it opens a world of his-torical difference, which thwarts our expectations. Clemens, you recall, had set up Webster's company to issue and sell *Huckleberry Finn*. The means of sale was subscription. Agents around the country were set up with ter-ritorial rights, and they went door-to-door selling subscriptions. Clemens insisted that the book would not come out until forty thousand subscriptions were sold. To assist in sales, agents were equipped with a prospectus for the book, which included an "abstract" of the book's "story," which I quote in full:

> the adventures of Huckleberry Finn [note that this is in fact the full title], Tom Sawyer and a negro named Jim, who in their travels fall in with two tramps engaged in *taking in* the different country towns

through which they pass, by means of the missionary dodge, the temperance crusade, or under any pretext that offers to *easily* raise a dishonest dollar. The writer follows these characters through their various adventures, until finally, we find the tramps properly and warmly clothed,—*with a coat of tar and feathers,*—and the boys and Jim escape their persecutions and return safely to their friends. (*HF*, 846; emphasis in original)

Huckleberry Finn is described as a (belated) local narrative of south-western humor. The King and Duke appear as the central selling point of the book; only the middle third of it, which is where they appear, plays any role in the publicity. Although this description focuses on two rogues, it presents a far less countercultural book than the one that has been read for most of the last fifty years. Huck is never alone with Jim, and the inclusion of Tom suggests that they are not fleeing but frolicking. The issue of slavery is so far buried that Jim's unfree status is not even mentioned, let alone that it might provide any motive for the travels.

I'm not accusing Clemens of misleading advertising; rather, I'm suggesting that these documents point to problems in our historical understanding of how *Huckleberry Finn* came into the world. This abstract was still used in the 1889 *Publishers' Trade List Annual* advertisement (*HF*, 850), long after it could be likely that the question of Jim's enslavement was being masked because of fear that the subject was not attractive to potential buyers.[17] This critical interpretation of the book's shape and substance—this abstract—was put out by the young publisher whose every arrangement enjoyed, according to the California editors, "the accompaniment of an unremitting barrage of advice, assistance, and interference from his employer" (*HF*, xlviii)—the author, Mark Twain. Even where evidence is not available, the editors are certain that all advertising material had "at least the author's tacit approval" (*HF*, 843).

Literary history exposes radically different understandings of what, in the most basic sense, *Huckleberry Finn* is about, and the efforts of literary historians to place the book expose the argumentative structure of literary history. The dialectic terms most basic to literary history are tradition

17. It was by no means uncommon for popular writings of the 1880s to address life under slavery. See, for an overview, chap. 8 ("The South Begins to Write") and chap. 9 ("The North Feels the Power of the Pen"), in Paul H. Buck, *The Road to Reunion, 1865–1900* (1937; reprint, New York: Vintage Books, 1959), 196–235, which, however, does not mention *Huckleberry Finn*, tacitly acknowledging its generic difference.

and innovation, and *Huckleberry Finn* has been placed solidly with both. As tradition, it has been understood as part of American romance, notably by Richard Chase (*The American Novel and Its Tradition*, 1957) and Leslie Fiedler (*Love and Death in the American Novel*, 1959), or as American pastoral by Leo Marx (*The Machine in the Garden*, 1964). As innovation, it has been seen as inaugurating the triumph of the vernacular in American prose, as by Henry Nash Smith, and, again, Leo Marx.[18] Although it will not be possible to develop this point further now, I emphasize that the sense of Twain as innovative has been especially fostered by those who wished to be innovative, notably the early American prose modernists Sherwood Anderson and Ernest Hemingway.[19]

The issue of linguistic innovation helps elucidate Twain's status as iconoclastic idol. I shall come finally to Twain's divergences from national narrative as exemplified by Fenimore Cooper's *Pioneers*, but my starting point will be Mark Twain's major work of literary criticism, one of the most successful, best known critical essays in English, "Fenimore Cooper's Literary Offenses."[20] As its title suggests, Twain's essay is a bill of indictment, an act of offense in the guise of judgment. The essay's force springs from the double cross of its opening. Twain begins parodically with three encomiastic epigraphs, in which the revered Cooper is roundly praised by Professors Lounsbury and Matthews and by the famous English novelist Wilkie Collins, but Twain's critique of Cooper makes his readers eventually find in the language of these authorities the same complacent wooliness he has found in Cooper. So Twain offers all the pleasure of a violent assault on the establishment.

18. See especially "The Vernacular Tradition in American Writing" (1958) and "The Pilot and the Passenger: Landscape Conventions and the Style of *Huckleberry Finn*" (1956), the two essays Marx placed first in his collection *The Pilot and the Passenger: Essays on Literature, Technology, and Culture in the United States* (New York: Oxford University Press, 1988), 3–36. Because of Marx's capacity to see Twain on both sides of the duality I am defining, he receives further attention in the book project from which this essay springs.

19. For Anderson, see the correspondence with Van Wyck Brooks in Edmund Wilson, ed., *The Shock of Recognition: The Development of Literature in the United States Recorded by the Men Who Made It* (Garden City: Doubleday, Doran, 1943), 1256–89; for Hemingway, see the famous line in *The Green Hills of Africa*: "All modern American literature comes from one book by Mark Twain called *Huckleberry Finn*" (New York: Scribner, 1935), 22.

20. Mark Twain, "Fenimore Cooper's Literary Offenses," in Wilson, ed., *The Shock of Recognition*, 582–94; hereafter cited in my text as FCLO.

But in this essay, Twain himself appears not as a wild man, a western rule breaker, but precisely in the role of a pseudo-neoaristotelian, enunciator of eighteen rules that Cooper can be shown to have violated. Twain's rational-technical authority stands against the traditional authority of Cooper, and the English, and the professors. Twain does not himself historicize his argument with Cooper, except for one moment when he speculates that perhaps Cooper's procedures would make sense if it were possible to believe that there ever "was a time when time was of no value to a person who thought he had something to say" (FCLO, 592). The very terms of Twain's concession point to its incredibility; time has been money in America at least since Ben Franklin, a century before Cooper. A time in which time had no value would be, by the very words, a worthless time. Twain treats Cooper as a contemporary, that is, as a fellow author confronting a timeless realm of practical rules.[21] Adapting terms from Roland Barthes, we could say Twain attempts to persuade us that Cooper's work is no longer writable and is readable only for those in a state of distraction, their levels of attention set at near zero.

Twain represents Cooper's failings as sensory, failures of eye and ear. Cooper's "ear was satisfied with the *approximate* word" (FCLO, 593; Twain's emphasis), not the "right word" (FCLO, 584), but only its "second cousin" (FCLO, 584). Because of his "poor ear for words," Cooper was guilty of "literary flatting and sharping": "You perceive what he is intending to say, but you also perceive that he doesn't *say* it" (FCLO, 593; Twain's emphasis). Sensorily handicapped as he was, Cooper "failed to notice that the man who talks corrupt English six days in the week must and will talk it on the seventh, and can't help himself" (FCLO, 592). Mark Twain does not believe in linguistic Sunday best. Cooper was not just half-deaf; he was half-blind, too. Balzac had adapted the tense alertness of Cooper's woodsmen to highlight the perceptual intensity required for life in Paris, but for Twain, Cooper was not "an observer" (FCLO, 586). Cooper could not "see the commonest little every-day matters accurately" (FCLO, 587). If he had, "his inventive faculty would have worked better; not more interestingly, but more rationally, more plausibly" (FCLO, 586). In one episode that Twain mockingly analyzes at length, Cooper's imprecision concerning

21. It is usual to contrast Twain's realist critique of Cooper with the mythic redemption of Cooper by D. H. Lawrence in *Studies in Classic American Literature*. I do not think it has been observed, however, that Twain's realism is, as I have argued, antihistorical, while Lawrence's mythic reading draws from a sharp sense of history on both large and small scales.

speed and distance means that "the inaccuracy of the details throws a sort of air of fictitiousness and general improbability" over the whole business (FCLO, 589).

Twain's vocabulary of judgment ("plausibly," "improbability") echoes the etymological history of its terms: Plausible and probable both originate as terms of social approbation but have come to be used as if they were absolutes, and so Twain versus Cooper. Nowadays, when to read Cooper at all requires, as Yvor Winters already argued fifty years ago, "an act of sympathetic historical imagination,"[22] it is clear that Twain's standards were those that most effectively served to emphasize the differences between the emerging standards of taste of his time, an emergence that he was actively fostering in this essay, and the standards of Cooper's time, still residual in Twain's. By downplaying his innovation, by emphasizing not tradition but rather the eye and ear, the plausible and probable—terms that are conventionally understood as unchanging nature—Twain sets his critique as little as possible in the realm of the overtly ideological. He might, for instance, have attacked Cooper on the grounds that Cooper was the "American Scott," a liability both on nationalist cultural grounds and, more particularly for Twain, because of Twain's well-established critique of the disastrous effects he argued Scott had exercised on southern culture.[23]

Yet Twain's technically rational standards of observation and consistency, based on the regularities of the natural world and human nature, rule out of court the possibility that people may speak in several distinct registers for different purposes, at different times, with different interlocutors. Twain insists on linguistic consistency as the index of a psychologically and socially unified identity. In *Huckleberry Finn*, the only characters who manifest the variable linguistic usages of which he accuses Cooper are the King and the Duke, and they are frauds. For Twain, their variation occurs because they are bad people, not because they are badly written. Cooper, however, offers a different view of linguistic instability. In *The Pioneers*, Cooper notes that Judge Temple, raised as a Quaker, tends to fall into Quaker idiom at moments of passion, as does his daughter to a lesser degree. Neither the Judge nor his daughter is a fraud, but neither has the kind of stability Twain requires. In the United States of the later nineteenth

22. Yvor Winters, "Fenimore Cooper, or The Ruins of Time," in *In Defense of Reason* (3d ed., 1947; Denver: Swallow, n.d.), 182.
23. See chapter 46 of *Life on the Mississippi*, "Enchantments and Enchanters," in Mark Twain, *Mississippi Writings* (New York: Literary Classics of the United States, 1982), 500–502.

century, as is emphatically the case now, questions of educating immigrants and members of culturally distinct, but long-settled, groups necessarily involved thinking through questions of what it might mean to use situationally variable languages, but this is no concern of *Huckleberry Finn*. Jim speaks for the book when he answers Huck's question, "Spose a man was to come to you and say *Polly-voo-franzy*—what would you think?" Jim answers, "I wouldn' think nuff'n; I'd take en bust him over de head" (*HF*, 97).

Huckleberry Finn as a whole, of course, does not confine itself to a single form of English. Twain's initial note on the language of his book proposes an agenda of dialect accuracy that has been studied and warranted by generations of scholars:

> In this book a number of dialects are used, to wit: the Missouri negro dialect; the extremest form of the backwoods South-Western dialect; the ordinary "Pike-County" dialect; and four modified varieties of this last. The shadings have not been done in a haphazard fashion, or by guess-work; but pains-takingly, and with the trustworthy guidance and support of personal familiarity with these several forms of speech. I make this explanation for the reason that without it many readers would suppose that all these characters were trying to talk alike and not succeeding. (*HF*, lvii)

For Twain, it is important that characters sound not like each other but each like her- or himself.

Yet Cooper, too, made *The Pioneers* serve as the repository for a great range of voices, as a registry for American idiosyncrasies of speech. Despite all that Twain says against his offenses, Cooper represents in *The Pioneers* a wide range of American immigrant, regional, professional, and ethnic linguistic varieties: representations of English spoken by American blacks and Indians; the socially pretentious Essex County, New England, talk of Tabitha the housekeeper and the Jacksonian-democratic New Englandism of Billy Kirby the Vermonter; the jargons of doctors and lawyers; English as spoken by the New York Dutch, a French émigré, and a Cornishman, as well as the cultivated transatlantic English of young Effingham, not to mention again the Temples and Natty.[24]

I want to develop further this comparison of *Huckleberry Finn* and

24. I am grateful to have these claims substantiated by the sharp insights and rich contexts of David Simpson, "The Languages of Cooper's Novels," chap. 5 in *The Politics of American English, 1776–1850* (New York: Oxford University Press, 1986), 149–201.

The Pioneers, because Twain's stylistic innovation in presenting an extended vernacular narrative of comprehensive scope and great emotional power has effectively rendered invisible a series of extraordinary similarities between these two works.[25] Once these similarities are recognized, it is then possible to define more precisely the divergences of Twain's literary narrative from Cooper's national narrative. Cooper's national narrative was grounded from its words on up in claims that were no longer representable aesthetically or politically to Twain and many of his contemporaries. National narratives held a positive understanding of the course of American history, and they believed it was a responsibility of culturally ambitious and important narrative not only to show but also to make explicit this understanding. Literary narratives denied any such responsibility, challenged any such understanding, and developed techniques to supersede such explicitness. American Studies has most often struggled to reincorporate literary narrative into a renewed national allegory, undertaking to explicate what was programmatically, even polemically, left silent.

The fundamental similarity I find between *Huckleberry Finn* and *The Pioneers* is the setting in place and time. Each book locates its action a full generation back in the setting of its author's childhood home. Living in New York City around 1820, Cooper looked back to the frontier days of Cooperstown, set in 1793. Living in Hartford around 1880, Twain set his action in the "Mississippi Valley . . . Forty to Fifty Years Ago" (*HF*, liii). Both books are sharply divided between satire and idyll. They satirically portray the small-town social interactions that make up much of the works' fictional substance, but they ecstatically evoke the beauties of the natural world that are set in contrast with town life. Both books locate important values in a smaller social group particularly linked to the natural setting. Moreover, in both books, this smaller, marginal group is homosocial but interracial. Leslie Fiedler has made the resemblances in the relations between Chingachgook and Natty Bumppo and Huck and Jim unforgettable points of reference for thinking about the history of American culture. In each case, a single individual is made to carry the burden of typifying a whole group. This technique has not been confined to novelists: Until the last few years, historians have almost inevitably written of "the Negro" and "the Indian" as if there were indeed only one such person.

---

25. See, however, the rapid connections to Cooper made in the intricate and magisterial opening pages of John Seelye's introduction to Mark Twain, *The Adventures of Huckleberry Finn* (Harmondsworth: Penguin, 1985), viii–xiv.

Both *The Pioneers* and *Huckleberry Finn* establish a crucial scene of conflict between the white outsider and the law, setting up an opposition between human nature and the state that reinforces the contrast between landscape and town. Both works rely on a mystery plot to bring about their conclusions, and in both the white outsider resists remaining within the bounds of the civilized scope that the book has delimited. Natty ends up "foremost in that band of Pioneers, who are opening the way for the march of the nation across the continent."[26] Huck aims to "light out for the Territory" (*HF*, 362).

Any single one of the resemblances I have drawn between *The Pioneers* and *Huckleberry Finn* might be merely trivial, or else part of a much larger network of fictional conventions, as some clearly are, but the total concatenation is very striking. The differences that appear on the ground of these resemblances help to define the historical shift from Cooper's time to Twain's, from a time when national narrative was still emergent to a moment when its authority was again, more effectively than in 1850, challenged by literary narrative.[27] In the context of my argument, the outstanding difference is that Twain isolates the historical setting of his book. Cooper, through his plot and his narrative voice, brings the frontier community of 1793 into conjunction with at least three historical epochs: with the period of colonial exploration and white-Indian relations; with the Revolutionary War, which brought the United States into existence as the sovereign authority replacing the British and which also significantly altered property relations within the white world and relations between whites and Indians; and finally, the narrator acknowledges the changes that have further transformed American life since the time of the novel's action.

In contrast, Twain's aesthetic choice requires that Huck have almost no historical perspective on the land he lives in, either in its local or national dimensions, and there is no narrative presence beyond Huck to open up a deeper past or to link his time and concerns to those of the time when Twain was writing. So rigorously dramatic is Twain's technique, by which any voice that appears must belong to a character, that he requires stage directions to set the novel's scene. The title page is inscribed "Scene: The

26. James Fenimore Cooper, *The Leatherstocking Tales, Volume I* (New York: Literary Classics of the United States, 1985), 465.
27. I do not claim that literary narrative wholly superseded national narrative in the 1880s. For example, *The Grandissimes* (1880), by George W. Cable, a writer closely associated with Twain during the later phases of the writing of *Huckleberry Finn*, is much more like Cooper than Twain in the respects I discuss.

Mississippi Valley; Time: Forty to Fifty Years Ago" (*HF*, liii). The Revolution is not part of Cooper's novel, but it is part of what makes the world of that novel intelligible, and it is therefore included by reference. The Civil War is not part of Twain's novel, and it is not in any way textually present, although without its having occurred, the meaning we read in *Huckleberry Finn* would be, we think, wholly different. When excerpts from *Huckleberry Finn* ran in the *Century* magazine (December 1884 through February 1885), they appeared in issues crammed with Civil War memoirs. In November 1884, the *Century* had begun a massive feature on the Civil War that was so popular, it ran for three years. Yet there is no evidence—whether in the papers of the editor, Richard Watson Gilder, in Twain's correspondence, or in any reviews or notices—that the conjunction of these materials was registered. It is certainly appropriate, even imperative, for historical criticism now to take such juxtapositions into account. My claim, however, is that we have failed, as yet, to take account of the formal absences and historical silences, which are primary data to be interpreted before we assimilate the work into a larger context. We must explain the blanks before we fill them in.

The difference I have been establishing between *Huckleberry Finn* and *The Pioneers* bears also on the way the mystery plot works in the two books. In *Huckleberry Finn*, both the mysterious death of Huck's Pap and the freeing of Jim take place within the time frame of the main narrative, while in *The Pioneers*, the mysteries have to do with events before the action of the book begins. In Cooper, the revelation of these events gives meaning to what had been obscure during the book's narration, but in *Huckleberry Finn*, as many readers and critics have observed, the revelation of the hidden events diminishes the meaning of what had seemed the book's action: Huck's flight from his Pap, Jim's flight from slavery. These motives are erased as fully as they are in the advertising prospectus. A similar erasure obscures *Huckleberry Finn*'s fictional representation of its being written. In the first sentence, Huck refers to *Tom Sawyer*, which was published in 1876. This suggests that an older Huck is narrating from a time near that of his book's 1885 publication date. But on the last page, Huck explains that he has composed his narrative almost immediately after the conclusion of its events, that is, some forty to fifty years before publication.

The conflicts between laws of the state and values taken as nature's are also handled very differently by Twain and Cooper. In *The Pioneers*, I find that readers feel pulled both ways between the claims of the law as represented by Judge Temple and the claims of custom and nature in Natty Bumppo; in contrast, I do not know of any reader who believes that Huck should have turned in Jim. Moreover, the crisis of judgment in chapter 31 of *Huckleberry Finn* is treated purely internally; Huck is by himself. He describes his decision in terms that evoke the sharp senses Twain valued and claimed but Cooper lacked. Huck repeats that he could "see" Jim (*HF*, 270), but this is only in memory; Jim is not there. Moreover, it is a crucial feature of Twain's scene that legal penalties never occur to Huck as he thinks over the situation, only religious retribution. All this is very different from *The Pioneers*. A full courtroom scene is mounted, in which the force and value of the law is presented, even as the actual legal agents are mocked and criticized.[28]

A comparable difference may be defined in the treatment of what I have called the registry of American voices. In *Huckleberry Finn*, readers have found no other voice with the authority of Huck's. In *The Pioneers*, however, many readers have found Natty's voice to exceed in authority Judge Temple's, or even the authorial narrator's. More broadly, in the terms that Bakhtin has made familiar to recent literary study, we may understand the different voices of *The Pioneers* as indices for the struggles among different social groups, while in *Huckleberry Finn* this is much less frequently and forcibly the case.[29] Indeed, as early as the narratives of the anti-Jacksonian, Whig Congressman Davy Crockett in the 1830s, a written folk-voice had been put to use for elite politics. The powerful voices of Pap in his tirade against the "govment" (*HF*, 33–34) and Colonel Sherburn against the lynch mob are isolated grotesques rather than integral parts of an action, while the kindly gospel teachings of Widow Douglas are simply forgotten at the moment Huck's mind turns in crisis to religious terror.

Huckleberry Finn emerges from these comparisons as a much more powerfully centered work than *The Pioneers* in the conjunction it effects between its hero and its narrative language. *Huckleberry Finn* is famous in critical tradition for displacing narrative and linguistic authority from the traditional centers to a character marginal in any number of defined ways, yet it is not certain that *The Pioneers* may not be a much more fundamentally multifocal, and, in that sense, uncentered, work. Cooper's concern is the process of civilization, which requires many human agents in a variety of roles. For instance, Cooper sets the values of property and mobility into

28. My thoughts on this legal issue owe much to Carol Kay, *Political Constructions: Defoe, Richardson, and Sterne in Relation to Hobbes, Hume, and Burke* (Ithaca: Cornell University Press, 1988), esp. 118–19, 185–87.

29. I argue more fully these issues, with reference to Bakhtin, in a related essay, to appear in a volume edited by Janice Carlisle.

historical tension through contrasting Natty and Effingham. Through the course of the book, they have lived and hunted together with Chingachgook, but after the Indian's death, Natty goes out West, while Effingham enjoys marriage and his rightful inheritance after the death of his long-missing and hidden father. Huck, in contrast, both plans to light out for the territory and also finds six thousand dollars rightly restored to him after Pap's death. Twain consolidates the values of Natty's mobility and Effingham's wealth into his single idealized figure of Huck.

Again, *Huckleberry Finn* is famous for bringing crucial moral issues to bear on and in the psyche of its protagonist, yet this, too, is a further centering; the form and fable of *Huckleberry Finn* reject the very possibility of public debate. After the political failures that had led to the Civil War, after the political failures that had brought Reconstruction to an end, Twain's literary narrative takes the obliquity of radical ellipsis. In Cooper's national narrative, the light of American nature had insured that Natty would feel right about what he did; in the national narrative of *Uncle Tom's Cabin*, the light of grace insured that readers who responded properly to the horrors of slavery would "feel right."[30] Huck Finn lives so as to feel right with no sanction beyond his own psyche, the imaginative construction of an autonomous self that is the cultural work of literary narrative.

30. Harriet Beecher Stowe, *Uncle Tom's Cabin or, Life Among the Lowly*, ed. Ann Douglas (Harmondsworth: Penguin, 1981), 624.

The Politics of Nonidentity: A Genealogy

Ross Posnock

Recently, historians have called for a comparative intellectual history as an alternative to the reigning methodology of contextualism. Instead of regarding the meaning of figures and ideas as inseparable from their development in specific circumstances in the past, comparative history recontextualizes and resituates them in "theoretical confrontations."[1] New and unexpected contexts result, with "the power to inform us about certain possibilities of the present—possibilities we had not seen before."[2] The following pages suggest new possibilities of understanding the political responsibility of intellectuals by constructing a theoretical confrontation between various figures active from 1904 to the present. Together they comprise a genealogy for what I call the politics of nonidentity. The genealogy extends from Henry James of *The American Scene* to Michel Foucault, and includes Randolph Bourne, John Dewey, and Theodor Adorno.

1. This last phrase is from John P. Diggins's book on Veblen, which lifts him from his American context and reads him against Marx and Weber. See *The Bard of Savagery* (New York: Seabury Press, 1978).
2. David Harlan, "Intellectual History and the Return of Literature," *American Historical Review* 94 (June 1989): 605.

1

The admittedly improbable lineage proposed here intends at least two challenges to the received wisdom of American cultural history: (1) that Henry James is bereft of political interests; and (2) that there is an irremediable antagonism between pragmatism (John Dewey, in particular) and the Frankfurt School (Adorno, in particular). But these two revisionary efforts are, ultimately, the means to a larger end and show that, despite unbridgeable differences too numerous to mention, these five figures share a certain style of cultural and political inquiry, whose guiding value is nonidentity and whose philosophical orientation is a pragmatic emphasis on creative, experimental action produced by historically embedded subjects.[3] I will define and refine this bald statement in the course of constructing a constellation that can illuminate resemblances and reveal nuances of a shared cultural practice, whose importance has been egregiously overlooked in a culture that, until recently, equated the intellectual and the aesthetic with a transcendent realm of value.

If anything can be said to unite the constellation I propose, it might be a negative bond: all five of these thinkers have been routinely accused of various degrees of political timidity, naïveté, and aloofness. A survey of opinion includes the following: "romantic defeatism" (Lewis Mumford on Bourne), flight from the intricate realities of power and politics, and refuge in the abstractions of scientism and social control (C. Wright Mills on Dewey), bland, naïve "platitudinous" rationalism (Reinhold Niebuhr on Dewey), "desperate adherence" to a hopelessly sterile, dead-end negativism (Habermas and a multitude of critics on Adorno), a disturbing amorality that minimizes human agency and "provides solely negative conceptions of critique and resistance" (Cornel West concurring with Edward Said on Foucault).[4]

---

3. A popular misunderstanding of pragmatism ignores its emphasis on creative experimentation and, instead, depicts its view of action as narrowly instrumental. Another critic who links Foucault with pragmatism is Mark Maslan in "Foucault and Pragmatism," *Raritan* 7, no. 3 (Winter 1988): 94–114. Keith Gandal implies the link in "Foucault: Intellectual Work and Politics," *Telos* 67 (Spring 1986): 121–34.

4. Lewis Mumford is quoted in Gary Bullert, *The Politics of John Dewey* (Buffalo, N.Y.: Prometheus Books, 1983), 72. C. Wright Mills, *Sociology and Pragmatism* (New York: Oxford University Press, 1966), 111–41; the Millsian indictment of Dewey is reaffirmed and expanded by Jeffrey Lustig, *Corporate Liberalism* (Berkeley: University of California Press, 1982), 150–94. Reinhold Niebuhr, *Pragmatism and American Culture*, ed. Gail Kennedy (Boston: Heath, 1950), 62. Jürgen Habermas, *Autonomy and Solidarity*, ed. Peter Dews (London: Verso, 1986), 158. See also Habermas's chapter on Adorno

Running through these influential, and often cogent, critiques from the Left is a thread that touches on the absence of a clearly identifiable, active political commitment in the social thought of Bourne, Dewey, Adorno, and Foucault. Instead of interpreting this absence negatively, as political paralysis or negativism, in the tradition of the critics surveyed above, I want to pursue an alternative reading that sees this absence as fertile and productive of an inquiry into the problematic status of agency—particularly the kinds of human action that would qualify as distinctly political. Ignored or minimized in the received wisdom is the possibility that James, Bourne, Dewey, Adorno, and Foucault sought to explore and promote new forms of human agency and political action that acquire power and value by deliberately eluding identification and direct affiliation.

The various critiques cited above implicitly pose answers to the question that will be explored in the following pages: What, for the intellectual, counts as politically responsible behavior? Before embarking on this task, it is worth remarking how participants in the recent debate over New Historicism frame and answer this question. In the highly politicized context of the present, the issue of responsibility pivots on how one conceives the relation of politics and criticism; proponents of oppositional criticism believe it is imperative to theorize one's practice, "not just to think about it [practice] in general terms but to evolve a critical model adequate not just to action but to a specific politics," to quote from Howard Horwitz's cogent account.[5] In contrast to this left New Historicist insistence on continuity between critical theory and political practice, right New Historicism (I borrow the labels from Gerald Graff) "affirms that cultural practice is a historical phenomenon rather than a theoretical necessity" (ICR, 801).

For the right New Historicism of Stephen Greenblatt or Walter Benn Michaels, "politics emerge in specific actions, not in the structure of cognition" that orients one's critical methodology (ICR, 801–802). Greenblatt's "implication that there is a difference between the status of knowledge and the content of action is controversial because it problematizes the political agency of criticism and theorization" (ICR, 802). According to right New

---

and Horkheimer in *The Philosophical Discourse of Modernity* (Cambridge: MIT Press, 1987), 106–30. Cornel West, *The American Evasion of Philosophy* (Madison: University of Wisconsin Press, 1989), 225–26.
5. Howard Horwitz, "'I Can't Remember': Skepticism, Synthetic Histories, Critical Action," *South Atlantic Quarterly* 87 (Fall 1988): 802; hereafter cited in my text as ICR.

Historicists, who are often called neopragmatists, there is no logical connection between politics and criticism; to conflate them is to believe that, in particular, forms of critical thinking inhere theoretically necessary political consequences, a belief that ultimately betrays a desire to transcend the contingency of historical conditions wherein political action is embedded (ICR, 802).

The claim that theory is a refuge from the contingencies of social practice is both affirmed and complicated by the thinkers discussed below. They affirm that politics emerge in a cultural practice rooted in a historical moment. But at certain moments when philosophies of radical practice have been discredited—as pragmatism and Marxism were, respectively, for Bourne and Adorno, who both were writing during world war—neutrality (Bourne) or Critical Theory (Adorno) can become the most effective practice of intellectuals. At these moments, theory or neutrality places one not on the aloof outside but in the turbulent inside. Which is to say that for those involved in the politics of nonidentity, practice takes various, unpredictable, anomalous forms. For James, Bourne, Dewey, and Adorno, cultural inquiry is never a theoretical necessity itself but a political response to historical events.

Here some explication of the term *nonidentity* would be useful. Nonidentity is Adorno's phrase and refers to several things, one being his refusal of totalizing, closed systems of thought, be they Hegel's, that culminate in Absolute Spirit's identity of the rational as the real, or Lukács's Hegelian-inspired identity of Truth with proletarian class consciousness. Adorno's antisystem, called negative dialectics, is born in the wake of Marxism's failure to honor its pledge to achieve Absolute Spirit by making the proletariat the telos of history. For Adorno, this idealist goal exemplifies identity thinking: a mode of thought that dissolves particularity or difference into the abstractions of concepts and categories. In identity thinking, unlike things become alike, as the universal devours the nonidentical, the particular. Adorno finds the motive of idealism to be rage at nonidentity. By fashioning an antisystem that renounces any synthesis, closure, or finality, Adorno defends the irreducibility of the nonidentical against the devouring power of the concept to impoverish experience.

But how can one, especially a philosopher, dispense with concepts and with identity? Adorno's answer is that one cannot dispense with them. The desire to do so and the impossibility of doing so collide in a contradiction that Adorno deliberately dwells on rather than resolves. This willed tension propels his thought. Thus, Adorno insists on the "untruth of identity" while recognizing that "identity is inherent in thought itself. . . . To think is to identify. . . . We can see through the identity principle, but we cannot think without identifying. Any definition is identification."[6]

Often ignored is that pragmatism, specifically William James's, also attacks the coercion of identity thinking. James's radical empiricism celebrates a pluralistic universe and pivots on a critique of Hegel, specifically Hegel's adherence to, in James's phrase, "the logic of identity."[7] James contrasts his open universe of uncertainty, novelty, and possibility to Hegel's sacrifice of contingency to the laws of his absolutist system. Under the sway of Bergsonian vitalism, James, in 1907, dramatically renounces identity logic in his quest for the flux and excess of pure experience free of the subjugation of concepts and words. In effect, James's is precisely the move that Adorno resists in his insistence on avoiding irrationalism for a dialectic of identity and nonidentity. Dewey refuses to follow William James in his plunge into the flux and is actually closer to Adorno, who begins *Negative Dialectics* with a critique of Bergson (a critique equally applicable to William James) and a salute to Dewey. By taking seriously Adorno's rarely noticed late praise of Dewey (which he repeats in *Aesthetic Theory*), I hope to encourage a rapprochement between two traditions of social theory usually deemed irreconcilable.

Adorno and Dewey's shared distrust of system and of identity thinking extends to an understanding of the very act of classification and identification as the defining ideological moves in establishing what Foucault calls a culture's "regime of truth."[8] Dewey and Adorno encourage our suspicion of categories, including those of intellectual and political identity— oppositional, radical, liberal, conservative. One could say that the Frankfurt motto *nicht mitmachen* (not playing the game) also becomes the creed (or anticreed) of Dewey after the First World War and of his student Bourne in 1915. All three spurn party affiliation, opting instead for what Adorno calls

6. T. W. Adorno, *Negative Dialectics*, trans. E. B. Ashton (New York: Seabury Press, 1973), 5; hereafter cited in my text as *ND*.

7. William James, *A Pluralistic Universe* (Cambridge: Harvard University Press, 1977), 46 and passim. Here I am necessarily simplifying the relation of Adorno, Dewey, and James to Hegel. It is safe to say that no one's relation to Hegel is simple. In general, the thinkers named above were suspicious of his idealist *system* but inspired by his dialectical *method*.

8. Michel Foucault, *Power/Knowledge*, ed. Colin Gordon (New York: Pantheon, 1980), 133.

the only genuine revolution: behavior that is "open and unguarded," free of the "anal deformations" of bourgeois subjectivity.[9] He dubs this mode of being mimetic—a protean and enigmatic concept that seeks to undermine the fixity of concepts by suggesting wordless, expressive, spontaneous behavior that renounces the urge to subjugate the alien.

The bias toward fixity and closure infects not only character structure but also rationalism's and idealism's habitual failure to take into account, says Dewey, "the ultimate evidence of genuine hazard, contingency, irregularity and indeterminateness in nature."[10] Like Foucault in our time, Dewey exposes the Western philosophical tradition as a set of exclusionary mechanisms, "classificatory devices" that deify the fixed and stable and relegate the "uncertain and unfinished" to the category of the unreal (EN, 47–48). Adorno's similar concern for the excluded, the nonidentical, is enacted on at least two levels: Not only does he attack identity thinking in cognition—the belief that concepts and their objects coincide "without leaving a remainder"—but he also critiques its social manifestation as the capitalist law of fungibility (the eradication of difference), which structures the process of commodity exchange.

2

In Henry James's American Scene (1907), these issues of identity and difference find compelling historical embodiment. There, the novelist, who once described himself as having been a lifelong and unwitting pragmatist, enacts a profoundly pragmatist cultural criticism that anticipates Dewey's mode of inquiry founded on a "cultivated naïveté of eye, ear and thought" (EN, 35). During his repatriation of 1904, James returns to his city of birth and traverses the polarities of New York, walking the streets of the teeming immigrant ghettos of the lower East Side and also surveying the "immense promiscuity" of the crowded lobby of the Waldorf-Astoria.[11] The latter site, presided over by "master-spirits of management," testifies

9. T. W. Adorno, quoted in Susan Buck-Morss, The Origin of Negative Dialectics (New York: Free Press, 1977), 189–306. The quotations come from a draft of an essay entitled "Notizen zur neunen Anthropologie" (Frankfurt am Main: Adorno Estate), which appears in a later volume of Adorno's Collected Works.
10. John Dewey, Experience and Nature (LaSalle, Ill.: Open Court Publishing Co., 1929), 60; hereafter cited in my text as EN.
11. Henry James, The American Scene (Bloomington: Indiana University Press, 1969), 103; hereafter cited in my text as AS.

to the triumph of the "amazing hotel-world," wherein operates, with exquisite finesse, "the general machinery" that constitutes America's "genius
for organization" (*AS*, 102, 103, 106). The "hotel-world" is James's "syn-
onym for civilization," particularly modernity's rationalizing, disciplinary imperative. The Waldorf presents the appalling and impressive spectacle of
a "realized ideal" of social control that produces "perfect human felicity"
by turning its patrons into an "army of puppets" who "think of themselves
as delightfully free and easy," so adroitly are they managed by masters of
hotel-spirit (*AS*, 102, 104, 107).

If the Waldorf has dissolved individual differences into a "gorgeous
golden blur" (*AS*, 105), in a more marginal part of town, the lower East Side
Jewish ghetto, nonidentity—what James calls "the obstinate, the uncon-
verted residuum" (*AS*, 124)—remains vital, yet also precarious. Although
hotel-spirit has yet to colonize this immigrant "margin," the aliens seem
likely grist for a "mechanism working with scientific force"—the Progressive
ideology of assimilation bent on forging national unity by constructing "the
'American' identity" (*AS*, 106, 124, 129). This identity compulsion produces
a static uniformity that threatens to devour the margin or residuum of difference and to turn all the subjects of democracy into the puppets of the Waldorf. To resist such passivity, the individual must tap the energy of the margin, James's word for the volatile space of "immense fluidity" that constitutes
the irreducible fact that America's "too formidable future" remains a "fath-
omless depth" beyond all technologies of control (*AS*, 401). Standing for
neither a "possible greater good" nor "greater evil," the margin represents
the indeterminate "mere looming mass of the *more,* the more and more
to come" (*AS*, 401). Throughout *The American Scene*, James's effort is to
exemplify, in his own marginal, oscillating status as returning native and
stranger, an alternative mode of being. By incarnating "the more," James
demonstrates what it means for the self to relax the repressions and rigidi-
ties of identitarian thinking.

I have argued elsewhere that James's attitude toward the immigrant—the most notorious feature of *The American Scene*—should not be
reduced to racism or anti-Semitism, for it insists on a complexity that encompasses a range of reactions.[12] James signals this commitment to multiple,
conflicting responses in the self-description he repeats throughout: As a

12. For elaboration on this point and on all of section 2, see my *Trial of Curiosity: Henry
James, William James, and the Challenge of Modernity* (New York: Oxford University
Press, 1991).

"restless analyst," he risks a "certain recklessness in the largest surrender to impressions" (*AS*, 3). He deliberately seeks shocks, as he told William James prior to his visit. His kinetic response to "the intensity of the material picture in the dense" (*AS*, 130) streets of New York is best described as mimetic, in that it mimes (rather than seeks to order) the density, volatility, and "thick growth" of "rich accretions" of the urban spectacle that he confronts (*AS*, 130, 123). From his preface onwards, James insists on flaunting his vulnerability to "the largest exposure to mistakes," an exposure that produces *The American Scene*: his "gathered impressions" that defiantly "stand naked and unashamed."[13] Above all, his fascination is exploratory, involving "intimate surrender"; he describes himself "plunging into" the "study of the innumerable ways" in which "alienism unmistakable, alienism undisguised and unashamed" is somehow "*at home*" in New York (*AS*, 125–26; James's emphasis).

Compelling James to such intense study is an uneasy and unexpected recognition of resemblance—"*he* was at home too, quite with the same intensity" as his foreign "companions" (*AS*, 125–26; James's emphasis). Neither affirming the Brahmin impulse to lament and decry the immigrant presence, nor endorsing the liberal Progressive effort to celebrate the absorptive power of the melting pot, Jamesian fascination works by a dialectic of identity and difference that acknowledges the former (the identity of himself and the immigrant) in the very act of insisting on the value of the latter ("the vitality and value" of difference, of retaining alien "color") (*AS*, 129, 128).

Although he finds alien difference imperiled by America's assimilative "mechanism," he is not without hope that the "obstinate residuum" will somehow remain (*AS*, 124). James doubts that the "process of shedding" alien identity will ever be definitive or complete: "isn't it conceivable that they [foreign qualities "ingrained in generations"] may rise again to the surface. . . . Do they burrow underground, to await their day again?" (*AS*, 129). Such "speculation," says James, is "irresistibly forced upon" him as a measure of his "interest" in the "'ethnic'" outlook (*AS*, 130). But he is apologetic for indulging in these "vague evocations" of "nebulous remoteness" for they depart from the strenuous empiricism of his scrutiny of the "formidable foreground" with its "pressure of the present and the immediate" (*AS*, 130). James is acutely aware that his peripatetic cultural criticism

13. In my edition of *The American Scene*, the preface is unpaginated, thus I cannot provide page numbers for these quotations.

must resist the "impulse irresponsibly to escape from the formidable foreground which so often, in the American world, lies in wait for the spirit of intellectual dalliance" (*AS*, 130).

What makes theoretical speculation regarding "ultimate syntheses, ultimate combinations and possibilities" irresponsible is its reliance on "distance," which reduces experience to the mental and insulates the body from the "chaos of confusion and change" that James begins relishing immediately upon disembarking (*AS*, 1). Thus, in a remarkably literal affirmation, James comes to enact in *The American Scene* the kind of cultural criticism he had sponsored in 1898, when he surveyed the "question of opportunities" confronting the American writer and critic in a vast "newspapered democracy" of unprecedented mass literacy.[14] These "conditions hitherto almost unobserved" are precisely those "that the critic likes most to encounter": the "strain and stress—those of suspense, life, movement, change, the multiplication of possibilities, surprises, disappointments . . . the endless play" of "deferred conclusions" (*EOL*, 652).

This statement virtually summarizes the premise animating what I have called the politics of nonidentity. In various contexts, Bourne, Dewey, Adorno, and Foucault give it various inflections: one calling it the experimental life of irony (Bourne); another, cultivated naïveté (Dewey); another, immanent critique (Adorno); another, describing it as the stance of the specific intellectual (Foucault). But they all share, with Henry James, a paradoxical effort that engages in public life and upholds intellectual responsibility while resisting conventional modes of engagement and responsibility. They perceive a most basic convention—affiliation with a particular political party—as passive submission to a preordained identity that shields one from the hazards of immersion. Instead, these thinkers articulate a politics by embodying it in a style of practice.

The paradox of trying to label a strategy committed to disrupting the impulse to identity can never be fully avoided. Yet, the style of practice described above can be called pragmatic as long as we stress pragmatism's challenge to fixed identity, a challenge expressed not simply in the principle but the *practice* of fallibilism, with its skepticism toward any claim to stable identity or single truth. Electing practice over epistemology, this stance reconceives philosophy (and cultural inquiry) along the lines Adorno does at the outset of *Negative Dialectics*— as a "mode of conduct" that "shields no

14. Henry James, *Essays on Literature: American and English* (New York: Library of America, 1984), 652; hereafter cited in my text as *EOL*.

primacy, harbors no certainty": the "crux is what happens in it, not a thesis or position" (ND, 33–34). Adorno goes on to remark that such an orientation makes philosophy "not expoundable . . . the fact that most of it can be expounded speaks against it" (ND, 33–34). Instead of renouncing philosophy, however, Adorno uses this antinomy as a "ferment to an emphatic philosophy" akin to "Dewey's wholly humane version" of pragmatism (ND, 33–34, 14). Here, Adorno marks his kinship with the pragmatic commitment to experience and to the "evasion" (borrowing Cornel West's recent word) of philosophy's traditional task of questing for certainty.

Dewey is famous for abandoning this quest. He "evaded" not only philosophy but also traditional kinds of political engagement. Peter Manicas argues that Dewey is best described as an anarchist whose most "instructive legacy" is a sustained effort to articulate a "third" ideology, neither liberal nor Marxist.[15] One might add that Dewey's effort, akin to James's and Adorno's, in effect, makes thirdness itself a governing value and perspective, as an emblem of the remainder (Adorno) or margin (James)—that which is suspended between conventional oppositions.[16] At certain historical moments, this quest for thirdness acquires a desperate pathos, as when Bourne asks, "Is there no place left, then, for the intellectual . . . who does not dread suspense?"[17] He raises the question in the face of "the terrible dilemma" he confronts in 1917: either support the war and "count for nothing because you are swallowed in the mass . . . or remain aloof . . . in which case you count for nothing because you are outside the machinery of reality" (RW, 317). Feeling betrayed by Dewey's support of war, Bourne seems to appeal directly to his former mentor for reply.

Dewey eventually answers Bourne, we shall see, by a commitment to nonidentity that is diversely enacted in his inexhaustible career. In helping to form, for instance, the League for Independent Political Action in 1929, Dewey is careful to insist that "the league is not a party and has no ambition to become a party"; he defines its "function" as "looking toward the organization of the desired new alignment . . . it aims to act as a con-

15. Peter Manicas, "Dewey and the Class Struggle," in Values and Value Theory in Twentieth-Century America, ed. M. Murphey and E. Flower (Philadelphia: Temple University Press, 1988), 67–81, especially 79.

16. Adorno calls his nonidentity thinking (that constructs constellations) a "third possibility beyond the alternative of positivism and idealism" (ND, 166).

17. Randolph Bourne, The Radical Will (New York: Urizen Books, 1977), 317; hereafter cited in my text as RW.

necting link . . . a symbol for one type of approach to the problem."[18] And Dewey accepts as praise the critique of the League program as "partial and tentative, experimental and not rigid": "We claim them as indications of our philosophy."[19] On another occasion, asked to speak on the subject of "The Need for a New Political Party," Dewey immediately revises his topic and title to "Needed—A New Politics." He urges "the necessity for a new kind of politics, a new kind of moral conception in politics . . . some fundamental rethinking of our social and political relations."[20]

If the familiar name for Dewey's new kind of politics is democracy, this identification does not take us very far, for democracy, in Dewey's view, is stubbornly resistant to fixed definition; indeed he describes it as a perpetual pursuit of an end that is a "radical end because it has not been adequately realized in any country at any time."[21] "As yet the full conditions, economic and legal, for a completely democratic experience have not existed."[22] With fascism on the march in 1939, Dewey draws the unsettling consequences of this claim: If democracy has yet to exist, we in the United States are deeply mistaken if we believe "democratic conditions automatically maintain themselves, or . . . can be identified with fulfillment of prescriptions laid down in a constitution" (FC, 87–88). In short, Americans are tempted into a dangerously ahistorical reification of democracy if they imagine it a fixed entity guaranteeing us immunity "from the disease" of totalitarianism.

In emptying political parties and democracy of stable identity, Dewey's advocacy of a politics of nonidentity is striking. All its proponents challenge traditional accounts not only of philosophy and political engagement but also of the intellectual's identity. "I think that intellectuals are abandoning their old prophetic function," Foucault remarks often in the 1970s; they are no longer "master[s] of truth and justice, . . . 'the bearer of universal values'" standing above the masses as moral exemplars of the "universality of justice and the equity of an ideal law."[23] In American culture, seeds of an analogous revision of intellectual identity are evident in Randolph Bourne. In 1916, he vigorously rejects Matthew Arnold's cultural

18. John Dewey, The Later Works (Carbondale: Southern Illinois University Press, 1986), 9:67.
19. Dewey, The Later Works, 9:67.
20. Dewey, The Later Works, 11:274, 280–81.
21. Dewey, The Later Works, 11: 299.
22. John Dewey, Freedom and Culture, in The Later Works, 13:115, 87–88; hereafter cited in my text as FC.
23. Foucault, Power/Knowledge, 126, 128, 132.

ideal, which imposed the "tyranny of the 'best' " as a "universal norm" (*RW*, 194). Bourne can be said to anticipate Foucault's distaste for the "Greek wise man, the Jewish prophet, [or] the Roman legislator" as a model of the intellectual but to decline to relinquish an investment in the force of moral outrage embodied in the "malcontent" possessed of a "skeptical, malicious, desperate, ironical mood" (*RW*, 347).

Yet, Bourne resists enthroning the malcontent intellectual (derived partly from Bourne's enthusiasm for Nietzsche) as oppositional in the sense of occupying a transcendent moral position. Indeed, he describes the ironist (his name for the kind of urban intellectual he envisions) as having "lost his egotism completely. He has rubbed out the line that separates his person-ality from the rest of the world. . . . He has not the faculty of brooding; he cannot mine the depths of his own soul . . . the flow and swirl of things is his compelling interest" (*RW*, 147–48). Here, in Bourne's depiction of the intellectual as exultantly weightless, radically permeable, the de-centered self of Jamesian immanence is emphatically confirmed, indeed heightened. But if Bourne's pleasure in urban immersion looks back to the restless ana-lyst of *The American Scene*, it also anticipates Foucault's "dream of the intellectual" who is "incessantly on the move, doesn't know exactly where he is heading nor what he will think tomorrow for he is too attentive to the present." [24] Such engagement, notes Foucault, relegates questions of clas-sification and program to the merely secondary. Thus Foucault limns what he calls the "specific" intellectual.

Here, James's restless analyst and Bourne's dynamic ironist join Foucault in a shared commitment to the nonidentity of the intellectual, whose task (quoting Bourne) will be to "keep the intellectual waters constantly in motion to prevent" the "ice" of "premature crystallization" from ever form-ing (*RW*, 317). The incessant, doomed effort to defer the inevitable ice is the burden of Dewey's pragmatist project, especially after he revises and clarifies it in the wake of Bourne's withering critique in 1917. Before discuss-ing this, I will continue the effort to break the ice that has frozen James's reputation in "premature crystallization" as a genteel elitist and impeccable formalist.

Part of the audacity and importance of *The American Scene* is its calculated break with a New England idealist cultural tradition. Fashioning an alternative cultural criticism informed by a pragmatic emphasis on con-text, James underscores rather than disguises his embeddedness: While

24. "Power and Sex: An Interview with Michel Foucault," *Telos* 32 (Summer 1977): 161.

professing to wield his analytical scalpel with aloof severity, he can't resist the pleasures of roaming around New York. "I defy even a master of morbid observation," he declares, "to perambulate New York unless he be interested . . . interest must be taken as a final fact" (*AS*, 110). "You can't escape" becomes James's watchword, and he calls himself a "victim of his interest" (*AS*, 108). His attitude implicitly challenges the idealist assumptions of the genteel tradition that embraced many of those whom he counted among his oldest friends, including such masters of "morbid observation" as Henry Adams and E. L. Godkin (*AS*, 110).

These two mainstays of the urban gentry are relevant here for their striking divergence from James's dialectical response to modernity. Because both men lack James's interest and his willingness to be its victim, it would be difficult to conceive Godkin and Adams walking the turn-of-the-century streets of New York and sharing James's rapt attention to the radically democratic sites that fill most of the gentry with fear and repugnance: the swarms of immigrants in the Bowery, Ellis Island, and Central Park. A few years before his visit to America, James reviews the last work of his old friend Godkin and finds its view of American democracy impoverished and bitter. In the course of his review, he describes a perspective opposed to Godkin's but (implicitly) close to James's own. It is one that "both takes the democratic era unreservedly for granted and yet declines to take for granted that it has shown the whole . . . of its hand" (*EOL*, 690). From this viewpoint, James finds the era "exciting" in "its inexorability and its great scale" (*EOL*, 690). He evokes these qualities in a suggestive image: "If . . . we are imprisoned in it, the prison is probably so vast that we need not even meditate plans of escape" (*EOL*, 690).

James's stance is immanent, for it is launched from inside and takes for granted what he (and later Bourne) calls the inexorable: man's confinement in what has created him—social and cultural conventions, practices, representations, and institutions. James is confident that these constructions can be renovated—"nothing here is grimly ultimate," he says (*EOL*, 693). But he is skeptical of attempts to abolish history, whether by class revolt (as in Marx), by man becoming a god in nature (as in Emerson), or by man returning to the flux (as in Bergson and late William James), to cite three such strategies. In the extremity of their response, these oppositional critiques are heroic hymns to man's Promethean powers, a grandeur absent in the immanent stance. A remarkable aspect of the status of immanent critique in America has been its virtual invisibility, so naturalized is the equation of critique and Promethean heroism. We tend to conceive cultural

critique as draped in the flamboyant colors of alienation and/or elitism—
be it patrician disdain, Populist resentment, 1960s counterculture, or modernism's arsenal of strategies to *épater les bourgeois*: dadaist mockery,
avant-garde hermeticism, and proletarian social realism, among others.

Although "the transcendent method, which aims at totality, seems
more radical than the immanent method, which presupposes the questionable whole . . . [t]he choice of a standpoint outside the sway of existing
society is as fictitious as only the construction of abstract utopias can be."[25]
Thus argues Adorno, who, like James, refuses an Archimedean position
above culture that "speaks the language of false escape" (*P*, 31). Adorno
also shares James's imagery; he finds no exit from what he calls the "open
air prison which the world is becoming" (*P*, 34).

Renouncing transcendence, be it in the form of theoretical speculation or as the ideological privilege of his class, James situates his cultural
pragmatism in what he calls man's "exposed and entangled state" as a
"social creature."[26] The political equivalent of entanglement—which is citizenship or membership—is of special concern in *The American Scene*.
James's commitment to heterogeneity, or nonidentity, is at once aesthetic
(for it is registered stylistically) and political, for his animating motive is "experimental deviation" from "the democratic consistency" (*AS*, 455, 55). Yet,
the politics of James's book have appeared virtually nonexistent to most
readers because they are embodied in the practice of "restless" analysis
rather than in a theory about that practice. T. S. Eliot's famous remark on the
absence of ideas in James seems dramatically confirmed in *The American
Scene*, where the density of metaphor that comprises Jamesian observation affords no outside point upon which either author or reader can gain
reflective distance from the restless mobility of American life. This saturation
is precisely what James finds compelling: "The subject was everywhere—
that was the beauty, the advantage," he remarks at the start of the book:
"It was thrilling, really, to find one's self in presence of a theme to which
everything directly contributed, leaving no touch of experience irrelevant"
(*AS*, 3).

Hopefully, this broad sketch makes it apparent that James's project
in *The American Scene* is nearly the opposite of the received opinion that
reads the book as apolitical at best, antipolitical at worst. James's is a

25. T. W. Adorno, *Prisms*, trans. Samuel and Shierry Weber (Cambridge: MIT Press,
1981), 31; hereafter cited in my text as *P*.
26. Henry James, *The Art of the Novel* (New York: C. Scribner's Sons, 1962), 65.

48

strenuous, public effort to offer an implicit alternative to a modern social order rapidly becoming depoliticized (and thus impoverished) by superbly efficient disciplinary mechanisms. By injecting "margin," or what a recent political theorist calls "greater slack in the institutional order," James hopes to foster a broader range of subjectivity.[27] His politicizing project assaults the genteel antimodernism typical of his social class in at least three ways: His aim is not the futile, nostalgic one of recovering the primitive flux and eradicating the "hotel-spirit"; rather, he seeks its renovation. His contempt is not for the messy, bewildering overflow of democratic hotchpotch but for the homogenizing of its diverse possibilities by the American genius for organization. And he remains convinced that modernity does not announce the degradation of the human spirit but is a compelling and uncompleted project with the potential to be creatively revised in less disciplinary directions.

If James's emphatic modernity is anomalous in the context of his own time and social class, it leaves him the ally of a younger generation, the famous one of 1910 known as the Young Intellectuals. Its leader is Randolph Bourne, often considered America's first self-conscious, modern urban intellectual. Nurtured by the ideas of William James and Bergson, Bourne is actually closest to another writer he admired—Henry James. Both reject monadic individualism and the pursuit of the primitive flux and oppose the assimilationist compulsions of progressivism bent on "colorless . . . uniformity" (*RW*, 254). While James cannot be said to share the exuberance of Bourne's romantic commitment to the teeming city of aliens as the crucible of modernity, both men start from the premise that urban modernity is inexorable. Bourne's allegiances align him not only with Henry James but also with his mentor at Columbia, John Dewey. I argue below that Bourne helps instigate in Dewey a mode of cultural and philosophical inquiry steeped in the values of nonidentity thinking. In short, he stimulates Dewey to politicize his thought. One consequence is that Dewey's postwar intellectual role becomes congruent in significant ways with that of the Frankfurt School, which was to critique sharply American pragmatism in the 1940s. These matters comprise the subject of the next two sections.

3

Reflecting "with almost disarming candor the spirit of the prevailing business culture" and "modern industrialism," American pragmatism is the

27. "Slack" is William Connolly's concept in *Politics and Ambiguity* (Madison: University of Wisconsin Press, 1987), 107.

product of a society that "has no time to remember and meditate," declares Max Horkheimer in his 1944 attack on pragmatism.[28] Pragmatism forfeits the responsibility of critique and replaces it with adjustment, just as it replaces truth with calculability and reason with instrumentality. Horkheimer declares of the pragmatists: "They are liberal, tolerant, optimistic, and quite unable to deal" with the possibility that truth "might turn out to be completely shocking to humanity at a given historical moment."[29]

At a particularly shocking moment—America's entry into the First World War—Randolph Bourne delivers a critique of pragmatism strikingly similar to Horkheimer's. "Hostile . . . to any attitude that is not a cheerful and brisk setting to work," Deweyan instrumentalism, says Bourne, provided an intellectual climate particularly conducive to encouraging a generation of students and intellectuals into a shameful capitulation to the war hysteria of 1917 (RW, 341). Nuanced thinking alert to differences is sacrificed in the passion for direct unquestioning action. Running through his famous cluster of war essays is a powerful critique of pragmatism, which tends to be lost or minimized by commentators who claim that Bourne's primary concern is to articulate a pacifist position.

But as the historian Paul Bourke has shown, Bourne's is not a pacifist stance. Indeed, he "was not talking about the war, at least not in any way that was relevant to the business of prosecuting or ending it."[30] Rather, Bourne's specific concern is with pragmatism's "craving for action," which Bourne finds nurtured by an unreflexive confidence in having control over events (RW, 314). Without in any way scanting the political pressures of 1917, Bourne brilliantly reveals that this moment of history has brought to a crisis a crucial philosophical issue: the status of human agency and will in pragmatism and its political counterpart, progressivism. Both have encouraged a "dread of intellectual suspense. . . . Neutrality meant suspense, and so it became the object of loathing to frayed nerves" (RW, 315). The political position of neutrality is correlative with a whole range of attitudes tabooed by pragmatism: "hesitations, ironies, consciences, considerations—all were drowned in the elemental blare of doing something aggressive" (RW, 315).

In his war essays, which practice a powerful neutrality, Bourne recovers this range of affective experience from political oblivion. His refusal

28. Max Horkheimer, Eclipse of Reason (New York: Oxford University Press, 1947), 50, 52.
29. Horkheimer, Eclipse of Reason, 51–52.
30. Paul Bourke, "The Status of Politics, 1909–1919: The New Republic, Randolph Bourne, and Van Wyck Brooks," Journal of American Studies 8 (1974): 171–202.

to crystallize enacts precisely the "creative attitude toward the war" that pragmatists are impotent to achieve (*RW*, 313). Bourne's creative effort depends less on a theoretical apparatus or political program than on crafting strategies that can recognize and repair what the historical moment has revealed: "the inadequacies of American democracy" (*RW*, 327).

Pivotal to Bourne's revisionary practice is irony, which he employs less as an aesthetic term than as descriptive of a quality of action that avoids crystallization by dissolving conventional oppositions, like passive/active. Bourne's experimental life of irony, in effect, sponsors the indeterminacy of thirdness as an alternative to the pragmatic emphasis on scientific control and mastery. "How soon their 'mastery' becomes 'drift,' " says Bourne about the smug certainty of the "realists" (*RW*, 330). His diction, of course, sneers at one of the bibles of progressivism—Walter Lippmann's *Drift and Mastery*. In Lippmann's famous words: "This is what mastery means: the substitution of conscious intention for unconscious striving. . . . Science is the unfrightened, masterful and humble approach to reality. . . . It is self-government." [31] Upon its publication in 1914, Lippmann's modernized Emersonian prometheanism sweeps up Bourne and many others. [32] With the coming of war, Bourne's own faith wanes in progressivism's politics of the national state and social control. Fading, too, is his belief in what grounded progressivism—its liberal ideology of autonomy and will. Bourne's and Lippmann's hero, William James, has preached this doctrine and has celebrated the freedom of pure experience, wherein all is "perfectly fluent . . . self-luminous and suggests no paradoxes." [33] For all his disagreements with James's individualism, Dewey, by 1917, has yet to sever decisively his own instrumentalism from the Jamesian optimism in man's untrammeled powers.

The war overturns—politicizes—everything, for it rudely brings James's pure experience, Dewey's purposive social control, and Lippmann's mastery face to face with what Bourne calls the "inexorable": "the absolute, coercive" situation of imperialist power (*RW*, 322). Above all, says Bourne, "the inexorable abolishes choices," and "nothing is so disagreeable to the pragmatic mind as any kind of an absolute" (*RW*, 322). Bourne is ready to cope with the inexorable, for he has always tempered his indi-

31. Walter Lippmann, *Drift and Mastery* (Madison: University of Wisconsin Press, 1985), 150–51.
32. My characterization here is borrowed from David Hollinger's "Science and Anarchy: Walter Lippmann's *Drift and Mastery*," in *In the American Province* (Baltimore: Johns Hopkins University Press, 1989), 50.
33. William James, *Essays in Radical Empiricism* (Cambridge: Harvard University Press, 1976), 45.

vidualism with irony, which provides a "sense of proportion" and alerts man to the fact that he "lives in a world of relations" (*RW*, 143). Because, as we have seen, the ironist is spared the egotistical illusion of masterful selfhood, he is able to feel a "bond of sympathy" that complicates and inhibits the craving for immediate action and simple answers (*RW*, 145). Recognizing the war as unavoidable, Bourne detects the pragmatists' blind spot: "that war doesn't need enthusiasm, doesn't need conviction, doesn't need hope to sustain it. Once maneuvered, it takes care of itself, provided only that" the industrial elite arrange for American capital to be placed "in a strategic position for world enterprise" at the war's end (*RW*, 321).

The ironist also pursues the consequences of his historicist insight for the intellectual's status. In light of the inexorable, the intellectual suffers an impotence that is socially constituted by the economic demands of the modern imperial state. Rather than merely lamenting this, Bourne boldly seeks to turn powerlessness into the impetus for a constructive skepticism, a "robust desperation" and a "heightened energy" of "apathy" (*RW*, 345, 317). Faced with the inexorable, one keeps "healthy," says Bourne, by a "vigorous assertion of values in which war has no part," as skepticism becomes a "shelter behind which is built up a wider consciousness" of opportunities for critical civic inquiry and experimental modes of intellectual practice (*RW*, 326).

Bourne's embrace of the inexorable exposes the political naïveté at the heart of pragmatism's vain humanism. When he contends that, "given efficiency at the top," our country at war "can do very well without our patriotism," Bourne, in effect, delivers an ultimatum to pragmatism's followers: become an "efficient instrument of war-technique," manipulated by economic and imperialist imperatives to which you are blind; or awake and reconstruct pragmatism on a new basis—one that takes the fact of "inexorable" capitalist efficiency, rather than free will and choice, as the fundamental given of modernity (*RW*, 321, 343).[34] In his last essay, "Old Tyrannies," he not only buries the old tyranny of individualism but, more important, reconstructs the modern subject in light of the inexorable: The self, he writes, "is a network of representations of the various codes and institutions of society" (*RW*, 171).

This portrayal of the modern subject as social text counts as Bourne's legacy, the other part of which implicitly demands that pragmatism reorient

34. Bourne expresses this momentous sense of the inexorable in his last two essays, "Old Tyrannies" and "The State." Critics, like Michael Walzer, have noted the extreme pessimism of both. Walzer says they are "not the authentic Bourne" (see *The Company of Critics* [New York: Basic Books, 1988], 63).

its political thinking or, more precisely, recognize thinking as political, that is, as conducted not in the blissful freedom of pure experience but rather in the "thick encrustations" of society and class (*RW*, 380). After 1917, John Dewey is nourished by both parts of Bourne's gift, and he proceeds to renovate his pragmatism in a Bournian direction.[35] While never becoming the "malicious," "malcontent" (*RW*, 347) skeptic that Bourne urges as the intellectual's social role, Dewey does reconceive philosophy as, in his words, "a critique of prejudices"—of the saturations—overlaying "life-experience" (*EN*, 34).

Dewey equates philosophy and critique in his masterpiece *Experience and Nature* (1925).[36] Here, he calls "totality, order, unity, and rationality" mere "eulogistic predicates" that artificially simplify existence when they are "used to describe the foundations and proper conclusions" of a system (*EN*, 27). In this work, Dewey's sustained critique of the naturalized fictions of subjectivism, objectivism, and liberalism provides the philosophical basis for a more nuanced and various (less narrowly rational and instrumental) understanding of selfhood and for the widening of his political vision in the late twenties and in the thirties. In Dewey's work, Bourne's "heightened energy" of tentativeness and experiment that relaxes the "power of will and purpose" becomes a powerful source of vitality in mapping strategies to ventilate the "inexorable" (*RW*, 153).

One way Dewey embraces Bourne's "inexorable" is by dismissing classical liberalism's premise that individuality is given already. Replacing it is a view of selfhood as a continuously precarious active process. Dewey is able to draw the political consequences: When the self is dynamically

35. In no way do I intend to suggest Bourne as a monocausal explanation for the new direction in Dewey's thought. While there is no prima facie evidence for my contention of Bourne's influence, there is the fact that Dewey confesses error regarding his prowar stance. Soon after the war, Dewey speaks of the "pious optimism" and "childish" "sentimentality" of those, like himself, who supported war, and his biographer George Dykhuizen implicitly links this self-critique to the impact of Bourne's criticisms (see *The Life and Mind of John Dewey* [Carbondale: Southern Illinois University Press, 1973], 166). Robert Westbrook's definitive study of Dewey, published after I completed the present essay, argues that, to a degree, "Dewey's postwar writing and activism constituted, in effect, a concession to Bourne's arguments." In particular, Dewey "shared Bourne's contempt for those who uncritically took the values of their culture for granted" (see *John Dewey and American Democracy* [Ithaca: Cornell University Press, 1991], 196 n. 2, 369).
36. Ironically, in this philosophical work, rather than in the social criticism of, for instance, *Individualism Old and New* (1931), Dewey's political vision is most provocative, albeit implicit. One reason is that Dewey relaxes his emphasis on social control.

conceived, "it is also seen that social modifications are the only means of the creation of changed personalities. Institutions are viewed in their educative effect—with reference to the types of individuals they foster."[37] Inquiry is thus socialized, and we are prompted to ask "what the specific stimulating, fostering and nurturing power of each specific social arrangement may be."[38] Abolished is the traditional separation between politics and morals.

By reuniting politics and morals, Dewey has repaired the precise defect that Bourne had detected: pragmatism's subordination of values to technique. By 1935, Dewey's politics will reflect this revision In his philosophy as he moves left to socialism: Whereas "earlier liberalism regarded the separate and competing economic action of individuals as the means to social well-being," we "must reverse the perspective and see that socialized economy," rather than private control by the few of the means of production, is the means by which the "flowering of human capacities" is accomplished.[39] Dewey has migrated far from the impoverished criteria of adaptation or adjustment where, in Bourne's words, "there is no provision for thought or experience getting beyond itself" (RW, 344). Instead of adjustment, caution, and regression, Bourne urges a "vision [that] must constantly overshoot technique" (RW, 344). Bourne's emphasis on overshooting vision is not vague aestheticism but a response to the defining condition of modern capitalism, what he calls in 1917 a "new age of surplus value, economic and spiritual" (RW, 470). A philosophy of adjustment reflects a "parsimonious world. It has no place in a world of surplus energy."[40] "An importunate and incalculable stream of desire," says Bourne, floods the modern subject; how to direct desire into "creative channels," rather than suppress it, constitutes the problem (RW, 470).

In 1935, Dewey identifies the elimination of scarcity and the advent of an "age of potential plenty" as two of the decisive changes rendering capitalism—a system built on scarcity and competition—historically obsolete (LSA, 42). "Capitalism is a systematic manifestation of desires and purposes built up in an age of ever threatening want" (LSA, 43). The "corrosive materialism" and possessive individualism that defined this system of

---

37. John Dewey, Reconstruction in Philosophy (Boston: Beacon Press, 1957), 196–97.
38. Dewey, Reconstruction in Philosophy, 196–97.
39. John Dewey, Liberalism and Social Action, in The Later Works, 11:63–64; hereafter cited in my text as LSA.
40. The contexts of Bourne's remarks are in a review of the neoclassicist culture critic Paul Elmer Moore.

desires must now be replaced by a "radical" liberalism that bypasses piece-meal reformism for "re-forming, in its literal sense, the institutional scheme of things" (*LSA*, 45).

This renovation of pragmatism on the basis of a surplus, rather than a scarcity, economy likely helps convince Adorno of Dewey's "wholly humane version" of pragmatism (*ND*, 14). Sounding remarkably like Bourne, Adorno, in 1941, critiques pragmatism's passive surrender to adjustment as the "historical index of all truth."[41] Adjustment is such an index "only as long as scarcity and poverty prevail in the world. Adjustment is the mode of behavior that corresponds to the situation of 'too little.' Pragmatism is narrow and limited because it hypostatizes this situation as eternal" (*P*, 93). The pragmatist, says Adorno, "represents poverty"; "himself regressive, [he] clings to the standpoint of those who cannot think beyond tomorrow, beyond the next step" (*P*, 92). In contrast, the dialectician refuses to perpetuate adjustment, "the domination of what is always the same" (*P*, 94).

Such domination inhibits thought, which involves for Adorno, as for Bourne's irony, "an element of exaggeration, of overshooting the object, of self-detachment from the weight of the factual."[42] Thus, the act of thinking "resembles play" and possesses "the element of irresponsibility, of blithe-ness springing from the volatility of thought" (*MM*, 127). This is the volatility produced by thought that encourages differences to circulate, rather than dissolve into, static identity. Mimetic behavior involves the capacity for ex-periencing the dynamism of nonidentity thinking in its demand that one be both distant and intimate, relaxed and alert, in an affective "field of ten-sion."[43]

Adorno's remarks of 1951 on thought's instability anticipate the open-

41. Adorno's remarks on pragmatism are in his essay on Thorstein Veblen, reprinted in *Prisms*, 93.

42. Theodor Adorno, *Minima Moralia* (London: Verso, 1978), 127; hereafter cited in my text as *MM*.

43. My understanding of the status of mimesis in Adorno's thought departs from Haber-mas's influential interpretation. He claims that in his hatred of instrumental reason, Adorno refuses to make mimesis anything but wordless impulse, the sheer opposite of reason. But Habermas ignores the fact that, in his final work, *Aesthetic Theory*, Adorno repeatedly discusses mimetic *behavior* and practice. In a corrective to Habermas, Fred Alford dem-onstrates that Adorno conceives mimesis as activity embodying an alternative to instru-mental reason, not a flight from it. See C. Fred Alford, *Narcissism: Socrates, the Frankfurt School, and Psychoanalytic Theory* (New Haven: Yale University Press, 1988), 113–14. For an informative, convincing exposure of Habermas's misreadings of Adorno, see R. Hullot-Kentor, "Back to Adorno," *Telos* 81 (Fall 1989): 5–29.

ing of *Negative Dialectics* fifteen years later, wherein, he writes that "philosophy can always go astray, which is the sole reason why it can go
forward" (*ND*, 14). John Dewey, says Adorno, has most recently recognized
this paradox. Adorno salutes Dewey's "corrective to the total rule of method"
as a way of keeping alive philosophy's "playful element"—its attraction to a
"sphere beyond control" that is tabooed by traditional views that construe
philosophy as a science (*ND*, 14). Dewey seeks to reach this sphere by
what he calls an act of "intellectual disrobing," and, thus, he urges philosophy to renounce "intellectual timidity . . . for speculative audacity . . .
sloughing off a cowardly reliance upon those partial ideas to which we
are wont to give the name of facts."[44] Dewey's disrobing looks back to
Bourne's plea in 1917 for "free speculation" to "tease, provoke, [and] irritate
thought" (*RW*, 346), and looks ahead to Adorno's remark in 1931 that "with
the disintegration of all security within great philosophy, experiment makes
its entry."[45]

Experiment, of course, is Dewey's pragmatist watchword. Like critical theory, pragmatism abolishes philosophy as a repository of eternal truth
and definitive authority. Adorno's question in 1931 is whether, "after the
failure of efforts for a grand and total philosophy," philosophy must be "liqui-
dated" (AP, 125). His answer: only if it persists in the "Cartesian demand"
that reality be studied as an absolute, autonomous, rational totality (AP,
132). Philosophy will survive if it "renounces the question of totality" and
"gives up the great problems" (AP, 126) of metaphysics in order to read
the "incomplete, contradictory and fragmentary . . . text" of history—"the
break-in of what is irreducible" (AP, 132).

Three years before Adorno's statement, Dewey had practiced a cultural inquiry into the bewildering text of history precisely along the experimental lines sketched above. This is the subject of the next section.

4

For leftist intellectuals in the mid-twenties, the most exciting social
experiment was occurring in Russia; no place seemed so bristling with
possibility and potential, with what Walter Benjamin calls "astonishing ex-

44. Dewey, *EN*, 35; *The Later Works*, 3: 10.
45. Adorno's remark is in his important, posthumously published essay of 1931, "The
Actuality of Philosophy," trans. B. Snow, *Telos* 31 (Spring 1977): 133; hereafter cited in
my text as AP.

perimentation . . . boundless curiosity and playfulness," as Moscow.[46] Dewey visits in 1928, two years after Benjamin. In his remarkable set of "Impressions of Soviet Russia," Dewey practices an inquiry in his specific sense of an activity demanding "surrender of what is possessed, disowning of what supports one in secure ease" (*EN*, 201). In Russia, Dewey becomes what Bourne cherished and yearned for—"the intellectual who cannot yet crystallize, who does not dread suspense" (*RW*, 317).

Dewey's disowning of ease for the precariousness of the uncrystallized begins with his abandoning of his presuppositions that communism and Marxist dogma had exhausted the meaning of the Russian Revolution. And then he surrenders to the exhilarated sense of curiosity and openness that suffuses the streets, museums, and schools. In short, Dewey sufficiently relaxes his self to mime playfully the mood of revolution, whose essence is not "merely political and economic" but "psychic and moral" in its "release of courage, energy, and confidence in life."[47]

The first sentence of his opening essay finds Dewey immersed in the presiding mood of tentativeness: "The alteration of Petrograd into Leningrad is without question a symbol, but the mind wavers in deciding of what" (ISR, 203). Registering the fact of change and the attendant indeterminacy, Dewey will manage to dwell in suspension, much as Russia dwells in a state of transition, allegedly to total communism. Both remain in an "intermediate stage," resisting "premature crystallization." With his mind "dazed" and "in a whirl of new impressions," Dewey, in Russia, approximates to a striking degree the open, unguarded spontaneity of Adorno's mimetic behavior. Yet in modifying the urge for conceptual definition, clarity, and control (attributes of instrumental reason), Dewey is far from oblivious to actuality, to the fragility of the Russian release of human power. For this release, notes Dewey, occurs "in spite of secret police, inquisitions, arrests, and deportations . . . [and] exiling of party opponents" (ISR, 211).[48]

46. Walter Benjamin, "Moscow," in *Reflections*, trans. E. Jephcott (New York: Harcourt, 1978), 106. See also his *Moscow Diary*, trans. Richard Sieburth (Cambridge: Harvard University Press, 1986), which overlaps with and enlarges upon the essay.
47. John Dewey, "Impressions of Soviet Russia," in *The Later Works*, 3: 204; hereafter cited in my text as ISR.
48. Dewey's stance has striking affinities with Benjamin's characteristic antisubjectivist effort to have his response to Moscow "be devoid of all theory" and "refrain from any deductive abstraction, from any prognostication, and even within certain limits, from any judgment." Dewey shares what Benjamin calls the refusal of "any programmatic sketch one might draw of the future" and a preference for allowing Moscow's "very new and disorienting language" to "speak for itself" (from *Moscow Diary*, 132).

Russia, then, uneasily straddles repression and liberation, a fragile balance to be shattered by Stalin's consolidation of power two years later. The country itself and Dewey's response to it are riven by paradox, or what he calls "disparity" (ISR, 210): He notes that his wavering, his refusal to draw definitive conclusions about Russia's future, will offend both orthodox Marxists and anti-Communists. (And upon his return, Dewey is indeed denounced by the Left and the Right). Dewey's wavering is founded on his suspicion that this "release of human powers on such an unprecedented scale," this psychic renovation in subjectivity prompted by economic revolution, necessarily arouses new energies that overshoot any preordained historical laws (ISR, 207). To Dewey, the "Marxian philosophy of history" has begun to "smell of outworn absolutist metaphysics and bygone theories of straight-line, one way 'evolution' " (ISR, 205).

This land of unlikeness breeds in Dewey differential or nonidentical cognition, what Bourne calls irony, the trope of disparity. Strikingly, Dewey elects irony to embody the suspended weight of difference: "There is a peculiar tone of irony that hangs over all [one's] preconceptions" that, in Russia, undergo "complete reversal" (ISR, 218, 244). Perhaps the most intriguing irony for Dewey is the possibility that the Russian Revolution, in "creative energy," has "no intrinsic, necessary connection with communistic theory and practice," and that "the like of it might exist in any large industrial center" (ISR, 214). Thus, Dewey urges our close study of the Russian experiment, and it came to inspire his own move to socialism in 1935 (ISR, 249).[49] His willingness to relax the power of will and purpose, to forego "systematic inquiries" (ISR, 213) and permit himself to be shocked and dazed, hanging suspended in absorbed, alert contemplation, encompasses a rare mode of action. His stance permits the experience of difference and contradiction without the imperial annexing of otherness into a system, or classification, or ideological commitment—the reflex of identity thinking. It instances, too, the "flowering of human capacity" that his "renascent liberalism" (LSA, 64) will strive for and that Adorno's emphasis on the mimetic aims to preserve amidst modernity's imperative of rationalization.

Dewey's experimental life of mimetic irony in Russia is, in itself, an exemplary achievement of the politics of nonidentity. The ability to perform the "toilsome labor of understanding," with its "precarious uncertainty," to steer

---

49. Not surprisingly, in the wake of the Moscow Trials, Dewey notes that it was a "bitter disillusionment to me personally" to see the collapse of a "highly important social experiment . . . from which we . . . could learn a great deal" (see The Later Works, 11: 335).

58

between the polarized abstractions of communism and anti-communism, while remaining politically astute and involved, has always been a rare feat, particularly among American intellectuals (*EN*, 46–47). Did not Dewey himself too often sound like the rationalist *malgre lui,* content with his own ceaselessly reiterated abstractions—intelligence and scientific method?

5

By the late 1930s, the text of history was shadowed by increasingly ominous uncertainties, as a European culture steeped in the Enlightenment seemed helpless to avoid the contagion of totalitarianism, a disease to which no liberal democracy, including American, had guaranteed immunity. Escaping from Germany in 1934, the Frankfurt Circle settled in New York in a building provided by Dewey's university—Columbia—and proceeded to spend seven years largely in isolation from Dewey and most other American intellectuals. In retrospect, the facts of geographical proximity and intellectual nonengagement produce many ironies but also a sense of wasted opportunity for exchange. This sense is made all the more acute because the ground of exchange, we shall see below, was fertile. What drives the practice of both Dewey and the Frankfurt School in the late thirties is a pursuit of "thirdness," a position unassimilable to two political traditions in crisis—liberalism and Marxism.

Frankfurt School Marxism underscores its nonidentical relation to orthodox Marxism by rejecting the latter's necessitarianism—its preordained laws of revolutionary praxis embodied in the proletariat. What they keep of Marxism is its critical method for interrogating the culture of capitalism. Two questions spark their most intense pursuit: How has capitalism so effectively smothered what Marxism ordained as the fulcrum of revolution—proletarian socialist consciousness? and, most disturbing of all, how has fascism penetrated so easily a social order founded on the moral and political values of Enlightenment liberalism? They dub their radically historical practice *Critical Theory*, Horkheimer's phrase from his position paper of 1937. That essay, as we shall see, reveals striking affinities with Dewey, particularly his important text of 1939, *Freedom and Culture*. Horkheimer's "Art and Mass Culture" of 1941 explicitly praises Dewey's *Art as Experience*.[50] These affiliations are all the more surprising given the ferocity and

50. Horkheimer contrasts Dewey favorably to Mortimer Adler—Dewey's most notorious opponent from the Right—in "Art and Mass Culture," in *Critical Theory: Selected Essays*,

notoriety of Horkheimer's attack on Deweyan pragmatism in 1944, which all but obliterated any sense of connection.

Nonidentity can be said to inhere in Critical Theory, for the latter thrives on an internal contradiction that strips theory of theory's defining identity: the metaphysical props of certainty and logical necessity. Thus, Horkheimer stresses that the historical significance of the work of Critical Theory "is not self-evident; it rather depends on men speaking and acting in such a way as to justify it. It is not a finished and fixed historical creation" (*CT*, 220). Therefore, unlike a conformist "philosophy that thinks to find peace within itself, in any kind of truth whatsoever," Critical Theory does not "bring salvation to those who hold it" (*CT*, 252, 243). Because "his profession is the struggle of which his own thinking is a part and not something self-sufficient and separable from the struggle," the Critical Theorist must adapt to "ever new situations" and thus is "caught up in an evolution" without a preordained telos (*CT*, 216, 238–39). Situated within time, not beyond it, Critical Theory is neither rooted ("the unproblematic expression of an already constituted society" as posited by fascist nationalism [*CT*, 210]), nor free-floating (a product of a neutral intellectual class that replicates the essentially abstract nature of bourgeois thought), nor "satisfied to proclaim with reverent admiration the creative strength of the proletariat" (*CT*, 214). Each of these stances constitutes an "evasion of theoretical effort" because they are founded on various fixed points above the struggle, vantages that, in offering a "guarantee of correct knowledge," provide a refuge from history (*CT*, 213).

At the time of Horkheimer's position paper of 1937, however, the dissolution of proletarian class consciousness still seems preventable; thus, Frankfurt ties to the working class are yet to be severed, because the prospect of serving this class as a "force within . . . to stimulate change" appears historically viable in prewar Europe (*CT*, 215). Because the Frankfurt School has so often been labeled elitist and resigned, there is a certain shock in reading Horkheimer describing the relation of theorist and oppressed class as one of "dynamic unity" (*CT*, 215) and equating critical thinking with "transformative activity" (*CT*, 232) grounded in the "hope of radically improving human existence" (*CT*, 233). With the advent of war, this unity

---

trans. M. O'Connell (New York: Continuum, 1982), 273–90; hereafter cited in my text as *CT*. Indeed, Horkheimer provides a thoroughly Deweyan critique of Adler's static principles and fixed values offered as an antidote to pragmatism's pernicious relativism. To this, Adler opposes a neo-Thomistic Christian metaphysics.

is shattered, and hope goes underground, as Critical Theory is forced to address itself to an "Imaginary witness."[51]

The Frankfurt School spurns the refuge of a fixed political program, or identity, in the name of history, not in denial of it. Yet no aspect of Frankfurt thought has been more controversial and less understood. The received wisdom continues to regard their reluctance to obey the stern responsibilities of Marx's Thesis Eleven—ceasing theory and initiating praxis—as the blatant forfeiture of radical engagement. Late in life, Adorno notes the dogmatic element in Marx's taboo on critique, a demand that harbored a "concealed wound" of nervous authoritarianism, suggesting that Marx "was not at all sure of it himself."[52] The fetishizing of Thesis Eleven is "founded in fear" of ambiguity and of thought "not immediately accompanied by instructions for action" (R, 166). The only escape from Marx's absolutizing of practice is "insatiable . . . open" thinking, neither prescribed nor predetermined, that "points beyond itself" (R, 166). This "emphatic" thinking functions as a "figuration of praxis," which is more truly involved in change than "mere obedience for the sake of praxis."[53] "Above all the force of resistance," such thinking is exploratory and provisional, "by no means secure; no security is granted it by existing conditions . . . nor by any type of organized force" (R, 168). This recalls how Dewey conceives genuine thinking: as an "event" that permits "no rest for the thinker, save in the *process of thinking*" (*EN*, 101, 99). Sustaining such restlessness is arduous; life is made easier for the individual, says Adorno, "through capitulation to the collective with which he identifies. He is spared the cognition of his impotence. . . . It is this act [of capitulation]—not unconfused thinking—which is resignation" (R, 167).

Critical Theory's discovery of energy in impotence, of power in refusal, like its efforts to avoid being "a finished and fixed historical creation,"

51. Max Horkheimer and T. W. Adorno, *Dialectic of Enlightenment*, trans. John Cumming (New York: Herder and Herder, 1972), 256; hereafter cited in my text as *DE*.

52. T. W. Adorno, "Resignation," *Telos* 35 (Spring 1978): 166; hereafter cited in my text as R.

53. In recent retrospective remarks, Leo Lowenthal has clarified Critical Theory's relation to praxis: "We had not abandoned praxis; rather, praxis had abandoned us. . . . In a mediating sense Critical Theory was always in favor of praxis. The essential difference between Critical and Traditional Theory was this: the problems that concerned us . . . were determined essentially by the given historical situation. . . . The essence of Critical Theory is really the inexorable analysis of what is" (see *An Unmastered Past* [Berkeley: University of California Press, 1986], 61–62).

has often been greeted with contempt (*CT*, 220). As Horkheimer notes as early as 1937, conventional political intellectuals "cannot bear the thought that the kind of thinking which is most topical, which has the deepest grasp of the historical situation, and is most pregnant with the future, must at certain times isolate its subject and throw him back upon himself" (*CT*, 214). Helmut Dubiel has shrewdly noted that such proud isolation "would be easy to dismiss . . . as megalomaniacal messianism. Yet, that would be unhistorical, for this self-interpretation is the result of a specific historical constellation"—the Nazi liquidation of the progressive intellectual class.[54] The Frankfurt insistence on the nonaffiliation of nonidentity mimics the conditions of a social world itself "untransparent" and illegible, where the self is "unsure of itself too," for its identity "lies in the future, not in the present" (*CT*, 211). With identity deferred, rooted in tension, the theorist's present status is incalculable: His position may be "relatively assured," but "he is also at times an enemy and criminal, at times a solitary utopian; even after his death the question of what he really was is not decided" (*CT*, 220).

The question of the Frankfurt political identity remains open and unsettling. One consequence of this willed indeterminacy has been the attenuated contemporary influence of Frankfurt theory. Thinkers as diverse as Habermas and Rorty allege that Adorno's unremitting negativism destroys any vestige of Enlightenment reason, embraces a romantic irrationalism, and thus offers little of value to contemporary social theory. In *Contingency, Irony and Solidarity* (1989), the foremost contemporary champion of Dewey finds Frankfurt theory of small use in constructing a postmodern bourgeois liberalism. According to Rorty, Horkheimer and Adorno have "nothing useful to suggest except what Ricoeur has aptly dubbed 'the hermeneutics of suspicion.'" Quoting a passage from *Dialectic of Enlightenment* regarding "blindly pragmatized thought," Rorty avers that they "did not try to show how 'pragmatized thought' might cease to be blind and become clear sighted. Yet various other writers—people who wanted to retain Enlightenment liberalism while dropping Enlightenment rationalism—have done just that."[55] Among these others, says Rorty, John Dewey is preeminent.

Unmentioned in Rorty's scenario is the fact that *Dialectic of Enlightenment* is a self-consciously provisional, transitional work (originally circulated in mimeograph under the title *Philosophical Fragments*), reflecting

54. Helmut Dubiel, *Theory and Politics*, trans. B. Gregg (Cambridge: MIT Press, 1985), 52.
55. Richard Rorty, *Contingency, Irony, and Solidarity* (New York: Cambridge University Press, 1989), 57.

the Frankfurt commitment to truth as historical "rather than an unchanging constant to be set against the movement of history" (*DE*, ix). Thus, it offers a critique of Enlightenment that is "intended to prepare the way for a positive concept of Enlightenment which will release it from entanglement in blind domination" (*DE*, xvi). This furnishes the context in which Adorno's late work (principally *Negative Dialectics* and *Aesthetic Theory*) is best read: as the continually renewed effort to adumbrate a positive Enlightenment founded on mimetic reason as a dialectical (not an absolute) alternative to instrumental reason. And Adorno locates mimetic reason not merely in an aesthetic utopia (as Habermas argues) but in potentialities of human behavior. The historical specificity of Adorno's emphasis on the mimetic is evident in the fact that his valuation of it is strengthened when he explores its antithesis—the pathologies of intolerance diagnosed in *The Authoritarian Personality* (1950).

Adorno's relish for collaboration in *The Authoritarian Personality* and in *Dialectic of Enlightenment* exemplifies his willingness to undertake intellectual labor in the spirit of a democratic faith akin to Dewey's. As we have seen, Dewey conceives his own work and that of political parties as exploratory, as looking toward possibilities and functioning as connecting links. This approach to politics demands a partial, tentative, open attitude of critical and political inquiry that is, according to Dewey in 1939, fatally absent in Marxism. While claiming to be "the only strictly scientific theory of social change," it has "violated most systematically every principle of scientific method" (*FC*, 117, 135).

Unlike the Frankfurt rejection of science as merely positivism and instrumentalism, Dewey's critique of Marxism is made in the name of science pragmatically conceived. He finds Marxism's claims to be scientific woefully "dated," a product of nineteenth-century science's emphases on necessity and a "*single* all-comprehensive law" rather than on the "*probability*" and "*pluralism*" that characterize modern science (*FC*, 125; Dewey's emphases). "In the name of science, a thoroughly anti-scientific procedure was formulated" so that a "monistic block-universe theory of social causation" was understood as obviating "the need for continued resort to observation and to continual revision of generalizations in their office of working hypotheses" (*FC*, 125). While seeking, like Marxism, "radical transformation of the present controls of production" and accepting "some sort of economic determinism," Dewey echoes the Frankfurt critique of economism (*FC*, 118). He urges replacing monocausal Marxism with a dynamic, interactional social model that refuses to isolate economics as *"the* cause of *all* social change" (*FC*, 118; Dewey's emphases).

Before concluding that Dewey's faith in science seems to conflict sharply with the Frankfurt position, it is worth recalling that his pragmatist view of science rejects what the Frankfurt School also rejects: the paradigm of Enlightenment rationalism embodied in the spectator theory of knowledge. This posits a passive subject observing a static object, the Cartesian dichotomy that had provided the epistemological foundation of Enlightenment science that splits subject and object, theory and practice. Free of the phobic Frankfurt reaction to science, Dewey reconstructs science as experimental inquiry, as active, revisionary pursuit rather than attainment of a fixed body of knowledge.[56]

Pragmatist science is anything but positivistic contentment with "prearranged routines" (*CT*, 286). The scientific attitude, says Dewey, "may almost be defined as that which is capable of enjoying the doubtful" and finding "delight in the problematic."[57] Borrowing the words of C. D. Darlington, Dewey describes the function of science as a "Ministry of Disturbance, a regulated source of annoyance, a destroyer of routine, an underminer of complacency."[58] Deprived of the experimental attitude, human beings come to dread change, to depend on antecedent realities, to avoid problems and difficulties. By sapping a sense of historical perspective and responsibility, a

56. In a discrimination Horkheimer rarely makes (and will fail to make in *Eclipse of Reason*, where he views Deweyan pragmatism as twentieth-century Baconianism in its effort to model intellectual life upon laboratory techniques), he distinguishes positivism from science and deplores the fact that scientific thought "is always confined within the limits of the various specialized disciplines" (*CT*, 285). This is in his 1941 essay that praises Dewey. In the same essay, he writes: "Economy of thought and technique alone do not exhaust the meaning of science, which is also the will to truth. The way toward overcoming positivistic thinking does not lie in regressive revision of science, but in driving this will to truth further until it conflicts with present reality" (*CT*, 286). For Horkheimer and Adorno, this radicalizing of science turns it into philosophy, the mode of thinking that sets aside the "indestructible and static" results of research for the hazards of interpretation, which proceeds "without ever possessing a sure key" (AP, 126). Liberating science from narrow disciplines and driving its will to truth into active critique precisely describes Dewey's pragmatist project of reconstruction, so often misunderstood (by Horkheimer and others) as scientism because of its emphasis on scientific inquiry. Yet, what Dewey means by inquiry is akin to what the Frankfurt School calls philosophy: Both are committed to the adventure of interpretation.
57. John Dewey, *The Quest for Certainty* (New York: Putnam, 1960), 251, 258.
58. Dewey, *Reconstruction in Philosophy*, xvii.

passive conformism corrodes the activist citizenry necessary for the health of democracy.

By 1939, Dewey is deeply troubled by American democracy's failing health. Although *Freedom and Culture* lacks the deliberately disturbing intellectual and stylistic audacity of *Dialectic of Enlightenment*, which indicts as pathological the entire Western rationalist tradition, Dewey's book is equally unflinching in its recognition of how susceptible the subjects of democratic mass culture are to totalitarian control. Of special concern in both works is the production of what Horkheimer and Adorno call pseudo-individuality addicted to the identity-thinking inculcated by mass media. The reign of James's Waldorf puppets seems to have arrived.

Horkheimer and Adorno find thinking an "antiquated luxury," and "the ability to make the effort required by judgment disappears. . . . The individual no longer has to decide what he himself is to do in a painful inner dialectic of conscience, self-preservation, and drives" (*DE*, 203). What results is that the "irrationality of the unresisting and busy adaptation to reality becomes more reasonable than reason for the individual" (*DE*, 204). Dewey draws the disturbing conclusion: "The serious threat to our democracy is not the existence of foreign totalitarian states. It is the existence within our own personal attitudes and within our own institutions of conditions similar to those which have given a victory to external authority, discipline, uniformity and dependence upon The Leader in foreign countries" (*FC*, 98). Among those attitudes is "racial prejudice against Negroes, Catholics, and Jews. . . . Its presence among us is an intrinsic weakness and a handle for the accusation that we do not act differently than Nazi Germany" (*FC*, 153). In the pithier, if less precise, formulation of *Dialectic of Enlightenment*, "The bourgeois . . . at odds with himself and everybody else, is already virtually a Nazi" (*DE*, 155).

Two years prior to *Freedom and Culture*, Dewey embodies, in tensely dramatic historical circumstances, a style of individual behavior and judgment that defies the culturally induced pathologies of passive adaptation and identity thinking. His old friend Sidney Hook helps persuade Dewey to chair the inquiry into the charges Stalin had brought against Trotsky in the Moscow Trials of 1936 and 1937. In his work for the Trotsky Inquiry, Dewey's unaffiliated stance of nonidentity is especially valuable politically; indeed, his presence as neither fellow traveler, party member, nor anti-Communist is crucial in legitimating the fairness of the proceedings. But Dewey is publicly vilified for his participation, the abuse far exceeding what he endures in 1928 upon returning from Russia. This time, he is attacked by many of the New York left; and most painfully, perhaps, *The New Republic*, long his principal journalistic forum, opposes the inquiry. Speaking for most of the Left, the magazine editorializes that they see "no reason . . . to take the Moscow Trials at other than its face value."[59]

Dewey's openness eludes, as well, what he finds as liberalism's endemic weakness: "unwillingness to face the unpleasant," to "shirk when unpleasant conditions demand decisions and actions."[60] Knowing he risks the "bitter disillusionment" of his personal hopes for the success of the Russian experiment, Dewey nevertheless takes action: Granting "that a chairman might be found . . . whose experience better fit[s] him for the difficult and delicate task to be performed," Dewey decides to accept the responsibility, because, as he says, "I have given my life to the work of education . . . and I realiz[e] that to act otherwise would be false to my life work."[61]

Beneath his characteristic blandness is the remarkable fact of the seventy-eight-year-old Dewey performing his most dramatic act of "intellectual disrobing" (*EN*, 35). The work of education, to which he has been committed for a lifetime, takes upon itself its own form of the inexorable—the ineradicable risk of error and failure. For Dewey, inquiry demands divestiture—the temporary shedding of the "intellectual habits we take on and wear when we assimilate" cultural norms (*EN*, 35). This "disrobing" is rooted in an openness close to ignorance. He admitted as much to Max Eastman: "I came to the work [of the Trotsky Commission] about as ignorantly innocent of knowledge of the historic record & personalities involved as anybody could be"; he would later note, "My ignorance was rather shameful."[62] Here, at the very moment he is burdened with momentous historical responsibility, Dewey flirts with the "irresponsibility," the "blitheness springing from the volatility of thought," that Adorno finds the necessary "license" of genuine thinking.[63]

Dwelling in ignorance, the "cultivated naïveté" that can be obtained only through "the discipline of severe thought" (*EN*, 35), Dewey relaxes the

59. *The New Republic*, 2 Sept. 1936. Also quoted by Sidney Hook, *Out of Step* (New York: Carroll and Graf, 1987), 231. In anger and disgust at the journal's betrayal of liberal principles, Dewey resigns as contributing editor.
60. Dewey, *The Later Works*, 11:319, 335.
61. Dewey, *The Later Works*, 11:309.
62. Dewey, *The Later Works*, 11:641.
63. Adorno, *MM*, 127. Of such license, Adorno writes: It is "resented by the positivistic spirit and [is] put down to mental disorder" (*MM*, 127). And, indeed, Dewey is accused of senility by opponents of the inquiry.

coercions of unwavering rationality and approaches that "calm disinterest-edness of spirit," which Bourne finds the mark of the "experimental atti-tude toward life" (RW, 154).[64] His willed vulnerability and surrender have powerful consequences, not only the exculpation of Trotsky. This verdict reverberates, indirectly helping to consolidate the Trotskyist movement and to galvanize the re-formation of Partisan Review.[65] Such are the rich fruits of Deweyan inquiry. Its fertility has its source in one commitment: honoring what Dewey calls the universe's "character of contingency" (EN, 42). This adherence to the precarious, says Adorno, produces "the concrete aware-ness of the conditionality of human knowledge," which alone leads us "to the threshold of truth" (MM, 128).

6

What should seem obvious by now is that, until Adorno's correc-tion in the sixties, the Frankfurt relation to Dewey amounts to a remarkable misprision that has created a resonant absence in mid-twentieth-century intellectual history. There are various possible motives for this misprision, in-cluding the trauma of the Holocaust, which encouraged a monolithic critique of Enlightenment liberalism and science, and the disturbing ambiguities in Dewey's thought, both in his attitude to science and in his organicist-idealist heritage, ambiguities that made it easy to dismiss him.[66] Whatever the rea-sons, the undeniable result has been an obscuring of affinities between Frankfurt Marxism and American pragmatism. One consequence has been further isolation of both movements, making it easier to consign them to the background of the concerns of contemporary cultural criticism; hence, Criti-

64. James T. Farrell, an eyewitness to the inquiry's proceedings, is struck by "Dewey's relaxation . . . a sign of an unsuspected strain of worldliness in his character" (see "Dewey in Mexico," in Reflections at Fifty [New York: Vanguard Press, 1954], 112).

65. For this effect of the inquiry's verdict, see Terry Cooney, The Rise of the New York Intellectuals (Madison: University of Wisconsin Press, 1989), 103–04; and Harvey Klehr, The Heyday of American Communism (New York: Basic Books, 1984), 359, 363.

66. My account of Dewey contests the received opinion that depicts Dewey's model of inquiry and society as an organic one that seeks homeostatic adjustment rooted in an ideal of wholeness, behind which stands the influence not only of Hegelian idealism but also his early love of Darwin, Comte, and Spencer. But adjustment in Dewey is an activity of making that does not reach closure because of the inherently problematic character of situations. This is to say that Hegel's dialectical method of conflict and negation is as im-portant to Dewey as Hegel's positing of unity. The legacy of fallibilism bequeathed Dewey by Peirce surely counts as the other challenge to the Hegelian bias toward integration.

cal Theory tends to be dismissed as elitist and paralyzed, pragmatism as conformist and technocratic. These caricatures have kept from view their shared legacy that enlarges the practice of cultural inquiry to embrace a range of possibilities in the intellectual's relation to politics, agency, and responsibility.

The pragmatist and Frankfurt challenges to the idealist elevation topple the intellectual from a position of privileged moral vision to a far less stable vantage. The genealogy constructed here is comprised of figures whose thought and experience are "no longer 'glued' to identity," a condition, says Adorno, that induces vertigo as an index of truth (*ND*, 31). The locus of this vertigo is on "the formidable foreground," in James's phrase (*AS*, 130), where mastery and certainty are renounced, where "distance is not a safety zone but a field of tension" (*MM*, 127), and where freedom, says Foucault, is not an essence but an "'agonism' . . . [a] reciprocal incitation and struggle, . . . [a] permanent provocation."[67] In this immanent space of "immense fluidity" that James designated the "margin" (*AS*, 401), oppositions like success and failure, passivity and resistance, impotence and power radically intermix. Here, says Dewey, "our knowledge swims in a continuum of indeterminacy."[68]

With an unmatched richness and creativity, Dewey confronts the inherent frustrations of a politics of nonidentity and lives upon its vertiginous ground. That he possesses an acute sense of the costs involved is evident, for instance, in his reply, in 1922, to a critique of pragmatism made by Bertrand Russell. Rather than agreeing with Russell that pragmatism is serenely triumphant in America, Dewey responds that, on the contrary, "its workings are paralyzed here. . . . Pragmatic faith walks in chains."[69] What this initially puzzling statement seems to suggest is that if one is really willing to abide in the pragmatic spirit of experimentation, reconstruction, and revision (the responsibility entailed by Peirce's fallibilism), then one is committed, says Dewey, to a "supremely difficult task. Perhaps the task is too hard for human nature. . . . Its demands are too high for human power." The pragmatic "faith may demonstrate its own falsity by failure." But, more dis-

67. Michel Foucault, "The Subject and Power," reprinted in Hubert L. Dreyfus and Paul Rabinow, *Michel Foucault: Beyond Structuralism and Hermeneutics* (Chicago: University of Chicago Press, 1983), 222.

68. Dewey, *The Later Works*, 6:275.

69. All quotations in this paragraph are from John Dewey, "Pragmatic America," in *Characters and Events*, ed. Joseph Ratner, vol. 2 (New York: H. Holt and Company, 1929), 545–46.

turbing, we may also be "arrested on the plane of . . . success." Indeed, "we
not only may do so, but we actually are doing so." In short, implies Dewey,
any way we look at it, we are inadequate to the temptations of fixed belief,
thus inadequate to the demands of pragmatism. In this light, Dewey's pragmatism is anything but brisk and sunny; indeed, his project is as impossible
as Adorno's negative dialectics, as endless a venture as James's "restless"
analysis. For all three, impossibility proves immensely fertile.

If, in 1917, Dewey's pragmatic faith lapses, he spends the next thirty-
five years revising and refining it, becoming splendidly adequate by sur-
rendering the desire to achieve adequacy. He has learned Bourne's bitter
lesson in the value of "intellectual suspense"; the intellect, Bourne has
noted, "craves certitude. It takes effort to keep it supple and pliable" (*RW*,
315). Yet, of course, Bourne has imbibed his pragmatic suppleness from
Dewey himself. In a dialectical reversal worthy of Adorno, Dewey turns his
student's taboo on "premature crystallization" into the impetus for virtually
unparalleled public engagement.

As I Lay Dying in the Machine Age

John T. Matthews

The cultural transformation marking the New South was structured by a central dialectic: the dynamic relation between modernization and modernism. Various plans to rejuvenate the South after World War I urged the adoption of modernized modes of production, including tenancy and credit reform for farmers; crop diversification; increased commodity consumption; technological improvements, such as electrification and mechanization; cooperatives for equipment and supply purchasing; improved housing; reforestation and erosion work; and the development of small, local industry.[1]

Despite significant differences in the panoply of New South programs (for example, differences over the degrees of commitment to northern capital and management techniques, or over the extent to which black fortunes

I wish to thank my colleagues Jon Klancher and Susan Mizruchi for insightful commentary on this essay.

1. This list is drawn from Michael O'Brien, *The Idea of the American South: 1920–1941* (Baltimore: Johns Hopkins University Press, 1979), 67. O'Brien summarizes Howard Odum's proposals in *Southern Regions of the United States* (Chapel Hill: University of North Carolina Press, 1936).

would be integrated into the envisioned future) and despite the persistence with which antebellum relations of class, race, and gender held sway— and even were actively refurbished beginning in the 1880s[2]—the South decisively mobilized itself for a renaissance through modernization. At the same time, many southern writers coming of age at the time of the New South's emergence during and after World War I gravitated to the novelties of international aesthetic modernism. Daniel Singal has pointed out that the earliest southern hospitality to literary modernism was extended by the Vanderbilt Fugitive group in the early twenties.[3]

The dialectical nature of these movements might be appreciated when we follow the transmutation of Vanderbilt modernism into Vanderbilt Agrarianism. With the publication of the notorious *I'll Take My Stand* in 1930, John Crowe Ransom, Allen Tate, Donald Davidson, and Robert Penn Warren signaled that the poets were ready to ratify what Singal has called "the shift to southernism" (*WW*, 200) that began in the mid-twenties. Their modernism, in the first place, already had had to recognize its dialectical relation to modernization, for the New South was essentially a product of southern Victorianism. In its confidence in technological progress, education, commerce, and industry, the New South stood squarely on the belated circulation through the post–Reconstruction South of Arnold's and Tennyson's mid-Victorian optimism (*WW*, 23). Aesthetic modernism allowed some southern writers both to welcome the breakup of a moribund Cavalier tradition of paradise lost and to dispute the progressive materialism boosting the bourgeois New South.

From this standpoint, it is not so difficult to understand the Agrarians' move from modernism to a renovated agrarian Old Southernism. The Fugitives' modernism, inspired by Pound and Eliot, formulated itself in opposition to the sentimentalism, historical escapism, and verbal lavishness of the extended romantic tradition in poetry through the turn of the century. At the same time, however, it initially allied itself with a social mentality rooted in Victorian progressivism. This synthesis of anti- and pro-Victorian im-

2. On the persistence of racism, for example, see C. Vann Woodward, *The Origins of the New South: 1877–1913* (Baton Rouge: Louisiana State University Press, 1951; republished in 1971 with a critical essay on recent works by Charles B. Dew), especially chapter 14, "Progressivism—For Whites Only." See also John David Smith, *An Old Creed for the New South: Proslavery Ideology and Historiography, 1865–1918* (Westport, Conn.: Greenwood Press, 1985).
3. Daniel Joseph Singal, *The War Within: From Victorian to Modernist Thought in the South, 1919–1945* (Chapel Hill: University of North Carolina Press, 1982); hereafter cited in my text as *WW*.

pulses gave way to modernism's antithetical departure from the processes of modernization. The modernist project develops doubts about technology and progress, particularly in the aftermath of World War I. High modernism's apparent uninterest in representing social reality—its abstractness and autonomy—constitutes a defense against an intolerable present and an unimaginable future.[4]

A new synthesis arises in the form of the Agrarians' reactionary antebellum mythology. This mythology depends on what Singal has called a "modernized and sanitized"[5] version of the myth of the Old South. Agrarianism "vehemently attacked the New South shibboleths of national reconciliation, industrialism, and the modernization of southern society, and called instead for the supremacy of tradition, provincialism, and a life close to the soil."[6] Michael O'Brien summarizes this relation in a way I find useful: "By modernism I mean that shift in sensibility that has been closely linked to, but not necessarily sympathetic with, the process of modernization, the growth of industry, cities, secularization, democratization, and a mass bureaucratic society. . . . Modernism is, in short, a sensibility in dialectic with modernization."[7] I have risked this extremely sketchy rehearsal of a full and nuanced body of work on southern modernism because, in what follows, I want to suggest how Faulkner's fiction of the early thirties engages the dialectic between modernization and modernism.

• • • •

At the very moment the Fugitive modernists were moving toward Agrarianism, Faulkner wrote his two most modernist works, *The Sound and the Fury* (1929) and *As I Lay Dying* (1930). What is striking about both is the extent to which they conform to the received understanding of the modernist work as one that is, according to Andreas Huyssen, "autonomous and totally separate from the realms of mass culture and everyday life."[8] "The major premise of the modernist work is the rejection of all classical

4. Peter Bürger distinguishes the avant-garde from modernism on the basis of the former's self-reflectiveness as a form of social criticism in *Theory of the Avant-Garde*, trans. Michael Shaw (Minneapolis: University of Minnesota Press, 1984).

5. Singal uses this phrase in discussing *The Unvanquished* as an example of Faulkner's ambivalent modernism (*WW*, 196).

6. Singal, *WW*, 198. See also O'Brien, *Idea of the American South*, 14.

7. O'Brien, *Idea of the American South*, xvii.

8. Andreas Huyssen, *After the Great Divide: Modernism, Mass Culture, and Postmodernism* (Bloomington: University of Indiana Press, 1986), 53; hereafter cited in my text as *GD*.

systems of representation, the effacement of 'content,' the erasure of subjectivity and authorial voice, the repudiation of likeness and verisimilitude, the exorcism of any demand for realism of whatever kind" (*GD*, 54).[9]

Everyone remembers that *As I Lay Dying* itself identifies one important frame of reference for its modernist aesthetic when Darl describes his mother's coffin resting on sawhorses in the blazing Gillespie barn as looking "like a cubistic bug."[10] This is a suggestive remark, for not only does it encourage taking the radical perspectivism and antimimetic abstractionism of the novel as Faulkner's attempt at literary cubism, it also illustrates "the exorcism . . . of realism" performed in section after section.

No other novel of Faulkner's so successfully establishes the autonomy of the modernist text. The abstractness of its form reinforces the abstractions that preoccupy its discourse. The aesthetic of literary high modernism appears in the novel's fragmented narrative: radical relativism generated by contradictory points of view, concentration on psychology rather than event (as if the narrative of mind *is* the story), stream of consciousness technique, and elaborate rhetorical complexity (elliptical syntax, metaphysical conceits, and belaborings of metaphor).[11] Such massive rejection of conventional realistic procedures sits well with the rarefied content.

To see modernism as a refusal to address the repellent expansion of commodity capitalism, technologization, and mass culture has been a mainstay of its detractors from at least Lukács forward. Yet, notice how the language of the market, to anticipate my analysis by way of a preliminary example, has saturated the most private formulations of personal identity. Darl struggles to deduce his existence through pure reason, but into his Cartesian meditations floats the paradox of commodity exchange: "I can

9. Donald Pease shows the roots of American modernism's suppression of context to lie in the aesthetics of post–Civil War writers, like Twain, who seek to lay to rest the trauma of violent political conflict. Pease discusses the cultural work performed by the modernist text's refusal of history and the modern critic's consonant preoccupation with high culture (at the expense of mass culture) in *Visionary Compacts: American Renaissance Writings in Cultural Context* (Madison: University of Wisconsin Press, 1987), especially 41–44. In what follows, I describe the dynamics of such an opposition in a modernist text and attempt to break down the grounds for it.

10. William Faulkner, *As I Lay Dying*, The Corrected Text (New York: Random House, Vintage, 1987), 201. All quotations are from this edition and are cited by page number only.

11. On the novel's exploration of figurality, see Patrick O'Donnell, "The Spectral Road: Metaphors of Transference in Faulkner's *As I Lay Dying*," *Papers in Language and Literature* 20 (1984): 60–79.

hear the rain shaping the wagon that is ours, the load that is no longer theirs that felled and sawed it nor yet theirs that bought it and which is not ours either, lie on our wagon though it does" (72). The Bundrens' function as "middlemen" in this transaction becomes a metaphor for Darl's selfhood— not an end but a means, not property held but property in circulation, not self-possession but severally possessed.

What a more dialectical approach to the question of modernization and modernism might demonstrate is the *process* by which the autonomy of the modernist work establishes itself. According to Adorno's dialectical analysis of aesthetics, the modern work constitutes itself in a process of opposition to the "empirical" world, to all that is not art: "It is by virtue of its separation from empirical reality that the work of art can become a being of a higher order, fashioning the relation between the whole and its parts in accordance with its own needs. Works of art are after-images or replicas of empirical life, inasmuch as they proffer to the latter what in the outside world is being denied them. In the process they slough off a repressive, external-empirical mode of experiencing the world." [12]

Huyssen's reading of Adorno specifies the elements of modern culture that modernism must engage. In the first place, the commodification of culture that emerges during the nineteenth century permanently alters society, and art's relation to it: "What, then, are the traces of this commodification of time and space, of objects and the human body, in the arts?" (*GD*, 18–19). Huyssen's question suggests the kind of tasks practical criticism might perform in light of Adorno's general principle that "the ideology of the art work's autonomy is thus undermined by the claim that no work of art is ever untouched by the social. But Adorno makes the even stronger claim that in capitalist society high art is always already permeated by the textures of that mass culture from which it seeks autonomy" (*AT*, 35).

The questions I want to put to Faulkner's modernist endeavor in *As I Lay Dying* are the following: (1) Where do we find the "substratum" (*AT*, 6) of empirical reality that the work of art seeks to separate itself from? (2) How does the modernist work mediate social reality by turning it into aesthetic form? (3) How does *As I Lay Dying* demonstrate that a modernism *open* to the forces of modernization retains an analytical capacity that earlier practitioners like the Vanderbilt Fugitives short-circuited and abandoned prematurely? and (4) How does Faulkner prevent his work from being en-

---

12. T. W. Adorno, *Aesthetic Theory*, trans. C. Lenhardt (London and New York: Routledge & Kegan Paul, 1972), 6; hereafter cited in my text as *AT*.

tirely determined by the demands of the modernized mass culture that it reflects upon?

Modernization and the Commodification of Culture, or, Cash Relations

It has always been tempting to view the Bundrens through the lens of Agrarian nostalgia for the endurance of the yeomanry. For all their self-ishness, cruelties, and obtuseness, Faulkner does put them in the position of triumphing epically and comically over their life and death tribulations. Despite the stench of the partially putrefied farm family toting its losses to town, the novel begrudgingly acknowledges a will to survival and, even more, a will to reorganize and prepare for the future.[13]

What I would like to suggest in this section is the extent to which the Bundrens do *not* represent simply the South's version of a natural relation to the universal rhythms of living, working, and dying. Nor is it enough to historicize their plight superficially—as that of a productive, self-sufficient farm family about to be ruined by modernization. Were this the case, *As I Lay Dying* might be taken as a kind of grotesque Agrarian fable, one that allegorizes a phase of lapsarian southern history: the loss of the self-sufficient yeoman farmer to the growth of larger-scale, mechanized, agri-business, to greater opportunities in the towns, to the homogenizations of mass culture and a consumer economy. Such a reading would place the novel as Faulkner's idiosyncratic contribution to the myth of the South's perpetual Fall, a myth then being rehabilitated by the Agrarians.[14] But such a view misjudges the degree to which the Bundrens have already been *constituted* by the dialectical history of capitalist agriculture, commodified economic and social relations, and the homogenizations of mass culture in the nineteenth-century South. What I hope to show in this first step of my analysis is that Faulkner's modernist treatment of the social reality indicated by the Bundrens' predicament is not entirely absorbed into the aesthetic of

13. See Warwick Wadlington, *Reading Faulknerian Tragedy* (Ithaca: Cornell University Press, 1987), 101–30, for an account of how voice seeks to overcome death.
14. On this point, I seek to challenge the nostalgia for the producer farmer that limits Susan Willis's otherwise compelling analysis of the onset of the consumer society in the South of *As I Lay Dying* ("Learning from the Banana," *American Quarterly* 39 [1987]: 586–600). Ironically, Willis's exaggeration of the agricultural South's earlier connection to the land (for all her awareness of Faulkner's criticism of the economic oppression it rested upon) coincides with the agrarian sentimentalized portrait of the yeoman farmer.

modernist abstraction that universalizes their story. Rather, the traces of very specific historical conditions appear in the novel, and they appear in such a way as to suggest that modernization is part of a dialectic internal to the workings of the novel and of the history it reflects upon.

Cash Bundren's devotion to his carpentry might best represent the ethos apparently being replaced by the mass reproduction of goods in a consumer society.[15] In opposition to machine-made production, Cash crafts Addie's coffin with as personalized a relation as imaginable between producer and consumer. He shapes every board with "the tedious and minute care of a jeweler" (70), holding each one up to his dying mother's inspection while she gazes at his labor from her window. The mother's interested image framed above Cash "is a composite picture of all time since he was a child" (44). Making this final receptacle for the one who has made him, Cash conceives the coffin as the most intimate expression of his natural reproductive relation with Addie.

Like the celebrant of a ritual, Cash resists all pressures to economize. He will not use ready-made boards from the barn; he will not shelter his work from the elements; he will not compromise the seemingly pointless extravagance of beveling every board. This handcrafted coffin, originating purely for its use function, destined never to possess exchange value, enjoying visibility only during the performance of the rite of burial, might represent art before the age of mechanization and commodification.

But Cash's relation to the ethos of use value, personalized production, and blood loyalties remains ambivalent throughout the novel. Cash professes regret that "folks seem to get away from the olden right teaching that says to drive the nails down and trim the edges well always like it was for your own use and comfort you were making it" (216). Nevertheless, he recognizes the continuity between the old ways and the new. Rationalizing Darl's removal after his act of arson, Cash insists that "there just aint nothing justifies the deliberate destruction of what a man has built with his own sweat and stored the fruit of his sweat into" (221). The reification of labor into a product that can be stored over time, possessed as property, and sold when the producer decides requires a conceptualization of labor and production that is fundamentally commodified.[16]

15. I discuss the novel's interest in forms of mechanical reproduction in "Faulkner and the Reproduction of History," in *Faulkner and History*, ed. Michel Gresset and Javier Coy (Salamanca: University of Salamanca Press, 1985), 63–76.
16. Gavin Wright claims that the crisis of labor was the distinguishing characteristic of the

Cash reveals this mentality regularly when he discusses the sanctity of what a man has produced for himself. But he also welcomes the advent of a much more technologically sophisticated and heavily mediated mass consumer market. Cash's graphophone represents the displacement of labor and gratification into reified form—into a commodity. The graphophone's music sounds to Cash as "natural as a music-band" (218), an illusion that mystifies the artifice of disembodying live music and reducing it to an object that can be stored and later returned to simulated life. (Note the analogue to Addie's postmortal speech.) The graphophone promises comfort and relaxation to the laboring man:

> Seems like when [a fellow] comes in tired of a night, it aint nothing could rest him like having a little music played and him resting. I have seen them that shuts up like a hand-grip, with a handle and all, so a fellow can carry it with him wherever he wants. (239)

Music has become private, portable property, limitlessly reproducible, subject only to the consumer's desire. The process of substituting commodity gratification for emotional loss carries over into Vardaman's longing for the red train he has seen in town, and to Dewey Dell's effort to distract him with the novelty of bananas. Commodification cuts the product off from the circumstances of its production, just as consuming the commodities helps divert the laborer from the weariness that pays for them.

The Byzantine complexity of petty finances in Faulkner's fiction is notorious. The Bundren family accounts actually flush the original economic sediment of the nuclear family to the surface at the moment of highest consumer desire (which is also the moment of greatest personal loss), for it is clear that the Bundren family has the meter running on all the relations that the myth of agrarian familiarity upholds against the assaults of modern commercialism. Money silently constitutes and openly mediates the family in the agricultural South. When Jewel begins sneaking off at night to earn cash for his horse, he is too tired to do his chores properly; Addie protects her favorite: "It was ma that got Dewey Dell to do his milking, paid her somehow" (115). Jewel's eventual purchase of the wild pony provokes a crisis of economic authority in the household. Jewel denies that he has bought the horse on Anse's "word"; it is not his father's credit (a precious commodity in the sharecropping South) but his own earnings that give Jewel

---

regional economy of the post–Emancipation South in *Old South, New South: Revolutions in the Southern Economy since the Civil War* (New York: Basic Books, 1986), especially 7.

the freedom to buy—and the freedom of buying. Anse has another reading, though: "You went behind my back and bought a horse. . . . Taken the work from your flesh and blood and bought a horse with it" (121). Addie sees the destructiveness of rendering labor in monetary terms, most horribly within the family, but she is helpless to articulate an alternative relation based on need and generosity: " 'Jewel,' ma said, looking at him. 'I'll give———I'll give———give———' Then she began to cry" (120).

I want to emphasize that the sudden rupture of the family by Addie's death precipitates a crisis that exposes the economic contradictions of the modern farm family and its extension, the community. The Bundrens' neighbors are drawn into a process that confronts the monetization of personal relations. Jewel's ferocious efforts to pay for the extra hay his horse will eat at Samson's or for the use of Tull's mule underscore the ambiguous fluidity of personal and financial dealings. The codes of hospitality and charity conflict with those of economic self-sufficiency. Anse constantly trades on this ambiguity as he casts himself on the goodwill of those he meets: "I reckon there are Christians here" (218).

Accordingly, Anse blames the expansion of state authority as much as any natural catastrophe for his troubles:

> Putting it [the road] where every bad luck prowling can find it and come straight to my door, charging me taxes on top of it. Making me pay for Cash having to get them carpenter notions when if it hadn't been no road come there, he wouldn't a got them; falling off of churches and lifting no hand in six months and me and Addie slaving and a-slaving, when there's plenty of sawing on this place he could do if he's got to saw. (32)

It is state paternalism in the twenties and thirties that replaces the individual father's authority in the modernized United States,[17] but such paternalism is a social transformation that, in *As I Lay Dying*, helps to expose the arbitrary authority of the father in the nuclear family. Anse and his ruggedly individualistic neighbors complain about state incursions, like roads and taxes. Anse even takes Darl's long-threatened incarceration as more

17. Though they are interested in the breakup of the "Oedipal family" as an index of social upheaval in the modernization of the South as it is reflected in *As I Lay Dying*, Wesley and Barbara Morris offer an extremely simplistic and traditional account of Faulkner's resistance to change, and they fail to grasp the complexity of the relation between social and aesthetic discourses. See their *Reading Faulkner* (Madison: University of Wisconsin Press, 1989), especially 26–38 and 150–75.

state meddling: "They would short-hand me just because he tends to his own business" (32), Anse puts it economically. Eventually, of course, the state's law does intervene in family affairs, forcing the Bundrens to choose between defending themselves against a lawsuit and sacrificing a son to the state asylum.

Contemporary upheavals in the South's labor practices derive from the dismantling of the chattel slavery system. After emancipation, labor is no longer a capitalized factor in production. The southern economy is forced to develop a new reliance on wage labor.[18] When Anse thinks of his and Addie's work as "slaving and a-slaving," he inadvertently points to the way the biological family was exploited as non-wage labor in the post–Civil War agricultural South. That Anse's offspring begin to earn their own money continues a history of emancipation for a variety of underclass sub-populations. Addie mocks patriarchal economic domination in her derisive balancing of the reproductive books: "I gave Anse Dewey Dell to negative Jewel. Then I gave him Vardaman to replace the child I had robbed him of. And now he has three children that are his and not mine" (162). But the next generation of dispossessed seems a little less pliant. Dewey Dell warns Anse off her cash: "Dont you touch it! If you take it you are a thief" (237).

Cora Tull occupies a transitional position in the history of commodi-fied relations and market involvement in the modernized South. On the one hand, in her egg business she has grasped the principles of deferring profit in order to maximize capital investment, of reinvesting profit to as-sure growth, and of the advantage of producing goods for sale rather than for personal consumption. She stocks the best breed of hens, accepts the fact that early losses mean that they "couldn't afford to use the eggs our-selves" (5), and organizes her banking business vertically, becoming her own supplier of eggs and trading for the rest of what she needs.

Cora's savvy seems to dissolve when she learns that Miss Lawing-ton's customer for her cakes has canceled the order, leaving her with a perishable stock. She refuses to enforce the agreement and rationalizes her potential losses: "Well, it isn't like they cost me anything" (6). The cakes cost her nothing monetarily, because she saves out the eggs above those she has contracted to sell, but she does not recognize the cost of her own labor: "But it's not like they cost me anything except the baking" (8). Cora cannot appreciate that her labor is already capitalized in her business, nor does she count the lost profit that the unsold eggs would have brought.

18. See Wright, *Old South, New South*, 84–90.

This "miscue" (8), as she calls it, suggests the naïveté of the novice merchandiser, but I think Cora's rationalization of loss also points to a fundamental contradiction in a commodity economy. The ideology of the market claims that producers are matched with consumers through mutual need, and that exchange proceeds according to a rationalized process of equivalence. Cora's defense of her customer's behavior rests on her conviction that the woman "never had no use for them now" (6). To Cora's mind, use value remains inseparable from exchange value. From this standpoint, Cora refuses to submit to the impersonal abstractions of the law of the market.

I have been attempting to identify the sedimented empirical reality in *As I Lay Dying* as the process of modernization. This process includes the commodification of social and economic relations, the permeation of mass-market desires and gratifications, and the mechanization of everyday life. Such changes merge to produce the Bundrens' keen appetite for products delivered by an increasingly sophisticated technology and market: cheap false teeth, exotic bananas, electric toys, mechanically reproduced music, even culturally produced popular knowledge, like animal magnetism. When we discover Dewey Dell window shopping for an abortifacient in Mottson, we have reached the deepest penetration of the market into individual mentality.

Dewey Dell's perfect inexperience as a purchaser of anything, let alone what Lafe leads her to believe she can buy at a town drugstore, makes her dependent upon the merchant's desire to sell. Moseley feels "her eyes full on me and kind of blank too, like she was waiting for a sign" (183). Though this unit of an expanding consumer market feigns indifference, it is primed for activation. Even before the shock of what she actually wants hits Moseley, he is already feeling sorry that he will be the agent of her corruption by cosmetics. He thinks she wants "some of this female dope" that will ruin her complexion: "It's a shame, the way they poison themselves with it. But a man's got to stock it or go out of business in this country" (184). Moseley lets market pragmatics rationalize his exploitation of a defenseless clientele, never sensing how the profit motive here conflicts with his moral indignation over Dewey Dell's request for something to end her pregnancy.

Like so many of the other desires in *As I Lay Dying*, even Dewey Dell's longing to be relieved of what grows within her has been deeply conditioned by the market. In the first place, by the late 1920s, virtually every state had had strict antiabortion laws on the books for nearly three decades. In the period between 1880 and 1900, "the United States completed its transition from a nation without abortion laws of any sort to a nation where abortion was legally and officially proscribed."[19] At least part of the strength of the antiabortion movement in the later nineteenth century involved the professionalization of medical practitioners.[20] These physicians were committed to scientific training and practice, founded the American Medical Association in 1847 to advance their cause, and attacked nonprofessional practitioners, who performed the great majority of abortions between 1840 and 1880. The morality of abortion could not be separated from its real and symbolic significance as a form of non-regular medicine. The illegalization of abortion consolidated the triumph of professionalized medicine in the United States by the 1880s (Mohr, 238–39).

If Dewey Dell finds herself up against the patriarchal state in her quest for an abortion in 1928, her mother found herself shackled to the patriarchal family in her efforts to control her body's reproduction. Addie describes her first pregnancy, with Cash, as the moment her "aloneness" is "violated" for the first time (158). Her second pregnancy is more betrayal than violation: "Then I found that I had Darl. At first I would not believe it. Then I believed that I would kill Anse. It was as though he had tricked me, hidden within a word like within a paper screen and struck me in the back through it" (158). Addie considers reproduction forced labor and immediately begins to plan her death wish. Her revenge plot lodges her protest that Anse should be the one to decide how many children she must bear ("Nonsense," Anse said; "you and me aint nigh done chapping yet, with just two" [159]), that Anse should be the name for the shape of her body "where I used to be a virgin" (159).

Addie's resentment of maternity may also be measured against the long and complex history of reproductive rights for women in the United States. Mid-nineteenth-century America witnessed sharp increases both in the number of abortions and in the acceptability of the practice. The abortifacient industry marketed dozens of "guaranteed" cures—"French lunar" pills, "renovating" pills, and so on. The drug industry was expanding just as the medical industry was, and women wanting to limit family size constituted a market prime for development. Up through the 1880s, apothecaries sold a variety of over-the-counter abortifacients, including cotton-root, which was

19. James C. Mohr, *Abortion in America: Origins of National Policy, 1800–1900* (New York: Oxford University Press, 1978), 226; hereafter cited in my text as Mohr.
20. The first crusade against abortion in the United States was launched by so-called regular physicians in the 1850s.

particularly popular in the South because of its long-standing reputation as a slave remedy for unwanted pregnancy (Mohr, 59–60). Profits from commercial abortifacients proved very high, and some of the country's largest drug firms entered the market by the 1870s (Mohr, 59).

Dewey Dell's confidence that she can get something at the drugstore must originate in a history of once lawful, now clandestine, trade in abortifacients for desperate, poor, and ignorant customers. But Dewey Dell's predicament also reflects substantial shifts in the status of women during the 1920s. If one recalls that the Nineteenth Amendment, granting women the right to vote, had finally been ratified in 1920, Dewey Dell's insistent and brazen demand to be served symbolizes the rise of an entire gender.

If we place Dewey Dell's desire to stop what she calls the "terrible . . . process of coming unalone" (56), we may read her behavior as part of a larger resistance to oppression by women in the modernized South. Like Addie, Dewey Dell describes pregnancy as the sensation of multiplying herself: the daughter feels "my body, my bones and flesh beginning to part and open upon the alone," as her mother thinks of having two children as being "three now" (159). Dewey Dell's quest for an abortion at least entertains the possibility of release from this process of mandated disintegration. The novel gestures toward other forms of potential emancipation—Cora's ventures into the marketplace in the face of her husband's doubtfulness, the power of education and other mass movements that put individuals in touch with the energies of progress (both Cora and Addie were schoolteachers), and women's enfranchisement at the ballot box.[21]

The female vote played a decisive role in Mississippi politics in the twenties.[22] An early indication of the effect of enfranchisement in 1920 was the candidacy of the first woman to run for office in Mississippi—in the 1922 senatorial contest. Belle Kearney polled nearly 12 percent of the popular vote but lost to James K. Vardaman in a three-way contest. (Vardaman was himself defeated in the runoff and retired from public life that year.) In 1923, the gubernatorial election drew one hundred thousand new voters, probably sixty-five thousand of them women. The front-runner and eventual winner

21. Anne Firor Scott recounts the emergence of professional and political opportunities for southern women in *The Southern Lady: From Pedestal to Politics, 1830–1930* (Chicago: University of Chicago Press, 1970).

22. Information in the following paragraphs is drawn from Albert D. Kirwan, *Revolt of the Rednecks: Mississippi Politics, 1876–1925* (Gloucester, Mass.: Peter Smith, 1964, originally published Lexington, Ky.: University of Kentucky Press, 1951).

of the governorship was Henry L. Whitfield. He campaigned on a platform of reduced taxes, even though he had advocated higher taxes in an earlier position as state superintendent of education under then-Governor Vardaman.[23] The Vicksburg *Herald* credited newly voting women with Whitfield's victory over the infamous Theodore Bilbo. (Whitfield was strongly supported by the Delta and central regions of the state, which would have included Faulkner's home county.) The appearance of Whitfield's name attached to Addie's emancipatory lover creates a political resonance for their alliance. Addie expresses the meaning of her liaison with Reverend Whitfield in theological and metaphysical imagery, but it is pertinent to think of a buried political edge to Addie's development of a private life apart from Anse and to her temporarily refusing her body to him (161).

Of course, Addie has had her own occupation before Anse comes a-courting so persuasively. She and Cora Tull could well have owed their careers as schoolteachers to the Progressivist policies of Governor James K. Vardaman, who was elected to office in 1903 after three attempts, the last successful because of the recent adoption of direct primary voting.[24] Vardaman campaigned for social and economic reforms common to the national Progressivist positions: the regulation of corporations, women's suffrage, educational improvements, and Prohibition.

By the time Vardaman tried to recover the Senate seat he had lost in 1918, he was reduced by discouragement and mental illness to virtual incapacity. During the senatorial campaign of 1922, he sat on platforms while others spoke for him. The Jackson *Daily News* summed up his plight derisively: "It would be just as sensible to go out to the Mississippi Insane Hospital, pick out one of the unfortunate inmates . . . and adorn him with a Senatorial toga."[25] It is likely that Vardaman Bundren was born and honorifi-

23. Faulkner's interest in state politics would have been heightened by his family's involvement. In 1919, his uncle managed the successful gubernatorial campaign of Lee Russell, son of a tenant farmer from south Lafayette County and onetime law partner of Faulkner's grandfather. Bill Faulkner accompanied his uncle on many of the candidate's local appearances. In the summer of 1922, his uncle himself ran for election to a district court judgeship, and Bill served as his chauffeur during the campaign (see Joseph Blotner, *Faulkner: A Biography*, 2 vols. [New York: Random House, 1974], 243–45).
24. Woodward, *Origins of the New South*, 275.
25. Kirwan, *Revolt of the Rednecks*, 302. Vardaman and his Progressivist successors, like Theodore Bilbo (governor from 1915–1919), contributed to two projects whose effects we see in *As I Lay Dying*: an ambitious road construction program and the improvement of public health facilities, like the mental asylum in Jackson, to which Darl is sent (it is named after Whitfield). The Faulkner family supported Vardaman's career, though they

cally named during this last hurrah, when Vardaman's loyal constituencies actually delivered him a plurality in the open election but were insufficient to win the runoff.

Disintegration

I have sought to re-embody *As I Lay Dying* in order to measure the vast effort of transmutation that produces one of modernist literature's most thematically abstract and aesthetically elite works. The negation of empirical reality, if we recall Adorno's description of the process, allows the modern work to transcend its opposite—that which is not art—at the same time the work remains in communication with that opposite. The particularity of the modernizing South does, I admit, have little ostensible effect in *As I Lay Dying*. Criticism of the novel properly attends to the philosophical, metaphysical, psychological, and technical issues that comprise its main interests. At the same time, however, we can uncover the novel's reflection on the processes that produce these interests. If modernization is the novel's sedimented material, how does modernist form attempt to disembody it in the process of turning it into art?

The plot of *As I Lay Dying* centers on a crisis of disintegration. The Bundren family, deprived of its wife and mother, struggles to mobilize itself. Burdened by the dead past, which continues to exercise its will ghoulishly over the present, the Bundrens momentarily lose their balance. The family is threatened with disintegration: Along the way, Addie disappears into a box, a river, and a hole in the ground; Jewel disappears into the countryside; Vardaman runs off; Cash slips under water; Dewey Dell vanishes into a basement; and Anse goes into a house for a long time. Eventually, the forces of reintegration muster themselves, but it is difficult not to read the story as a fable of social upheaval, as I have suggested, with the modernization of the South implied both in the Bundrens' move to town and in their centrifugal impulses away from the broken forms of family and community.

The novel's replete imagery of dismemberment and disunification may be represented by a passage in which Vardaman thinks of Jewel's horse, invisible in the barn:

It is as though the dark were resolving him out of his integrity, into an unrelated scattering of components—snuffings and stamp-

---

never permitted him or the similarly lowborn Lee Russell to be favored by their social intimacy.

> ings; smells of cooling flesh and ammoniac hair; an illusion of a
> co-ordinated whole of splotched hide and strong bones within which,
> detached and secret and familiar, an *is* different from my *is*. I see him
> dissolve—legs, a rolling eye, a gaudy splotching like cold flames—
> and float upon the dark in fading solution; all one yet neither; all
> either yet none. (52)

Addie's death is a synecdoche for a whole set of disintegrative events in the
novel's world. The New South's partial rejection of the ways of antebellum
gentility; the ruptures induced by emancipatory movements among formerly
subjugated populations like blacks, poor whites, and women; the economic
endangerment of the small farmer; modernism's rejection of realism and
traditional modes like epic or tragedy—all these create the sensation of
disintegration, dissolution, disembodiment. Faulkner himself once said that
to write about the disappearance of the aristocratic South of the Sartorises
was to attempt "if not the capture of that world and the feeling of it as you'd
preserve a kernel or a leaf to indicate the lost forest, at least to keep the
evocative skeleton of the dessicated [sic] leaf."[26]

I want to recall the ambivalence that early modernism displayed
toward the disintegrative force of modernization. For example, technology,
the expression of the masses' desires and their gratification, the redistribu-
tion of wealth and means of production, the extension of enfranchisement,
and so on nourished utopian hopes.[27] As small farmers attempted to amass
some capital by selling their labor and other goods (like timber) on the market, they hedged against extreme reliance on cotton, whose prices fell after
World War I and whose production was nearly ruined by heavy rains in the
late twenties—the worst occurring in 1929, the summer before Faulkner
began *As I Lay Dying*.

As the coherence of the world from the standpoint of certain privileged racial, class, and gender positions begins to disintegrate, new voices
and subjectivities emerge. In *The Sound and the Fury*, the morose grief of
the Compson brothers for their lost Caddy figures in part a pathologically
nostalgic aristocracy moaning over its dispossession. By the last section of
that novel, however, it becomes clear that the whole world does not share
this mentality. Dilsey emerges from the ruination of the Compson house to

26. This quotation is from an unpublished manuscript in the Yale University Library, but it
is quoted here from Blotner, *Faulkner*, 531–32.
27. Huyssen describes how the avant-gardist movements embraced the emancipatory
potential of the machine age in *GD*, 12–13.

mark out the "endin" of one historical period and the "beginnin," perhaps, of another.[28] Idiocy, suicide, paranoia, hypochondria, delusion—these are not everyone's destinies, only those cast down, like the Compsons. The analytical potency of Faulkner's fiction forces us to ask *who* experiences these changes as disintegration.

As I Lay Dying also openly worries that modernization will lead to greater misery. The novel's imagery reflects the fear that humans themselves are becoming technologized. Consider the interest in prosthodontics and graphophonic simulations of live sound. The hardworking Tull describes his mistrust of introspection "because [man's] brain it's like a piece of machinery: it wont stand a whole lot of racking. It's best when it all runs along the same, doing the day's work and not no one part used no more than needful" (64). As Cash saws the coffin boards singlemindedly, Darl sees the "in and out of that unhurried imperviousness as a piston moves in the oil" (69). Similarly, Darl describes Jewel and Vernon wading across the flooded river: "It is as though [the surface] had severed them both at a single blow, the two torsos moving. . . . It looks peaceful, like machinery does after you have watched it and listened to it for a long time" (149). Surely these anxieties derive from a historical fear that the proletariat in industrialized countries will increasingly become deadened extensions of machinery.

Such views of the dangers of modernization would be fairly commonplace within the general post–World War I modernist project of rejecting the dream-turned-nightmare of technology and the vulgarities of social realism.[29] The difference in a writer like Faulkner arises from his refusal to reconcile the ambivalence toward modernization. The ambivalence remains in active dialectical relation, and the efforts to reconcile the differences are subject to conscious reflection within As I Lay Dying.

Disembodiment

The body of social material that constitutes the sediment of any work of art must be negated, left behind in the process that establishes the work's required autonomy. Modern art—artistic production with a desacralized cultural function—must seek autonomy for itself; it is not ordained by ritualistic or other supramundane authority. The work of art constitutes its identity and

28. William Faulkner, *The Sound and the Fury* (New York: Vintage Books, 1987), 344.
29. Huyssen observes that Adorno conceived of modernism as "a reaction formation to mass culture and commodification" (*GD*, 24).

86

autonomy by mediating the "substratum" of content through artistic form. Adorno formulates this relation between art and social reality:

> It is by virtue of its separation from empirical reality that the work of art can become a being of a higher order, fashioning the relation between the whole and its parts in accordance with its own needs. . . . We can say that art's opposition to the real world is in the realm of form; but this occurs, generally speaking, in a mediated way such that aesthetic form is a sedimentation of content. (*AT*, 8–9)

The sediment of content becomes such through a *process* of sedimentation. I want to try to describe the way *As I Lay Dying* transmutes the empirical realities I have been describing above. In this modernist text's foregrounding of formal problems, we see the effort to mediate the ambivalence toward modernization. In Adorno's terminology, "the unresolved antagonisms of reality reappear in art in the guise of immanent problems of artistic form. . . . The aesthetic tensions manifesting themselves in works of art express the essence of reality in and through their emancipation from the factual facade of exteriority" (*AT*, 8). Adorno's emphasis on the dynamic process of sedimentation, of "sloughing off" a "repressive, external-empirical mode of experiencing the world" (*AT*, 6) distinguishes his approach from a primitive distinction of form and content.

Early in *As I Lay Dying*, Darl describes the peculiar pitch of the Bundren house. Because it slants downhill, a "feather dropped near the front door will rise and brush along the ceiling, slanting backward, until it reaches the down-turning current at the back door: so with voices. As you enter the hall, they sound as though they were speaking out of the air about your head" (18). Here, Darl identifies what I will call the disembodiment effect, which characterizes almost every major facet of the novel. The image of voices loosed in the air, floating bodiless around the listener's head, precisely marks the status of voice and body in the novel.

Some of the most brilliant criticism of *As I Lay Dying* describes the varieties of disembodiment. In *The House Divided*, Eric Sundquist gives the problem its fullest treatment in a chapter organized around the relation of the novel's rhetoric to its themes of death and grief: "The book is obsessively concerned with problems of disembodiment, with disjunctive relationships between character and narration or between bodily self and conscious identity."[30] Sundquist elaborates on the disjunctions that plague

30. Eric Sundquist, *Faulkner: The House Divided* (Baltimore: Johns Hopkins University Press, 1983), 29; hereafter cited in my text as *HD*.

the characters' efforts to affirm the integrity of identity, of voice and body, of one mind and another, of word and deed. The entire novel, according to Sundquist, engages the author and reader in a process analogous to grieving, in which one expresses "an identity that is most intensely and passionately present even as it passes away."[31]

One goal of my earlier examination of the substratum of social antagonisms in the novel was to put us in a position to resituate this disembodiment effect. The typical view largely grants the work's "seclusion" from social reality; Sundquist, for example, notes that although it continues Faulkner's exploration of "the intimate family brutalities" in the earlier *The Sound and the Fury* and *Sanctuary*, *As I Lay Dying* "can, more than any of his major novels, be read independently" (*HD*, 28). As "a compendium of . . . problematic techniques," that is, the novel floats free of its social ground. I propose that the disembodiment manifested formally in *As I Lay Dying* constitutes the sedimentation of social disintegration.

I have used the term *modernization* to encompass various strains of social disintegration indicated in *As I Lay Dying*. The literal traces of this disintegrative process share the idea of disembodiment: Addie's decorporealization into metaphor ("My mother is a fish" [74]), memory, and print; Dewey Dell's quest to disburden herself of another's body ("And I am Lafe's guts" [54]); Darl's efforts to project himself telepathically into others' bodies; Jewel's yearning to rigidify and so deaden his body; Cash's willingness to inanimate one limb; and so forth. In all these quarters, we find suggestions of the larger processes of the work, which seek to mediate the emancipatory, yet deadening, antagonisms of social disintegration by formalizing them. Thus, the formal disjunctions of speaker and utterance,

---

31. *HD*, 42. Two other studies of formal disembodiment will secure my point. Stephen M. Ross has meticulously distinguished the mimetic voices of *As I Lay Dying* (i.e., those that create the illusion of personalized speech) from the textual voice of the novel (that element of the discourse that resists anthropomorphism and has the status of pure writing) in "'Voice' in Narrative Texts: The Example of *As I Lay Dying*," *PMLA* 94 (March 1979): 300–310. This line of analysis establishes the disembodiment of voice into writing and describes an irreconcilable fissure in the novel's discourse. Ross's categories explain the discrepancies between the language on the page and the characters' expressions they are supposed to represent. Likewise, Patrick O'Donnell subtly uncovers the "ambivalence of metaphor" in *As I Lay Dying*. He demonstrates that metaphors are "signs of the *relationality* of language conceived as a series of semantic shifts" (see O'Donnell, "Spectral Road," 63). O'Donnell demonstrates that language signifies through the slipping contact of signifier and signified, and that this conceptualization of metaphor informs the imagery describing the uncertain relation between surface and depth, inner and outer, embodiment and essence.

figure and meaning, radical perspectivism and coherent narrative, and so on function to "express the essence of reality" by disguising "the factual facade of exteriority" (*AT*, 8).

Faulkner concentrates the activities of disguise in his author surrogate Darl so that he can examine them critically. In so doing, Faulkner comes to distinguish one modernist aesthetic that is exhausted from another that will prove productive. Darl's reference to the "cubistic bug" identifies his aesthetic procedures: In the earlier part of the sentence, he describes the barn's "conical facade with the square orifice of doorway broken only by the square squat shape of the coffin" (201). Darl's cubism substitutes formal intricacy for the reality of a blazing barn; it converts the issue of his agency in destroying property into a question of geometry. Darl relies on two principal methods of modernism in treating experience in *As I Lay Dying*: he aestheticizes and he universalizes.

The first technique instances his poetic temperament and artistic eye.[32] Describing Cash's hard work in finishing the coffin, Darl transforms the grime of spent energy and labor into a beautifully rendered moment:

> The lantern sits on a stump. Rusted, grease-fouled, its cracked chimney smeared on one side with a soaring smudge of soot, it sheds a feeble and sultry glare upon the trestles and the boards and the adjacent earth. Upon the dark ground the chips look like random smears of soft pale paint on a black canvas. The boards look like long smooth tatters torn from the flat darkness and turned backside out. (67)

Notice how the material reality of Cash's work first becomes an intensely aesthetic effect and then becomes de-substantialized into the abstract image of tatters of darkness reversed. The modulations toward disembodiment practiced in this passage characterize Darl's regular efforts to expunge a certain kind of reality through aesthetic treatment. The verbal version of aestheticization appears in the following passage, in which Darl's playful musical effects conspire to make Addie's expressions meaningless: "The breeze was setting up from the barn, so we put her under the apple tree, where the moonlight can dapple the apple tree upon the long slumbering flanks within which now and then she talks in little trickling bursts of secret

32. On the poetic effects of Darl's style, see François L. Pitavy, "Through Darl's Eyes Darkly: The Vision of the Poet in *As I Lay Dying*," *William Faulkner: Materials, Studies, and Criticism* 4 (July 1982): 37–62.

and murmurous bubbling" (195). Darl turns the "talk" of Addie's decomposition into alliterative and pictorial abstraction.

Darl's complementary treatment of his material universalizes its meaning. Having bought cement in Mottson to repair Cash's leg, the Bundrens must find a bucket and water to mix it. As they pause, Darl notices that Dewey Dell still carries the package supposed to contain Mrs. Tull's cakes:

> "You had more touble [sic: for "trouble"] than you expected, selling those cakes in Mottson," I say. How do our lives ravel out into the no-wind, no-sound, the weary gestures wearily recapitulant: echoes of old compulsions with no-hand on no-strings: in sunset we fall into furious attitudes, dead gestures of dolls. Cash broke his leg and now the sawdust is running out. He is bleeding to death is Cash. (191)

The discourses of economics and labor frame Darl's cosmic despair. He responds to his sister's desperation by generalizing to the point of vertigo, arriving at a protective irony that is mostly verbal posturing. Making his brother into a sawdust-leaking doll underscores Darl's talent for the metaphysical conceit, but it also identifies him with the cerebral retreats from politics and history practiced by Mr. Compson, not to mention the Vanderbilt modernists.[33]

Reintegration

The danger for all cultural products in an age of consumption is that they will be neutralized through commodification. Faulkner fought this battle strenuously. One thinks of his slamming "shut a door between me and all publishers' addresses and book lists"[34] in order to write at least one book—*The Sound and the Fury*—that need not defer to consumer taste. On the other hand, Faulkner also understood that the market presented the only way the novelist could reach the readers who would confer literary immortality. He constantly wrote for film and short story markets because, in effect, they were financing his art fiction. Faulkner's engagements with the nascent culture industry in the United States bring him to the brink of being able to see a profound shift in the status of the work of art:

33. See Richard Moreland's account of modernist irony as a component of the Agrarians' social outlook in *Faulkner and Modernism: Rereading and Rewriting* (Madison: University of Wisconsin Press, 1990), 23–26.

34. William Faulkner, "An Introduction for *The Sound and the Fury*," ed. James B. Meriwether, *The Southern Review*, n.s., 8 (October 1972): 710.

> Just as art works become commodities and are enjoyed as such, the commodity itself in consumer society has become image, representation, spectacle. Use value has been replaced by packaging and advertising. The commodification of art ends up in the aesthetization of the commodity. (*GD*, 21)

As well as this description fits the elementary negotiations of consumer society by the Bundren family, it also describes the product of high cultural commodification, the modernist novel itself.

That *As I Lay Dying* is produced by the very processes it critiques may be seen in the traces of reification apparent in Faulkner's own comments about writing it. He referred to this novel as his tour de force and said that he could write it so exceptionally fast (six weeks, without changing a word—some exaggeration, but not much) because he knew every word before he began. Composed with the hum of the University of Mississippi's power station in the background, in the hours Faulkner worked on the night shift, *As I Lay Dying* takes on the sheen of a highly technical, even machine-made object.

Cash's graphophone quietly reminds us of the technologically reproduced, illusorily prosthetic qualities of novels themselves—mass-produced, mass-consumed goods that simulate life and speech, and that gratify us imaginatively when life is full of discontentment and loss. As the crisis of bereavement begins to move toward resolution, we might wonder whether the novel functions like the graphophone that eases Cash's odd hours, or like the bananas that console the novel's two disappointed shoppers. If *As I Lay Dying* wraps up its story of misery by reintegrating it into a tragicomic narrative of aesthetic virtuosity—if it is, again, like the graphophone, "all shut up as pretty as a picture" (241)—does it not fail in the modernist project of resisting and transmuting the forces of modernization and commodification?

Darl's impulse to integrate the complex and intractable realities of his world into abstract structures represents a danger in the modernist project. *As I Lay Dying* rejects the sort of falsifying modernism represented in Darl's overly aesthetic and universalized responses to his material. His incarceration at the end of the novel figuratively confirms Faulkner's repudiation of the sort of art that too effortlessly fills the gaps of a story, that too readily composes itself abstractly, and that too hastily universalizes its meaning. Unfeeling as the remark may seem, I wonder if Cash is not right in concluding about Darl that "this world is not his world; this life his life" (242). For Faulkner to proceed into the 1930s with his great fiction of social and historical analysis, he needed to exorcise the strictly aestheticist impulse of his modernism. Instead, the critical, self-reflective modernism he forged became a powerful instrument for *making* a world out of this world, a life out of this life.

Decomposition

Does Cash really believe that the music coming from the new Mrs. Bundren's graphophone is *as* natural as a music band? Are we to believe that Cash means to replace one Mrs. Bundren with another in his story without noting their difference? Do bananas make Vardaman as happy as the red train would have? At many points, *As I Lay Dying* seeks to pass off replicas and substitutes as the real thing. Here, the novel sees into the core of mass culture—in which image replaces substance, reproduction eliminates the very idea of an original, commodification masks the circumstances of production. Yet, the novel also resists its own impulses by sabotaging the faithful workings of biological, mechanical, and social reproduction. Slips, miscues, gaps, and hesitations interfere with the powerful drive toward reintegration.

One kind of textual interference shows up in the novel's many ellipses. The notorious example belongs to Addie: "The shape of my body where I used to be a virgin is in the shape of a   and I couldn't think *Anse*" (159). In this disruption of syntax, Addie produces a problem, some resistance, a hesitation about the authority males have to name, possess, and take the woman's intactness. Compare a similar moment in Moseley's section, just after he has furiously sent Dewey Dell back to the custody of her father, brother, boyfriend, "or the first man you come to on the road." He goes on to think, "But it's a hard life they have; sometimes a man . . . . if there can ever be any excuse for sin, which it cant be" (187; ellipses in original). The breaking off of Moseley's sentence allows him to entertain genuine sympathy for Dewey Dell's plight and likely victimization. In gaps like these, we are invited to think about problems from conflicting standpoints, to evaluate the pressures silencing discourse, as well as those producing it.

The small snarls in the plot line also produce moments of reflective pause. An example occurs at the point the Bundrens enter Jefferson, when the stinking coffin overtakes several blacks on the road: "'Great God,' one says; 'what they got in that wagon?'" (212). Jewel "whirls" on the insulter but attacks the wrong person: "'Son of a bitches,' he says. As he does so he is abreast of the white man, who has paused. It is as though Jewel had gone blind for the moment, for it is the white man toward whom he whirls" (212). Darl jumps in to defuse the confrontation, but the moment spotlights the relation between racial and class strife. In Darl's judgment, Jewel would have to be "blind" to identify a white man as his adversary. Poor whites, especially hill farmers like the Bundrens, took their interests to be in direct competition with those of blacks. They consistently supported the otherwise progressive, but virulently racist, policies of politicians like James Vardaman, who was known as "The White Chief" for good reason. The irony of the moment involves its revelation of an authentic ground for conflict between whites. Jewel sulks that the white man has insulted them out of snobbery: "Thinks because he's a goddamn town fellow" (213). At moments like these, the novel makes us sort out the way racial conflict is an ideological construct that deflects potentially more productive class conflict in the South.

Perhaps the most potent sort of hesitation in the novel derives ultimately from Addie's death and from the numerous ways it disrupts the reproduction of everyday reality. Addie's more or less abrupt departure stops a lot of folks dead in their tracks. For all his cruelties and selfishness, the most touching victim may still be Anse. Addie's death makes Anse confront a dilemma. Repeatedly, narrators portray him as looking silently out over his land. The first time we see him meditating, Jewel has insisted that he decide about whether he wants his sons to haul one more load of lumber despite Addie's imminent death. Anse "gazes out across the land, rubbing his knees" (16). He is thinking about a real problem: the conflict between emotional and economic obligations. The summer of 1929 saw ruinous floods destroy cotton crops, whose value had fallen steadily throughout the decade.

The farmer's silent meditation on what is happening to farmland in the South possesses great poignancy when the social transformations of modernization are borne in mind. How many other times Anse and Darl are described as staring at their land! Here is Tull on Anse: "His eyes look like pieces of burnt-out cinder fixed in his face, looking out over the land" (27–28). Over and over, Darl broods "with his eyes full of the land" (32; see also 23 and 106). Dewey Dell might make fun of Anse's immobility, but there is a serious side to the image she offers: Anse "looks like right after the maul hits the steer and it no longer alive and dont yet know that it is dead" (55). The analogy echoes Addie's remark that Anse "did not know he was dead" (160). One wonders if farmers like the Bundrens could already feel that they were sociological corpses.

My analysis of the reflective and potentially critical modernism of *As I Lay Dying* would not be complete unless I observed that opportunities to think descend on the characters as a kind of enforced leisure. Tull, for example, accompanies Anse and the younger Bundrens across the sunken bridge through a torrent and finds himself looking back in amazement at his own farm: "When I looked back at my mule it was like he was one of these here spy-glasses and I could look at him standing there and see all the broad land and my house sweated outen it like it was the more the sweat, the broader the land; the more the sweat, the tighter the house because it would take a tight house for Cora" (125). This moment of almost perfect defamiliarization comes on the heels of Tull's crossing the river. A child has led him, "like he [Vardaman] was saying They wont nothing hurt you. Like he was saying about a fine place he knowed where Christmas come twice with Thanksgiving and lasts on through the winter and the spring and the summer, and if I just stayed with him I'd be all right too" (125). This is a very odd juxtaposition of perceptions—they quite nearly read like hallucinations. The logic joining them arises from the utopian content of Vardaman's drive toward town, that consumer paradise where everyone is made a child by wanting something better than he or she is entitled to, where every worker fantasizes about leaving the sweated-out land and sweated-out house on the other side of the river.

In these moments of reflection, we may begin to appreciate how Faulkner's modernist aesthetic reequips itself for his major novels of the thirties. Leaving idle metafiction, like *Mosquitoes*, behind, radically interrogating and finally exorcising the effete poeticism of Quentin Compson and Darl Bundren, Faulkner prepares for an experimentalism deeply implicated in the search for truth about the South in *Light in August* and *Absalom, Absalom!* The way for Faulkner's aesthetic to keep the dialectic between modernization and modernism critically charged is to resist with the force of decomposition the impulse toward reintegration and commodification. The objects furnished by mass culture mark the very discontent they would neutralize. When Vardaman sees the toy train in Jefferson again, he says, "It made my heart hurt" (199). We understand his pure longing here. Later, he experiences that same hurt when he sees the Gillespies' barn burning: "Then it went swirling, making the stars run backward without falling. It hurt my heart like the train did" (208). To make a book that refuses to solve its difficulties, that remains in communication with the sediment of reality it frames and forms, that forces its participants to think deeply about their lives, is to make a book that reproduces with a critical difference the conditions of its own making. It is to make a book that continues to hurt the heart.

Failed Cultural Narratives: America in the Postwar Era and the Story of *Democracy*

Alan Nadel

Joan Didion begins *Democracy* by describing the novel she had started to write but which no longer seems tenable. As she develops her notes out of the "jettisoned cargo" (a recurrent image in the book) of her unfinished narrative, we learn that the story she intended to write focused on the family and affairs of Inez Christian, who grew up on Hawaii just after World War II, where her family ("in which the colonial impulse had marked every member"[1]) had become prosperous, involved primarily in real estate and construction. In 1955, Inez married Harry Victor, a sort of Kennedy Democrat, who became a United States Senator and then a failed presidential hopeful toward the end of the Vietnam era. This marriage uniting the Christians and the Victors, with their interests in the Pacific perimeter, had allegorical potential, underscored by the fact that prior to her marriage Inez had had an affair with Jack Lovett, a CIA operative also specializing in Pacific operations, and during the course of her marriage had kept in distant contact with him. The crucial event anchoring these fictions was

1. Joan Didion, *Democracy* (New York: Pocket Books, 1984), 26; hereafter cited in my text as *D*.

the murder of Inez's sister, Janet Ziegler, and her sister's apparent lover, Wendell Omura (a Hawaiian congressman), by Inez's father, Paul Christian. Although Paul Christian's motive was never made clear, it may have had something to do with his siding with Janet's husband, Dick Ziegler, "who made a modest fortune in Hong Kong housing and lost it in the development of windward Oahu" (D, 25), against Paul's brother, Dwight Christian, who had "construction contracts in Long Binh and Cam Ranh Bay," and who "used Wendell Omura to squeeze Dick Ziegler out of windward Oahu and coincidentally out of the container business" (D, 26). This family catastrophe coincided with the collapse of the American-backed government in Vietnam and was followed, shortly thereafter, by the death of Jack Lovett and Inez's estrangement from her husband.

Didion makes clear the symbolic potential of her unwritten—or at least unorganized—narrative in passages like the following: "In that prosperous and self-absorbed colony the Christians were sufficiently good-looking and sufficiently confident and, at least at the time Inez was growing up, sufficiently innocent" (D, 27), or, "The Christians, like many island families, had surrounded themselves with the mementos of their accomplishments, with water colors and painted tea cups and evidence of languages mastered and instruments played, framed recital programs and letters of commendation and souvenirs of wedding trips and horse shows and trips to China" (D, 53–54). In the symbolic sub-text, Inez Victor represents Americans facing the dissolution of their patriarchal, hegemonic conception of themselves. Their protocol, manners, status, and Christian morality have been reduced to a series of photo opportunities, euphemisms, and captions—a collage of images that mask a history of infidelity. Their father figure is, it has become clear, insane—he is obsessed with taking sides and settling issues through homicidal violence. Faced with this hypocrisy, the American (Inez) remains a Victor in name only—as she and her father had been Christians in name only—refusing any of the other associations connected with her husband or nation.

This allegorical reading explains the novel Didion was unable to write; it glosses not the narrative that Democracy contains but the one that it was supposed to contain. In this way, Didion's book is not about the allegories we use to define our position in the world but about the erosion of our ability to believe in our personal and national allegories.

Throughout the post–World War II era, democracy has been the name we have given to a narrative of American global politics. Recounted as it was on the pages of Time and Newsweek and on national television networks, the narrative called democracy placed Americans in the roles of reader and viewer of a series of adventures, in which the heroes and villains were clear, the desirable outcomes known, and the undesirable outcomes contextualized as episodes in a larger narrative that promised a happy ending.

To effect that narrative, we adopted a foreign policy called *containment*. It started under President Truman as a form of financial aid to stabilize non-Soviet bloc countries in the economically shaky period of recovery from the destruction caused by World War II and was first introduced in Truman's address to a joint session of Congress on March 12, 1947. Truman requested financial aid for Greece, aid deemed "imperative if Greece is to survive as a free nation,"[2] and for Turkey, because the "future of Turkey is clearly no less important to the freedom-loving peoples of the world than the future of Greece" (AJSC, 5). Truman also requested authority to dispense American personnel to supervise the use of the appropriated money and to train "selected Greek and Turkish personnel" (AJSC, 8). The principle behind this program was the explicit belief that "it must be the policy of the United States to support free peoples who are resisting subjugation by armed minorities or outside pressures" (AJSC, 8).

Even in Truman's speech, however, *democracy* was a questionable name for the rubric governing the story of American foreign aid, for Turkey, as one of the two exemplary cases, many believed, was hardly a fit example then—any more than it is now—of a democracy. One of the skeptics, in fact, was George Kennan, director of Secretary of State George Marshall's Policy Planning Staff. Kennan's 1947 essay, published anonymously in *Foreign Affairs*, introduced the word *containment* and articulated the philosophical underpinnings of American foreign policy for nearly half a century to follow. Whether this essay crucially influenced American policy, or whether it merely articulated an already extant consensus in the Truman administration,[3] it nevertheless focuses most sharply America's understanding of its Cold War role.

It does so by juxtaposing two kinds of narrative. The first assembles

2. Harry S. Truman, "Address to Joint Session of Congress, March 12, 1947," reprinted in *Caging the Bear: Containment and the Cold War*, ed. Charles Gati (New York: Bobbs-Merrill, 1974), 3; hereafter cited in my text as AJSC.
3. John Lewis Gaddis (in *Strategies of Containment: A Critical Appraisal of Postwar American National Security Policy* [New York: Oxford University Press, 1982]) is perhaps the most accomplished scholar on the issue of containment. He argues that although Kennan was reflecting and summarizing already formulated policy, he also had been a chief architect of that policy, having persuasively used within the administration the same arguments he makes in the essay.

98

background material in order to construct a profile of the Soviet mentality, and the second projects scenarios of American response to that mentality. Kennan's narrative of democracy thus stands in sharp contrast to Didion's. Written at opposite ends of the Cold War, his is an imaginative construction of the future (i.e., a fiction), while hers is an imaginative reconstruction of the past (i.e., a history).

Prior to Didion's history stands Kennan's story. His story is one as steeped in the conventions of psychological realism as hers is in the conventions of postmodern meta-fiction. Implicitly equating the body politic with the human body, Kennan undertakes delineating the "political personality" of that body—a difficult task of "psychological analysis"—so that Soviet conduct could "be understood and effectively countered."[4] This unquestioned need to counter the Soviets motivates Kennan's analysis, one that shows this political analysand to be full of contradictions: flexible and intransigent, impetuous but patient, monomaniacal and monolithic but filled with enough hidden rivalries and disagreements to doom it, committed to ideology above pragmatics but also using ideology as a mere excuse for practical actions, part of the long-term political landscape but also likely to collapse with the first transition of power.

Kennan's subject, in other words, is not only hostile but also so clearly schizoid that Kennan's metaphor—the "political personality of Soviet power" (SSC, 571)—cannot control its disparate properties. For Kennan, the power changes from a "personality" to a fluid: "Basically the [Soviet] antagonism remains. It is postulated. And from it *flow* many of the phenomena which we find disturbing in the Kremlin's conduct of foreign policy: the secretiveness, the lack of frankness, the duplicity, the wary suspiciousness, and the basic unfriendliness of purpose" (SSC, 572; my emphasis). These paranoic characteristics run with fluidity from their schizoid source and, "like the postulate from which they flow, are basic to the internal nature of Soviet power" (SSC, 572). The "internal nature" becomes in Kennan's rhetoric a source of essential fluids, and Soviet aggression becomes a form of incontinence: "Its political action is a fluid stream which moves constantly, wherever it is permitted to move, toward a given goal. Its main concern is to make sure it has filled every nook and cranny available to it in the basin of world power. But if it finds unassailable barriers in its path, it accepts these philosophically and accommodates itself to them" (SSC, 575).

4. "X" (George F. Kennan), "The Sources of Soviet Conduct," *Foreign Affairs* 25 (July 1947): 566; hereafter cited in my text as SSC.

With incontinence as the implicit problem, Kennan recommends we not try to change the essential nature of the fluid but rather to limit its flow with "a long-term, patient but firm and vigilant *containment* of Russian expansive tendencies" (SSC, 575; my emphasis). Linking this prolonged policy to a projection of Soviet economic impotence (SSC, 578), Kennan's rhetoric suggests that the fluid's fearful nature is its seminal quality and that containing the flow long enough will make Soviet impotence apparent or cause a mutation. In the eventual ascent of new leaders, Kennan suggests, "strange consequences could flow for the Communist party" (SSC, 579).

But the United States must do more than prevent Soviet flow by "entering with reasonable confidence upon a policy of firm containment designed to confront the Russians with unalterable counterforce at every point where they show signs of encroaching upon the interests of a peaceful and stable world" (SSC, 581); it must also make the source of that flow "appear sterile and quixotic" (SSC, 581), not by counterforce, but by counterexample. If America projects an image of potency through decisiveness, power, and spiritual vitality—a function of internal, as well as external, affairs—containment will be effective by making the Soviets appear, in contrast, less potent and attractive. This appearance will deprive the Soviets of partners, of receptors for their seminal flow, with the goal being "to increase enormously the strains under which Soviet policy must operate . . . and in this way to promote tendencies which must eventually find their outlet in either the breakup or gradual mellowing of Soviet power. [For the Kremlin cannot] face frustration indefinitely without eventually adjusting itself in one way or another" (SSC, 582).

These increased strains, attempts to frustrate by containing the flow —suggesting a model less akin to a great statesman than to Aristophenes' Lysistrata—do not constitute the foundations of a foreign policy so much as they do the motivations for a national narrative, a point implicit in Kennan's closing paragraphs:

> Thus the decision will really fall in large measure in this country itself. The issue of Soviet-American relations is in essence a test of the overall worth of the United States as a nation among nations. To avoid destruction the United States need only measure up to its own best traditions and prove itself worthy of preservation as a great nation.
>
> Surely, there was never a fairer test of national quality than this. In the light of these circumstances, the thoughtful observer of Russian-

American relations will find no cause for complaint in the Kremlin's challenge to American society. He will rather experience a certain gratitude to a Providence which, by providing the American people with its implacable challenge, has made their entire security as a nation dependent on their pulling themselves together and accepting the responsibilities of moral and political leadership that history plainly intended them to bear. (SSC, 582)

Although this national narrative rather consistently informs Cold War thinking—even, arguably, through the 1980s—the specific actions impelled by this narrative were, from the outset, subject to debate. As John Lewis Gaddis points out, "there has developed a kind of cottage industry among Cold War scholars devoted to elucidating 'what Kennan really meant to say.'"[5] Gaddis himself, noting consistent distinctions between policy and

5. Gaddis, *Strategies of Containment*, 26. One might even argue that the entire history of the Cold War and, equally, its entire historiography could be constructed around revised interpretations of Kennan's essay and revised evaluations of the policies and practices mandated by each interpretation. It would take a separate bibliographical essay to delineate the scholarship on this issue. Gaddis provides an extensive bibliography. Early critiques of Kennan came most notably from Walter Lippman (*The Cold War: A Study in U.S. Foreign Policy* [New York: Harper & Row, 1947]) and Hans Moganthau (*In Defense of National Interest* [New York: Knopf, 1951]), both of whom contested less the adversarial relationship with the Soviet Union than the appropriate American approach to the problem. In 1959, William A. Williams (*The Tragedy of American Diplomacy* [New York: World Publishing Co., 1959]) initiated a "revisionist" approach to containment, identifying American policy as expansionism motivated by economic necessity. Throughout the 1960s and early 1970s, revisionist interpretations abounded, locating the origins of the Cold War chiefly in American policies rather than in Soviet policies. Some of the most important include: Gar Alperovitz, *Atomic Diplomacy: Hiroshima and Potsdam* (New York: Simon & Schuster, 1965); Richard J. Barnet, *The Roots of War: The Men and Institutions behind U.S. Foreign Policy* (New York: Antheneum, 1972); D. F. Flemming, *The Cold War and Its Origins, 1917–1960* (New York: Doubleday, 1961); David Horowitz, ed., *Containment and Revolution* (Boston: Beacon, 1967); Joyce Kolko and Gabriel Kolko, *The Limits of Power: The World and United States Foreign Policy, 1945–1954* (New York: Harper & Row, 1972); and Lawrence S. Wittner, *Cold War America: From Hiroshima to Watergate* (New York: Praeger, 1974). In the 1970s, revisionism came under scrutiny, ranging from the vitriolic attacks of Robert James Maddox, *The New Left and the Origins of the Cold War* (Princeton: Princeton University Press, 1973), to the more moderate studies: Raymond Aron, *The Imperial Republic: The United States and the World, 1945–1973*, trans. Frank Jellinek (Englewood Cliffs, N.J.: Prentice-Hall, 1974); Alonzo L. Hamby, *The Imperial Years: The U.S. since 1939* (New York: Weybright & Talley, 1976); and Adam B. Ulam, *The Rivals: America and Russia since World War II* (New York: Viking, 1971). Two collections of essays with entries by a number of these scholars provide a good cross-

implementation, delineates in *Strategies of Containment* the ways successive administrations acted in accordance with their understandings of the policy. These included the expansion of economic support, a series of military treaties, a global rather than a merely European perspective, a network of covert actions, and active military interventions that either supported or suppressed sundry insurgencies.

While I cannot here summarize Gaddis's superb work, one aspect of Gaddis's approach is important to note. Rather than presume that the national narrative of containment required or caused specific acts, Gaddis examines the actions of an administration so as to reconstruct that administration's interpretation of the national narrative. In so doing, he demonstrates that under the common name of containment we have generated numerous, often contradictory or mutually exclusive, stories, each grounding its authority in the claim that it is part of the same story. Without claim to that story, none of the narratives would have the authority to generate the actions committed in its name; at the same time, the claim to a common narrative renders the narrative itself incoherent.

Although it is neither Gaddis's thesis nor goal, one could argue that the evidence and analysis in *Strategies of Containment* demonstrate that the "strategic," as Michel de Certeau says, on the scale of contemporary history, in general, is "transformed, as if defeated by its own success," so that "what was represented as a matrix-form of history [becomes] a mobile infinity of tactics."[6] *Strategies of Containment* thus constitutes the narrative of a narrative, a narrative that neither generates events nor results from their sum; rather, it is a narrative completely divorced from its constituent events, a free-floating signifier designating an infinity of possible referents.

In this context, the containment policy developed, almost exactly during the span of Jack Lovett's professional career, into a narrative of expansion, of spreading democracy. The policy of containment thus suggested that the narrative democracy contained would also "contain" the spread of communism. Although containment was the name of the policy that was supposed to effect that narrative, the narrative's expansive quality could no longer contain all of its disparate elements without becoming democracy in name only.

----

section of the debate at the end of the Vietnam era over the policy of containment: Gati's *Caging the Bear,* and Thomas G. Paterson, ed. *The Origins of the Cold War* (Lexington, Mass.: D. C. Heath, 1970).
6. Michel de Certeau, *The Practice of Everyday Life,* trans. Steve Rendell (Berkeley: University of California Press, 1988), 41.

Like the novel *Democracy*, the term *democracy* has thus become the name of the narrative it does not contain, or, as Didion's narrative strategies suggest, the narrative it intended to contain but never did, overburdened by "facts" that cannot be legitimized within the governing fiction, and fictions that cannot be legitimized by the facts. In this sense, the novel is profoundly elegiac, marking as it does not the story of democracy but its loss—lost either in its inability to be contained by Kennan's fictions or to be reconstructed by Didion's history—lost, in other words, in its own narrativity.

The "author" is also elegized, albeit with ambivalence, in that Didion's narrative reveals a rejection not only of authorial authority but also of its political implications. If narrative, de Certeau has suggested, is always an attempt to colonize the Other,[7] then constructing the narrative of *Democracy* will unavoidably implicate its author in the colonialist activity it attempts to expose, for a narrative's authority always relies on a referent outside the narrative, the part that always remains different from the narrative itself, the part that is not the same as the language that refers to it. That difference, de Certeau has shown, legitimizes a narrative, because without that difference, it would only claim to be referring to itself. At the same time, however, that difference means a narrative never captures its referent, only devises conventions and strategies to disguise its inadequate authority. These conventions and strategies define the hegemonic activity, an activity, as Wlad Godzich points out, whose paradigm can be found in the quest of chivalric romances, the goal of which is to reduce the other "to (more of) the same."[8] Didion's *Democracy*, I shall attempt to demonstrate, not only exposes the personal and national cost of propagating America's colonialist narrative but also investigates both the author's and the reader's complicity in the narrative by attacking the conventional boundaries between reader and text, fact and fiction.

• • • •

The complex relationship between fact and fiction is suggested by the book's first sentence, a disembodied assertion that may or may not be factual. The sentence contains an image of America's ascent to atomic power: "The light at dawn during those Pacific tests was something to see"

7. See Michel de Certeau, *Heterologies: Discourse on the Other*, trans. Brian Massumi (Minneapolis: University of Minnesota Press, 1986).
8. Wlad Godzich, "The Further Possibility of Knowledge" (Foreward), in Certeau, *Heterologies*, xiii.

(*D*, 11). Actually, it contains Jack Lovett's assessment of those tests, or, even more accurately, Joan Didion's account of a conversation with her protagonist, Inez Victor. In the conversation, Inez recounts her conversation with Jack Lovett, in which he describes the tests. The tests take place .in 1952 and 1953; the conversation between Jack and Inez takes place in the spring of 1975; the conversation between Didion and Inez six months later. The sentence, furthermore, is presented without quotation marks. We don't know, therefore, who the speaker and/or the audience is, and we don't know the context, or, in this case, contexts. Learning the contexts, moreover, makes the speaker and audience of this unquoted assertion even more ambiguous. We simply have an ostensive statement of fact: The light at dawn during those Pacific tests was something to see. But what is the claim being made? Is it a claim about the light, given to us on the authority of Jack Lovett; or a claim about Jack's response to the light, given to us on the authority of Inez Victor; or a claim about Inez's conversation, given to us on the authority of Joan Didion, a character who narrates the story of *Democracy*? Is it that Joan Didion is a professional novelist who made several notes, invented several settings, and made several plans for telling the story named *Democracy*? She is also a professional journalist, one who had taken several notes, conducted several interviews, clipped several magazine articles, and saved several photos, also in the interest of telling the story of *Democracy*. Yet, as we discover, all her research and invention, all her method and technique, has made it harder to tell the story, not easier.

The status of the first sentence thus typifies the problem presented by the book and repeatedly foregrounded by its narrator: that the methods for writing truthfully, in fiction, journalism, or history, are not techniques for establishing adequate authority but rather techniques for masking the absence of that authority.

As it will later, with the interview, for example, firsthand knowledge in the book's opening pages proves itself to be inadequate. But if our knowledge of the event—the shot—cannot be acquired from the senses, what does it take to behold Jack Lovett's vision? This question is the quintessential question of authorial authority. By what means do we acquire the reality of a story? Was the light at dawn something to behold? Is Didion presenting this as a fact established on the authority of Jack Lovett's observation, or is she presenting it merely as the fact that it was Jack Lovett's observation.

And, moreover, who is Jack Lovett? To know that would be to know more than the novel will allow—it would be to know among other things, and most important, what values inform his observation. As Didion implies, authors have the power to tell us these things (i.e., to define characters), which is exactly the power that differentiates novelists from journalists. In foregrounding herself in both the role of journalist and of novelist, however, Didion also foregrounds the conflict between the two roles: Whereas the journalist depends on received information, the novelist depends on invented information. At the same time, however, Didion knows that invented information depends as greatly on powers of observation as received information does on the ability to invent connections between bits of information. The problem of this symbiosis becomes further complicated because information never arrives in a pure form; rather, it comes framed by a series of inventions and imaginings. Other people's accounts, deceptions, and self-deceptions, their censorship and self-censorship, their selective observations and more selective memories, render reportage as much the filter of fictions as fiction is the invention of reportage; the journalist is always already one more fictional frame. The professional journalist creates a particularly problematic frame, Didion suggests, because the professional journalist has learned to appropriate experience in the interest of writing about it. Didion's attempts, in this light, to gather and organize her material, become foregrounded as *Democracy*'s plot. The story of the novel's authorship, in other words, becomes one more fiction, in many ways indistinguishable from the fictions it frames.

The second chapter of *Democracy* thus introduces that crisis in authorial authority, beginning with the one-sentence paragraph: "Call me the author" (*D*, 16). This play on Melville points to the dissolution of authorial authority. When Melville says, "*Call* me Ishmael," he acknowledges that his authority to name is stipulative, not essential, by calling attention to its arbitrary nature. Didion, on the other hand, by retaining the authority but dispensing with the name, reveals that the names in all narratives have only one source and that the author, in pretending to be someone else, is employing a technique to disguise the source, even if that source is to be accepted solely on a stipulative basis. Whereas both Melville's and Didion's versions foreground the arbitrary nature of authorial authority, Melville's version does so by exercising the authority in a stipulative fashion, and Didion's version does so by replacing the authority with a tautology that reduces that authority to pure stipulation. By alluding to Melville's biblical allusion, Ishmael, Didion's version of authority becomes a version of another author's version of authority, and thus it does not so much claim authority as it refers to an infinite regress in versions of that claim.

This regress of versions is further underscored by Didion's rejection of her already qualified claim. The opening sentence becomes one she cannot employ. Nor can she assert her authorial presence in the third person ("*Let the reader be introduced to Joan Didion, upon whose character and doings much will depend of whatever interest these pages may have, as she sits at her writing table, in her own room in her own house on Welbeck Street*" [*D*, 16]), as she tells us "Trollope might begin this novel" (*D*, 16). She lacks the authority to start the novel in either the first or third person. "I have no unequivocal way of beginning it," she states, "although I do have certain things in mind" (*D*, 16). Even this assertion is qualified by the fact that "Call me the author" unequivocally begins the second chapter, just as "The light at Dawn during those Pacific tests was something to see" unequivocally begins the first, no matter how many re-contextualizations follow either sentence. Neither sentence equivocates; what Didion equivocates is her willingness to give a statement representative status.

Didion acknowledges this problem in an observation that merges her roles as journalist and novelist:

> My point is this: I can remember a moment in which Harry Victor seemed to present himself precisely as he was and I can remember a moment when Dwight Christian seemed to present himself precisely as he was and I can remember such moments about most people I have known, so ingrained by now is the impulse to define the personality, show the character, but I have no memory of any one moment in which either Inez Victor or Jack Lovett seemed to spring out, defined. (*D*, 81)

The events Didion, as a journalist, discusses in this passage are not amalgamations of sensory data but moments when her imagination converted data into a presentation. Clearly, the people were not presenting themselves *to* Didion nor did they necessarily know that their behavior comprised a presentation. The moments when people *seemed* to present themselves, in other words, are the moments when Didion defines them by virtue of imagining a semblance between specific acts and definitive qualities. This semblance, of course, exists not in nature but under the rubric of an author, who, of necessity, must pretend that acts define characters and, as well, that these acts emanate from the actors rather than the author (just as a reporter must pretend that the interviewee is the source of the information). Didion implies that she knows this is the author's pretense, moreover, when she tells us that these moments are the function not of the way people behave but of her ingrained impulse—the impulse of a fiction writer, without which a journalist would be dysfunctional, because without that impulse a journalist could not render a coherent version of events. Without the context of a coherent version, events cannot acquire meaning, and if events do not acquire meaning, then journalists cannot acquire events, nor can readers, or novelists, or any other form of colonizer.

Yet, Didion focuses exactly on the failure of that impulse, in regard to her novel's central characters. Inez and Jack are hard to read and, hence, hard to write about; in other words, they are hard to acquire, hard to incorporate into a narrative, and hard to contain. Their actions, rather than representing Didion's acquisition of characters, represent the failure of Didion's impulse, her loss of authority, and her inability to turn events into narrative.

To put the question of authority another way, we could ask of the character Joan Didion what she asks of her characters: At what moment does Didion seem to present herself precisely as she is? How does the author define herself? Like Inez and Jack, she seems to evade definition by virtue of existing beyond the limits of her own capacity for observation and definition.

We can posit that the moment when an author speaks to us is the moment when, *by definition,* she appears precisely as she is. Regardless of what we call her, regardless of what she calls herself, regardless of whether we refer to her (or she refers to herself) in the first or the third person, the text always already defines her as author. But the author of *Democracy*, as we have noted, uses the text both to foreground and to reject those definitions. She goes on to reject the details, characters, and plans for the novel she was planning to write, and she finally rejects the possibility of narrative itself, in an unsettling tally sheet of possession and lack:

> I began thinking about Inez Victor and Jack Lovett at a point in my life when I *lacked* certainty, *lacked* even that minimum level of ego which all writers recognize as essential to the writing of novels, *lacked* conviction, *lacked* patience with the past and interest in memory; *lacked* faith even in my own technique.
>
> Cards on the table.
>
> I *have:* "colors, moisture, heat, enough blue in the air," Inez Victor's full explanation of why she stayed on in Kuala Lampur. Consider that too. I *have* those pink dawns of which Jack Lovett spoke. I *have* the dream, recurrent, in which my entire field of vision fills with rainbow, in which I open the door onto a growth of tropical green . . . and watch

the spectrum separate into pure color. Consider any of these things long enough and you will see that they tend to deny the relevance not only of personality but of narrative, which makes them less than ideal images with which to begin a novel, but we go with what we *have*. (*D*, 17; my emphasis)

What Didion *has* tends to deny the relevance of narrative, and what she *lacks* is the authority nonetheless to assert that relevance.

Didion is thus raising the question of what it means to be the author of *Democracy*. What does the narrative of *Democracy* contain, and what kind of authority is necessary to tell it? How is it relevant to its audience and to its author? By raising these questions, Didion destabilizes the authority not only for her own text but for the text of American hegemony authored globally since World War II under the name *democracy*.

For the word *democracy*, as we have noted, names not a unified narrative but a compendium of fictions. So does the novel *Democracy*. *Democracy*'s fictions include the stories Didion's characters invent to cope with the political necessities of their lives, their personal deceits, and their self-deceits. About her husband's chronic absence from their home in Hawaii, Inez's mother, Carol Christian, for example, advises her daughters, " 'When a man stays away from a woman it means he wants to keep their love alive' " (*D*, 24), and when Carol abandons her family in Hawaii, Janet and Inez's grandmother characterizes Carol's departure as "a sudden but compelling opportunity to make the first postwar crossing on the reconditioned *Lurline*" (*D*, 22). After twenty years of marriage to a public figure, Inez "ha[s] come to view most occasions as photo opportunities" (*D*, 48). When Inez's teenage daughter, Jessie, is found using heroin, each therapist she visits produces another fiction. The first implies that the problem lies in Inez's "substance habituation" (namely, cigarettes) (*D*, 61). The second "believe[s] that the answer [lies] in a closer examination of the sibling gestalt. The third employ[s] a technique incorporating elements of aversion therapy" (*D*, 61).

Democracy also includes the fictions characters invent for public or political reasons. Jack Lovett's first wife describes his profession as "army officer," and his second wife describes it as "aircraft executive." His visa application identifies him as a "businessman," and his business cards identify him as a "consultant in international development." Janet similarly invents incidents in her sister's childhood for a *CBS Reports* interview, and, in the interest of her husband's nomination bid, Inez has to develop what

Harry's aid, Billy Dillon, calls a "special interest": "She insisted, unexpectedly and with some vehemence, that she wanted to work with refugees, but it was decided that refugees were an often controversial and therefore inappropriate special interest" (*D*, 54). Inez's interests, in other words, do not determine her "special interest," which is special by virtue of being a fiction especially constructed in the interest of a campaign policy.

In prepping Inez for an AP interview, Dillon thus provides her a catalog of convenient fictions:

> "The major cost of public life is privacy, Inez, that's an easy shot. The hardest part about Washington life is finding a sitter for the Gridiron Dinner. The fun part about Washington life is taking friends from home to the Senate cafeteria for navy-bean soup. You've tried the recipe at home but it never tastes the same. Yes, you do collect recipes. Yes, you do worry about the rising cost of feeding a family. Ninety-nine percent of the people you know in Washington are basically concerned with the rising cost of feeding a family. Schools. Mortgages. Programs. You've always viewed victory as a mandate not for a man but for his programs. Now: you view defeat with mixed emotions. Why: because you've learned to treasure private moments."
> (*D*, 50)

Dillon prefaces these fictions, furthermore, with yet another fictional frame: that the fictitious statements do not comprise the material of an interview any more than they do the material of the life to which they ostensibly refer. Rather, they are volleys in a game of tennis.

Nor has Inez the power not to play the game by trying to make a nonfictitious statement—that the major cost of public life is "memory, mainly" (*D*, 48)—any more than she can by trying to expose the fictional contexts that frame the interview:

> "Here's an example. . . . You looked up the clips on me before you came here."
> "I did a little homework, yes." The woman's finger hovered over the stop button on her tape recorder. . . .
> "That's my point."
> "I'm afraid I don't quite—"
> "Things that might or might not be true get repeated in the clips until you can't tell the difference."
> "But that's why I'm here. I'm not writing a piece from the clips. I'm writing a piece based on what you tell me."

"You might as well write from the clips," Inez said. Her voice was reasonable. "Because I've lost track. Which is what I said in the first place." (*D*, 50–51)

Inez, in other words, has played this figurative game of tennis about her life frequently, as evidenced by the existence of many clips. Having served up numerous fictions about herself, Inez, by the nature of the game, has rendered herself the least reliable witness to her own life and, therefore, the person least qualified to correct or contradict the clips.

The reporter at least *acts* as though she misses that point, for her role as reporter depends on privileging firsthand information. If Inez can add nothing to the clips, then not just the interview but the reporter herself is perfunctory. For Inez, playing inside the lines means repeating the fictions already in the clips, as if they referred to an external truth; for the reporter, it means reporting the fictions as if they were not repetitions. Since the reporter's ultimate function, moreover, is to generate yet another clip, the validity of the clips themselves must be preserved at the same time as they must be seen as lacking, as needing some form of supplementation. The clips thus are always already present at interviews, as both the necessary authority and the necessary lack. When Inez tries to indicate the way in which they empower the game, she threatens the game itself, as evidenced by the reporter's verging on turning off the recorder and thus converting Inez's statements into silence.

The reporter's role, of course, is not to convert Inez's speech into silence but into a news clip. The story thus goes out "INEZ VICTOR OFTEN CLAIMS SHE IS MISQUOTED" (*D*, 51), creating a clip that effectively reverses the implications of Inez's assertion. The term *misquote* implies the possibility of an accurate quote and, more importantly, it implies that Inez can distinguish between the actual statement and its deformed version; in other words, she can distinguish between the events of her life and those news clips which distort it. Inez refuses, however, to make such a distinction, because she sees her life as fashioned by news clips. Since those media representations (news clips, photos, and captions) comprise, moreover, the genre known as current events, the fictions include all the sources of contemporary history. As Didion portrays it, then, the sources of historical evidence are not events or facts but an endless chain of re-contextualizations, wherein events are always generated by fictional frames and are decoded by them, as well.

This relationship is particularly well exemplified in the book's description of Harry Victor's 1969 visit to Jakarta, on which he is accompanied by his family, by Inez's sister, Janet, by Billy Dillon, and by a special female aide, Frances Landau. They are met at the Jakarta airport by Jack Lovett. A personal and/or public fiction frames each character's presence, in a life so infused with official fictions that Inez cannot correlate the specific fiction to the specific occasion:

> One of many occasions on which Harry Victor descended on one tropic capital or another and set about obtaining official assurance that human rights remained inviolate in the developing (USAID Recipient) nation at hand.
> One of several occasions during those years . . . in which Inez got off a plane and was met by Jack Lovett.
> Temporarily attached to the embassy.
> On special assignment to the military.
> Performing an advisory function to the private sector. . . .
> Inez did not remember exactly why Janet had been along (some domestic crisis, a ragged season with Dick Ziegler or a pique at Dwight Christian, a barrage of urgent telephone calls and a pro forma invitation), nor did she remember exactly under what pretext Frances Landau had been along (legislative assistant, official photographer, drafter of one preliminary report or another). (D, 90–91)

With the as yet unwritten news clip framing their discourse, Victor and Dillon articulate the fictions that define the visit:

> "Let's get it clear at the outset, I don't want this visit tainted," Harry Victor had said.
> "No embassy orchestration," Billy Dillon said.
> "No debriefing," Harry Victor said.
> "No reporting," Billy Dillon said.
> "I want it understood," Harry Victor said, "I'm promising unconditional confidentiality."
> "Harry wants it understood," Billy Dillon said, "he's not representing the embassy." (D, 91)

The stipulation "no reporting," like all the other stipulations, of course, actually specifies how the visit is to be reported: as an unofficial, unorchestrated, unreported visit. All the stipulations articulated here are meaningful only if the visit is reported, a point underscored by Harry's holding a press conference during the visit and Dillon's negotiating with reporters to move it out "in time for Friday deadlines at the New York *Times* and the Washington

Post" (*D*, 95). Without the clips, the visit doesn't exist, because the visit is a performance with the clips, themselves, as the initial audience. As Jack Lovett says to Harry and Dillon, " 'You don't actually see what's happening in front of you. You don't see it unless you read it. You have to read it in the New York *Times*, then you start talking about it. Give a speech. Call for an investigation. Maybe you can come down here in a year or two, investigate what's happening tonight' " (*D*, 96–97). Because it identifies the initial event as the report, and not the incident that the report alleges to describe, Lovett's assertion glosses the structure of *Democracy* as a network of re-contextualized rhetorical situations. The news report becomes a rhetorical situation making possible other rhetorical situations that re-contextualize the initial report and that mandate further re-contextualizations.

Democracy's structure is also glossed by Harry's press conference, in which he asserts that "the rioting in Surabaya reflected the normal turbulence of nascent democracy" (*D*, 95). Just as Lovett's did, Harry's assertion reveals the gap between event and reportage, for Harry's statement defines the event—rioting, a grenade lobbed into the embassy commissary—as normal democratic activity. In order to do so, he constructs an implicit narrative—the story of democracy—with distinctly normal stages from nascence to maturity. Only by knowing the whole story, by knowing that Jakarta will become a mature democracy, can one define the current riots. The riots evidence not democracy's failure but democracy's beginning, at least according to the wire service clips, filed in time to be picked up by the *Post* and the *Times*. The story of democracy thus becomes one constructed by the media, and Lovett accordingly captions Harry " 'a congressman'. . . . 'Which means he's a radio actor' " (*D*, 99).

Harry seems, indeed, to view his own life as part of an abstract political narrative. Announcing over cocktails, at a London dinner party filled with European dignitaries, that he had slept the preceding night on a carrier in the Indian Ocean, for example, Harry "seem[s] to perceive the Indian Ocean, the carrier, and even himself as abstracts, incorporeal extensions of policy" (*D*, 81). This proclivity to imply narratives that blur the distinction between his public and private self can be seen, as well, in Harry's public statement after the murder of Congressman Omura (by Harry's father-in-law), "expressing not only his sympathy and deep concern but his conviction that this occasion of sadness for all Americans could be an occasion of resolve as well . . . resolve to overcome the divisions and differences tragically brought to mind today by this incident in the distant Pacific" (*D*, 149). Even in context, it is difficult to tell what divisions and differences Harry intends, or exactly how this "incident" reflects them. As the evocation of all abstractions tends to, Harry's statement attempts simultaneously to extend distance and to diminish it by making the incident close enough to affect "all Americans" but located in that abstract place, the "distant Pacific." For those—including a member of Harry's immediate family—in the vicinity of the incident, the site is neither distant nor Pacific. But their immediate response is to turn the incident into a distant abstraction so that it will have the kind of immediacy for them that Harry implies it does for "all Americans": the immediacy of a good novel, or today's newspaper, or *People* magazine.

In this way, Inez and Dillon, Dick Ziegler, and the Christians all work at converting the incident, for themselves, as well as for everyone else, into a good read. These attempts represent personal policies of containment. As Ziegler (who was being driven out of the container business, to be replaced by Wendell Omura's brother) says to Dillon, "There's considerable feeling we can contain this to an accident" (*D*, 114). Dillon, realizing that Ziegler's strategy of containment would not work, attempts his own strategy of containment, one that starts with a visit to Omura's cousin by marriage, Frank Tawagata, to ask for "a reading": "A reading on where the markers are, what plays to expect" (*D*, 141). Dillon wants to get a reading so that he may generate one, one that conforms to the reading implied in Harry's statement, one that would contain Paul's fate in the category of treatment rather than punishment, and, especially, one that would isolate the murderous behavior from the political and financial circumstances surrounding it: "It had been agreed, above all, that no purpose would be served by further discussion of why Wendell Omura had introduced legislation hindering the development of Dick Ziegler's Sea Meadow, of how that legislation might have worked to benefit Dwight Christian, or what interest Wendell Omura's brother might recently have gained in the Chriscorp Container Division" (*D*, 143).

Paul Christian, too, constructs his identity as something to be read for public consumption. On his return to Hawaii, Paul presents himself as destitute, taking a room at the YMCA. "He had never to anyone's knowledge spent an actual night there, but he frequently mentioned it. 'Back to my single room at the Y,' he would say as he left the dinner table . . . and at least one or two of the other guests would rise, predictably, with urgent offers. . . . By way of assent Paul Christian would shrug and turn up his palms. 'I'm afraid everyone knows my position,' he would murmur, yielding" (*D*, 125). At one point, Dwight Christian realizes that his brother "[is] no longer presenting himself as a victim of his family's self-absorption" but as "the deliberate victim of the family's malice" (*D*, 128). Paul is neither, of course, or he is both, depending on how one defines victimization.

Both roles, moreover, are seen here as functions of presentation and self-presentation. Paul's activities, like Harry's, in other words, form kinds of foreign policies, ways of presenting oneself to the world, of making one's position known through a composite of assertions, actions, gestures, and references. Paul and Harry are representing themselves metonymically (i.e., using the techniques of a writer to create their identities). Their failure of narrative authority thus becomes synonymous with the failure of presentation and self-presentation, in other words synonymous with the inability to author a coherent foreign policy, a failure replicated in several ways throughout the novel: Paul's policy, culminating in the physical and emotional destruction of his entire family, is completely disastrous. Harry's self-presentation becomes both a failed political policy and a failed personal policy. Similarly, Lovett's policy fails, as does the policy of the government for which Lovett works. All are policies of containment.

The boundaries between narratives of personal policy and narratives of national policy are, in fact, hard to maintain, because if our narrative of national hegemony contained both the free world and the Communist world, it also contained the readers who consumed this narrative, making them participants in the narrative by virtue merely of the fact that they had consumed it. At the same time, it also protected them by containing them within that narrative in the privileged position of readers, implicated only vicariously in the narratives with which they identified. The narrative of democracy thus affected their personal lives only to the extent to which they chose to identify with the text (i.e., made consumer decisions). By participating in this narrative named democracy, Americans were able to decide on an individual basis how much they each wanted to become involved.

But the characters in *Democracy* can no longer achieve the appropriate distance, nor can they erect the appropriate borders between their personal lives and their national narratives. Similarly, Didion cannot exercise the author's choice to divorce her characters' failures from her own. Instead, from the outset, as we have noted, and throughout the book, she exposes directly both her techniques and her shortcomings as author.

Early in the novel, for instance, Didion presents a list of details she has "abandoned," "scuttled," "jettisoned"—details that comprise what is commonly called the background, details that, as she makes clear, are not so much facts as they are prior stories: "those very stories with which most people I know in those islands confirm their place in the larger scheme"

(*D*, 19). These are the stories an author, like a society, normally needs to situate the present. They are the stories, in other words, that the present usurps to colonize the past. But the past is reduced for Didion to headlines, captions, and photos, "the shards of the novel I am no longer writing. . . . I lost patience with it. I lost nerve" (*D*, 29). Patience and nerve are the two traits necessary to assert connections between those shards (i.e., convert them into narrative). First looks, she tells us later, must also be privileged "not only by novelists but by survivors of accidents and by witnesses to murders . . . anyone . . . forced to resort to the narrative method" (*D*, 31). Again, Didion calls attention to a technique for creating emphasis, showing that it is a fictional device upon which truthful reportage depends. Like so many of the other fictional devices Didion can, and unavoidably does, employ, this one is presented in such a way as to call into question the authority it normally asserts.

Didion has her self-conscious attention to technique function as a form of reader-alert, a warning to all readers that they can be manipulated by techniques, techniques to which they willingly consent in what they believe are special circumstances, but which they also demand without realizing it in their general reading of reality. Later, she articulates this "narrative alert" (*D*, 155) more fully:

> As a reader you are ahead of the narrative here.
>
> As a reader you already know that Inez Victor and Jack Lovett left Honolulu together that spring. One reason you know it is because I told you so, early on. Had I not said so you would have known it anyway: you would have guessed it, most readers being rather quicker than most narratives, or perhaps you would have even remembered it, from the stories . . . in the newspapers and on television. (*D*, 152)

This passage not only makes the reader a partner in the creation of stories (in novels, in newspapers, or on television) but also subtly implies the fictional status of the reader as the person who reads, believes, and, by narrative convention, helps author fictional events. By convention, by accord, by treaty, author and reader maintain the borders and accept the myths necessary to privilege the fictional state. This is a code that Didion knows well: "I know the conventions and how to observe them, how to fill in the canvas I have already stretched; know how to tell you what he said and what she said and know above all, since the heart of narrative is a certain calculated ellipsis, a tacit contract between writer and reader to surprise and be surprised, how not to tell you what you do not want to know" (*D*, 154).

Knowledge, in other words, serves the interest of narrative. What the reader will know, by tacit contract, will be determined by the story the reader wants, which, also by tacit contract, will be the story the author provides. This set of allegiances and contracts, wherein the author decides what the reader wants to know and the reader agrees to let the author make this decision, prevails for the novel Didion intended to write, the narrative intended for *Democracy*, the one for which she has lost patience and nerve. The version of *Democracy* before us, however, will not contain those conventions; its author "no longer [has] time for the playing out" (*D*, 155).

She also will not accept the responsibility for doing so. In the spring of 1975, at the same time that the Victors and the Christians are trying to contain their personal catastrophes and the American policy of containment collapsed in Vietnam, Didion is teaching a seminar at Berkeley on "the idea of democracy in the work of certain postindustrialist writers" (*D*, 68) as reflected in the author's style "(the hypothesis being that the way a writer constructed a sentence reflected the way that writer thought)" (*D*, 68). She tells her class to consider "the political implications of both the reliance on and distrust of abstract words, consider the social organization implicit in the use of the autobiographical third person" (*D*, 69). Then, quoting a textbook assignment on her own writing, cited at the beginning of the novel, she tells the reader (or herself): *"Consider, too, Didion's own involvement in the setting: an atmosphere results. How?"* (*D*, 69; Didion's emphasis). This request casts the readers in the same role as the class, that of people trying to understand the political implications of the ways narratives are constructed.

At the same time, however, it casts Didion in two roles: the first as director of the scrutiny; the second as the scrutinized object; in both cases, in other words, as author, for the author directs and controls the scope of observation, the boundaries, the outcome. In so doing, however, the author also reifies a process. The narrative that —by contractual agreement—appears to be unfolding achieves this appearance by having been fixed and, therefore, insulated from the vicissitudes of change, from the possibilities of intervention, and from the effects of criticism and scrutiny. The author's involvement is thus everywhere and nowhere, functioning with absolute power and absolute impunity, the two conditions that militate against democratic activity. To assert the traditional power of the author thus means to deny the requisite conditions of democracy—limited power and complete culpability. The responsibility for constructing the narrative of *Democracy* necessarily entails violating the conditions of democracy. As Didion's shifts in perspective make clear, furthermore, the reader shares responsibility for these violations by implicitly participating in a hierarchical relationship, wherein the referents of a text are subordinate to its narrative, the narrative is subordinate to the author's control, and the author's control is subordinate to the reader's scrutiny. The conditions that surround the text, the author, and the reader remain safely out of bounds.

If Didion questions her own willingness to produce the traditional narrative for the traditional reasons, her refusals, she makes clear, result not from a lack of skill but from reluctance to employ her skill without accepting responsibility for the consequences. This can be seen in how extensively her statements about authoring *Democracy* apply, as well, to authoring American foreign policy: "Let me establish Inez Victor" (*D*, 42), she says, locating her heroine in "the Territory of Hawaii" (*D*, 42) as part of the Christian family marked by "the colonial impulse" (*D*, 26). Inez herself thus becomes the establishment of one more Christian colony, one more territorial claim, serving the special interest of *Democracy*.

Maintaining that colony and expanding from it require unimpeded senses of direction and goal, strong powers of concentration and confidence, without which it becomes impossible to sustain the delicate balance that narrative demands in order to institute the illusion of truth. As Didion notes:

> Aerialists know that to look down is to fall.
>
> Writers know it too.
>
> Look down, and that prolonged spell of suspended judgment in which a novel is written snaps, and recovery requires that we practice magic. (*D*, 103)

"That prolonged spell of suspended judgment," which permitted America to expand its policy of containment, can only exist contained within these strictly delimited boundaries, and even then only with vigilant maintenance of offices aimed at propping up the illusion: "We straighten our offices, arrange and rearrange certain objects, talismans, props. Here are a few of the props I have rearranged this morning" (*D*, 103). One prop is a postcard of the Kuala Lampur International Airport with a banner reading " 'WELCOME PARTICIPANTS OF THE THIRD WORLD CUP HOCKEY' " (*D*, 104). The wording is replete with irony. The word *world* is distributed in the sentence in such a way as to identify the underdeveloped nations and also an international sporting event. The sign greets participants in that sporting event and also identifies the country as a welcome participant in the Third World.

The welcome becomes even more ironic given the fact that Kuala Lampur is where Inez ends up, tending to refugees. From the ironic perspective, the sign couples the citizens of the Third World with the international sport of the First World, in a subordinate relationship to which they willingly submit.

That ironic perspective, however, is one of the props of Didion's narrative as much as it is a prop of American foreign policy, and as such it is one Didion can no longer employ. As she makes clear, "The morning I bought this postcard was one of several mornings . . . when I believed I held this novel in my hand" (*D*, 104), just as the authors of American foreign policy believed, in their increasingly rarer optimistic moments, that they held democracy in their hands and could offer it to the welcome participants of the Third World, in a form of global gamesmanship. But the novel, like the foreign policy, has gotten out of hand. The policy that offers democracy has become a narrative that does not contain it, and the failure of containment describes Didion's final view of *Democracy*:

> It has not been the novel I set out to write, nor am I exactly the person who set out to write it. Nor have I experienced the rush of narrative inevitability that usually propels a novel toward its end, the momentum that sets in as events overtake their shadows and the cards fall in on one another and the options decrease to zero.
> Perhaps because nothing in this situation encourages the basic narrative assumption, which is that the past is prologue to the present, the options remain open here. (*D*, 220–21)

The basic narrative assumption creates a sense of inevitability and thus allows a novel to manifest destiny. In rejecting that assumption, Didion makes clear, she is denying the manifest destiny of *Democracy* and of the foreign policy that resembles it. In so doing, she reveals the facts of American history to be the function of a dubious narrative convention.

Didion also does this by mixing several kinds of facts: the facts of her life, the facts of her attempts to write *Democracy*, the facts of the lives, events, and settings she has jettisoned, the facts of the lives, events, and settings that remain, the facts of American history during the period covered by the narrative, the facts of her meetings with the characters. Didion further erodes the boundary between her life and the narrative she produces by introducing herself as a character in the novel, so that Inez Victor becomes not only Didion's creation but also her acquaintance. "Under different auspices and to different ends" (*D*, 31), she and Inez work for *Vogue* magazine in 1960. Through Inez, she first meets Jack Lovett, who is a good contact for Didion after she leaves *Vogue* and is working as a reporter. In 1971 and 1973, she has discussions with him about Inez. Didion also recalls "being present one morning in a suite in the Hotel Doral in Miami, amid the debris of Harry Victor's 1972 campaign for the nomination" (*D*, 49), when the AP reporter tries to interview Inez. After reading a newspaper story about Janet's murder, Didion tries to call Inez in New York. Didion visits Dwight Christian at his home, and she attends a dinner party in London with Harry. She corresponds with Inez in Kuala Lampur in 1975, and in August of 1975 she spends several days on Martha's Vineyard talking to Harry and Billy Dillon. Later that year, Didion flies to Kuala Lampur to see Inez.

From these fictitious experiences and interviews, Joan Didion the character constructs her narrative, aided by information she has gleaned from the media. She refers to articles, photos, headlines, or captions from over thirty news publications (the *New York Times* is mentioned ten times), sometimes citing the specific date and edition to let the reader identify with journalistic and historical accuracy the sources of the fictitious information discovered by the fictitious character Joan Didion, the author.

By foregrounding her roles as author and as character and by mixing the levels of fact, Didion denies the reader the same distance she has denied herself. If this distance has been the privilege of postwar Americans, Didion's rejected narrative reveals the ways in which that privilege was inscribed in and erased by the name of democracy, which has failed to contain its story in such a way as to make Americans its eternal authors and consumers. In this way, Didion defines the contemporary American culture as framed by our failed narrative, which, in turn, is framed by our futile efforts to consume it and thus reclaim the roles of reader and author, the privileged position from which involvement is a matter of personal choice.

As Didion presents it, democracy becomes one more signifier divorced completely from its signified, existing, as Jean Baudrillard has pointed out, simply to the extent that it participates in codes of consumption.[9] As an object of consumption, democracy has had extensive currency in post–World War II America, becoming perhaps the most conspicuous of our political and social consumables. We have defined ourselves and

9. See Jean Baudrillard, *Selected Writings of Jean Baudrillard*, ed. Mark Poster (Stanford: Stanford University Press, 1988). Baudrillard's work articulates the ways in which the total divorce of the sign from its referent in contemporary consumer society makes consumption an activity devoid of gratification rather than a method for meeting needs. The American quality of consumerism is implicit, I think, in his discussion and informs his book-length analysis, *America*, trans. Chris Turner (New York: Verso, 1988).

created our personal narratives by participating in its codes even more completely than we have by purchasing cars or by watching movies. In our consumer-oriented society, democracy has been the narrative of consumer preference.

We have come, in other words, to regard our narratives as consumer choices. Didion emphasizes this not only by commenting on her understanding of narrative technique and reader expectation—namely of production and consumption—but also by pointing out that Inez's daughter Jessie regards her heroin use not as "an act of rebellion, or a way of life, or even a bad habit of particular remark; she consider[s] it a consumer decision" (*D*, 162). With the sense that she—like all Americans in the narrative of democracy—is a consumer and not a participant, Jessie displays the same imperviousness that Harry did when he visited Jakarta (and elsewhere) in 1969; she goes to Saigon in 1975 because she heard that there are "some pretty cinchy jobs" there (*D*, 113): "because she believed that whatever went on there was only politics and that politics was for assholes, she would have remained undeflected, that March night in 1975, the same night as it happened that the American evacuation of Da Nang deteriorated into uncontrolled rioting, by anything she might have seen or read in a newspaper" (*D*, 166).

In this way, the collapse of Da Nang intersects inextricably with the breakdown in the Victors' insularity and impunity. Although Jessie continues to function with the distance of a consumer, or, more exactly, because she does, that distance is destroyed, and, despite her personal narrative, she becomes converted from consumer to refugee, a member of that group for which Inez had not been allowed to show a special interest.

Inez's inability to show a special interest thus becomes synonymous with her loss of special privilege, a point Inez recognizes in April of 1975 as she listens to the short wave in an apartment in Vientiane for the encoded announcement of America's final withdrawal—the message "mother wants you to call home" followed by a recording of "White Christmas":

> Inez thought about Harry in New York and Adlai at school and Jessie at B.J.'s and it occurred to her that for the first time in about twenty years she was not particularly interested in any of them.
>
> Responsible for them in a limited way, yes, but not interested in them.
>
> They were definitely connected to her but she could no longer grasp her own or their uniqueness, her own or their difference, genius, special claim. What difference did it make in the long run

what she thought, or Harry thought, or Jessie or Adlai did? What difference did it make in the long run whether any one person got the word, called home, dreamed of a white Christmas? The world that night was full of people flying from place to place and fading in and out and there was no reason why she or Harry or Jessie or Adlai, or for that matter Jack Lovett or B.J. or the woman in Vientiane on whose balcony the rain now fell, should be exempted from the general movement.

Just because they believed they had a home to call.

Just because they were Americans.

No.

En un mot bye-bye. (*D*, 197)

The elegiac qualities of this passage, and of the whole novel, are unmistakable. Like all elegies, the novel marks an unbroachable gap and then seeks a context that will make the gap seem smaller. The gap marked here, however, is between events and the privileged position from which they can be elegized, the position of the author who can contain inside his or her vision the limits of the gap. The book, in other words, is an elegy for the strategies of elegy, which it thus reveals as another version of the myth of containment.

Resisting History: *Rear Window* and the Limits of the Postwar Settlement

Robert J. Corber

> This is not to say that the Communist "interest" is a legitimate one, or that the Communist issue is irrelevant. As a conspiracy, rather than as a legitimate dissenting group, the Communist movement is a threat to any democratic society.
> —Daniel Bell, "Interpretations of American Politics"

> We've become a race of Peeping Toms.
> —Stella, in *Rear Window*

In the preface to *An End to Innocence* (1955), his first critical work, Leslie Fiedler registers his misgivings about publishing a book of literary criticism in which so many of the essays are political. He sees himself as primarily a "literary person," and when he writes of politics, he does so only reluctantly.[1] But because he has lived through a crisis in liberalism that seems to him "a major event in the development of the human spirit" (1:xxiii), he feels justified in addressing issues not ordinarily considered lit-

---

1. *The Collected Essays of Leslie Fiedler* (New York: Stein and Day, 1971), 1: xxii; hereafter cited in my text by volume and page numbers only.

erary. Indeed, although he lacks a specialized knowledge of politics and is only an indifferent researcher, he believes his training as a literary critic makes him peculiarly well qualified to analyze recent political events. For the very reason that he is primarily a "literary person," he can subject events, such as the Rosenberg trial, to a "close reading" (1:xxii). His training in the "newer critical methods" (1:xxiii) enables him to provide an analysis of the contemporary crisis in American culture that does not scant ambiguity or paradox but that gives "to the testimony of a witness before a Senate committee or the letters of the Rosenbergs the same careful scrutiny we have learned to practice on the shorter poems of John Donne" (1:xxiii).

Why would Fiedler believe that close reading, a critical practice most closely associated, at the time he was writing, with *Scrutiny*, a journal famous for emphasizing the autonomy of the text, was the best critical tool for analyzing the crisis in liberalism? Did he understand the newer critical methods, or did he mistakenly think they were compatible with a materialist understanding of culture? Fiedler's "readings" of recent political events suggest that he did indeed understand the newer critical methods, for despite its tendency to interpret the text in isolation from its historical context, close reading *was* the best critical tool for him to use. He had no interest in providing a materialist critique of postwar American culture; rather, he wanted to show that materialist criticism could not adequately explain the American situation. On the one hand, Fiedler's analysis of the crisis in liberalism seems to acknowledge the historicity of the subject, its construction by a plurality of already existing discourses that guarantee its insertion into history; on the other hand, it seems to deny the subject's discursive construction in a specific historical context. Fiedler stresses the incoherence of political identities, their fracturing by changing historical conditions. In "Hiss, Chambers, and the Age of Innocence," for example, originally published in *Commentary* in December 1950, he reduces history to the Freudian uncanny. The subject experiences its insertion into history as the return of the repressed. Despite our attempts to forget our political past, "like some monumental bore, it grabs us by the lapels, [and] keeps screaming into our faces the same story over and over again" (1: 3). The subject, in other words, can never escape history. Although it tries to repress the past, the past returns, like the uncanny, to remind it of its own historicity.

Yet, the subject's insertion into history is always uneven. Indeed, its very historicity disconnects it from its political past, which is why it experiences its political past as uncanny. Although Fiedler claims that the subject must accept its own connection to the past to achieve "moral adulthood"

(1: 4), he argues that "it is a painful thing to be asked to live again through events ten years gone, to admit one's identity with the person who bore one's name in a by now incredible past" (1: 4). History, in other words, actually prevents the subject from constructing a coherent political identity. The subject feels disconnected from its political past because, historically, it is. The network of discourses in which the subject is constructed is constantly shifting, and thus its political identity remains fractured, incoherent: "It is hardest of all to confess that one is responsible for the acts of the past, especially when such acts are now placed in a new and unforeseen context that changes their meaning entirely" (1: 4). For Fiedler, then, the subject's very historical production cuts it off from history. Society's constantly changing historical conditions militate against the achievement of a fixed, stable political identity.

Fiedler's theorization of the subject as both produced by and cut off from history is crucial to his reading of Hiss's perjury trial and its significance for liberalism. He accuses Hiss of refusing to acknowledge his own insertion into history. By insisting that he was innocent, Hiss "failed all liberals, all who had, in some sense and at some time, shared his illusions (and who that calls himself a liberal is exempt?), all who demanded of him that he speak aloud a common recognition of complicity" (1: 23). Hiss's denial under oath that he had committed treason not only implied that his commitment to the Popular Front was historically justified but that liberals should remain faithful to their "illusions." In the altered historical conditions of postwar American society, however, such a position was no longer acceptable. While Hiss could, perhaps, justify his former Stalinization because of the Depression, his continuing allegiance to the Communist party, indicated by his refusal to admit his guilt, was incompatible with America's economic recovery. The Popular Front critique of American culture had become irrelevant. Thus, in claiming that he was innocent, Hiss denied America's changing historical conditions, and in denying America's changing historical conditions, he refused to acknowledge his own shifting relation to discourse.

To establish Hiss's resistance to his own insertion into history, a resistance that allows him to remain loyal to the legacies of the New Deal, Fiedler compares him to Henry Julian Wadleigh, one of Chambers's former contacts at the State Department and a witness at Hiss's trial. He considers Wadleigh, with his disheveled appearance and acquired Oxford accent, a "comic version" (1: 7) of Hiss. Like Hiss, Wadleigh confessed his guilt and declared his innocence at the same time. Although he readily admitted passing secret documents to Chambers while he was an employee at the

State Department, he denied that his activities had betrayed American interests. Showing no sign of contrition, he claimed that history justified his actions. In so doing, he ignored his own historicity. He refused to believe that the altered conditions of postwar American society no longer justified fellow traveling: "Wadleigh has learned nothing. He cannot conceive of having done anything *really* wrong. He finds in his own earlier activities only a certain excessive zeal, overbalanced by good will, and all excused by—Munich" (1: 7). In maintaining his innocence, in other words, Hiss, like Wadleigh, refused to see the way in which the Cold War radically altered the meaning of his political identity. Although his fellow traveling in the 1930s could, perhaps, be excused because of the European appeasement of Hitler, the Cold War placed his commitment to the Popular Front in a new and unforeseen context that, in retrospect, rendered it treasonous.

Fiedler blames Hiss's and Wadleigh's resistance to history, their unwillingness to accept their shifting construction as political subjects, for the crisis in liberalism. According to Fiedler, prominent leftist intellectuals exerted an influence over public policy during the New Deal that far exceeded their numbers, and McCarthy's exposure of many of them as Communists threatened to discredit their legacies. Fiedler is prepared to accept that liberal intellectuals in the 1930s were justified in affiliating themselves with the Communists, since they could assume that the Communists shared their moral values, those of the "old Judeo-Christian ethical system, however secularized" (1: 22). Subsequent political events, however, demonstrated that the Communists "had ceased to subscribe to a political morality universally shared, whatever its abuses, until 1917" (1: 22). As a result, liberal intellectuals now had a moral obligation to confess their former fellow traveling, for only by confessing their former fellow traveling could they reclaim the New Deal and its social welfare programs for the postwar settlement. This does not mean, however, that admitting their complicity with the Stalinization of American culture in the 1930s would be a way of connecting with their past; rather, it would be a way of exorcising a part of their history better left behind them. Fiedler claims that "the Hiss case marks the death of an era, but it also promises a rebirth if we are willing to learn its lessons" (1: 24). Confessing their own participation in the Stalinization of American culture would be tantamount to acknowledging that their relation to discourse had shifted because of America's economic recovery: They were no longer Stalinized leftist subjects; they were subjects of the liberal consensus.

The structure of Fiedler's essay repeats formally his argument that the open acknowledgment of the ties between the liberals and the Communists during the 1930s would lead to a "rebirth" of liberalism. By waiting to admit his own liberalism until the end of his essay, he enacts the very break with the past he is proposing as a solution to the liberal crisis. He carefully conceals his liberalism throughout "Hiss, Chambers and the Age of Innocence" and claims to be providing an "unbiased look" (1: 9) at the proceedings of the House UnAmerican Activities Committee and its investigation of Hiss. In so doing, he seems to deny his own insertion into history. In stating that his reading of Hiss is "unbiased," he places himself above history. He supposedly does not have a vested interest in claiming that the trials of fellow travelers, such as Hiss, threaten to damage liberalism irreparably. At the same time, however, by acknowledging his own liberalism at the end of the essay, he implies that there is no escaping history. History resembles the Freudian uncanny: Regardless of our attempts to repress it, it inevitably returns. Fiedler can no longer conceal his liberalism and must therefore admit it. Still, he confesses his own history of fellow traveling as a way of putting it behind him. Because he accepts that America's growing prosperity refuted the Popular Front critique of American culture, he can provide an "unbiased look" at the significance of Hiss's trial for liberalism. In a sense, he *is* above history. His recognition that his own relation to discourse has shifted renders him immune to ideology, which is why he can subject Hiss's trial to a close reading.

Despite its emphasis on America's changing historical conditions, Fiedler's close reading of Hiss's perjury trial seeks to discredit the sort of materialist critique of American culture favored by Popular Front intellectuals. His claim that Hiss, in committing perjury, denied his own historicity as a subject, allows him to substitute psychological for historical categories of analysis. History does not adequately explain Hiss's continuing Stalinization. Hiss could never acknowledge that postwar American prosperity contradicted the Marxist analysis of the capitalist relations of production, because to do so would have been to change "the whole meaning of his own life, turned what had perhaps seemed to him his most unselfish and devoted acts, the stealing of State Department documents, into shameful crimes—into 'treason'!" (1: 11). It does not occur to Fiedler that Hiss's continuing allegiance to the Popular Front reflected deeply held political convictions, or that, as a political agent, he *chose* to remain committed to a materialist critique of American culture. Rather, Hiss's history of involvement with the Communist party could only represent the acting out of a barely repressed oedipal drama: "It was as if Alger Hiss had dedicated himself to fulfilling, along with his dream of a New Humanity, the other dream his father had passed on to him with his first name—from rags to riches" (1: 14). Fiedler makes a similar argument about Chambers. Chambers's Stalinization as a Popular Front intellectual was also psychologically, rather than ideologically, motivated. According to Fiedler, Chambers discovered "in the revolution an answer to the insecurity and doubt which had brought his brother to suicide, [and] himself to months of despair and near paralysis" (1: 15). Ultimately, then, Fiedler acknowledges the historicity of the subject only to deny it. Psychology, rather than history, provides the most adequate explanation for Hiss's and Chambers's discursive construction as Popular Front intellectuals.

I have been discussing "Hiss, Chambers, and the Age of Innocence" in such detail because I want to argue, in what follows, that Fiedler's denial of history and the psychologizing of political behavior it enabled were crucial to the establishment of the postwar settlement known as the liberal consensus. I intend to show that Fiedler's essay participated in an extended ideological struggle among liberal intellectuals for hegemonic control over the postwar settlement.[2] Liberal intellectuals had exerted hegemonic control over the American political system since the 1930s. Until the rise of McCarthyism, they had succeeded in containing within the parameters of their own thought the reasoning and calculation of all forms of political opposition. Because of the success of the New Deal, even conservatives took for granted the need for limited government intervention in the economy. McCarthyism, however, threatened to undermine this hegemonic control by exposing many of the intellectuals responsible for the New Deal as Communists or fellow travelers. Suddenly America, under the New Deal, appeared no different from the Soviet Union. The public repudiation of their former ties to communism offered liberal intellectuals a solution. By distancing themselves from the more extreme elements on the Left, they could remain loyal to the legacies of the New Deal without alienating large segments of the American electorate. Liberal intellectuals, in other words, constantly needed to renew the hegemony of the social welfare state in order for it to remain

2. For a good discussion of the role of liberal intellectuals in shaping the postwar settlement, see Andrew Ross, No Respect: Intellectuals and Popular Culture (New York: Routledge, 1989), 1–64. See also Geraldine Murphy, "Romancing the Center: Cold War Politics and Classic American Literature," Poetics Today 9, no. 4 (1988): 737–47. Murphy relates the idea, common to American studies, that the characteristically American literary form is the romance rather than the novel to what she calls the "vital-center liberalism" of the Cold War.

hegemonic. This meant that they had to enter into vigorous debate not only with their conservative opponents but with the more radical elements of the ruling liberal coalition, because the exposure of those elements by the conservatives threatened to discredit the achievements of the New Deal.

But liberal intellectuals not only had to contest and contain all forms of political opposition, including those within their own ruling coalition; they also had to gain control over the way in which Americans thought and lived their relations to the world.[3] The postwar settlement needed to occur on a cultural, as well as a political, level to win the free and spontaneous consent of the American people. Thus, the liberals had to extend their hegemony beyond the political to the cultural realm. For the postwar settlement to remain hegemonic, it needed to operate unconsciously, to determine, without appearing to do so, a definition of reality to which Americans would consent spontaneously because it seemed to go without saying. This meant that the liberals had to limit the fund of interpretive possibilities available to the American people for understanding their own lived experience. Only by establishing the authoritative descriptions of American culture would they gain control over the discursive construction of the postwar subject.

That they were largely successful in accomplishing this I will show by examining Alfred Hitchcock's *Rear Window* (1954) in relation to the postwar settlement. I will argue that Hitchcock's film tried to recuperate the cinematic apparatus from its contamination by the emergence of the national security state. The series of repressive legislative acts that established the national security state authorized the appropriation of the cinematic apparatus and its technology for internal security purposes.[4] Hitchcock's film openly acknowledges the taint of this appropriation. Its hero, the photojournalist L. B. Jeffries, or "Jeff" (James Stewart), deploys the techniques of

3. For the most authoritative discussion of this aspect of hegemony, see Antonio Gramsci, *Prison Notebooks: Selections*, trans. Quintin Hoare and Geoffrey N. Smith (New York: International Publishers, 1971). See also Stuart Hall, "The Toad in the Garden: Thatcherism among the Theorists," in *Marxism and the Interpretation of Culture*, ed. Cary Nelson and Lawrence Grossberg (Chicago: University of Illinois Press, 1988), 35–57.
4. These acts were: the Smith Act (1940), the Taft-Hartley Act (1947), the McCarran Internal Security Act (1950), the McCarran-Walter Act (1952), and the Communist Control Act (1954). For a detailed discussion of these acts and their impact on leftist politics in general, see David Caute, *The Great Fear: The Anti-Communist Purge under Truman and Eisenhower* (New York: Simon and Schuster, 1978). For a history of leftist politics in Hollywood and the impact of McCarthyism on the film industry, see Larry Ceplair and Steven Englund, *The Inquisition in Hollywood: Politics in the Film Community, 1930–1960* (Berkeley: University of California Press, 1979).

the national security apparatus to spy on the neighbors of his Lower East Side apartment complex. To be sure, he lacks the listening devices, hidden cameras, and microfilm of the FBI and the CIA, but his telephoto lens allows him to scrutinize even the remotest corners of his neighbors' apartments and to discover their most carefully guarded secrets. Yet, in admitting its complicity with the government persecution of suspected Communists, homosexuals, lesbians, and other "undesirables," *Rear Window* was simply adopting Fiedler's strategy in "Hiss, Chambers, and the Age of Innocence." It readily admits that its technology facilitated the systematic repression of basic civil liberties (the right to free speech, the freedom of association) as a way of reclaiming that technology for the postwar settlement. Implicit in the film's "confession" of its own tainted past is a critique of McCarthyism. The film pathologizes Jeff's constant surveillance of his neighbors by suggesting that he suffers from an arrested sexual development. By alluding to the McCarthy witch hunts in this way, the film repudiates its own "fellow traveling." Although it cannot deny that in the past the cinematic apparatus lent its technology to the national security state, it can recuperate that technology for the liberal consensus by indirectly attacking the government surveillance of suspected Communists, homosexuals, and lesbians as a form of psychopathology.

Liberal Pluralism and the Denial of Political Agency

In a postscript to "McCarthy and the Intellectuals," an essay originally published in *Encounter* in August 1954 but included in *An End to Innocence*, Fiedler identified McCarthy's hearings on the Army as one of the low points of the postwar period. Although the hearings irreparably damaged McCarthy, they failed to result in an official censure of his conduct, and administration officials shamefully tried to mollify him. When Secretary of the Army Robert T. Stevens finally stood up to the Wisconsin senator, he displayed, according to Fiedler, only a "last-minute, useless kind of courage" (1: 85). But what bothered Fiedler most about the hearings was that they were televised. Their coverage on television implicated the entire nation in the "whole ignoble affair" (1: 85), not just those directly involved in it. According to Fiedler, television elicited from the American people a voyeuristic curiosity about the political process. Americans did not watch the hearings out of a sense of civic duty but because they wanted to see McCarthy make a spectacle of himself. Thus, they were complicitous with the shameful proceedings: "It was not only that nobody directly involved in the circus managed to perform with distinction or tact, but that even those not directly implicated, the nation itself, sat transfixed for weeks before their television receivers in a voyeuristic orgy" (1: 85). Television, in other words, threatened to transform American politics into a spectacle in which politicians "preened for the cameras" (1: 85).

Fiedler's argument that television threatened to reduce American politics to a form of entertainment was typical of the liberal critique of postwar American culture. The liberal historian, Richard Hofstadter, for example, in "The Pseudo-Conservative Revolt," his contribution to *The New American Right* (1955), a collection of essays on the postwar crisis in liberalism edited by Daniel Bell, warned that television threatened to erode the distinction between the public and the private spheres traditional to liberal democracy.[5] Televised coverage of committee hearings enabled the American people to feel as though they were directly participating in them. According to Hofstadter, the use of television has "brought politics closer to the people than ever before and [has] made politics a form of entertainment in which the spectators feel themselves involved."[6] For this reason, television threatened to undermine, rather than strengthen, the democratic process. Although it seemed to involve the American people more directly in the democratic process, it encouraged them to treat the public sphere as an extension of the private. Hofstadter claimed that because the McCarthy hearings had been televised, politics "had become, more than ever before, an arena into which private emotions and personal problems can be readily projected" (*NAR*, 52). For Hofstadter, then, television promoted the privatization of the public sphere. It encouraged the American people to regard the political process as a form of entertainment intended for their own private consumption.

Hofstadter's claim that television facilitated the privatization of the

5. I have chosen to discuss this particular collection of essays because it includes contributors from a broad spectrum of academic disciplines (history, sociology, political science, linguistics) and because its critique of postwar American culture was representative of the vital-center liberalism discussed by Murphy in "Romancing the Center." Other examples of "vital-center" critiques of postwar American culture that would serve my argument equally well include, but are not limited to, Arthur M. Schlesinger, Jr., *The Vital Center: The Politics of Freedom* (Boston: Houghton Mifflin, 1949), and Lionel Trilling, *The Liberal Imagination* (New York: Viking, 1950).

6. Richard Hofstadter, "The Pseudo-Conservative Revolt," in *The New American Right*, ed. Daniel Bell (New York: Criterion, 1955), 52. Subsequent references to this text will be cited as *NAR*.

public sphere suggests that what he and other liberal intellectuals were afraid of was not so much that television might transform American politics into a spectacle but that American politics as a form of spectacle was changing because of television.[7] After all, American politics had always been a form of spectacle.[8] Structured according to a propagandistic model of communication, it had positioned the voter as a spectator. The political sphere never fostered rational, enlightened debate about the common good, as the liberals implied when they attacked television, but it depended on the skillful manipulation of public opinion through the careful control of information. Television, however, as the primary mode of mass communication in postwar America, threatened this communicative model. It enabled the American people to actively interpret, rather than passively receive, political messages. Televised coverage of committee hearings undermined the traditional model of political communication: It broke down the structural separation between the source of the political message and its intended recipient. Because television created the illusion that the American people were participating directly in the McCarthy hearings, it allowed them to see themselves as the producer, rather than the consumer, of the political message. In projecting their own personal problems onto the political arena, they were giving meaning to what they saw, producing their own texts and interpreting them according to their own personal histories.

Daniel Bell's introduction to *The New American Right*, "Interpretations of American Politics," explains more fully why liberal intellectuals were afraid that the privatization of the public sphere through television would erode the democratic process. Bell argued that the privatization of the public sphere had led to an "ideologizing" of American politics, or a reduction of American politics to a series of divisive and irresolvable ideological conflicts. Traditionally, the American political process had been pragmatic rather than

---

7. For a discussion of television that sees the spectacle form of American politics as in crisis, see Paolo Carpignano, Robin Anderson, Stanley Aronowitz, and William Difazio, "Chatter in the Age of Electronic Reproduction: Talk Television and the 'Public Mind,'" *Social Text* 25/26 (1990): 33–55. See also John Fiske, *Television Culture* (London: Routledge, 1988). Fiske persuasively refutes the liberal critique of television that sees television as constructing a passive spectatorial subject who substitutes television viewing for meaningful political action.

8. Even the contributors to Bell's collection of essays were aware of the spectatorial aspect of American politics. See Bell's discussion of the "cider election" of 1840, which he identifies as a turning point in American politics in "Interpretations of American Politics," in *The New American Right*, 22–23.

ideological. It had enabled competing special interest groups to reach a consensus through bargaining with each other: "The saving glory of the United States is that politics has always been a pragmatic give-and-take rather than a series of wars-to-the-death" (*NAR*, 27). But the tendency of Americans to project their personal problems onto the political arena had radically transformed the political process. The privatization of the public sphere through television encouraged Americans to confuse political issues with moral ones. Ironically, although Americans had become more relaxed in the area of traditional morality, they had become "moralistic and extreme in politics" (*NAR*, 20). As a result, the American political process was no longer a pragmatic "give-and-take." It had shifted from "specific interest clashes, in which issues can be identified and possibly compromised, to ideologically-tinged conflicts which polarize the groups and divide the society" (*NAR*, 27). This development threatened to destroy the democratic process: "The tendency to convert issues into ideologies, to invest them with moral color and high emotional charge, invites conflicts which can only damage a society" (*NAR*, 27).

Although the contributors to *The New American Right* agreed with Fiedler that the most appropriate categories for understanding political behavior were psychological rather than historical, unlike him, they were interested in developing a materialist understanding of postwar American culture. They related McCarthyism and the "ideologizing" of the political process directly to the economic prosperity of the postwar period. At the same time, however, they carefully distinguished their materialism from that of the Stalinized intellectuals who had been exposed by McCarthy. For example, in "The Intellectuals and the Discontented Classes," sociologists David Riesman and Nathan Glazer argued that in periods of economic prosperity "ideology tends to become more important than economics" (*NAR*, 66) in determining political behavior. In "Social Strains in America," sociologist Talcott Parsons simply dismissed Marxist categories as not applicable to American economic structures: "The United States of course has a class structure; but it is one which has its primary roots in the system of occupational roles, and in contrast to the typical European situation it acts as no more than a brake on the processes of social mobility" (*NAR*, 121). These rejections of Marxist theory and its explanatory powers served primarily as disclaimers. By arguing that the category of class could not adequately explain the structure of American society, the contributors to Bell's collection of essays made clear that they were working within a liberal, rather than a Marxist, intellectual tradition.

But in carefully distinguishing their critical practice from that of the Popular Front, they were also adopting Fiedler's strategy in "Hiss, Chambers, and the Age of Innocence." Like Fiedler, they were committed to recuperating liberalism from its association with the Stalinization of American culture in the 1930s. In claiming that Marxist theory was not applicable to American society, they repudiated their former ties to the Popular Front. Parsons readily conceded that there had been a great deal of Communist infiltration of American society in the 1930s when "considerable numbers of the intellectuals became fellow travelers" (*NAR*, 130). Because of the postwar economic recovery, the Stalinization of leftist intellectuals could no longer be justified. The Communist party had "drastically repudiated the procedures of constitutional democracy" (*NAR*, 131), and thus liberal intellectuals who remained committed to the Popular Front critique of American culture were truly enemies of the state. Moreover, America's economic recovery rendered the Marxist critique of the capitalist relations of production irrelevant. American prosperity required new categories of analysis, categories that could explain the continuing disaffection of large segments of the American population, despite the postwar economic recovery. Parsons complained that the fellow traveling of liberal intellectuals rendered liberalism vulnerable to attack from conservatives. Citing the Popular Front, conservatives could attack liberalism "on the grounds that association with Communist totalitarianism makes anything liberal suspect" (*NAR*, 132). Here, Parsons tried to reclaim the liberal intellectual tradition for a materialist critical practice that could explain America's continuing social tensions without recourse to the category of class. Recourse to the category of class would only prove that liberalism had indeed been irreparably damaged by its history of fellow traveling.

The contributors to *The New American Right*, then, tried to develop a materialist critique of American culture that remained faithful to the liberal intellectual tradition at the same time that it retrieved that tradition from its tainted past. For them, the most important factor in American society was the desire for status; only the desire for status could adequately explain McCarthyism and the scapegoating of ethnic and religious minorities. For example, in "The Sources of the 'Radical Right,'" Seymour Martin Lipset claimed that while leftist political movements committed to economic reform usually gained strength during periods of unemployment and economic depression, status politics predominated "in periods of prosperity, especially when many individuals are able to improve their economic position" (*NAR*, 168). According to Lipset, the material prosperity of immigrant families in periods of economic recovery rarely translated into social acceptance. More established American families felt threatened by the economic success of immigrant families and therefore refused to accept them into the middle and upper classes. Compounding this rejection was the tendency of well-to-do immigrants to misunderstand the class structure. They viewed "the status hierarchy as paralleling the economic structure; they believe[d] that one need only move up the economic scale to obtain the good things of the society. But, as they move[d] up economically, they encounter[ed] social resistance" (*NAR*, 193). For this reason, they tended to become ardent supporters of McCarthy; his populism appealed to their resentment of the more privileged sectors of American society.[9]

The problem with this critique was that it still had recourse to the category of class. On the one hand, the contributors to Bell's collection claimed that in American society class and status existed independently of each other; on the other hand, they inadvertently showed that they were directly related to each other. Well-to-do immigrant families felt entitled to a higher social status because, economically, they belonged to the middle and upper classes; more established American families tried to exclude well-to-do immigrants from the middle and upper classes because such immigrants lacked social status. Bell's contributors, in other words, denied that class and status were intimately connected to each other, despite the evidence provided by their own examples. Their definition of class was too narrow; they conceived of class as a purely economic category. Still, their materialism required them to conceive of class in purely economic terms. Limiting their definition of class to the purely economic one enabled them to separate America's economic and social systems. By establishing the existence of a status hierarchy that was independent of and not parallel to the economic ladder, they could focus on the social, rather than on the economic, structures of American society. In this way, they provided an analysis of American culture more faithful to the liberal intellectual tradition. Although their critical practice was materialist, it considered social status the most important category for understanding American culture. They were clearly not working within the Marxist intellectual tradition because they as-

9. Michael Rogin persuasively refutes this interpretation of McCarthyism in *The Intellectuals and McCarthy* (Cambridge: MIT Press, 1967). He shows that the most active supporters of McCarthyism were not populists but rank and file members of the Republican party who thought that an anti-Communist platform would undermine Democratic control of the House and Senate.

sumed that the social structure functioned independently of the economic structure.

Moreover, by isolating American social and economic structures from each other, they avoided the economic determinism of the Popular Front. Focusing on the status hierarchy rather than on the economic ladder allowed them to psychologize political behavior. Despite their materialism, they argued that psychology, rather than material conditions, ultimately determined political behavior. McCarthyism and the scapegoating of religious and ethnic minorities could best be explained psychologically. In periods of economic prosperity when the possibility of social mobility was greatest for religious and ethnic minorities, the desire for status could become pathological. Richard Hofstadter, for example, claimed that because immigrant families were "unable to enjoy the simple luxury of assuming their own nationality as a natural event, they are tormented by a nagging doubt as to whether they are really and truly and fully American" (*NAR*, 48). Compounding this "nagging doubt" was the resistance they encountered as they climbed the economic ladder. Rejected by the middle and upper classes, they developed "an enormous hostility to authority, which cannot be admitted to consciousness, [and which] calls forth a massive overcompensation which is manifest in the form of extravagant submissiveness to strong power" (*NAR*, 47). This tendency to reduce McCarthyism to a form of psychopathology was typical of the contributors to Bell's collection. Talcott Parsons also felt that the most useful categories for understanding McCarthyism were psychological rather than political. He claimed that in periods of dramatic structural change, such as the one America was experiencing, irrational behavior in the form of political extremism was inevitable: "There will tend to be conspicuous distortions of the patterns of value and of the normal beliefs about the facts of situations. These distorted beliefs and promptings to irrational action will also tend to be heavily weighted with emotion, to be 'overdetermined' as the psychologists say" (*NAR*, 127).

In substituting psychological for historical categories of analysis, the contributors to *The New American Right* were following Fiedler's example in *An End to Innocence*. In "Afterthoughts on the Rosenbergs," originally published in *Encounter* in 1953, Fiedler argued that the Rosenbergs should have been pardoned.[10] Although he had no doubt they were guilty, he felt

10. Andrew Ross discusses this essay and its relation to the postwar debate over highbrow, middle-brow, and low-brow culture in *No Respect*, 15–41. For a reading of *An End to Innocence* that is more sensitive to the subtleties of Fiedler's critical project,

they deserved clemency on humanitarian grounds: "Under their legendary role, there were, after all, *real* Rosenbergs, unattractive and vindictive but human" (1: 33). Indeed, the real tragedy of their case was that they seemed to deny their own humanity. They defined their identities solely in political terms: "For even at the end the Rosenbergs were not able to think of themselves as real people, only as 'cases,' very like the others for which they had helped fight" (1: 38). For this reason, they provided an especially graphic example of the tensions in American society between the public and the private spheres: "In the face of their own death, the Rosenbergs became, despite themselves and their official defenders, symbols of the conflict between the human and the political, the individual and the state, justice and mercy" (1: 33). Fiedler's series of binary oppositions here is revealing. He wanted to open up a space in American culture in which politics could not intervene and thus he needed to reify the distinction between the public and the private spheres. His argument required him to exclude politics from the network of discourses in which the subject was constructed. The subject of the liberal consensus had to see its "humanity" in constant and irresolvable conflict with the state. According to Fiedler, the subject's political identity was purely a function of its relation to the state. It entered into this relation only when exercising its rights as a citizen. Thus, its political identity was an artificial construct of the democratic process rather than an extension of its "real" humanity and could never exhaust its subjectivity, as the Rosenbergs mistakenly believed.

To exert hegemonic control over the postwar settlement, the contributors to *The New American Right* similarly needed to reify the distinction between the public and the private spheres. They agreed with Fiedler that the subject's political identity was only operative when it entered into direct relation to the state. They felt that the privatization of the public sphere through television encouraged the subject to see its political identity as an extension of its own personal history. As a form of mass communication, television constructed a subject whose political behavior was psychologically motivated. By denying political agency in this way, their analyses of postwar American culture enabled them to oversee the postwar settlement. They provided a vision of American society in which the political process remained free from the "taint" of ideology. Pluralistic democracies not only tolerated ethnic and religious diversity but strictly maintained the distinction

see Donald E. Pease, "Leslie Fiedler, the Rosenberg Trial, and the Formulation of an American Canon," *boundary* 2 17, no. 2 (1990): 155–98.

between the public and the private spheres. Thus, liberal Democrats would never permit any one special interest group to dominate, or claim a monopoly of, the political system, as the Republicans had under McCarthy's leadership.

Rear Window and the Psychopathology of Surveillance

Alfred Hitchcock's *Rear Window* participated in this extended ideological struggle among liberal intellectuals for hegemonic control over the postwar settlement. It performed the necessary cultural work by extending the liberal consensus beyond the political system to the cultural realm. Critics usually interpret *Rear Window* as Hitchcock's critique of the voyeuristic economy of the filmic system.[11] Jeff's constant scrutiny of his neighbors through his telephoto lens reduces spectatorial pleasure to a form of voyeurism. Jeff represents the spectator, transfixed by the events in the apartment complex opposite his window, which acts as a kind of screen. The spectator readily identifies with Jeff, since, like him, she or he is immobilized in a chair and must limit her or his activity to looking. Consequently, she or he feels complicit with Jeff's transgressive desires. Because she or he derives pleasure from looking at the images on the screen, she or he, too, must be fixated at an infantile stage of psychosexual development. Although it seems to me that *Rear Window* does indeed conceive of spectatorial pleasure as a form of fetishistic scopophilia, this reading does not adequately explain why the film would want to discredit the cinematic apparatus. In particular, it fails to identify the historical conditions that would have made the film's critique of its own system of representation possible. Critics who use *Rear Window* to substantiate Lacanian theories of the cinematic apparatus conflate Hitchcock's critique of spectatorial pleasure with their own.[12]

11. See, in particular, Jean Douchet, "Hitch et son public," *Cahiers du Cinema* 113 (November 1960): 7–15. See also Alfred Spoto, *The Art of Alfred Hitchcock* (New York: Doubleday, 1979), 237–49, and Laura Mulvey, "Visual Pleasure and Narrative Cinema," in *Feminism and Film Theory*, ed. Constance Penley (New York: Routledge, 1968), 57–68. For a persuasive feminist critique of these readings of Hitchcock's film, see Tania Modleski, *The Woman Who Knew Too Much: Hitchcock and Feminist Theory* (New York: Methuen, 1988), 73–85.
12. For an excellent discussion of the emergence of narrative cinema as the dominant form and its dependence on identification as its primary mode of address, see David Bordwell, Janet Staiger, and Kristin Thompson, *The Classic Hollywood Cinema* (New York: Columbia University Press, 1985). For a discussion of "primitive" cinema and the radically

The film does not so much critique the voyeuristic economy of the cinematic apparatus as it tries to retrieve it from its contamination by the emergence of the national security state.

The consolidation of the national security state had reduced voyeurism to a surveillance practice. In appropriating the technology of the filmic system, the national security apparatus politicized voyeuristic pleasure. According to the specular logic of the national security state, voyeurism was no longer a private form of erotic pleasure but a mode of political behavior intended to expose potential enemies of the state. In mobilizing spectatorial pleasure for its own purposes, the national security state guaranteed that the individual would not so much watch others for erotic pleasure as scrutinize them for any indication of political and/or sexual deviance that conflicted with the nation's security interests. The cinematic apparatus was directly implicated in this politicization of voyeurism. The filmic text allowed the spectator to experience legitimately voyeuristic pleasure in a public space. Consequently, it facilitated the appropriation of spectatorial pleasure by the national security apparatus. In a sense, voyeurism had already become a form of public pleasure through the institutionalization of the filmic system as a narrative form that guaranteed the spectator's total absorption in the diegesis.[13] The filmic system contributed to the politicization of voyeurism in other ways, as well. It resembled television in that it undermined the structural separation between the source of the message and its intended recipient critical to propagandistic models of communication. Every aspect of the cinematic apparatus, from the darkened auditorium to the placement of the projector behind the spectator, conspired to make the

---

different way in which it positions the spectator, see Miriam Hansen, "Early Cinema— Whose Public Sphere?" in *Early Cinema: Space, Frame, Narrative*, ed. Thomas Elsaesser (London: British Film Institute, 1990), 228–46. See also Tom Gunning, "The Cinema of Attractions: Early Film, its Spectator and the Avant-Garde," in Elsaesser, *Early Cinema*, 56–62.

13. Feminist film theorists have recently begun to challenge this masculinist conception of spectatorial pleasure. See, in particular, Mary Ann Doane, *The Desire to Desire: The Woman's Film of the 1940s* (Bloomington: Indiana University Press, 1987). See also Teresa de Lauretis, *Alice Doesn't: Feminism, Semiotics, Cinema* (Bloomington: Indiana University Press, 1984), and Modleski, *The Woman Who Knew Too Much*. The problem with these feminist challenges to Lacanian theories of the cinematic apparatus is that they rely on a psychoanalytic understanding of female subjectivity and therefore do not adequately address the historicity of filmic pleasure, its discursive construction in a specific historical context and in relation to hegemonic social and political structures.

spectator confuse her- or himself with the characters on the screen.[14] In so doing, it collapsed the distinction between the public and the private spheres. The spectator mistakenly saw her- or himself as the producer, rather than the consumer, of the images projected on the screen. For this reason, filmic discourse helped to insert the spectator into a McCarthyite, rather than a liberal, subject position.

The filmic system was even more directly implicated in the politicization of voyeurism. In the early 1950s, Hollywood studios produced a series of low-budget, Cold War propaganda films, such as *I Was a Communist for the FBI* (1951) and *My Son John* (1952), which justified the politicization of the private sphere.[15] These films encouraged the spectator to scrutinize her or his psyche for any indication of sexual and/or political deviance that might throw doubt upon her or his loyalty. The "enemy within" was not limited to the Communists, homosexuals, and lesbians who had supposedly infiltrated the federal government but included the individual's own psyche. The site of unconscious, potentially transgressive desires, the psyche constantly threatened to betray the individual and, by extension, the nation's security interests. Ironically, such films politicized privacy as a way of preserving it. Although, obviously, it would be absurd to reduce Hitchcock's cinematic practices to the crude propaganda of *My Son John* or *I Was a Communist for the FBI*, he nevertheless participated in Hollywood's attempt to legitimate the national security state through the use of the cinematic apparatus. As I have shown elsewhere, *Strangers on a Train* (1951) exploited the voyeuristic economy of the filmic system for the purposes of internal security.[16] It tried to conscript the spectator for the national security state by addressing her or him libidinally. It showed that the spectator could derive voyeuristic pleasure from clandestinely observing and exposing homosexuals and lesbians who "passed" as heterosexuals. For this reason, it legitimated the right of the state to regulate the sexual practices of all Americans, whether homosexuals or heterosexuals, in the name of national security.

14. For a discussion of this aspect of the cinematic apparatus, see Jean-Louis Baudry, "The Apparatus," *Camera Obscura* 1 (1977): 104–28. See also Christian Metz, *The Imaginary Signifier*, trans. Celia Britton, Annwyl Williams, Ben Brewster, and Alfred Guzzetti (Bloomington: Indiana University Press, 1982), 1–87.

15. Michael Rogin discusses these films in detail in "Kiss Me Deadly: Communism, Motherhood, and Cold War Movies," *Representations* 6 (1984): 1–36.

16. Robert J. Corber, "Reconstructing Homosexuality: Hitchcock and the Homoerotics of Spectatorial Pleasure," *Discourse* 13, no. 2 (1991): 58–82.

Hitchcock pathologizes spectatorial pleasure as a form of fetishistic scopophilia in *Rear Window* because he wants to acknowledge the corruption of voyeuristic pleasure by the rise of McCarthyism. In suggesting that cinematic viewing   merely another form of surveillance, the film tries to repudiate Hitchcock's own contaminated practices as a director, practices that involved him, however indirectly, in the government persecution of suspected Communists, homosexuals, and lesbians. But the film also wants to reclaim voyeurism as a private form of erotic pleasure. It conflates voyeurism with the surveillance practices of the national security state in order to show that voyeuristic pleasure had become corrupt. Its representation of filmic pleasure directly implicates the filmic system in the rise of McCarthyism. It suggests that the national security state had successfully mobilized voyeuristic desire for the clandestine scrutiny and subsequent exposure of potential enemies of the state. According to the film, the specular logic of the filmic text helped to create the conditions for McCarthyism. Because of its voyeuristic structures, the filmic text constructs a spectatorial subject who is fixated at an infantile stage of psychosexual development and who therefore derives pleasure from violating the privacy of others. As a photojournalist, Jeff is a representative subject of the mass media. His spying on his neighbors is merely an extension of his photojournalism. Scrutinizing their activities through his telephoto lens acts as a substitute for his lack of photo assignments during his convalescence. His work as a photojournalist paves the way for his transformation into a Peeping Tom. He simply transfers the pleasure he derives from looking at the world through his camera to scrutinizing his neighbors' most private activities.

Thus, rather than representing the voyeuristic economy of the filmic text as necessarily corrupt and corrupting, Hitchcock's film tries to show that under the scopic regime of the national security state voyeurism had become a surveillance practice. Jeff's voyeuristic practices are rooted in the establishment of a national security apparatus that legitimated the use of the camera for intruding on the privacy of others. His abuse of voyeuristic pleasure is directly related to a set of specific social conditions in which privacy had become politicized. In shot after shot, the film tries to restore voyeuristic pleasure to the private sphere by stressing the autonomy of the camera's look. Since the camera's look exists independently of Jeff, the spectator is ultimately responsible for determining its structure. Jeff does not always see what the camera sees. When Lars Thorwald (Raymond Burr), for example, leaves his apartment with a woman the morning after he has murdered his invalid wife, the camera moves back through Jeff's apartment window and shows him asleep in his wheelchair. Thus, the camera can operate independently of Jeff; the structure of its look does not depend on him. Even from the very beginning, the film emphasizes the independence of the camera's look from Jeff's corrupt use of it by constantly shifting between objective and subjective point-of-view shots. In the opening shots, for example, the camera pans the courtyard of Jeff's Lower East Side apartment complex and briefly introduces us to each of his neighbors: Lars Thorwald, a jewelry salesman, and his nagging invalid wife; Miss Torso, a dancer who practices her sexually suggestive dance routines in front of her window; a middle-aged, alcoholic musician suffering from composer's block; a middle-aged couple who sleeps on the fire escape; and Miss Lonelyhearts, a middle-aged spinster unable to find the man of her dreams. It then moves back through Jeff's apartment window and shows Jeff asleep in his wheelchair sweating profusely in the ninety-degree heat. Here, the film makes a point of not adopting Jeff's point of view. But if Jeff has not been controlling the camera's look, then the spectator has: He or she is the one who has derived pleasure from looking at Jeff's neighbors. In this way, the opening shots try to distinguish the voyeuristic economy of the filmic text from the scopic regime of the national security state by returning voyeuristic desire to the spectator's own psychical structures.

In attributing Jeff's corrupt use of the camera to the rise of McCarthyism, the film tries to show that voyeuristic desire can be rehabilitated for the liberal consensus. At the same time that the film acknowledges the contamination of its own voyeuristic economy by the scopic regime of the national security state, it tries to construct alternative forms of voyeuristic pleasure that are not political. For example, although Jeff's girlfriend, Lisa Freemont (Grace Kelly), derives pleasure from observing Jeff's neighbors, she does not treat them as objects of public scrutiny; rather, she identifies with them. Indeed, she initially resists observing them because she does not want to violate their privacy. She tells Jeff that his interest in their activities is "diseased." She only becomes interested in them when she discovers Miss Lonelyhearts and Miss Torso, women with whom she can identify.[17] Whereas Jeff watches Miss Lonelyhearts with amused detachment, Lisa

17. Modleski makes a similar point in The Woman Who Knew Too Much, pp. 80–81, but she tries to claim that Lisa's empathy for Miss Lonelyhearts and Miss Torso represents an alternative way of looking that is not voyeuristic. The implication of her argument is that it would be politically incorrect for the feminist-identified woman to derive pleasure from looking at others.

identifies with the lonely spinster when she pretends to entertain a lover. When Jeff tells Lisa that she has nothing in common with Miss Lonelyhearts, she replies: "Oh! You can see my apartment from here?" She apparently knows what it is like to spend evenings alone fantasizing about the man of her dreams. She has a similar reaction to Miss Torso. When Jeff derisively compares Miss Torso to a "queen bee with her pick of the drones," Lisa defends her. She knows how she would feel in a similar situation: "I'd say she's doing a woman's hardest job—juggling wolves." She feels sure that Miss Torso does not love any of the men she is entertaining in her apartment, even the "prospering-looking one" she allows to kiss her on the balcony. When Jeff asks her how she can be so sure, she says, "You *said* it resembled my apartment, didn't you?"

Laura Mulvey has argued that Lisa does not truly become an object of Jeff's desire until she breaks into Lars Thorwald's apartment.[18] As she frantically searches the apartment for the murdered Mrs. Thorwald's wedding ring, Jeff observes her through his telephoto lens, thereby treating her as one of his neighbors: She is no longer an active subject of desire who aggressively pursues him but rather an object he masters through scrutinizing her. While Mulvey is quite right to call attention to the intensification of Jeff's desire for Lisa in this scene, she misinterprets its significance. Jeff's fetishistic and scopophilic pleasure in looking at Lisa through his telephoto lens as she searches for the incriminating ring is important not so much because it allows him to master her but because it indicates an important shift in the voyeuristic structure of his gaze. Looking at Lisa through his telephoto lens not only intensifies his voyeuristic pleasure but also returns it to the private sphere. His interest in his neighbors' activities is no longer "diseased" but personal. In placing Lisa in danger, Thorwald's sudden return works to reconfigure Jeff's interest in him. Jeff can no longer observe Thorwald's murderous activities through his telephoto lens without becoming directly involved in them, since they now threaten Lisa. This shift in his way of looking becomes apparent even earlier in the film when Miss Lonelyhearts is assaulted by a man she has picked up in a bar and brought back to her apartment for a drink. At first Jeff watches in fascination but then abruptly turns away ashamed. Echoing Tom Doyle (Wendell Corey), the detective Jeff has asked to investigate Thorwald, Jeff says, "[Tom] might have gotten hold of something when he said it's pretty private stuff going on out there." For the first time in the film, Jeff is unable to use his camera

18. Mulvey, "Visual Pleasure," 65–66.

to maintain a distance between himself and his neighbors. He looks away in shame because he feels complicit with the assault. He can no longer treat Miss Lonelyhearts as an object for his own private consumption: He realizes that he, too, has violated her by constantly observing her through his telephoto lens.

The structure of Jeff's voyeurism, then, gradually shifts over the course of the film. Although he continues to derive pleasure from observing his neighbors, he no longer treats them as objects of public scrutiny; rather, he begins to connect with them by identifying with them. This shift is perhaps most apparent in the film's climactic scene. Here, he tries to defend himself from Thorwald, who has entered his apartment to confront him, by popping the flash of his camera in Thorwald's face. But this recourse to his camera fails. Though momentarily blinded by the flash, Thorwald recovers his sight and manages to push Jeff out his apartment window into the very space he has refused to enter except through his telephoto lens. He can no longer maintain a distance between himself and his neighbors through his camera; he is as much a part of the apartment complex as they are. Indeed, he is no different from them, Thorwald included, for his methods of exposing Thorwald place him equally outside the law. He constantly encourages Doyle to violate Thorwald's constitutional rights. He refuses to believe that Doyle cannot legally search Thorwald's apartment or open the trunk he has sent to his wife in upstate New York without a search warrant. He does not understand that even criminals have rights; in his view, suspicion alone should provide sufficient grounds for Thorwald's arrest. The film's critique of the McCarthyite subject corroborates Fiedler's in "Afterthoughts on the Rosenbergs." Jeff's observations of Thorwald reduce him to a "case." As a subject of the mass media, Jeff refuses to acknowledge Thorwald's "humanity"; he does not realize that, as a private individual, he has an obligation to show mercy even to murderers. Ironically, when Doyle tells him that Thorwald must have gone to the train station with his wife because he later told the building superintendent he had, Jeff dismisses the report as "a secondhand version of an unsupported story by the murderer himself." He fails to realize that his own story is secondhand and unsupported, and that, in systematically violating Thorwald's constitutional rights, he, too, is guilty of breaking the law.

The shot/reverse shot structure of the film's climactic scene visually expresses Jeff's problematic relation to the law. Shots of Jeff sitting in his wheelchair in the dark directly facing Thorwald are crosscut with shots of Thorwald standing in the doorway obscured by shadows. Because all we see is Jeff's darkened silhouette, he and Thorwald seem virtually indistinguishable from each other; indeed, Jeff looks even more sinister and menacing than Thorwald. While it is true that Thorwald has murdered his wife and should be exposed, Jeff, in relentlessly pursuing him, has violated his "humanity." We even experience a moment of sympathy for Thorwald when he desperately pleads with Jeff: "Say something. . . . Tell me what you want from me." Here, the film reveals the "real" Thorwald under the murderer and in so doing tries to insert the spectator into a liberal subject position. It forces her or him to acknowledge that Thorwald is not a "case" but a human being who deserves her or his compassion. Moreover, the shot/reverse shot structure of this scene enacts formally the reversal of Jeff's voyeuristic relation to Thorwald in the plot. Jeff is no longer scrutinizing Thorwald; rather, Thorwald is scrutinizing him. It is *his* mysterious behavior that is now open to question: Why has he been observing Thorwald through a telephoto lens, writing him anonymous notes, and surreptitiously telephoning him to arrange secret meetings? The structure of this scene, in other words, locates Jeff outside the law. It establishes a resemblance between him and the very murderer he has been trying to expose: Like Thorwald, he has been caught in the act of breaking the law and must now confess his guilt.

In trying to reprivatize the voyeuristic economy of spectatorial pleasure, Hitchcock's film demonstrates its support for the postwar settlement. The film's emphasis in the climactic scene on Jeff's resemblance to Thorwald indirectly ratifies the liberal critique of postwar American culture. Jeff's constant surveillance of his neighbors collapses the distinction between the public and the private spheres. The ability of Jeff's telephoto lens to penetrate even the remotest corners of his neighbors' apartments makes privacy impossible. Jeff reduces even his neighbors' most intimate activities to a form of entertainment for his own private consumption. Thus, there is no aspect of their personal life free from public scrutiny. In exposing their privacy to public scrutiny in this way, Jeff politicizes the private sphere. In the context of the McCarthy witch hunts, his surveillance of his neighbors' activities is a political act. A McCarthyite, rather than a liberal, subject, he inappropriately takes on the role of the state in trying to expose Thorwald. He fails to understand that his identity as a neighbor is in direct conflict with his identity as a citizen. Rather, he sees his relation to the state as an extension of his "real" self, a self overly inserted in mass culture.

Not surprisingly, Jeff's politicization of the private sphere polarizes the neighbors; they become increasingly suspicious of each other. When the middle-aged couple who sleeps on the fire escape discovers their dog has been strangled, the wife angrily accuses the whole apartment complex of having done it. Because they treat each other not as neighbors but as spies, they are all guilty of the dog's death: "Neighbors [should] like each other, [should] speak to each other." Although, obviously, such a comment is most applicable to Thorwald, the neighbor who strangled the dog, it also pertains to Jeff. Jeff neither likes nor speaks to his neighbors. His only contact with them is through his telephoto lens, and thus he, too, is complicitous with the "ideologizing" of the apartment complex, despite his refusal to become involved in it except vicariously. In his mind, his neighbors are all potentially guilty of the most brutal crimes. But Jeff has done more than contribute to the politicization of the private sphere; he has also facilitated the privatization of the public sphere. His suspicions of Thorwald are psychologically, rather than politically, motivated. He pursues Thorwald not because he wants to bring him to justice but because he derives voyeuristic pleasure from doing so. Thus, he has allowed the scopic regime of the national security state to corrupt his voyeuristic desire. His voyeurism is no longer a private form of erotic pleasure but a surveillance mechanism. If he truly wanted to act on behalf of the state, he would try to transcend his cultural specificity instead of allowing his construction as a subject of the mass media to determine his political behavior.

The correlation in the film between Jeff's voyeuristic interest in his neighbors and the McCarthy witch hunts indicates the extent to which progressive liberal intellectuals had succeeded in exerting hegemonic control over the production of the postwar subject. The film follows the example of the contributors to *The New American Right* in suggesting that the tensions in American society between the public and the private spheres were structurally necessary. It shows that Jeff's subjectivity is always in excess of his identity as a citizen of the state. In so doing, it tries to insert the spectator into a liberal subject position.[19] At the same time, however, that the film tries to

19. This attempt on the part of the film to make available to the spectator a liberal interpretation of reality to which she or he will consent spontaneously leads me to question Ina Rae Hark's recent analysis of Hitchcock's so-called political films. Hark claims that Hitchcock's "political films" (which of Hitchcock's films are not political? one might legitimately ask) "challenge citizens to break suture and disrupt those performances designed to lull them into complacent reliance upon authority." See "Keeping Your Amateur Standing: Audience Participation and Good Citizenship in Hitchcock's Political Films," *Cinema Journal* 29, no. 2 (1990): 14. Although I would agree with Hark that Hitchcock's films (and not just those she identifies as political) try to position the spectator as a "good" citizen,

conscript the spectator for the postwar settlement, it inadvertently exposes the contradictions in the liberal critique of postwar American culture and its theorization of the subject. In particular, it identifies the distinction between the public and the private spheres as nothing more than a structuring fiction of pluralistic democracies. Ironically, according to Hitchcock's film, the only way to restore the distinction between the public and the private spheres is by modeling the private on the public: The private sphere must function as a pluralistic democracy. In this way, the film emphasizes the interpenetration of the public and the private spheres in pluralistic democracies. The private sphere becomes the primary site for the construction of the liberal subject, a subject who consents freely and spontaneously to the postwar settlement, because it unconsciously conceives of liberal democratic principles as based on common sense.

This contradiction in the film's own proposed solution to the postwar crisis is perhaps most obvious in its representation of Jeff and Lisa's relationship. The film structures Jeff and Lisa's relationship according to the pluralistic model of democracy proposed by the contributors to *The New American Right* as a solution to the postwar crisis. The film represents their relationship as a pragmatic "give-and-take" and insists that the only way in which they can contain their differences is by compromising with each other. Basically incompatible, Jeff and Lisa represent competing special interests. They are both equally committed to their careers, Jeff as a photojournalist, Lisa as a model, and thus it does not seem likely they will ever marry. Although Lisa is obviously head over heels in love with Jeff and aggressively pursues him, Jeff refuses to marry her because, as he tells Stella (Thelma Ritter), the insurance company nurse who comes to his apartment every day to massage him, she is "too perfect." She could never adapt to the hardships of his photo assignments. Moreover, whereas he wants a wife who would accompany him to out-of-the-way places, like Kashmir, she wants him to quit his job at the magazine and open a studio in New York. Despite their differences, however, Jeff and Lisa do eventually reach a compromise. In watching Lisa search Thorwald's apartment for the incriminating wedding ring, Jeff realizes that she is not "too perfect."

I would argue that what constitutes good citizenship for Hitchcock varies from historical moment to historical moment. I would also argue that Hitchcock's films, rather than challenging the spectator to break suture, work actively to absorb her or him in the diegesis. The abhorrence of totalitarianism Hark attributes to Hitchcock clearly did not extend to his own authoritarian performances.

If she can face the murderous Thorwald when he returns to his apartment unexpectedly, then she can adapt to the hardships of remote places, like Kashmir.

By the end of the film, Lisa also demonstrates a willingness to compromise. She no longer urges Jeff to remain in New York with her; rather, she prepares to accompany him on his photo assignments. Her willingness to compromise is most obvious in the final shots of the film. The film ends the way it began: with a pan of the apartment complex. This time, however, the pleasure we derive from observing Jeff's neighbors works to depoliticize the voyeuristic economy of the filmic text. Our interest in them has become wholly personal. We enjoy looking at them because they have finally resolved their problems: Miss Lonelyhearts has met and fallen in love with the middle-aged alcoholic musician who no longer suffers from composer's block; the middle-aged couple who sleeps on the fire escape has gotten a new dog; and Miss Torso's soldier boyfriend has returned home from the Korean War. Repeating its movement in the opening shots of the film, the camera then moves back through the window of Jeff's apartment and shows Jeff dozing in his wheelchair, with a smile on his face. It then cuts to Lisa, who is lounging on a couch in front of Jeff's apartment window, reading the sort of book he would enjoy, *Beyond the High Himalayas*. Slowly panning her, it carefully notes what she is wearing item by item: penny loafers, an old pair of blue jeans, and a red sport shirt—all items Jeff himself might wear on one of his assignments. Here, appropriately enough, Lisa expresses her willingness to make concessions through her clothes. She will accompany Jeff anywhere, even beyond the high Himalayas, if it will make him happy. But she also uses her clothes to show that there are limits to what she will concede. Lest we think she has completely abandoned her interests for Jeff's, the final shot of the film shows her stealing a glance at him to see if he is still asleep and then quickly exchanging the book she has been reading for a copy of *Harper's Bazaar*. While she is willing to give up her modeling career for Jeff, she insists on maintaining her own separate identity. Fashion has retained its importance for her, as her clothes in this scene make clear.

The film, then, tries to resolve the postwar crisis by extending the liberal consensus beyond the political to the cultural realm. Its representation of Jeff and Lisa's relationship insists that liberal democratic principles can provide the most effective structures for everyday life. Neither Jeff nor Lisa should try to dominate their relationship. Although they should certainly protect their own interests, they should not press their individual claims too aggressively; to do so would be to "ideologize" their relationship. Rather, they should try to identify the interests they have in common through bargaining with each other. In this way, their relationship helps to restore the distinction between the public and the private spheres. In particular, it re-contains Jeff's voyeurism in the private sphere. Lisa's willingness to make concessions returns her to the privatized space of the middle-class nuclear family. In giving up her modeling career, she no longer exposes herself to public scrutiny but becomes an object of private consumption for Jeff. The final shots of her lounging on Jeff's couch try to extend this re-containment of voyeuristic pleasure beyond Jeff to the male heterosexual spectator. The fragmentation of her body, its fetishization by the camera, insures that the male heterosexual spectator will similarly treat her as an object of private consumption. In slowly panning her, the camera allows the male hetero-sexual spectator to elude the threat of castration signified by her image. Her fragmented body guarantees the totality and coherence of his own, and thus he can return her look without fear of castration.

Here, however, the film contradicts its own critique of McCarthyism and the politicization of the private sphere through the rise of the mass media. In trying to insert the male heterosexual spectator into a voyeuristic subject position that is not political, it enacts the very collapse of the distinction between the public and the private spheres it seeks to reverse. The only way in which the male heterosexual spectator can treat Lisa as an object of private consumption is in the public space of the darkened auditorium. Moreover, because Jeff and Lisa's relationship enacts the liberal consensus on a private level, it functions as an extension of the public sphere. It guarantees their free and spontaneous consent to the postwar settlement by fostering rational, enlightened debate about their common good. Thus, the film ultimately suggests that the political identity of the liberal subject *should* wholly saturate its humanity, for if the subject's humanity did not coincide perfectly with its political identity, then it might make political claims based on its identity as a gendered and/or racialized subject. For the liberals to maintain their hegemonic control over American culture, the liberal subject has to act as a political agent in the private, as well as in the public, sphere.

I have been claiming that Jeff and Lisa's relationship resembles a pluralistic democracy because the film clearly wants us to see it in those terms. I have also wanted to show that the film's representation of their relationship as a sort of pluralistic democracy suggests that the liberals had extended their hegemonic control of the political to the cultural realm. The film accepts unequivocally the applicability of liberal democratic principles to all aspects of American life. Now, however, I want to argue that the pragmatic "give-and-take" of Jeff and Lisa's relationship is all one-sided. Lisa gives more than she takes. To be sure, Jeff finally agrees to marry her, but only after she has proven to him that she can make the necessary adjustments to his career as a photojournalist. The film inadvertently calls attention to the political double bind in which the liberal consensus placed women and other historically disenfranchised groups. Lisa must not press her claims *as a woman*. Whereas Jeff, as a man, has a right to both a sexually satisfying marriage and a highly successful career, she does not. For her to insist otherwise would be to confuse her identity as a woman with her political identity. In claiming that she, too, has a right to a highly successful career, she would be acting as a feminist. Yet, not to press her claims is already to confuse her identity as a woman with her political identity. She willingly abandons her career because she realizes that as a middle-class married woman in postwar American society she has no right to one. Ultimately, then, Hitchcock's film enacts the very limits of the liberal consensus. It tries to show that what Lisa loses in the public sphere (a highly successful career), she gains in the private (a sexually satisfying marriage), a claim it would hardly make if she were a man. Thus, the film is willing to accommodate her interests, but only within the confines of the privatized space of the middle-class nuclear family.

Queer Nationality

Lauren Berlant
Elizabeth Freeman

Now the skins felt powerful and human.
They became lords of sounds and lesser things.
They passed nations through their mouths.
They sat in judgement.
—Zora Neale Hurston, *Their Eyes Were Watching God*

We Are Everywhere. We Want Everything.
—Queer Nation, Gay Pride Parade, New York, 1991

I Pledge Allegiance to the F(l)ag

At the end of Sandra Bernhard's film *Without You I'm Nothing*, the diva wraps herself in an American flag. This act, which emblazons her in-

We thank our collaboratrixes: Claudia L. Johnson, Tricia Loughran, Deborah N. Schwartz, Tom Stillinger, AK Summers, Michael Warner, the Gay and Lesbian Studies Workshop at the University of Chicago, and the Cultural Forms/Public Spheres study group at the Center of Psychosocial Research.

terpretation of Prince's "Little Red Corvette," culminates her performance of feminine drag, feminist camp. Staging not a cross-dressing that binarizes sex but a masquerade that smudges the clarity of gender, Bernhard frames *woman* within a constellation of sexual practices whose forms of publicity change by the decade, by subcultural origin, by genres of pleasure (music, fashion, political theater), and by conventions of collective erotic fantasy. Having sexually overdressed for the bulk of the film, Bernhard strips down to a flag and a sequined red, white, and blue G-string and pasties, and thus exposes a national body—her body. This national body does not address a mass or abstract audience of generic Americans, nor does it campily evoke a "typical" American citizen's nostalgia for collective memory, ritual, and affect. Bernhard flags her body to mark a fantasy of erotic identification with someone present, in the intimate room: it is a national fantasy, displayed as a spectacle of desire, and a fantasy, apparently external to the official national frame, of communion with a black woman whose appearance personifies authenticity.

At the same time, also in 1990, Madonna responded to a civic crisis marked by voter apathy among youth by performing in a pro-voting commercial stripped down to a bikini and wrapped alluringly in an American flag. In this commercial, the blond bombshell is flanked by a black man and a white man, both of whom are dressed in the clone semiotic that flags a certain East Coast urban gay community style. These men sing "Get Out and Vote" in discordant comic harmony with Madonna, while they wave little flags and she flashes her body by undulating a big one.

On March 24, 1991, the *Chicago Tribune Magazine* featured the Gulf War as a fashion event. Adding to the already widely publicized rush by citizens to own their very own gas masks and military fatigues, supplementing the fad for patriotic tee shirts and sweatshirts bearing American flags and mottoes like "These Colors Won't Run," this style section, titled "Red, White, and You," featured the new rage in feminine fashion: red, white, and blue. Mobilized by the patriotic furor generated by the war, women en masse were signifying through the color combination and not the icon, capitalizing on the capacity of the flag's traces to communicate personal politics without explicit polemic. The dissolution of the flag into flagness also protected the consumer from being charged with desecrating the flag, should it become stained with food or sweat, or singed with the dropped ashes of a cigarette.

In 1991, *RFD*, a magazine for rural gays with connections to the Radical Faeries, featured the image of a naked young white man with an erection on a pedestal, set against the background of an American flag. Two captions graced this portrait: "BRING OUR BOYS HOME AND WHOLE THIS SOLSTICE PEACE NOW!" and "What could be more American than young, hard man/boy flesh?"

A rhetorical question? Having witnessed this rush to consume the flag, to fuse it with the flesh, we conclude that at present the nation suffers from *Americana nervosa*, a compulsive self-gorging on ritual images. This grotesque fantasy structure was paraded in the 1988 presidential election by the Republican flap over whether citizens should be legally obliged to say the Pledge of Allegiance. It was further extended from mass public struggle into the Supreme Court by constitutional battles over whether the flag should be exposed to mortality's contagion in the form of its own ashes or dirt, and it has recast national patriotism as a question not of political identity but of proper public expression, loyal self-censorship, and personal discipline. No longer is the struggle to secure national discursive propriety located mainly on the general terrain of "freedom of speech," state policies against certain sexual practices, and the regulation of privately consumed sexual images within the U.S. mail: The struggle is now also over proper public submission to national iconicity and over the nation's relation to gender, to sexuality, and to death.

If, in the wake of the election and the remilitarization of America, official patriotic discourse casts the American flag in an epidemic crisis and struggles to manage its public meaning through a sublime collective manufactured consent, the consumption of nationality in the nineties appears motivated not by a satisfaction that already exists but by a collective desire to reclaim the nation for pleasure, and specifically the pleasure of spectacular public self-entitlement. Queer Nation has taken up the project of coordinating a new nationality. Its relation to nationhood is multiple and ambiguous, however, taking as much from the insurgent nationalisms of oppressed peoples as from the revolutionary idealism of the United States. Since its inception in 1990, it has invented collective local rituals of resistance, mass cultural spectacles, an organization, and even a lexicon to achieve these ends. It aims to capitalize on the difficulty of locating the national public, whose consent to self-expression founds modern national identity.[1]

1. There is yet no anthology or full history documenting Queer Nation, and its redefinitions in the print media are ongoing. For some contemporary accounts of QN, see the following articles: Allan Bérubé and Jeffrey Escoffier, "Queer/Nation," *Outlook: National Lesbian and Gay Quarterly* 11 (Winter 1991): 13–15; Alexander Chee, "A Queer Nation-

Queer Nation's outspoken promotion of a national sexuality not only discloses that mainstream national identity touts a subliminal sexuality more official than a state flower or a national bird but also makes explicit how thoroughly the local experience of the body is framed by laws, policies, and social customs regulating sexuality. Queer Nation's tactics of invention appropriate for gay politics both grass roots and mass-mediated forms of countercultural resistance from left, feminist, and civil rights movements of the sixties—the ones that insisted that the personal is political, engaging the complex relation between local and national practices. Also, in the retro-nostalgia impulse of postmodernism, QN redeploys these tactics in a kind of guerrilla warfare that names all concrete and abstract spaces of social communication as places where "the people" live and thus as national sites ripe both for transgression and legitimate visibility.[2] Its tactics are to cross borders, to occupy spaces, and to mime the privileges of normality—in short, to simulate "the national" with a camp inflection. This model of political identity imitates not so much the "one man one vote" caucus polemic mentality of mainstream politics but the individual and mass identities of consumers: Queer Nation, itself a collection of local affinity groups,[3] has produced images, occupied public spaces of consumption, like bars and malls, and refunctioned the culture of the trademark. Exploiting the structures of identification and the embodied and disembodied scenes of erotic contact, substitution, publicity, and exchange so central to the

---

alism," *Outlook: National Lesbian and Gay Quarterly* 11 (Winter 1991): 15–19; Esther Kaplan, "A Queer Manifesto," in Guy Trebay's article "In Your Face," *Village Voice* 14 (August 1990): 36; Kay Longcope, "Boston Gay Groups Vow New Militancy against Hate Crimes," *Boston Globe*, Wednesday, 21 Aug. 1990: 25, 31; Maria Maggenti, "Women as Queer Nationals," *Outlook: National Lesbian and Gay Quarterly* 11 (Winter 1991): 20–23; Deborah Schwartz, "'Queers Bash Back,'" *Gay Community News*, Monday, 24 June 1990: 14–15; Randy Shilts, "The Queering of America," *The Advocate* 567 (1 Jan. 1991): 32–38; Guy Trebay, "In Your Face," *Village Voice*, 14 Aug. 1990, 35–39.

2. Bérubé and Escoffier, "Queer/Nation," 13–14.

3. These affinity groups include ASLUT, "Artists Slaving Under Tyranny"; DORIS SQUASH, "Defending Our Rights in the Streets, Super Queers United Against Savage Heterosexuals"; GHOST, "Grand Homosexual Organization to Stop Televangelists"; HI MOM, "Homosexual Ideological Mobilization Against the Military"; LABIA, "Lesbians and Bisexuals in Action"; QUEER PLANET, an environmental group; QUEER STATE, which deals with state governments; QUEST, "Queers Undertaking Exquisite and Symbolic Transformation"; SHOP, "Suburban Homosexual Outreach Program"; UNITED COLORS, which focuses on experiences of queers of color. For the extended list, see Bérubé and Escoffier, "Queer/Nation," 15.

allure of nationalism and capitalism, Queer Nation operates precisely in the American mode.[4]

In this article, we seek to understand the political logic of Queer Nationality and to trace the movement's spectacular intentions and effects. We will, in the next three sections, describe Queer Nation in its strongest tactical moments, as when it exploits the symbolic designs of mass and national culture in order to dismantle the standardizing apparatus that organizes all manner of sexual practice into "facts" of sexual *identity*,[5] as when it mobilizes a radically wide range of knowledge—modes of understanding from science to gossip—to reconstitute information about queerness, thus transforming the range of reference "queer" has by multiplying its specifications.[6] Whether or not Queer Nation survives as an organization past the present tense of our writing,[7] the movement provides us with these discursive political tactics not simply as fodder for history but also as a kind of incitement to reformulate the conditions under which further interventions

4. Our construction of the manifold publics, polities, and symbolic cultures that traverse American life emanates from a number of sources: Benedict Anderson, *Imagined Communities* (London: Verso, 1983); Lauren Berlant, *The Anatomy of National Fantasy: Hawthorne, Utopia, and Everyday Life* (Chicago: University of Chicago Press, 1991); Alice Echols, *Born to be Bad: Radical Feminism in America, 1967–1975* (Minneapolis: University of Minnesota Press, 1989); Elizabeth Freeman, "Pitmarks on the History of the Country: The Epidemic of Nationalism in Hawthorne's 'Lady Eleanore's Mantle'" (unpublished manuscript, University of Chicago, 1990); George Mosse, *Nationalism and Sexuality* (Madison: University of Wisconsin Press, 1986); Linda J. Nicholson, ed., *Feminism/Postmodernism* (New York: Routledge, 1990); Iris Marion Young, "Polity and Group Difference: A Critique of the Ideal of Universal Citizenship," *Ethics* 9 (January 1989): 250–74, and *Throwing Like a Girl and Other Essays in Feminist Philosophy and Social Theory* (Bloomington: Indiana University Press, 1989).

5. For the political need to postminoritize cultural experience through the manipulation of representational codes, see David Lloyd, "Genet's Genealogy: European Minorities and the Ends of the Canon," in *The Nature and Context of Minority Discourse*, ed. Abdul R. JanMohamed and David Lloyd (New York: Oxford University Press, 1990), 369–93.

6. Three essays that argue for the need to re-taxonomize sexual identity have inspired this essay: Esther Newton and Shirley Walton, "The Misunderstanding: Toward a More Precise Sexual Vocabulary," in *Pleasure and Danger*, ed. Carole Vance (Boston: Routledge, 1984), 242–50; Gayle Rubin, "Thinking Sex," in *Pleasure and Danger*, 267–314; and Eve Kosofsky Sedgwick, *Epistemology of the Closet* (Berkeley: University of California Press, 1990), 1–63.

7. This death knell was sounded as early as June 1991, in Toronto, according to *Xtra!*, a Toronto publication. Cited in "Quotelines," *Outlines* 5, no. 1 (June 1991): 7. We have since heard that reports of its death have been greatly exaggerated.

into the juridical, policy, and popular practices of contemporary America must be thought and made.[8]

This demands an expanded politics of description. We might say, "an expanded politics of *erotic* description," but crucial to a sexually radical movement for social change is the transgression of categorical distinctions between sexuality and politics, with their typically embedded divisions between public, private, and personal concerns. The multiplicity of social spaces, places where power and desire are enacted and transferred, need to be disaggregated and specified. The abstract, disembodied networks of electronic visual, aural, and textual communication, the nationalized systems of juridical activity and official public commentary, the state and local political realms that are not at all simply microcosmic of the national: All coexist with both the manifestly pleasuring or moneymaking embodiments of local, national, and global capitalism, and with the random or customary interactions of social life—this sentence could, and must, go on interminably. These spaces are hard to describe, because they are all unbounded, dialectically imagined, sometimes powerful, and sometimes irrelevant to the theory, practice, and transformation of sexual hegemony. Whatever they are, at the moment they are resolutely national. Queer Nation's nationalist-style camp counterpolitics incorporates this discursive and territorial problem, shifting between a utopian politics of identity, difference, dispersion, and specificity and a pluralist agenda, in the liberal sense, that imagines a "gorgeous mosaic" of difference without a model of conflict. Our final section, "With *You* Out We're Nothing," supports and extends Queer Nation's contestation of existing cultural spaces but seeks to reopen the question of nationalism's value as an infidel model of transgression and resistance, for the very naturalizing stereotypes of official nationality can inflect even the most radical insurgent forms. In other words, this is an anti-assimilationist narrative about an anti-assimilationist movement. It must be emphasized, however, that disidentification with U.S. nationality is not, at this moment, even a theoretical option for queer citizens: As long as PWAs require state support, as long as the official nation invests its identity in the pseudo-right to police nonnormative sexual representations and sexual practices, the lesbian, gay, feminist, and queer communities in the United States do not have the privilege to disregard national identity. We are compelled, then, to read America's lips. What can we do to force the officially constituted nation to speak a new political tongue?

8. See Andrew Ross, *No Respect: Intellectuals and Popular Culture* (New York: Routledge, 1989), 135–70.

Recently, official America has sought to manage an explicit relation between national power and the vulnerable body by advertising an
unironic consecration of masculine military images and surgical incisions
into the borders of other sovereign nations. Queer Nation, in dramatic contrast, produces images in response to the massive violence against racial,
sexual, gendered, and impoverished populations within the U.S. borders,
a violence emblematized by, but in no way limited to, the federal response
to AIDS. A brief history of the movement will help to explain the genesis
of its polymorphous impulses. Founded at an ACT UP New York meeting in April 1990, Queer Nation aimed to extend the kinds of democratic
counterpolitics deployed on behalf of AIDS activism for the transformation
of public sexual discourse in general. Douglas Crimp and Adam Rolston's
AIDS DEMO GRAPHICS is to date the fullest and most graphic record
of ACT UP's intervention into local, state, and national systems of power
and publicity.[9] This specification of mainstream sites of power was made
necessary by federal stonewalling on the subject of AIDS treatment, support, and education among institutions in the political public sphere, where
the bureaucratic norm is to disavow accountability to vulnerable populations. ACT UP recognizes the necessity to master the specific functions of
political bureaucracies and to generate loud demands that these live up to
their promise to all of "the people." Among other strategies, it exploits the
coincidence between national and commercial spectacle by pirating advertising techniques: An alliance with the political artists called Gran Fury has
produced a sophisticated poster campaign to transform the passive public
space of New York into a zone of political pedagogy. Queer Nation takes
from ACT UP this complex understanding of political space as fundamental to its insistence on making all public spheres truly safe for all of the
persons who occupy them, not just in psychic loyalty but in everyday and
embodied experience. To be safe in the national sense means not just safe
from bashing, not just safe from discrimination, but safe *for* demonstration,
in the mode of patriotic ritual, which always involves a deployment of affect,
knowledge, spectacle, and crucially, a kind of banality, ordinariness, and
popularity:

> Through its activism Queer Nation seeks to redefine the commu-
> nity—its rights, its visibility—and take it into what's been claimed as
> straight political and social space. "QUEERS READ THIS" asks to
> be read as the accompanying declaration of nationalism. It says: In

9. Douglas Crimp and Adam Rolston, *AIDS DEMO GRAPHICS* (Seattle: Bay Press,
1990).

156

this culture, being queer means you've been condemned to death; appreciate our power and our bond; realize that whenever one of us is hurt we all suffer; know that we have to fight for ourselves because no one else will. It says, this is why we are a *nation* of queers, and why you must feel yourself a part. Its language seems to borrow from other, equally "threatening" power movements—black nationalist, feminist separatist.[10]

The key to the paradoxes of Queer Nation is the way it *exploits* internal difference. That is, QN understands the propriety of queerness to be a function of the diverse spaces in which it aims to become explicit. It names multiple local and national publics; it does not look for a theoretical coherence to regulate in advance all of its tactics: all politics in the Queer Nation are imagined on the *street*. Finally, it always refuses closeting strategies of assimilation and goes for the broadest and most explicit assertion of presence. This loudness involves two main kinds of public address: internal, for the production of safe collective Queer spaces, and external, in a cultural pedagogy emblematized by the post–Black Power slogan "We're Here. We're Queer. Get Used to It." If "I'm Black and I'm Proud" sutures the first-person performative to racial visibility, transforming the speaker from racial object to ascendant subject, Queer Nation's slogan stages the shift from silent absence into present speech, from nothingness to collectivity, from a politics of embodiment to one of space, whose power erupts from the ambiguity of "here." Where?

Inside: I Hate Straights, and Other "Queeritual" Prayers

Nancy Fraser's recent essay on postmodernity and identity politics argues that countercultural groups engage in a dialectic with mainstream public culture, shifting between internal self-consolidation and reinvestment of the relatively essentialist "internal" identity into the normalizing discussions of the mass public sphere.[11] In this dialectic, the subaltern indeed becomes a speaking player in her own public identity, for the public is an intelligibly "dominant" space characterized by collective norms. Fraser's model does not work for Queer Nation, which neither recognizes a single internal or privatized interest nor certifies one mainstream whose disposition

10. See Kaplan, "A Queer Manifesto," 36; Kaplan's emphasis.
11. Nancy Fraser, "Rethinking the Public Sphere: A Contribution to the Critique of Actually Existing Democracy," *Social Text* 25/26 (1990): 56–80.

constitutes the terrain for counterpolitics. This distinguishing mark of Queer Nation—its capacity to include cultural resistance, opposition, and subcultural consolidation in a mix of tactics from identity politics and postmodern metropolitan information flows—will thus govern our inside narrative. We will shuttle between a dispersed variety of Queer National events, falsely bringing into narrative logic and collective intentionality what has been a deliberately unsystematized politics.

If there is one manifesto of this polyvocal movement, defining the lamination of a gay liberation politics and new gay power tactics, it is, famously, the "I Hate Straights" polemic distributed as a broadside at the Gay Pride parades in New York and Chicago in the summer of 1990. "I Hate Straights," printed (at least in Chicago) over the image of a raised clenched masculine fist, is a monologue, a slave narrative without decorum, a manifesto of rage and its politics. Gone, the assimilationist patience of some gay liberation identity politics; gone, the assertive rationality of the "homosexual" subject who seeks legitimacy by signifying, through "straight" protocols, that "civilization" has been sighted on the cultural margin.[12]

"I Hate Straights," instead, "proceeds in terms of the unavoidable usefulness of something that is very dangerous."[13] What is dangerous is rage, and the way it is deployed both to an "internal" audience of gay subjects and an "external" straight world. The broadside begins with personal statements: "I have friends. Some of them are straight. Year after year, I see my straight friends. I want to see them, to see how they are doing . . . [and] [y]ear after year I continue to realize that the facts of my life are irrelevant to them and that I am only half listened to." The speaker remains unheard, because straights refuse to believe that gay subjects are in exile from privilege, from ownership of a point of view that American social institutions and popular cultural practices secure: "Insiders claim that [gays] already are" included in the privileges of the straight world. But gay subjects are excluded from the privileges of procreation, of family, of the public

---

12. Identity is linked to territorialization, both geographical and ideological. We mean to offer an account of a subcultural *topology,* a description of how modern space requires negotiating a complex relation between situated identities and mobilized *identifications.* The shifting terrain in the meaning of the phrase *gay community* symptomatized in Queer Nation's practices has been splendidly explicated by Richard Herrell's "Symbolic Strategies of Chicago's Gay and Lesbian Pride Day Parade," in Gilbert Herdt, ed., *The Culture of Gay Men* (forthcoming).

13. Gayatri Chakravorty Spivak, "In a Word. *Interview," Differences* 1 (Summer 1989): 129.

158

fantasy that circulates through these institutions: Indeed, it seems that only the public discipline of gayness keeps civilization from "melt[ing] back into the primeval ooze."

In the face of an exile caused by this arrogant heterosexual presumption of domestic space and privilege, the speaker lights into a list of proclamations headed by "I hate straights": "I" hates straights on behalf of the gay people who have to emotionally "take care" of the straights who feel guilty for their privilege; "I" hates straights for requiring the sublimation of gay rage as the price of their beneficent tolerance. "'You'll catch more flies with honey,'" the speaker hears; "Now look who's generalizing," they say, as if the minoritized group itself had invented the "crude taxonomy" under which it labored.[14] In response, the flyer argues, "BASH BACK . . . LET YOURSELF BE ANGRY . . . THAT THERE IS NO PLACE IN THIS COUNTRY WHERE WE ARE SAFE."

The speaker's designation of "country" as the space of danger complexly marks the indices of social identity through which this invective circulates. "I" mentions two kinds of "we": gay and American subjects, all of whom have to "thank President Bush for planting a fucking tree" in public, while thousands of PWAs die for lack of political visibility. Here, the nation of the Bush and the tree becomes a figure of nature that includes the malignant neglect of AIDS populations, including, and especially (here), gay men. Straights ask the gay community to self-censor, because anger is not "productive": Meanwhile, the administrators of straight America commit omissions of policy to assert that healthy heterosexual identity (the straight and undiseased body) is a prerequisite to citizenship of the United States. The treatise goes on to suggest that the national failure to secure justice for all citizens is experienced locally, in public spaces where physical gay bashing takes place, and in even more intimate sites like the body: "Go tell [straights to] go away until they have spent a month walking hand in hand in public with someone of the same sex. After they survive that, then you'll hear what they have to say about queer anger. Otherwise, tell them to shut up and listen."

The distribution of this document to a predominantly gay population at Gay Pride parades underscores a fundamental Queer Nation policy. *Visibility* is critical if a safe public existence is to be forged for American gays, for whom the contemporary nation has no positive political value. The cities where Queer Nation lives already contain local gay communities, locales

14. See Sedgwick, *Epistemology of the Closet*, 1–63.

that secure spaces of safe embodiment for capital and sexual expenditures. For Queer Nation, they also constitute sites within which political bases can be founded. This emphasis on safe spaces, secured for bodies by capital and everyday life practices also, finally, constitutes a refusal of the terms national discourse uses to frame the issue of sexuality: "Being queer is not about a right to privacy: it is about the freedom to be public . . . [i]t's not about the mainstream, profit-margins, patriotism, patriarchy or being assimilated. . . . Being queer is 'grass roots' because we know that every-one of us, every body, every cunt, every heart and ass and dick is a world of pleasure waiting to be explored. Everyone of us is a world of infinite possibility." Localness, here transposed into the language of worldness, is dedicated to producing a new politics from the energy of a sentimentally and erotically excessive sexuality. The ambiguities of this sexual geography are fundamental to producing the new referent, a gay community whose erotics and politics are transubstantial. Meanwhile, in the hybrid Queer/ American nation, orthodox forms of political agency linger, in modified form: For example, Queer Nation proclaims, "An army of lovers cannot lose!" But this military fantasy refers in its irony to a set of things: counterviolences in local places, sixties movements to make love, not war, and also the invigo-rated persecution of queer subjects in the United States military during the Reagan/Bush years.

Thus, too, the self-proclaimed "Queeritual" element in some Queer Nation productions exceeds secular American proprieties, as in broadsides that replace "I pledge allegiance to the flag" with "I praise life with my vulva" and "I praise God with my erection." [15] Although we might say that this queer-ituality is reactionary, reflecting a suprapolitical move to spiritual identity, we might also say that this is literally conservative, an attempt to save space for hope, prayer, and simple human relations—a Queer Nation "Now I lay me down to sleep." These pieties assert the luck the praying subjects feel to be sleeping with someone of their own sex, thus promoting homosexuality in the way Queer Nation wants to do, as a mode of ordinary identifica-tion and pleasure. But these prayers also parody the narrative convention of normative prayer to find a safe space for eluding official and conven-tional censorship of public sexuality: *Thing* magazine reports, indeed, that

15. We cite the texts in their entirety. "I Praise Life": "I praise life with my vulva. I thank the gods for all the women who have kissed my lips. I praise life." "I Praise God": "I praise God with my erection. I thank God for all the men I've slept with. I praise God." They were created in 1990 by Joe Lindsay of Queer Nation Denver.

the broadside has come under criticism for seeming to promote promiscuity.[16] In our view, the prayers counter the erotophobia of gay and straight publics who want to speak of "lifestyles" and not of sex. Finally, just as the genre of the circulating broadside reveals how gay and straight populations topographically overlap, so does this use of prayer itself avow the futility of drawing comprehensive affective boundaries between gay and straight subjects. Queer Nation's emphasis on public language and media, its exploitation of the tension between local embodiment and mass abstraction, forfeits the possibility of such taxonomic clarity.

Outside: Politics in Your Face

On February 23, 1967, in a congressional hearing concerning the security clearance of gay men for service in the Defense Department, a psychiatrist named Dr. Charles Socarides testified that the homosexual "does not know the boundary of his own body. He does not know where his body ends and space begins."[17] Precisely, the spiritual and other moments of internal consolidation that we have described allow the individual bodies of Queer Nationals to act as visibly queer flash cards, in an ongoing project of cultural pedagogy aimed at exposing the range and variety of bounded spaces upon which heterosexual supremacy depends. Moving out from the psychological and physical safe spaces it creates, Queer Nation broadcasts the straightness of public space, and hence its explicit or implicit danger to gays. The queer body—as an agent of publicity, as a unit of self-defense, and finally as a spectacle of ecstasy—becomes the locus where mainstream culture's discipline of gay citizens is written and where the pain caused by this discipline is transformed into rage and pleasure. Using alternating strategies of menace and merriment, agents of Queer Nation have come to see and conquer places that present the danger of *violence* to gays and lesbians, to reterritorialize them.

Twenty-three years after Dr. Socarides' mercifully brief moment of fame, New Yorkers began to display on their chests a graphic interpretation of his fear for the national defense. The tee shirt they wore portrays a silhouette of the United States, with the red tint of the East Coast and the blue tint of the West Coast fading and blending in the middle. Suddenly, the heartland of the country is a shocking new shade of Queer: Red, white, and

16. Robert Ford, "Sacred Sex: Art Erects Controversy," *Thing* 4 (Spring 1991): 4.
17. John D'Emilio, *Sexual Politics, Sexual Communities* (Chicago: University of Chicago Press, 1983), 216.

blue make lavender. This, Queer Nation's first tee shirt, extends the project of an earlier graphic produced by Adam Rolston, which shows a placard that reads "I Am Out, Therefore I Am." But Queer Nation's shirt locates the public space in which the individual Cartesian subject must be out, transforming that space in order to survive. Queer Nation's design maps a psychic and bodily territory—lavender territory—that cannot be colonized and expands it to include, potentially, the entire nation. This lamination of the country to the body conjoins individual and national liberation: Just as Dr. Socarides dreaded, the boundaries between what constitutes individual and what constitutes national space are explicitly blurred. "National Defense" and "Heterosexual Defense" become interdependent projects of boundary maintenance that Queer Nation graphically undermines, showing that these colors *will* run.

While the Queer Nation shirt exploits heterosexist fears of the "spread of a lifestyle" through dirty laundry by publicizing its wearer as both a gay native and a missionary serving the spread of homosexuality, not all of their tactics are this benign. The optimistic assertion that an army of lovers cannot lose masks the seriousness with which Queer Nation has responded to the need for a pseudo-militia on the order of the Guardian Angels. The Pink Panthers, initially conceived of at a Queer Nation meeting (they are now a separate organization), provided a searing response to the increased violence that has accompanied the general increase of gay visibility in America. The Panthers, a foot patrol that straddles the "safe spaces" described in the first section and the "unsafe spaces" of public life in America, not only defend other queer bodies but aim to be a continual reminder of them. Dressed in black tee shirts with pink triangles enclosing a black paw print, they move unarmed in groups, linked by walkie-talkies and whistles. In choosing a uniform that explicitly marks them as targets, as successors of the Black Power movement, and as seriocomic detectives, the Panthers bring together the abstract threat implicit in the map graphic described above, the embodied threat implicit in individual queers crossing their subcultural boundaries, and the absurdity that founds this condition of sexual violence.

The Panthers' slogan is "Bash Back." It announces that the locus of gay oppression has shifted from the legal to the extralegal arena, and from national-juridical to ordinary everyday forms.[18] The menace of "Bash Back" reciprocates the menace of physical violence that keeps gays and lesbians

18. John D'Emilio, "Capitalism and Gay Identity," in *The Powers of Desire*, ed. Ann Snitow, Christine Stansell, and Sharon Thompson (New York: Monthly Review Press, 1983), 108.

162

invisible and/or physically restricted to their mythically safe neighborhoods. But rather than targeting specific gay bashers or lashing out at random heterosexuals, the Panthers train in self-defense techniques and travel unarmed: "Bash Back" simply intends to mobilize the threat gay bashers use so effectively—strength not in numbers but in the presence of a few bodies who represent the potential for widespread violence—against the bashers themselves. In this way, the slogan turns the bodies of the Pink Panthers into a psychic counterthreat, expanding their protective shield beyond the confines of their physical "beat." Perhaps the most assertive bashing that the uniformed bodies of the Pink Panthers deliver is mnemonic. Their spectacular presence counters heterosexual culture's will not to recognize its own intense need to reign in a sexually pure environment.

While the rage of "Bash Back" responds to embodied and overt violence, Queer Nation's "Queer Nights Out" redress the more diffuse and implicit violence of sexual conventionality by mimicking the hackneyed forms of straight social life. Queer Nights Out are moments of radical desegregation with roots in the civil rights era lunch counter sit-ins; whereas the sixties' sit-ins addressed legal segregation, these queer sorties confront customary segregation. Invading straight bars, for example, they stage a production of sentimentality and pleasure that broadcasts the ordinariness of the queer body. The banality of twenty-five same-sex couples making out in a bar, the silliness of a group of fags playing spin the bottle, efface the distance crucial to the ordinary pleasures straight society takes in the gay world. Neither informational nor particularly spectacular, Queer Nights Out demonstrate two ominous truths to heterosexual culture: (1) gay sexual identity is no longer a reliable foil for straightness; and (2) what looked like bounded gay subcultural activity has itself become restless and improvisatory, taking its pleasures in a theater near you.

Queer Nights Out have also appropriated the model of the surprise attack, which the police have traditionally used to show gays and lesbians that even the existence of their subcultural spaces is contingent upon the goodwill of straights. Demonstrating that the boundedness of heterosexual spaces is also contingent upon the (enforced) willingness of gays to remain invisible, queers are thus using exhibitionism to make public space psychically unsafe for unexamined heterosexuality. In one report from the field, two lesbians were sighted sending a straight woman an oyster, adding a Sapphic Appetizer to the menu of happy hour delights. The straight woman was not amused.[19] Embarrassment was generated—the particular

19. Trebay, "In Your Face," 36.

embarrassment liberals suffer when the sphere allotted to the tolerated exceeds the boundaries "we all agree upon." Maneuvers such as this reveal that straight mating techniques, supposed to be "Absolutely Het," are sexual lures available to any brand of pleasure: "Sorry, you looked like a dyke to me."[20] This political transgression of "personal space" can even be used to deflect the violence it provokes. Confronted by a defensive and hostile drunk, a QN gayboy addresses the room: "Yeah, I had him last night, and he was terrible."

In this place of erotic exchange, the army of lovers takes as its war strategies "some going down and butt-fucking and other theatricals."[21] The genitals become not just organs of erotic thanksgiving but weapons of pleasure against their own oppression. These kinds of militant-erotic interventions take their most public form in the Queer Nation kiss-in, in which an official space, such as a city plaza, is transfused with the juices of unofficial enjoyment: Embarrassment, pleasure, spectacle, longing, and accusation interarticulate to produce a public scandal that is, as the following section will reveal, Queer Nation's specialty.

Hyperspace: "Try Me On, I'm Very You"[22]

In its most postmodern moments, Queer Nation takes on a corporate strategy in order to exploit the psychic unboundedness of consumers who depend upon products to articulate, produce, and satisfy their desires. Queer Nation tactically uses the hyperspaces created by the corporeal trademark, the metropolitan parade, the shopping mall, print media, and, finally, advertising to recognize and to take advantage of the consumer's pleasure in vicarious identification. In this guise, the group commandeers permeable sites, apparently apolitical spaces through which the public circulates in a pleasurable consensual exchange of bodies, products, identities, and information. Yet, it abandons the conciliatory mode of, for instance, Kirk and Madsen's plan to market "positive" (read "tolerable") gay images to straight culture.[23] Instead, it aims to produce a series of elabo-

---

20. The "Absolutely Het" series, parodies of the ads for Absolut vodka, were produced by the anonymous group OUTPOST.
21. Trebay, "In Your Face," 39.
22. From Deee-Lite's song, "Try Me On, I'm Very You," on the album *World Clique*. Elektra Entertainment, 1990.
23. Marshall Kirk and Hunter Madsen, *After the Ball: How America Will Conquer its Fear and Hatred of Gays in the '90s* (New York: Doubleday, 1989). Kirk and Madsen advise the gay community to present nonthreatening images of homosexuality to straight culture,

rate blue-light specials on the queer body. The Queer National corporate strategy—to reveal to the consumer desires he/she didn't know he/she had, to make his/her identification with the product "homosexuality" both an unsettling and a pleasurable experience—makes consumer pleasure central to the transformation of public culture, thus linking the utopian promises of the commodity with those of the nation.

One particular celebrity oscillates between local/embodied and corporate/abstract sexual identification: "Queer Bart" stars on a tee shirt produced by Queer Nation in the summer of 1990. Queer Bart reconfigures Matt Groening's bratty white suburban "anykid," Bart Simpson, into the New York gay clone: He wears an earring, his own Queer Nation tee shirt, and a pink triangle button. The balloon coming out of his mouth reads, "Get used to it, dude!" Like all bodies, Queer Bart's body is a product that serves a number of functions. In the first place, he provides a countertext to the apparent harmlessness of the suburban American generic body: Queer Nation's Bart implicitly points a finger at another bootleg tee shirt, on which Bart snarls, "Back off, faggot!" and at the heterosexuality that Normal Bart's generic identity assumes. In the second place, the original Bart's "cloneness," when inflected with an "exceptional" identity—Black Bart, Latino Bart, and so on—not only stages the ability of subcultures to fashion cultural insiderhood for their members but also reinscribes subcultural identity into mainstream style. The exuberant inflection of Bart Simpson as queer speaks to the pleasures of assuming an official normative identity, signified on the body, for those whom dominant culture consistently represents as exceptional.

Queer Nation's reinflection of Bart's body, which, precisely because it *is* a body, readily lends itself to any number of polymorphously perverse identities, graphically demonstrates that the commodity is a central means by which individuals tap into the collective experience of public desire. Queer Bart, himself a trademark, is a generic body stamped with Queer Nation's own trademarked aesthetic, which then allows the consumer to publicly identify him- herself as a member of a trademarked "nation."[24] Thus,

a "marketing campaign" designed to win mainstream approval for the bourgeois homosexual at the cost of eliminating drag queens, butch lesbians, transsexuals, etc., from visibility.

24. For a discussion of the relationship between the trademark, commodity identification, and the colonized American body, see Lauren Berlant, "National Brands/National Body: *Imitation of Life*," in *Comparative American Identities: Race, Sex, and Nationality in the Modern Text, Selected Papers from the English Institute*, ed. Hortense J. Spillers (Boston: Routledge, 1991), 110–40.

Bart embodies the non-spaces we will discuss in the following paragraphs: His own unboundedness as a commodity identity exploits the way that the fantasy of being something else merges with the stereotype to confer an endlessly shifting series of identities upon the consumer's body.[25]

The genealogy of the Queer Bart strategy extends from the Gay Pride parades of the 1970s, when, for the first time, gay bodies organized into a visible public ritual. In addition to offering gays and lesbians an opportunity to experience their private identities in an official spectacle, the parades also offered flamboyant and ordinary homosexuality as something the heterosexual spectator could encounter without having to go underground—to drag shows or gay bars—for voyeuristic pleasure or casual sex.[26] In the last twenty years, the representation of "gayness" in the Gay Pride parade has changed, for its marching population is no longer defined by sexual practice alone. Rather, the current politicization of gay issues in the metropolitan and civic public spheres has engendered broadly based alliances, such that progressive "straights" can pass as "queer" in their collective political struggles.[27] As a result, the Gay Pride parade no longer produces the ominous gust of an enormous closet door opening; its role in consolidating identity varies widely, depending on what kind of communication participants think the parade involves. While Gay Pride parades have not yet achieved the status in mainstream culture of, for instance, St. Patrick's Day parades (in which people "go Irish for a day" by dressing in green), they have become pluralistic and inclusive, involving approval-seeking, self-consolidating, and saturnalian and transgressive moments of spectacle.[28] Although Queer Nation marches in traditional Gay Pride parades, it has updated and complicated the strategy of the parade, recognizing that the planned, distanced, and ultimately contained nature of the form offers only momentary displacement of heterosexual norms: After all, one can choose not to go to a parade, or one can watch the scene go by without becoming even an imaginary participant.

25. A powerful and extensive exploration of the role of this "stereotyped fantasy body" in the black gay voguing subculture is provided by Jenny Livingston's documentary film, *Paris is Burning*. See also Berlant, "National Brands/National Body."
26. On the history of the Gay Pride parade, see D'Emilio, *Sexual Politics, Sexual Communities*.
27. See Ross, *No Respect*.
28. See Richard Herrell, "Symbolic Strategies." Herrell discusses how Chicago politicians annually assume at the parade pseudo-Irish last names, such as "Mayor Richard O'Daley." The stigma attached to various cultural groups might well be discerned by such a litmus test: The unthinkable prospect of "Mayor Richard Gayley" suggests that there is, as yet, no such thing as "honorary" symbolic homosexuality.

In parades through urban American downtowns, Queer Nationals often chant, "We're here, we're queer, we're not going shopping." But shopping itself provides the form of a tactic when Queer Nation enters another context: The Queer Shopping Network of New York and the Suburban Homosexual Outreach Program (SHOP) of San Francisco have taken the relatively bounded spectacle of the urban pride parade to the ambient pleasures of the shopping mall. "Mall visibility actions" thus conjoin the spectacular lure of the parade with Hare Krishna-style conversion and proselytizing techniques. Stepping into malls in hair-gelled splendor, holding hands and handing out fliers, the queer auxiliaries produce an "invasion" that conveys a different message: "We're here, we're queer, *you're* going shopping."

These miniature parades transgress an erotically, socially, and economically complex space. Whereas patrons of the straight bar, at least, understand its function in terms of pleasure and desire, mall-goers invest in the shopping mall's credentials as a "family" environment, an environment that "creates a nostalgic image of [the] town center as a clean, safe, legible place."[29] In dressing up and stepping out queer, the Network uses the bodies of its members as billboards to create what Mary Ann Doane calls "the desire to desire."[30] As Queer Shoppers stare back, kiss, and pose, they disrupt the antiseptic asexual surface of the malls, exposing them as sites of any number of explicitly sexualized exchanges—cruising, people-watching, window-shopping, trying on outfits, the purchasing of commodities, and having anonymous sex.[31]

The inscription of metropolitan sexuality in a safe space for suburban-style normative sexual repression is just one aspect of the Network's critical pedagogy. In addition, mall actions exploit the utopian function of the mall, which connects information about commodities with sensual expressivity and which predicts that new erotic identities can be sutured to spectacular consuming bodies. The Queer Shopping Network understands the most banal of advertising strategies: sex sells. In this case, though, sex sells not

---

29. See Anne Friedberg, "Flaneurs du Mal(l)," *PMLA* 106 (May 1991): 419–31. Whereas Friedberg analyzes the mall as theater, an illusory and ultimately nonparticipatory realm, we would argue that "mall erotics" extend beyond the consumer/commodity exchange she describes to include visual consumption of other people as products.

30. Mary Ann Doane, *The Desire to Desire* (Bloomington: Indiana University Press, 1987).

31. A letter in *Raunch* reveals that Southglenn Mall in Denver, Colorado, where guess-which-one-of-us hung out every Saturday for her entire adolescence, also used to contain one of the best arrays of glory holes in the country. Imagine my delight. Boyd McDonald, *Raunch* (Boston: Fidelity Publishing, 1990).

substitutions for bodily pleasures—a car, a luxury scarf—but the capacity of the body itself to experience unofficial pleasures. While the Network appears to be merely handing out another commodity in the form of broadsides about homosexuality, its ironic awareness of itself as being on display links gay spectacle with the window displays that also entreat the buyers. Both say "buy me"; but the Queer Shopping Network tempts consumers with a commodity that, if they could recognize it, they already own: a sexually inflected and explicitly desiring body. Ultimately, the mall spectacle addresses the consumer's own "perverse" desire to experience a different body and offers *itself* as the most stylish of the many attitudes on sale in the mall.

Queer Nation exploits the mall's coupling of things and bodies by transgressively disclosing that this bounded, safe commercial space is also an information system where sexual norms and cultural identities are consolidated, thus linking it with Queer Nation's final frontier, the media. As it enters the urban media cacophony, Queer Nation scatters original propaganda in the form of graffiti, wheatpasted posters, and fliers into existing spaces of collective, anonymous discursive exchange. While the mall circulates and exchanges bodies, print media circulates and exchanges information in the most disembodied of spaces. Queer Nation capitalizes on the abstract/informational apparatus of the media in a few ways, refunctioning its spaces for an ongoing "urban redecoration project" on behalf of gay visibility.[32] First, it manipulates the power of modern media to create and to disseminate cultural norms and other political propaganda: QN leeches, we might say, onto the media's socializing function. Second, QN's abundant interventions into sexual publicity playfully invoke and resist the lure of monumentality, frustrating the tendency of sexual subcultures to convert images of radical sexuality into new standards of transgression.

In addition to manufacturing its own information, Queer Nation's mass mediation takes on a more ironic "Madison Avenue" mode, "queering" advertisements so that they become vehicles of protest against and arrogations of a media that renders queerness invisible, sanitary, or spectacularly fetishized. More ambiguous than the tradition of political defacement from which it descends—feminist spray-painting of billboards with phrases like "this offends women," for example[33]—Queer Nation's glossy pseudo-advertisements involve replication, exposure, and disruption of even the

32. We first heard this phrase at Queer Nation Chicago, Spring 1991.
33. See Jill Posener's photoessay on the British and Australian feminist billboard spray-painting movement, in *Louder than Words* (New York: Pandora Press, 1986).

semiotic boundaries between gay and straight. The group's parodies and reconstructions of mainstream ads inflect products with a sexuality and promote homosexuality as a product: They lay bare the queerness of the commodities that straight culture makes and buys, either translating it from its hidden form in the original or revealing and ameliorating its calculated erasure. In short, the most overtly commercial of Queer Nation's campaigns, true to the American way, makes queer good by making goods queer.

One form this project takes is an "outing" of corporate economic interest in "market segments" with which corporations refuse to identify explicitly. The New York Gap series changes the final *P* in the logo of stylish ads featuring gay, bisexual, and suspiciously polymorphous celebrities to a *Y*. For the insider, these acts "out" the closeted gay and bisexual semi-celebrities the Gap often uses as models. But the reconstructed billboards also address the company's policy of using gay style to sell clothes without acknowledging debts to gay street style: Style itself is "outed," as are the straight urban consumers who learn that the clothes they wear signify gay.

Whereas the Gap ads confront both the closetedness of a corporation and the semiotic incoherence of straight consumer culture, another series addresses the class implications of advertising's complicity in the national moral bankruptcy. A series of parody Lotto ads exposes the similarities and differences between the national betrayal of poor and of gay citizens. The "straight" versions of a series of advertisements for New York's Lotto depict generic citizens of various assimilated genders and ethnicities, who voice their fantasies about sudden wealth underneath the caption "All You Need is a Dollar Bill and a Dream." The ads conflate citizenship and purchase, suggesting that working-class or ethnic Americans can realize the American dream through spending money. One of Queer Nation's parody ads shows an "ordinary citizen" in one of the frank, casual head-and-shoulders poses that characterize the real ads. The caption reads, "I'd start my own cigarette company and call it Fags." The Queer Nation logo appears, along with the slogan "All You Need is a Three-Dollar Bill and a Dream." Again, the ads link citizenship with capitalist gain, but the ironized American dream cliché also establishes the group's resistance to a liberal "gay business" approach to social liberation, in whose view capitalist legitimation neutralizes social marginality. QN recognizes that the three-dollar bill remains nonnegotiable tender. The transformed caption reveals that the lottery's fundamental promise does not hold true for the nation's gay citizens in terms of the freedom to pursue sexual pleasure, which costs more than any jackpot or bank account has ever amassed.

In posing as a countercorporation, a business with its own logo, corporate identity, and ubiquity, Queer Nation seizes and dismantles the privileges of corporate anonymity.[34] It steals the privilege that this anonymity protects, that of avoiding painful recrimination for corporate actions. As it peels the facade of corporate neutrality, Queer Nation reveals that businesses are people with political agendas, and that consumers are citizens to whom businesses are accountable for more than the quality of their specific products: Abstracting itself, Queer Nation embodies the corporation. The Lotto ad finally promises an alternative to the capitalist dream machine: Its Queer Nation logo, juxtaposed against the "All You Need is a Three-Dollar Bill and a Dream" caption, appeals to the consumer to invest in its own "corporate" identity.

The Queer Nation logo itself, then, becomes a mock twin to existing national corporate logos: Just as red, white, and blue "Buy USA" labels, yellow ribbons, and flag icons have, by commodifying patriotism, actually managed to strengthen it, so does the spread of Queer Nation's merchandise and advertising expand its own territory of promises.[35] Because Gap clothes and lottery fantasies confer identities as much as flag kitsch does, Queer Nation has the additional power to expose or transform the meaning of these and other commodities—not simply through the reappropriation that camp enacts on an individual level but through collective mimicry, replication, and invasion of the pseudo-identities generated by corporations, including the nation itself.

Queer Nation's infusion of consumer space with a queer sensibility and its recognition of the potential for exploiting spaces of psychic and physical permeability are fundamental to its radical reconstitution of citizenship. For in the end, an individual's understanding of himself as "American" and/or as "straight" involves parallel problems of consent and local control: Both identities demand psychic and bodily discipline in exchange

---

34. Paradoxically, actual corporations have in turn exploited Queer Nation's/Gran Fury's recognizable style to produce mock gay ads, such as the Kikit billboard, which portrays two "lesbians"—actually an androgynous heterosexual couple—kissing.

35. The *New York Times* devoted a full section to paid advertisements supporting the Persian Gulf invasion and to commercial ads linking patriotism with purchase. Included were an ad for a Steuben glass flag paperweight, a Bloomingdale's spread saluting fathers' "devotion to family and country alike," and—in the most sinister pun of our times (apart from, perhaps, "Saddamize Hussein")—a Saks Fifth Avenue ad with the caption "A woman's place is in the home of the brave and the land of the free" (*New York Times*, Sunday, 9 June 1991).

for the protection, security, and power these identities confer. If the official nation extracts public libidinal pleasure as the cost of political identity, queer citizenship confers the right to one's own specific pleasures. In the final analysis, America, understood not as a geographic but as a symbolic locus in which individuals experience their fundamental link to 250 million other individuals, is the most unbounded of the hyperspaces we have been describing. The official transformation of national identity into style—of flag into transvestite "flagness"—offers Queer Nation a seamless means of transforming "queerness" into a camp counternationality, which makes good on the promise that the citizen will finally be allowed to own, in addition to all the other vicarious bodies Queer Nation has for sale, his mighty real, his very own national body.

With *You* Out We're Nothing, and Beyond

We have territorialized Queer Nation and described the production of a queer counterpublic out of traditional national icons, the official and useful spaces of everyday life, the ritual places of typical public pleasure (parades, malls, bars, and bodies), and the collective identities consumers buy in the mode of mass culture. The effect of casting gay urban life and practices as ongoing and scandalously ordinary is simultaneously to consolidate a safe space for gay subjects and also to dislocate utterly the normative sexual referent. If nationality as a form of fantasy and practice provides a legal and customary account of why American citizens in the abstract are secure *as heterosexuals*, Queer Nation exploits the disembodied structure of nationality by asserting that xenophobia would be precisely an inappropriate response for a straight community to have toward gay Americans. By asserting that straight and gay publics are coextensive with Americans at large, QN shows that the boundaries that might secure distinctions between sexual populations are local (like neighborhoods), normative (like taxonomies), and elastic (like latex). But these distinctions, in any event, must not be considered national, and in this sense Queer Nation's relay between everyday life and citizens' rights seems fitting.

Yet if Queer Nation tactically engages the postmodernity of information cultures, cutting across local and disembodied spaces of social identity and expressivity to reveal the communication that already exists between apparently bounded sexual and textual spaces, the campaign has not yet, in our view, left behind the fantasies of glamour and of homogeneity that characterize American nationalism itself. We might comment on the mas-

culine apriori that dominates even Queer spectacle; we might further comment on the relative weakness with which economic, racial, ethnic, and
non-American cultures have been enfolded into queer counterpublicity.[36] In
short, insofar as it assumes that "Queer" is the only insurgent "foreign"
identity its citizens have, Queer Nation remains bound to the genericizing
logic of American citizenship and to the horizon of an official formalism—
one that equates sexual object choice with individual self-identity. We concede the need to acknowledge the names people use for themselves, even
when they originate in the service of juridical and medical discipline. Popular forms of spectacle and self-understanding are crucial for building mass
cultural struggle. But it is not enough to "include" women, lesbians, racial
minorities, and so on in an ongoing machine of mass counternationality.
Achieving the utopian promise of a Queer Symbolic[37] will involve more than
a story of a multicultural sewing circle sewing the scraps of a pink triangle
onto the American flag, or turning that flag, with its fifty times five potential
small pink triangles, into a new desecrated emblem; more than a spectacle
of young hard girl/woman flesh outing the pseudo-abstraction of masculine
political fantasy. Queer culture's consent to national normativity must itself
be made more provisional.

We have argued that America has already become marked by a
camp aesthetic in the nineties. Camp America enrages, embarrasses, and
sometimes benignly amuses official national figures and gives pleasure to
the gay, the African American, the feminist, and the left-identified communities who understand that to operate a travesty on the national travesty is
to dissolve the frame that separates national fantasy from ordinary bodies.
But the verb *dissolve* is a temporal fantasy, of course: Tactical interventions, such as Dred Scott's flag doormat in Chicago's Art Institute or Kelly

36. Charles Fernandez, "Undocumented Aliens in the Queer Nation," *Out/Look* 12 (Spring
1991): 20–23.

37. Our reference to a "Queer Symbolic" follows Berlant's analysis of the official "National
Symbolic," which coordinates political affect in American life and extends the notion of a
political counter-lexicon to the current practices of Queer Nation. The National Symbolic
is defined as "the order of discursive practices whose reign within a national space . . .
transforms individuals into subjects of a collectively held history. Its traditional icons, its
metaphors, its heroes, its rituals, and its narratives provide an alphabet for a collective consciousness or national subjectivity; through the National Symbolic, the historical
nation aspires to achieve the inevitability of the status of natural law, a birthright. This
pseudo-generic condition not only affects profoundly the citizen's subjective experience
of her/his political rights, but also of civil life, private life, the life of the body itself" (Berlant,
The Anatomy of National Fantasy, 20).

and Ronnie Cutrone's transformation of the flag into a sheet for polymorphous lovemaking in New York, have momentarily disintegrated national
abstractness by turning bodies into national art and actually making censorship law look silly. These gestures were potentially dangerous and legally
scandalous: But contained in museums/galleries, they depended on the
usual protections of free high "artistic" expression to purchase the right to
scandalize national iconography. At a time when existing laws against public and private sex are being newly enforced, the class distinction between
sexual art and sex practices must be replaced by an insurgent renaming of
sexuality *beyond* spectacle.

In other words, the exhibition of scandalous direct contact between
oppositional stereotypes of iconic America and its internally constructed
Others—say, between the "body" and the "nation"—solves as spectacle a
problem of representation and power that is conceptually much harder to
solve. But the indeterminate "we" from which we are writing, comfortable
on neither side of most taxonomies, seek to occupy a space of a more complexly dimensional sexuality and political identity than these simple sutures
suggest. This is, as Monique Wittig contends, not simply a question of "de-
dramatiz[ing] these categories of language. . . . We must produce a political
transformation of the key concepts, that is of the concepts which are strategic for us."[38] As a gesture toward mapping this unsanctioned terrain, let
us return to the problem of Sandra Bernhard: her pasty body wrapped in
the flag, her extremely (c)little "red corvette," and her desire to seduce
cathartically an African American woman through a lesbian erotics that manipulates sentimentality, national parody, and aesthetic distance. This final
seductive moment, when Bernhard "accidentally" stutters, "Without me/you
I'm nothing," is framed by the "you" she addresses to the audience in the
film's opening monologue. There, Bernhard wishes the impossible—that
"you," the disembodied, autoerotic spectator, would traverse the space of
aesthetic and celluloid distance to kiss her right "here," on a facial place
where she points her finger; no such contact with the audience happens in
the frame of the film. In the end, after the masquerade, the racial, regional,
ethnic, and class drag, and during the American striptease, the film stages
a response that goes beyond the star's original request: the generic black-
woman-in-the-audience about whom the film has periodically fantasized in

38. Monique Wittig, "The Straight Mind," in *Out There: Marginalization and Contemporary Cultures*, ed. Russell Ferguson, Martha Gever, Trinh T. Minh-ha, and Cornel West
(Cambridge: MIT Press, 1990), 51–57.

nonnarrative, naturalistic segments writes on the café table with a lipstick, "FUCK SANDRA BERNHARD." This syntactically complex statement—a request, a demand, and an expletive—situates the black woman as an object of desire, as an author of feminine discourse, and as an image of the film's hopelessly absent audience: Her proximity to Bernhard's final lesbian-nationalist striptease thus suggests neither a purely sentimental "essential-ist" lesbian spectacle, nor a postmodern consumer feminine autoerotics, nor a phallocentrically inspired lust for lesbian "experience," but all of these, and more.

In this encounter, Bernhard tries to merge national camp with lesbian spectacle.[39] She produces scandalous erotic pleasure by undulating between the impossibility of laminating the flag onto her body and the equal impossibility of ever shedding the flag altogether: As she peels off her flag cape, she reveals three more in the form of a red, white, and blue sequined G-string and patriotic pasties, leaving us no reason to think that this exponential multiplication of flags would ever reach its limits. This undulation of the body and the flag, which eroticizes the latter as it nationalizes the former, is coterminous with the tease and the denial of the cross-race, homoerotic address to her consumer—the black-woman-in-the-audience. That is to say, the political liberation the flag promises and the sexual liberation its slipping off suggests makes a spectacle of the ambiguity with which these subjects live American sexuality.

Bernhard's refusal to resolve her feminine and sexual identities into a lesbian love narrative also illustrates how the eroticization of female spectacle in American public culture frustrates the political efficacy of transgressive representations for straight and lesbian women. The film imagines a kind of liberal pluralistic space for Bernhard's cross-margin, cross-fashion fantasy of women, but shows how lesbophobic that fantasy can be, insofar as it requires aesthetic distance—the straightness of the generic white woman-identified-woman—as a condition of national, racial, *and* sexual filiation. Her desire for acceptance from the black-woman-in-the-audience perpetuates the historic burden black women in cinema have borne to represent embodiment, desire, and the dignity of suffering on behalf of white

---

39. We have been orally instructed on the genealogy of camp counterpolitics and its intersection with radical sexuality by Richard Herrell and Pam Robertson. For textual support, see Esther Newton, *Mother Camp: Female Impersonators in America* (Chicago: University of Chicago Press, 1979); Ross, *No Respect*; and Pamela Robertson, "Guilty Pleasures: Camp and the Female Spectator" (unpublished manuscript, University of Chicago, 1990).

174

women, who are too frightened to strip themselves of the privileges of white heterospectacle. Thus, in addition, the rejection Bernhard receives from the black-woman-in-the-audience demonstrates the inability of cinematic public spectacle to make good on its teasing promise to dignify feminine desire in any of its forms. Bernhard's inability to bridge the negativity of anyone's desire focuses the lens on female spectacle itself, staging it as a scene of negativity, complete with producer, consumer, audience resistance, and the representation of multiple and ambiguous identifications.

The failed attempt to represent and to achieve a lesbian/national spectacle foregrounds the oxymoronic quality of these two models of identification. In the remainder of this essay, we mean to explain how this failure to conflate sexual and political spectacle can provide material to transfigure Queer as well as American Nationality—not to commandeer the national franchise for our particular huddled masses but instead to unsettle the conventions that name identity, frame expressivity, and provide the taxonomic means by which populations and practices are defined, regulated, protected, and censored by national law and custom. Lesbian national spectacle emerges here as the measure of a transitory space, a challenge to revise radically the boundaries of the normative public sphere and its historical modes of intelligibility, among which are male homosociality, a very narrowly defined set of public "political" interests, and garbled relations between politics and affect.[40] We understand that to define sexual expressivity as public political speech, and to resist censorship by expanding the range of erotic description, is simultaneously to exercise a fundamental privilege of American citizenship and to risk forsaking the refuge of camp. These are risks that queers/Americans cannot afford to pass on. Indeed, the question of whether female/lesbian sexuality can come into any productive contact with the political public sphere is a founding problem of lesbian political writing of the last fifteen years, and this problem is a problem for us all, by which we refer to "us" Queers and "us" Americans.

Female subjects are always citizens in masquerade: The more sexual they appear, the less abstractable they are in a liberal corporeal schema. Lesbian theory's solution to this dilemma has been to construct *imaginable* communities, which is to say that America's strategies for self-promotion have not worked for lesbians, who have historically and aesthetically often

40. For an aligned project, see Scott Tucker, "Gender, Fucking, and Utopia," *Social Text* 27 (1991): 3–34.

embraced the "space-off" in expatriate expression of their alienation from America.[41] The female body has reemerged in the safe spaces of lesbian political theory outside of the political public sphere, in tribal structures that emphasize embodied ritual and intimate spectacle as a solution to the indignities women, and especially lesbians, have had to endure. The blinking question mark beside the word *nation* in Jill Johnston's separatist *Lesbian Nation*; the erotogenic metamorphoses of the body, sex, and knowledge on the island of Monique Wittig's *The Lesbian Body*; and even the personal gender performances central to Judith Butler's sexual self-fashioning in *Gender Trouble* all reveal an evacuation of liberal nationality as we know it.[42] But for what public?

Separatist withdrawal into safe territories free from the male gaze secures the possibility of nonpornotropic embodiment in everyday life and aesthetic performance by emphasizing intimacy, subjectivity, and the literally local frame.[43] We do not mean to diminish the benefits of separatist expatriation: In its great historical variety, separatist withdrawal has expressed a condition of political contestation lesbians and gays already experience in America and has used the erotics of community to create the foundation of a different franchise. However, by changing the locus of spectacle—transporting it over state lines, as it were—lesbian theory has neglected to engage the political problem of feminine spectacle in mass society. Even Butler's metropolitan polymorphous solution to the politics of spectacle limits the power of transgression to what symbolic substitution on the individual body can do to transform custom and law. And as Queer Nation has shown us, no insistence on "the local" can secure national intimacy and national justice, where spectacle is intimacy's vehicle, and the vehicle for control. If the spectacle of the body's rendezvous with the flag has seemed to yoke unlike things together, the distance between persons and collective identities must also be read not only as a place to be filled up by fantasy but as a

41. See Teresa de Lauretis, *Technologies of Gender* (Bloomington: Indiana University Press, 1987), and Bertha Harris, "The More Profound Nationality of Their Lesbianism: Lesbian Society in the 1920's," in *Amazon Expedition: A Lesbian Feminist Anthology*, ed. Phillis Birky et al. (New York: Times Change, 1973), 77–88.
42. Judith Butler, *Gender Trouble* (New York: Routledge, 1990); Jill Johnston, *Lesbian Nation* (New York: Simon and Schuster, 1973); Monique Wittig, *The Lesbian Body*, trans. David Le Vay (Boston: Beacon Press, 1986).
43. Hortense J. Spillers, "Mama's Baby/Papa's Maybe: An American Grammar Book," *Diacritics* 17 (Summer 1987): 65–81.

negative space, a space where suddenly the various logics of identity that circulate through American culture enter into relations of contradiction and not simple analogy.

Along this axis, the negativity of national life for nonwhite and/or nonmale queers has reemerged in a more radical diacritic, the queer fanzine.[44] We move away from the word *lesbian* and toward these descriptions of negative identity because it is this space—the space of nonidentification with the national fantasy of the white male citizen—that is both the symptom of even "queered" Enlightenment nationality and also the material for its refunctioning. As a rule, underground fanzines make explicit their refusal of a property relation to information and art, repudiating the class politics of mainstream gay for-profit journals, like *The Advocate* and *Outweek*, and shunning the mock Madison Avenue production values of Queer Nation, Gran Fury, and ACT UP.[45] BIMBOX writes that the magazine is free because "the truth is, you have already paid for BIMBOX. We have all paid for it—dearly. We have paid for it in blood and we have paid for it in tears. Unrelenting pain is our credit limit, and we are cursed with interminable overdraft protection."[46] Xerox collage, desktop publishing, and other phototechniques have combined in a medium of comic and political communication, whose geographically isolated examples have converged into the infocultural version of the tribe, a network.[47] Thus, the contest over the territory of the Queer Symbolic has resulted in what Bitch Nation, a manifesto in the Toronto fanzine BIMBOX, calls a civil war.

The fanzines' only shared identity is in their *counterproductivity*—a multifold mission they share with other sexual radicalisms to counter American and Queer National cultures' ways of thinking about political tactics

44. Citational proprieties in the "University of Chicago Style" are both inappropriate and virtually impossible with regard to the zines. Here is a selected list of those we consulted to make these generic observations: *BIMBOX* 2 (Summer 1990); *Don't Tell Jane and Frankie* (undated); *Dumb Bitch Deserves to Die* 2 (Winter 1989); *The Gentlewomen of California* 6 (undated); *Holy Titclamps* 6 (Fall 1990); *Homoture* 2 (undated); *Manhattan Review of Unnatural Acts* (undated); *Negativa* 1–3 (March–May 1991); *No World Order* (1990); *Screambox* 1 and 2 (November 1990, May 1991); *Sister/My Comrade* (Winter 1991); *Taste of Latex* 4 (Winter 1990–1991); *Thing* 4 (Spring 1991).
45. See Crimp and Rolston, *AIDS DEMO GRAPHICS.*
46. *BIMBOX* 2 (Summer 1990).
47. In May 1991, the Randolph Street Gallery of Chicago hosted the first international queer fanzine conference called "SPEW: The Homographic Convergence."

and sexual intelligibility.[48] In the first place, the zines show that "obscenity" itself is political speech, speech that deserves constitutional protection: Transforming "the American flag into something pleasant," Sondra Golvin and Robin Podolsky's "Allegiance/Ecstasy" turns "i pledge allegiance" into an opportunity to add "my cunt helplessly going molten," "her clit swelling to meet my tongue," "my fist knocking gently at her cunt" to the national loyalty oath.[49] Additionally, the zines have widened the semantic field of sexual description, moving sexual identity itself beyond known practical and fantastic horizons—as when BIMBOX imagines "fags, dykes, and USO's (*Unidentified Sexual Objects*)." But they are also magazines in the military sense, storehouses for the explosives that will shatter the categories and the time-honored political strategies through which queers have protected themselves. Queer counterspectacle might well be read as a means for aggressively achieving dignity in the straight world; in the zine context, however, these spectacles are also icons that require smashing. The suspicion of existing tactics and taxonomies runs deep: "Dykes against granola lesbians. Fags against sensitive gay men. And bitches against everyone else."[50]

Along with joining queer culture's ongoing politics of dirty words, then, some zines engage in what would seem to be a more perverse activity: the aggressive naming and negation of their own audience. If citizenship in the Queer Nation is voluntary and consensual, democratic and universalist in the way of many modern nationalisms, the application for citizenship in the Bitch Nation, for example, repudiates the promise of community in common readership, the privileges of a common language, and the safety of counteridentity. "And—don't even bother trying to assimilate any aspect of Bitch Nation in a futile attempt to make your paltry careers or lame causes appear more glamorous or exciting. We won't hesitate to prosecute—and the Bitch Nation court is now in session!!"[51] As Bitch Nation endangers the reader who merely quotes, abstracts, and appropriates zine culture, many zines engage in a consumer politics of sexual enunciation, forcing

48. Rubin, "Thinking Sex"; and Lisa Duggan, "Sex Panics," in *Democracy: A Project by Group Material*, ed. Brian Wallis (Seattle: Bay Press, 1990), 209–12.
49. Sondra Golvin and Robin Podolsky, "Allegiance/Ecstasy," *Screambox* 1 (November 1990): 20–21.
50. *Don't Tell Jane and Frankie*, no page number.
51. We understand the risk we take in citing *Bitch Nation* against its stated will. We look forward to our punishment at the hands of editrix G. B. Jones, who "takes her girls like Tylenol–2 at a time" (see *Don't Tell Jane and Frankie*).

the reader to see where she is situated, or to resituate herself politically and culturally: Thus, when the cover of *Thing* magazine proclaims that "She Knows Who She Is," it mobilizes the common gay use of the feminine pronoun in the ventriloquized voice of the woman's magazine to categorize "insiders" by attitude rather than by gender or sexual identity, disarming many different kinds of essentialism through arch indirect address.

This move to materialize the spectator as *different* from the spectacle with which she identifies has powerful political force for women, whose collective and individual self-representations are always available for embarrassment, and most particularly for lesbians, whose sexual iconography has been overdetermined by the straight porn industry. By reversing the direction of the embarrassment from the spectacle toward the spectator, the zines rotate the meaning of *consent*. In severing sexual identity from sexual expressivity, the spectacle talks dirty to *you*, as it were, and you no longer have the privilege to consume in silence, or in tacit unconsciousness of or unaccountability for your own fantasies. As *Negativa*, a Chicago lesbian fanzine, puts it, "What you looking at, bitch?" (see figure 1).

Linked complexly to the enigma of consensual sex is that of consensual nationality, which similarly involves theories of self-identity, of intention, and of the urge to shed the personal body for the tease of safe mutual or collective unboundedness. American and Queer National spectacle depend upon the citizen's capacity to merge his/her private, fractured body with a collectively identified whole one. Uncle Sam points his finger and says he wants *you* to donate your whole body literally and figuratively to the nation, and Queer Nation uses the allure of commercial and collective embodied spectacle to beckon *you* toward a different sort of citizenship. But the fanzines' postnational spectacle disrupts this moment of convergence: Just as *you*, the desiring citizen, enter the sphere of what appears to be mutual consent, an invisible finger points back at you. It unveils your desire to see the spectacle of homoculture without being seen; it embarrasses you by making explicit your desire to "enter" and your need for "permission" to identify; and it insists that you declare your body and your goods and that you pay whatever political and erotic duty seems necessary.

Thus, like Queer Nation, the zines channel submission and bitterness into anger and parody. Queer Nation and allied groups struggle to reoccupy the space of national legitimation, to make the national world safe for just systems of resource distribution and communication, to make it safe for full expression of difference and rage and sexuality. Parody and camp thus become the measure of proximity to the national promise, as well as

Figure 1. From *Negativa*, by AK Summers

180

the distance from access to its fulfillment. Gestures of anger, parody, and camp in the zine network, by contrast, represent a disinvestment in authenticity discourse that moves beyond the intelligibility of gender, of sexual object choice, and of national identity by cultivating a passionate investment in developing the negative for pleasure and politics. In their drive to embody *you,* the citizen/spectator/reader/lover, by negating your disembodiment, the zines represent the horizon of postpatriarchal and postnational fantasy.

Even in their most parodic manifestations, gestures of sexual and national intelligibility—both oppressive and emancipatory—are part of a process of making norms. The zines acknowledge the necessity, and also the reality, of stereotypical self-identity and at the same time try to do violence to normative forms that circulate in America. In staging the process by which stereotypes become hybrid forms, their clarifying function as sites of identity and oppression exhausted, the zines do more than deconstructively put the icon "under erasure."[52] The negated stereotype remains available: Mass politics requires a genuinely populist currency. But the stereotype is expensive. The fanzines' gestures in countering national political sovereignty, then, lead us in another direction. They suggest a space of politics in which to be "out" in public would not be to consent parodically to the forms of the political public sphere but to be *out beyond* the censoring imaginary of the state and the information culture that consolidates the rule of its names. We support Queer Nation and ACT UP's commitment to occupy as many hegemonic spaces as possible in their countering moves. What we seek to describe, in addition, is the value in converting the space of negativity that distinguishes Queer American identity into a discursive field so powerful that the United States will have to develop a new breed of lexical specialists to crack the code of collective life in a hot war of words about sex and America, about which the nation already finds itself so miserably— and yet so spectacularly—archaic.

52. On the national stereotype and hybrid identities, see Homi K. Bhabha, "The Other Question: Difference, Discrimination and the Discourse of Colonialism," in *Out There,* 71–87.

Engendering Paranoia in Contemporary Narrative

Patrick O'Donnell

Paranoia is one of the more prominent issues taken up by contemporary North American novelists since 1960. Writers as divergent in matters of style and subject as Norman Mailer, Philip Roth, Joseph Heller, Robert Coover, Thomas Pynchon, Diane Johnson, Joseph McElroy, John Barth, Kathy Acker, Saul Bellow, Marge Piercy, Don DeLillo, William Gaddis, Ishmael Reed, and Margaret Atwood have represented paranoid characters, communities, schemes, and lifestyles; history, technology, religion, patriarchy, and bureaucracy have all been viewed as motivated systems that oppress the masses and disenfranchise the preterite. Of course, to generate a list of writers who, despite their differences, seem mysteriously to agree to represent *paranoia* as a way of knowing or acting in their fiction is a paranoid act, especially if one were to argue that this is the result of the operation of some manipulated cultural paradigm (conceived by whom? enforced by what agency?). Paranoia, like power after Foucault, ranges across the multi-discursivity of contemporary existence; it is as present in most of the current debates over canonicity and cultural literacy as it was in the debates about the "domino theory" that took place during the Vietnam War and that recur with disturbing frequency in American foreign policy.

For the purposes of this essay, I will refer to *cultural paranoia* as an intersection of contiguous lines of force—political, economic, epistemological, ethical—that make up a *dominant reality* (or *episteme,* or *paradigm,* or *habitus,* or *structure of feeling*) empowered by virtue of the connections to be made between materiality, as such, and the fictional representations or transformations of that materiality which come to affect its constitution.[1] In my definition, cultural paranoia is not content but method: a way of seeing the multiple stratifications of reality, virtual and material, as interconnected or networked. In essence, this is to use a paranoid method (seeking the meeting point between political and epistemological lines of force) to elucidate the paranoia of contemporary narrative. However limited and self-enclosed it may be, looking at paranoia in this way partially reveals (and partially conceals) the nature of the compact and the engendering of paranoia as an element that partakes of and informs a contemporary American ideology.

Since paranoia has so much to do with the mystified, hegemonic enactments of power, the representation of paranoia in the artificial plots of fiction can, indeed, be seen as a site where epistemology and ideology meet. As a way of knowing, paranoia is a mode of perception that notes the connectedness between things in a hyperbolic metonymizing of reality. It can be conflated with—is the mirror image of—the more blatant monolithic and incorporative aspects of "late capitalism," defined by Fredric Jameson as a "world system" whose features include the emergence of "transnational business[,] . . . the new international division of labor, a vertiginous new dynamic in international banking and the stock exchanges (including enormous Second and Third World debt), new forms of media interrelation-

---

1. The familiar terms I cite here are lifted at large from a heterogeneous assortment of social and critical texts/authors: thus, *episteme* comes from Foucault; *paradigm* from Kuhn; *habitus* from Bourdieu; and *structure of feeling* from Raymond Williams. What is interesting in this assortment is the number of terms that have, of necessity, it seems, been invented to describe a cultural dominant; conceivably, doing so is, in itself, a paranoid activity that assumes there is one or more forms of thought and action that can be said to characterize a culture. Tautologically, these ways of thinking about thought and action—much as they critique whatever forms of cultural and discursive dominance they describe—are (self-admittedly, for many of these critics) produced by and within them. This, I will argue, is also the case for those novels I discuss that both critique paranoia, or represent it as liminal, "outside the system," and, at the same time, *produce* paranoia.

ship (very much including transportation systems such as containerization), computers and automation, the flight of production to Third World areas."[2] The conflation of epistemology and politics in cultural paranoia is particularly pressing, as I will show, when apparent forms of resistance to political or narrative systems actually comply with the evolving story of hegemony. The romanticized opposition to cultural domination, for example, in which the individual perceives him- or herself to be part of a community of underground men and women opposed to the dominant culture, becomes, in novels of cultural paranoia, the disguised infiltration of that culture into every hidden corner of contemporary existence. There is complicity here, as well as connection. In the work of four male writers—Norman Mailer's *Executioner's Song*, Thomas Pynchon's *Crying of Lot 49*, Don DeLillo's *Running Dog*, and Joseph McElroy's *Lookout Cartridge*—I will discuss these manifestations of paranoia as means to transforming information into knowledge and to formulating identity as part of a paranoid community. Alternatively, Diane Johnson's work, *The Shadow Knows*, poses a critique of the neat fit between cultural domination and paranoid preterition, our Puritan inheritance.[3] In the comparisons I draw between these authors, I will suggest how cultural paranoia arises from the construction of the "knowing" subject negotiated within our social and political economies.

1

In his revisionary view of Foucauldian notions of power, Jean Baudrillard writes of the "transparency principle" operative in a culture that pursues the following set of edicts: "Let everything be produced, be read, become real, visible, and marked with the sign of effectiveness; let everything be transcribed into force relations, into conceptual systems or into calculable energy; let everything be said, gathered, indexed and registered. . . . Ours is a culture of 'monstration' and demonstration."[4] In this arena of the "hyperreal," where information is capital, where performance replaces interpretation, and where the most valued form of mystification is the exultation of the

2. Fredric Jameson, *Postmodernism, or, The Cultural Logic of Late Capitalism* (Durham: Duke University Press, 1991), xix.
3. Sacvan Bercovitch, *The Puritan Origins of the American Self* (New Haven: Yale University Press, 1975). This work provides a comprehensive analysis of "Puritan" identity and its historical lineaments.
4. Jean Baudrillard, *Forget Foucault*, trans. Nicole Dufresne (New York: Semiotext(e), 1987), 21–22.

obvious, what I educe in work-in-progress to be the manifestation of cultural paranoia in contemporary narrative finds its true home.[5] If, following Baudrillard, everything is visible and marked by or transcribed into capitalized relations of force and energy, then paranoia becomes the means by which connections are forged between disparate material realms: Everything is known; everything is related; the anecdotal becomes the conspiratorial; accident becomes design. Further, paranoia, under these conditions, can be viewed as the binding force of the nation or the community: What brings people together, as it were, is the sense that they are the wary participants in an unfolding historical plot over which they have no control, but through which they gain visible identity as historically unified subjects.

Certainly the Mormon community of Provo, Utah—the community Norman Mailer describes in *The Executioner's Song*—is unified by the disciplinary spectacle of Gary Gilmore's trial and execution. The quiet streets of the western city suggest that Provo is a paragon of sanity, cleanliness, and order, "laid out in a checkerboard," with "very wide streets and a few buildings that were four stories high. It had three movie theaters. Two were on Center Street, the main shopping street, and the other was on University Avenue, the other shopping street. In Provo, the equivalent of Times Square was where the two streets crossed. There was a park next to a church on one corner and diagonally across was an extra-large drugstore."[6] Gary Gilmore, the murderer who made headlines by insisting upon his own execution, enters Provo as a wild card in a stacked deck; he is taken in by this sanitized community, only to contaminate it with acts of ambiguously random violence, killing two men on consecutive days—men who offer no resistance to the small-time robberies he is in the act of committing, suggesting that it was homicide, not robbery, that Gilmore was after in the first place. For the community of Provo, Gilmore's violent, unmotivated

5. Tentatively entitled *Always Connect: Cultural Paranoia in Contemporary American Fiction*. At this point, I do not trace the representation of paranoia in psychoanalytic theory since Freud's "Schreber" case; rather, I argue, in a limited sense, that it is the representation of a cultural perception of subject-object relations. Later work on this project, however, will attempt to make more explicit connections between cultural paranoia and the homophobia inherent in the Freudian representations of paranoia. The classic reflection on paranoia as a form of cultural representation can be found in Richard Hofstadter's "The Paranoid Style in American Politics," in *The Paranoid Style in American Politics and Other Essays* (New York: Alfred A. Knopf, 1965), 3–40.
6. Norman Mailer, *The Executioner's Song* (Boston: Little, Brown, 1979), 23; hereafter cited in my text as *ES*.

incursions can only be recontained in the plots and counterplots of legal proceedings, in the orderly (but, as it turns out, very messy) ritual of execution by rifle squad, and in the aftermath of the stories the community tells about Gilmore in an attempt to explain him.

Seemingly against his own rhetorical intentions, Mailer forges a myth out of this tabloid scenario. Apparently taking a hands-off attitude toward his subject, Mailer abnegates "himself" from *The Executioner's Song*. Posing as a transcriber who compiles Baudrillardian indexes of public "monstrations"—what everyone says and thinks about Gilmore—Mailer conveys the impression that the Gilmore story is a heteroglossiac fantasy, where we "hear" dozens of disparate voices and "see" a multiplicity of perspectives in the hundreds of hours of taped interviews (most of them not conducted by Mailer himself) with the story's principals. In this verbal collage, "Mailer's" function is to listen and to arrange; the arrangement itself appears to follow the historical lines of force and the sequential pattern of events as they unfold, unintruded upon by the authorial recording angel. Yet, who compares the intersection of Center Street and University Avenue in Provo to Times Square, that American carnivalesque site which Robert Coover exploited as the scene of ritual sacrifice in his parody of paranoia, *The Public Burning*, and who thus, implicitly, tags Gilmore as sacrificial victim-to-be? Who surveys the order of these streets? Who divides the novel's voices into its two books, entitled "Eastern Voices" and "Western Voices" (clearly a play on Cold War politics, as well as on traditional American geopolitical polarities)? As in *Why Are We in Vietnam?* Mailer seems compelled to fabricate parallels between the anecdotal (for *The Executioner's Song* is, above all, a compendium of anecdotes about Gary Gilmore) and the historical, thus converting the subject of contingent events into the subject of history, the focal point of its patterns and orders. These, in Mailer's antihermeneutic epistemology, are ultimately unknowable and uninterpretable, but they exist nevertheless, and we are the subjects/victims of their ravelings.

Gilmore passes easily from cipher to symbol as the novel progresses, and in the end, it makes no difference who or what Gilmore is or has been. When he becomes a public spectacle—the disciplinary subject of *The Executioner's Song*'s history—he also becomes public property; his words, letters, poems, thoughts, and memories are fully capitalized. In Mailer's hands, Gilmore, publicized like Marilyn Monroe or Jack Abbot, becomes what can be made of him; passing into a spectacular history, these characters are transformed into fluid identities subject to rates of exchange as they become the symbolic reservoirs of public consensus. What first appears to be Gilmore's contingent, accidental identity is increasingly given over to a conception of Gilmore as the fated punisher/victim of Mormon theodicy (or, if one wishes, in more secular terms, of post–Vietnam War America).

It turns out, for example, that Gary Gilmore and his girlfriend, Nicole Baker, both own Ford Mustangs of exactly the same model and year; Gary has his painted blue to match Nicole's after they meet. Jim Barrett, one of Nicole's former husbands, leaves Provo for "Cody, Wyoming, with a friend of his also named Barrett," at the same time that Nicole finds a house in Spanish Fork, where she will briefly share her life with Gilmore, "like something funky out of a fairy tale" (*ES*, 117). Nicole's mother, Kathyrine, is the spitting image of her half-sister, Kathy. Ida Damico has a twin sister, Ada, who is deceased. Max Jensen, the gas station attendant Gilmore kills, has a sister and a wife who share the same name—Colleen. Gibbs, Gilmore's cellmate in the Logan County Jail, has "a kid sister living in Provo who was married to a fellow named Gilmore" (*ES*, 367). The maiden name of Grace McGinnis, a dedicated teacher who attempts to help Gary's brother avoid the family curse of violence and early death, is Gilmore. And so on: The doublings and repetitions of the novel begin to add up to something—a "synchronicity," as Mailer titles one of the chapters. The word *paranoid* is used not only in reference to Gilmore, who may be so because of massive doses of Prolixin given to him in prison, but also in reference to Brenda Nicol, Gary's cousin (note that her last name is the same as the first name of Gary's lover), to Nicole herself, to her former husband Kip, to her sister April, to Gilmore's mother Bessie, to Debbie Bushnell on the day of her husband's death, to Gibbs, to John Woods, one of Gilmore's psychologists, and so on. Paranoia is contagious in *The Executioner's Song*, and almost every one of its dozens of characters is afflicted with it at some point or another. Moreover, it seems that almost everyone—from the soft-brained Dennis Boaz, who first attempts to break the Gilmore story and who specializes in esoterica and believes in obscure theories of numerology, to the most hard-nosed reporter in the field—has some sense that things are happening according to some kind of plan or pattern. Theories about reincarnation, the conspiracy of Mormonism, prison surveillance systems, and remarkable historical parallels (e.g., George Latimar, chairman of the Utah Board of Pardons, which will decide upon Gilmore's execution, turns out to have been the chief civilian defense attorney in the Lt. William Calley trial) are conflated to such an extent in the novel that it would be nearly impossible *not* to think that Gilmore is more than he appears to be, that he stands at the crossroads of events converging upon the apocalyptic, nihilistic, media-made postmodern antihero.

Bolstering this conception, Mailer represents the community of Provo as engaging in identical speech-acts in reference to Gilmore, almost as if, despite the variety of speakers, his presence generates a common, homogeneous language issuing from a single communal body—this, clearly in contrast to the hundreds of recorded voices one "hears" in the novel. Mont Court, Gilmore's probation officer, describes Gilmore as "supernice" and himself as "neither a hard-nose, nor superheat" (*ES*, 53); Spencer McGrath, Gary's boss, notes that Gary and Nicole seem to be in "super-good shape" (*ES*, 63–64); Pete Galovan, a Mormon missionary, suffers from "superexcitement" (*ES*, 130); Gary tells Nicole a "supergross" prison story (*ES*, 141); April is "superfreaky" (*ES*, 166); Nicole feels "double-loyal" to Gary and regards Roger Eaton, another lover, as "superclean" and "supersweet" (*ES*, 177); Dean Christiansen, Ben Busnell's bishop, bears a "super-Mormon" name (*ES*, 258); Gilmore describes events in a letter as "supershitty" (*ES*, 360); Jerry Scott, a prison guard, resents the fact that everyone is "extra nice" to Gilmore (*ES*, 448); Kip, Nicole's former husband, regards her as a "super chick" who is "superdaring" (*ES*, 514); Dennis Boaz regards Barry Farrell, soon to be Schiller's co-writer on the Gilmore story, as a "superpipeline" (*ES*, 629); and Gilmore, in an interview, suggests that "you don't have to be superintelligent to get away with shit" (*ES*, 798).

This collation of coincidental tic and expression into communal grammar is evidence of the "overvoice" of *The Executioner's Song*, and it reflects what I take to be the insertion of Mailer's intention—more pointedly, his paranoid authorial presence—into events that otherwise would appear to be random. Mailer is the orchestrator here, the one who generates a narrative recording machine whose narrator takes clear note of these communal speech patterns and amazing coincidences, even if he refuses to comment on them. Indeed, merely "taking note," in these instances, is a form of commentary exhibiting a belief in synchronicity, in the fatality of systems and institutions that lead Gilmore to murder and that generate Gilmore as the exemplary subject of a disciplinary history. Even more, Mailer, through overvoicing, heroicizes Gilmore precisely because he sees in him someone who fulfills the wholly paranoid pattern of history that interests Mailer most: the oedipal pattern, in which the revolutionary, amoral son takes on not the father, in the usual sense, but the paternal system, attempts to overturn it, and then, in a contradictory act of submission and revolt, demands that the system keep its word and fulfill its mission by exacting just punishment from the former victimizer, and now victim, of that very system. For Mailer, in the most direct sense, these actions, whereby Gilmore becomes the central spectacle of a capitalist system's manifold and intersecting plots, are what gives his life and death a meaning: Gilmore, disciplined and commodified, brought out into the open and made obvious, is "worth something." Only in the egotism of the oedipal nightmare of Gilmore's life—a life spread over, as it were, the entire community of speakers in *The Executioner's Song*—can Mailer elicit, or, rather, *dub in,* the impression that this "true life story" makes sense.[7] For Mailer, the blending of individual voices into the communal voice is what makes Gilmore significant. In this way, the purported radicality of heteroglossia is made over into a cultural consensus that is technologized (put on tape) and commodified (inscribed in a best-selling novel), a process that confers authority upon this story comprised, precisely, *of* many transcribed voices.

In *The Executioner's Song*, a novel written in the aftermath of Vietnam, everyone—from Gilmore to the priest to whom he utters his last words—thinks that *Gilmore* must *mean* something, that he must be a sign of the design of a totalized cultural order. In Provo, it seems, there is really no random violence. The novel's communal consensus—its cultural paranoia—works in many ways and has many filiations, but perhaps most remarkable, particularly for the representation of cultural paranoia I will address later in Diane Johnson's work, *The Shadow Knows*, is its inherent and contradictory homophobia and homoeroticism. *The Executioner's Song* is, above all, a tale of verbal, legal, and monetary exchanges between men. The Gilmore story passes between reporters, from Dennis Boaz, to Larry Schiller, to Norman Mailer. In Provo, men confer death on each other: In exchange for the four bullets Gilmore intends to fire into his two male victims, four male riflemen shoot four bullets straight into his heart. He is punished, in the end, by the judges of the Mormon patriarchy and the United States Supreme Court. His tales of incarceration are replete, as one would expect, with examples of male rape and male eroticism in prison. Amidst the bevy of male exchanges of scripts, bullets, sentences, and semen, there is the figure of Nicole Baker, whom Gilmore frequently refers to as his "elf," and whose "promiscuity," in some minds, is what leads Gilmore to murder in the first place.

---

7. For a discussion of Mailerian romantic egotism in the realm of technology—a situation enacted in *The Executioner's Song* as "Gilmore" is rendered via tape recorder—see Joseph Tabbi, "Mailer's Psychology of Machines," *PMLA* 106 (1991): 238–50.

Gilmore is obsessed with the idea of possessing Nicole in life and death, to the extent that he talks her into a failed mutual suicide pact, and Boaz/Schiller/Mailer are obsessed with the idea of getting hold of Baker's letters to Gilmore—clearly not only because they are interested in their historical value. As the Gilmore story evolves in *The Executioner's Song*, Nicole Baker emerges as the object of scriptive and bodily exchanges in a world of violent, ambitious men: She is the medium and catalyst, as it were, for male rivalries that are acted out over her body and the sought-after texts of her letters and interviews. Gilmore reminds Nicole, whose voice, in the mind of the novel's narrative authority, "never stumbled when it told the truth," that in an early letter "you talk of climbing in my mouth and sliding down my throat with a strand of your hair to mend the worn spot in my stomach" (*ES*, 486–87; italics deleted). In this grotesque image, supposedly generated by Nicole herself, the female body becomes the consumable item of the cultural imaginary as Nicole is incorporated into Gilmore's soon-to-be executed body in the final spectacle of a paranoid semiotic regime.[8] In his afterword, Mailer notes that he has edited some of Gilmore's letters in order to match the expression with the quality of mind he senses in a man he, apparently, never met; on the other hand, he does not mention making even minor changes in Nicole's telegraphic and, often, ungrammatical letters. Baker, then, is one kind of transparency amongst many in *The Executioner's Song* whom men talk over or talk through in order to get at Gilmore, to determine the significance and nature of his act. Unlike Gilmore, who becomes "something" in the communal mind, Nicole remains a corporeal cipher, a siren across or for whose faintly homoerotic body men murder and punish each other. Mailer's version—his engendering—of cultural paranoia demands a kind of epistemology that explains and connects things together in a disciplinary pattern of law and order that governs the free-market economy in which Gilmore's story could be bought and sold. *The Executioner's Song* implicitly affirms Gilmore's decision to make the system keep its word about the train of male exchanges he has initiated: an eye for an eye, a tooth for a tooth, a bullet for a bullet. In this, the contradictions of Mailer's

8. The phrase "semiotic regime" is derived from the work of Gilles Deleuze and Félix Guattari, who refer to any semiotic system as a "regime of signs"; the paranoid regime of signs I discuss here would be for Deleuze and Guattari a "semiotic" regime, that is, a linguistic system that strives for tautological self-containment. See Deleuze and Guattari, "587 B.C.–A.D. 70: On Several Regimes of Signs," in *A Thousand Plateaus: Capitalism and Schizophrenia*, trans. Brian Massumi (Minneapolis: University of Minnesota Press, 1987), 111–48.

novel are most evident: Gilmore comes off as one of Mailer's existential criminal antiheroes—a figure of resistance that fouls up the system; yet, his acts call that very system to order: his freakishness (what Pynchon would call "ambiguity" and DeLillo "secrecy") is transformed into the human-izing, explanatory grammar of community consensus. Taking place in the far reaches of the new west, *The Executioner's Song* is a western story that articulates Gilmore as a leading symbol in the dominant cultural imaginary upon which systems of discipline and their victims depend and suffer. In Pynchon, DeLillo, and McElroy, this story takes on further dimensions as "a way of thinking about thinking," wherein the resistance to what Mailer represents as an oedipal cultural order (its oedipal nature suppressed in the scriptive labyrinths of these authors) becomes the means of its enabling.

2

Within the realm of the obvious, saturated by information overload, the paranoid subject is disempowered by virtue of the all-encompassing plots and systems that surround her; paradoxically, she is empowered as one in a growing army capable of reading the signs of these plots and power relations, not to resist or escape them but to formulate an ironic, streetwise attitude toward them. One knows she is part of a series of orches-trated events over which she has no control, but knowing it confers a kind of legitimacy upon the knower: She can be manipulated but she can't be fooled about being manipulated; she is always prepared for the revelation of deeper plots, more layered conspiracies.

This description approximates the situation of Oedipa Maas, pro-tagonist of Thomas Pynchon's *The Crying of Lot 49*. In the novel, Oedipa, co-executor of the vast Pierce Inverarity empire, slowly discovers that her powers of dispensation have been accompanied by both an insider's knowl-edge of an oppositional postal system and a cluster of marginalized com-munities—from Inamorati Anonymous, for those who are addicted to love and, thus, must live as isolates, to AC-DC, the Alameda County Death Cult. Increasingly sensitive to and suspicious of the proliferation of signs indica-tive of Trystero, a vast conspiratorial umbrella under which all the plots and sects she encounters operate, Oedipa drives the freeways of southern Cali-fornia and looks out upon endless suburbs that resemble Mailer's Provo: "a vast sprawl of houses which had grown up all together, like a well-tended crop, from the dull brown earth; and she thought of the time she'd opened a transistor radio to replace a battery and seen her first printed circuit."[9] In a Walpurgisnacht of revelations, she walks the streets of San Francisco observing the sign of the Trystero (a muted post horn) as the city lies spread out, anatomized: "The city was hers . . . she had safe passage tonight to its far blood's branchings, be they capillaries too small for more than peering into, or vessels mashed together in shameless municipal hickeys, out on the skin for all but tourists to see" (*TCL49*, 117).

Oedipa is trapped in the hermeneutic circle, arguably, the philosopher's trope for paranoia. She either possesses secret knowledge of an increasingly obvious conspiracy—thus assisting in its construal—and is the victim of sinister global machinations stretching across a millennium, or she is just another crazy housewife in suburban America victimized by a patriarchal culture that forces her to such extremes in the quest for articulation. She awaits, even as the novel ends, some final, apocalyptic revelation, "the direct, epileptic Word, the cry that might abolish the night" (*TCL49*, 118), and, a true child of the fifties, she is admirably prepared for her role in Pynchon's sardonic conflation of conservative politics and academic training: "Where were secretaries James and Foster and Senator Joseph, those dear daft numina who'd mothered over Oedipa's temperate youth? In another world. . . . Among them they had managed to turn the young Oedipa into a rare creature indeed, unfit for marches and sit-ins, but just a whiz at pursuing strange words in Jacobean texts" (*TCL49*, 104). In these characterizations, Oedipa becomes what might be termed the paranoid Cold War subject formed within the cybernetic economy of contemporary America. Literate, suspicious, and sensitive (like any good New Critic) to the subtleties of paradox and ambiguity, the more information Oedipa gathers, the more connections she finds, confirming her sense that she is part of some tangled network of linkages whose origins and ends ever recede into obfuscation as the information mounts. She is part of something bigger, and she appears to be taken in at the end—as are many of Pynchon's readers—by the promise of some singular revelation that will explain it all as she awaits the voice of the prophetic auctioneer, Loren Passerine, about to announce the sale of a lot of forged postage stamps.[10] Placed within this

9. Thomas Pynchon, *The Crying of Lot 49* (1966; reprint, New York: Harper & Row, 1986), 24; hereafter cited in my text as *TCL49*.
10. For an example of an interpretation of *The Crying of Lot 49* which argues that Oedipa is on the verge of a sacred revelation, see Edward Mendelson, "The Sacred, the Pro-

hushed roomful of buyers, shills, and hermeneuts (in a typical Pynchonian contradiction, a community of insiders—the power elite—oddly similar in its constitution to the preterite communities she has discovered in the streets), Oedipa is about to fulfill the promise of her upbringing: A daughter of Joe McCarthy, Oedipa will hear the word and fulfill the destiny of "the true paranoid for whom all is organized in spheres joyful or threatening about the central pulse of [her]self" (*TCL49*, 128–29).

Pynchon's infamous "ambiguity" prevents us from stabilizing any further the arcing contradictions of his vision in *The Crying of Lot 49*—a vision which, growing more complex in the encyclopedic narratives of *Gravity's Rainbow* and *Vineland*, thus accruing more material and information, has become the basis for an academic industry.[11] In a replay of the modern/postmodern dialectic, *The Crying of Lot 49* moves between the obfuscated mysteries of modernist symbolic depth and the surfaces of the contemporary "hyperreal." The inherent indeterminacies of this movement are analogous to Oedipa's confusion about whether she is really part of a labyrinthine plot or just making it all up: ambiguity and confusion, within the regime of a totalizing cultural paranoia and its attendant political consequences, comply with its advancement.[12] In Pynchon's contradictorily patent and suppressed engendering of paranoia, Oedipa is aptly named as the female questor in pursuit of the truth; she reduplicates, rather than subverts, the oedipal desire for a singular truth and an origin to the order of things. And Pynchon, himself, has taken on the peculiar role he assigns Oedipa in *The Crying of Lot 49*. Both a cult figure and a best-selling author, both liminal and at the center of that manifestation of the dominant culture labeled (by some) postmodernism, he has disappeared as an intentionality into the interpretive plots constructed for him by "well-meaning" critics. It is perfectly consistent with the logic of cultural paranoia that his invisibility as a public personality has served as an enticement for the proliferation of "information" about Pynchon, including apocryphal stories about his youth, insider's

fane, and *The Crying of Lot 49*," in *Individual and Community: Variations on a Theme in American Fiction*, ed. Kenneth Baldwin and David Kirby (Durham: Duke University Press, 1976), 182–222.

11. Thomas Schaub's *Pynchon: The Voice of Ambiguity* (Urbana: University of Illinois Press, 1981) offers the most far-reaching discussion of ambiguity in Pynchon.

12. I am indebted here to Donald Pease's arguments concerning the relation between modernist versions of indeterminacy and the "Cold War consensus" in his *Visionary Compacts: American Renaissance Writings in Cultural Context* (Madison: University of Wisconsin Press, 1987), 7–12.

gossip about his travels and his next novel, and privately circulated annotations to his works. Here, networks of communication and communities of informational exchange are formed around the conservation of the text and the mystified authorial source of the text's plots. Intentionally or not, he may be said in this way to foster paranoia, as well as to fabulate it.

The novels of Don DeLillo do not indulge in Pynchon's transitionally late modernist enjambments of ambiguity and circuitry; rather, as Tom LeClair has argued, DeLillo writes the novel of information systems, of Baudrillard's "hyperreal," where everything is visible and on the surface.[13] The tone of such works as *Libra*, *White Noise*, *The Names*, and *Running Dog* is jaded and anxious: Yes, everything is connected; yes, we are part of plots and systems of capital and informational exchange over which we have no control; no, there is nothing we can do about it, at least not in the usual senses of political engagement or resistance. In *Running Dog*, DeLillo presents the reader with an assemblage of crosshatched plots, secret agents, politicians, collectors of erotic art, and, supposedly, a secret pornographic film recording Hitler's sexual exploits during his last days in the bunker. All are red herrings in DeLillo's demystification of the romance of secrecy: Even the film of Hitler is a failure, as it records the maniac dictator at a children's birthday party playing the role of an avuncular clown. The monstrosity of this historical recording (these children are the ones who will die in the parental murder-suicides of the final moments in the bunker) is lost upon those who would vend it. Since this is the age of overexposure and pornography, the film is, Baudrillard would claim, just another example of the overwhelming "order of visible and calculable phenomena: objects, machines, sexual acts, or gross national product."[14] Everybody wants to see the formerly hidden, the opaque "private life" exposed; no one wants to see Hitler acting within a normalized familial framework: "Pornography is there," Baudrillard suggests, "only to reactivate th[e] lost referent in order to prove *a contrario*, by its grotesque hyperrealism, that there is however some *real* sex somewhere."[15]

The case is put clearly in a conversation between Moll Robbins, the female lead of *Running Dog* and a parodic recapitulation of Oedipa Maas, and Glen Selvy, a secret agent with multifarious political connections:

13. See Tom LeClair, *In the Loop: Don DeLillo and the Systems Novel* (Urbana: University of Illinois Press, 1987).
14. Baudrillard, *Forget Foucault*, 22.
15. Baudrillard, *Forget Foucault*, 15n. (Baudrillard's emphasis).

> "What is it like, secrecy? The secret life. I know it's sexual. I want to know this. Is it homosexual?"
>
> "You're way ahead of me," he said.
>
> "Isn't that why the English are so good at espionage? Or why they seem so good at it, which comes to the same thing. Isn't it rooted in national character?"
>
> "I didn't know the English controlled world rights."
>
> "To what?"
>
> "Being queer," he said.
>
> "No, I'm saying the link is there. That's all. Tendency finds an outlet. I'm saying espionage is a language, an art, with sexual sources and coordinates. Although I don't mean to say it so Freudianly.
>
> "I'm open to theorizing," he said. "What else do you have?"
>
> "I have links inside links. This is the age of conspiracy."
>
> "People have wondered."
>
> "This is the age of connections, links, secret relationships." [16]

In an age when sexuality is organized according to lines of force ("sources and coordinates"), even incorporated, secrecy is reconfigured as the obvious—the "always already" known—waiting to be mapped; "hiddenness" becomes merely the precondition for materialization. In this corporate environment, every form of human activity, including subversion and "theorizing," aspires to the condition of espionage. In this system, as we know from John LeCarré's sinister and cynical novels, patriotic and political affiliations are merely the cover for articulation and positioning within a single, vast "language" or monolithic system of communication devoted to obfuscating (in the contained processes of encoding and deciphering) the transparency of its signs.

As Baudrillard suggests, the hyperbolic referentiality and connectedness of a novel like *Running Dog* is due, in part, to a desire for "the real," for the materiality, or "worldliness," that lies behind all of the information. Like Baudrillard, DeLillo conceives of contemporary reality as a palimpsest of representations, so that, in the novel, any quest for the "real" Hitler results in the accumulation of the unprofitable representations of him that remain. In this and all of his novels, DeLillo seemingly offers an escape or alternative to the monolithic reign of cultural paranoia, just as Mailer offers oral consensus as complicit response to the machinery of the state, or as Pynchon

16. Don DeLillo, *Running Dog* (1978; reprint, New York: Vintage, 1979), 111; hereafter cited in my text as *RD*.

offers modernist ambiguity as a countereffect to postmodern cybernetic binarity. If everything is a matter of representation, the novel might argue, then perhaps (again, conceiving of paranoia as an epistemological issue) how we *see* representations can transform the nature of what Baudrillard terms the *reality effect*.

In *Running Dog*, a senator enmeshed in political conspiracies remarks to Moll that the moderator of a television show upon which he has recently been interviewed is "all image. . . . He's a bunch of little electronic dots, that's all he is" (*RD*, 31). The senator unwittingly suggests that one might undermine the overwhelming effects of televised images by regarding them not as reality, not even as representations of reality, but as what they are materially—transmissions of colored, electronic dots. DeLillo suggests that the de-totalization of representation, the replacement of the paranoid, macroscopic "hyperreal" with what Guattari and Deleuze refer to as the "rhizomic" or "molecular," the breaking down of the image into a series of "particles that do not divide without changing in nature," whose "movements are Brownian" and whose "quantities are intensities, differences in intensity" might be seen as an alternative to the paranoid activities of making connections in a punning reversal of "networking." [17] But, of course, we are culturally constrained to connect any dots we might see floating about; moreover, the dominance of the orders of representation in *Running Dog* (itself a form of representation in a late capitalist culture wherein its author is becoming more famous, more familiar as a representation, because of the success of his critiques *of* representation) suggests that the perceptual variations of de-totalization—essentially, parodies of representation—will be quickly reincorporated into another image connected with other images, providing a "view" of the real. Hence, DeLillo and Pynchon implicitly define the activity of subjectivity within paranoid political and epistemological orders as a form of resistance to totalization, but the very nature of the resistance itself—for Pynchon, preterition, for DeLillo, molecularization—is homologous to the formation of the repressive orders in the first place.

In Joseph McElroy's *Lookout Cartridge*, as in *Running Dog*, there is a futile quest for a missing film, purportedly a montage of "English life" rendered by the American filmmakers Cartwright and Daggar DiGorro. Cartwright, the novel's protagonist, searches for the experimental film amidst a labyrinthine assemblage of characters and plots, recalling its disjointed

17. Deleuze and Guattari, *A Thousand Plateaus*, 33.

sequences: a softball game played by American expatriates in an English park; a meeting of druids at Stonehenge; the social activities of a weekend at a circular English country house; a conversation between an American draft dodger and an anonymous friend in a bare room; the antics of vacationing Brits in Corsica. As Cartwright recounts the filming of each scene, he realizes that Dagger, who has also disappeared, has managed the casting and production in such a way that the same characters appear in widely scattered shots, seemingly, "meeting" in the film to exchange secret messages. Cartwright begins to suspect that Daggar is using the film as a way of communicating with co-conspirators in a political plot that may involve anything from the hiding of American war resisters to a terrorist attack upon a roomful of singing schoolchildren.

The outlines of *Lookout Cartridge* are familiar within the terms of cultural paranoia: Cartwright, like Oedipa Maas, processes masses of unassimilated information (about the Mayan calendar, Catherwood's explorations of Central America, techniques of film editing, Bunel's engineering feats, the nature of liquid crystals) only to discover that everything is connected to everything else, and that he is the subject or victim of a monolithic scheme whose ends, even and especially in acts of resistance, he unwittingly advances. While Pynchon and DeLillo portray, respectively, ambiguity and parody as forms of complicitous narrative resistance, McElroy fragments the narrative process itself, thereby framing the forced juxtapositions, displacements, and de-contextualizations of the avant-garde within the schematic of cultural paranoia. Cartwright's function in the novel is that of a "lookout cartridge," a technological advance over Mailer's author/transcriber, which, apparently, indiscriminately records everything within its range without filtering out background noise. While this allows for the possibility of random information and noise to seep through, for pure chance connections and patterns to emerge (the illusion created by a Pollock composition), Cartwright suggests that even the most spontaneous upsurge of event, text, noise, or response into the "inchoate" will result in design or geometry:

> And at this instant, hearing Sub [Cartwright's friend] come out of the kitchen and stand on the threshold of the littered living room and not speak, I found that though my power to prove my feeling about computers—about miles of memory, or abstract numbers switched out of the blue into the real angular turns of a machine or the actual relation of two electric currents—stirred inchoate though contained inside a circle of broken connections that could get long or short or

acquire right angles and stern diagonals while being still this circle of known emotions and words and people, my power to turn that inchoate into a statement was, as if half unwilled, finding itself in the new movements after the ruin of the film that my pulses from moment to moment were deciding to make.[18]

The style of this passage is characteristic of McElroy's novel: loose, rambling, and syntactically skewed. Yet, we see that Cartwright insists on the "half unwilled" systematizing of the instinctual, as if the human mind is constrained to convert the casual into the causal, the pulsings of spontaneity into statement and decision, as if, in short, it were a computer generating and assembling random numbers.

In ways more extreme than Pynchon or Mailer—the former relying upon postmodern indeterminacy, the latter upon the romance of consensus to cheat or "humanize" paranoia—McElroy, in *Lookout Cartridge*, portrays a thoroughly hegemonic universe, where the mirroring of human cognitive processes in technology (and vice versa) is so complete that it is impossible to tell where the mind ends and the machine begins. This cybernetic rendering of contemporary reality is familiar enough at this point with such cultural manifestations as the movie *Robocop* or Transformers, children's toys that can be converted from machine, to warrior, to machine again.[19] In the end, Cartwright finds pieces of the film and destroys them, possibly as a futile protest against the novel's tangled plots and against those who cultivate them, those for whom the film has served as code and courier. Cartwright concludes with a reflection about the contaminating, oddly nonegotistical nature of his retrospective paranoia: The "initial system highly improbably would indeed have yielded increasing probabilities, things coming together . . . but only if that system had to begin with one system and not many systems which I had to forget in the living, and whose multiple impingements I had easily imagined operating through me in the chance of my life but operating through this impure semiconductor like many parts of *me* or as through one terminal albeit moving. But that was not the case" (*LC*,

18. Joseph McElroy, *Lookout Cartridge* (1974; reprint, New York: Carroll & Graf, 1985), 214; hereafter cited in my text as *LC*.
19. For fascinating discussions of the cybernatization of contemporary literature and material culture, see Gabrielle Schwab, "Cyborgs and Intertexts: On Postmodern Phantasms of the Body and Mind," in *Intertextuality and Contemporary American Fiction*, ed. Patrick O'Donnell and Robert Con Davis (Baltimore: Johns Hopkins University Press, 1989), 191–213; and Donna Haraway, *Simians, Cyborgs, and Women: The Reinvention of Nature* (New York: Routledge, 1991).

525). For Cartwright, there is not one Trystero but an infinite number of plots crisscrossing each other, and not one Oedipa upon whom the whole plot impinges but hundreds of Oedipas working at different states of awareness on the local level. Things do not come together in *Lookout Cartridge*, yet the novel suggests that this de-centered form of paranoia, like the avant-garde film, serves analogous sinister ends because dominant political and ideological processes can proceed apace while the forces of resistance are relegated to the micropolitical tier. McElroy's novel equates epistemological specialization to complicity with assimilative cultural and political forces. In the narrowed range of the specialist's angle of vision (that of the scientist, anthropologist, or literary critic), it appears that he is at the center of over-lapping conspiracies, or that he is peering through layered complexities and getting at the underlying order of things; meanwhile, to personify, the larger political processes grind on, all too content to leave him the field.

I have been arguing that in these four dense, encyclopedic, highly allusive works, paranoia is represented as a way of coming to terms with a complex reality, but that the perceptual orders which evolve within the arena of our contemporary imperialistic and incorporative cultural environ-ment will reflect, as what is materially "there," its overarching designs; the nature and specificity of the designs themselves are inevitably obscured by the size and intricacy of the revealed plot or plots. What are, in fact, "literary" alternatives to the formation or finalization of plots—counterplot, heteroglossia, ambiguity, fragmentation, and encyclopedic inflation—result in the advancement of the plot. If the plot is, at once, narrative, economic, and political (and the works I have been discussing clearly insist on the conflation of these), then the double bind of the contemporary episteme I have been calling *cultural paranoia* becomes apparent. Traditional ways of knowing and perceiving, "deconstructed" in these recent novels, are shown to accommodate a political process—in the great American tradition of consensus—that assimilates, capitalizes, and homogenizes in the very obfuscation of that process all that falls outside its purview. So much, we might say, for the touted radicalism of the avant-garde, "multi-voicedness," the pragmatic "realism" of oral consensus and communities of belief, or the self-consciousness of experimental metafiction, were it not that these authors, arguably, forge a tautology to tell a truth about what that tautology does not include.

3

An alternative version of the causes and effects of contemporary cultural paranoia exists in Diane Johnson's largely ignored *The Shadow Knows*. In this work, Johnson, a Victorian scholar and author of several novels, a series of biographical sketches depicting the "lesser lives" of several nineteenth-century women, and a biography of Dashiell Hammett, portrays a woman continually beset by fears that she is about to be murdered. N., as the narrator refers to herself, is a recently divorced mother of four young children living in a low-rent housing district of north Sacramento and is pursuing a graduate degree in linguistics. In the midst of an affair with a married man, Andrew, N. is suddenly beleaguered with threats from an unknown assailant: The door to her house is battered with an ax, the window of her car is covered with vomit, and her companion and housekeeper, Ev, is physically assaulted in a laundry room. *The Shadow Knows*—a preemptory rejoinder to recent misogynist affirmations of the nuclear family in films such as *Fatal Attraction* and *Someone to Watch Over Me*—recounts a week in N.'s life during which she is compelled to come to terms with the embodiment of her anxieties about her identity as one who knows and sees the magnitude of her victimization.

N., who reveals her married name to be Hexam, suggestive of her paranoia (she is "hexed") and her role as a victimized woman (reminiscent of Lizzie Hexam of Dickens's *Our Mutual Friend*), does believe that there is a plot to murder her. As the novel unfolds, she runs through the list of suspects—her ex-husband, her ex-maid Osella, who has been making obscene phone calls to her, Andrew's wife, and her best friend Bess—and so exposes her troubled personal life to the scrutiny of the reader, who is implicitly asked to take on the role of confessor while verifying that there is, indeed, something going on here. The novel proceeds through a series of personal disasters that neither confirm nor deny N.'s status as a paranoid victim: Ev dies suddenly of pancreatitis (though N. believes she has been murdered); N. miscarries the child she has conceived with Andrew; after a series of indecisive moves, Andrew returns to his wife; Bess confesses to N. that she has, for years, hated her and resented her supposedly promiscuous activities. Johnson's novel has all of the earmarks of a soap opera, a genre whose conventions inscribe the putative feminine desire to be violated; hence, in the end, N.'s fears are "confirmed" not by murder but by rape. *The Shadow Knows* thus brings to bear upon the phenomena of paranoia several leading questions: How is paranoia gendered and

200

engendered? Where and how, in its range, do the "personal" and the "political" meet? In the case of N., is it a defense against external evils or the projection of guilt and self-victimizing desire?

These questions suggest that *The Shadow Knows*, unlike the other novels I've discussed, "personalizes" paranoia by taking the issue of paranoia out of the realm of the consensual hyperreal and converting it into what may appear, on the surface, to be a rather outdated existentialist dialectic moving between the "inner" and "outer" life. Johnson, however, makes this conversion in such a way as to suggest that the projections of passion, longing, revenge, jealousy, and hatred found in this disturbing novel both disguise and abet the cultural forces that lie behind the victimization of women. Variously stereotyped by friends, relatives, neighbors, and police as "the other woman," the promiscuous divorcée, the careless mother, the hysteric, N. is enclosed in a threatening environment that takes its revenge upon any woman who resists its normalizing processes by pressuring its victims into the state of paranoia where hegemonic reality and marginalized inwardness are so split up, so separated, that the "paranoid" can only engage in the "narcissistic" activity of bringing them back together—at times, violently.

N., faced with extreme circumstances, resorts to what Julia Kristeva terms a "paranoid-type mechanism" that is "the inevitable product of . . . a denial of the sociosymbolic contract and its counterinvestment as the only means of self-defense in the struggle to safeguard an identity."[20] Thus, N. is continually marked for exhibitions of abjection and hysteria that further separate her from the existing order and that designate her as victim or paranoid: She screams at the "Famous Inspector" (the police detective assigned to investigate Ev's death) that Ev has been murdered when all evidence points to the contrary; she hemorrhages from a miscarriage in a public parking lot. The manifestations of N.'s paranoia involve recurrent incidents where inwardness and exteriority are brought to meet, where what is intuited or imagined and what is "real" coincidentally or prophetically merge. The condition of separation forced upon her (when a neighbor suggests she spend her money fixing up the outside of her house, not the inside, for the sake of property values; when N. declares that "outside I am a round-faced little woman with round breasts and toes, surrounded by round babies; I

20. Julia Kristeva, "Women's Time," in *Feminist Theory: A Critique of Ideology*, ed. Nannerl O. Keohane, Michelle Z. Rosaldo, and Barbara C. Gelpi (Chicago: University of Chicago Press, 1982), 46.

look like a happy moon—now who would have thought that I am riddled and shot through invisibly with desperate and sordid passions, raging passions and egotism, insecurity and lust?"[21]) results in its opposite. Thus, N. cites as evidence of the "interrelation among passions and things unceasing" her, seemingly, ludicrously exaggerated violent passion with Andrew: "When we were first in love [we] wrecked each other's houses. It was peculiar. I mean physically wrecked them with crowbars and such, and it seemed quite natural and called-for" (SK, 28). She looks out for (or she "makes up," or naturalizes) the "interrelation among passions and things unceasing" with increasing anticipation as the evidence mounts that someone is planning an act of violence against her. By the time of her rape she is relieved that the violence is not as bad as what she had been expecting: "I don't know. I felt happy. Anything bad can happen to the unwary, and when life sends you the coup de grâce you have a way of knowing. So I felt better then, thinking well, that was the coup de grâce and here I still am" (SK, 276). This is the rhetoric of a survivor in a paranoid system that has so thoroughly converted her to that system that she will remain content (now that the "worst" has happened) with her liminal status. N. "becomes herself" in the end, but her identity is that of the shadow, otherness beat into airy thinness, inside and outside joined in the shadow's single dimension, outrage transformed into the street wisdom of the "spiritually sly":

> I feel better. You can change; a person can change. I feel myself different already and to have taken on the thinness and lightness, like a ghost slipping out from his corporeal self and stealing invisibly across the lawn while the body he has left behind meantime smiles stolidly as usual and nobody notices anything different. You can join the spiritually sly, I mean. Well, maybe I'm making too much of this. I mean your eyes get used to the dark, that's all, and also if nothing else you learn to look around you when you get out of your car in a dark garage. (SK, 277)

The Shadow Knows thus critiques the romance of that complicitous, "marginalized" identity (Gilmore, Oedipa Maas, Selvy) that is fostered in the male paranoid novels I have mentioned. It stands as a judgment upon the paranoid system it represents—a system that disguises its inclusions so well that N.'s alteration to the status of shadow could be conceived

21. Diane Johnson, The Shadow Knows (New York: Alfred A. Knopf, 1975), 8; hereafter cited in my text as SK.

as revolutionary. As countercritique to the binary versions of cultural paranoia projected by DeLillo, McElroy, and Pynchon, Johnson's novel warrants
that N.'s paranoia arises out of gender-specific anxieties transformed into a
series of cultural relations that then, at a later stage, become homogenized
into the all-powerful conspiracy that represses the preterite in Pynchon, or
the nomadic in McElroy. What stands in *The Executioner's Song* as the
transparent text upon which is inscribed a primary function of cultural paranoia—the exchange of women's bodies—is brought to the fore of Johnson's
novels as the engendering element of cultural paranoia. Johnson engages
the "before" of cultural paranoia, one of its founding moments; in so doing,
she reveals the underlying motives of a system of mastery that encourages
paranoia and offers epistemology as resistance to it.

In a telling moment, N. reflects upon not her own anxiety but what
she refers to as "that inchoate masculine fear" that leads to the resentment
of bad mothers and other "abnormal" versions of womanhood:

> A smirk of comprehension and disgust overspreads the features of
> the Famous Inspector: this is a neglectful, a resentful mother he is
> dealing with, the sort that gets murdered all the time and the children
> put in foster homes, usually a good thing, too. Ah, it is not reason
> which congeals the wellsprings of the Famous Inspector's sympathy,
> but that he is a man. It is that inchoate masculine fear they all have.
> Where does it come from? It must be that sometime in his life every
> little baby boy, rosy in his bath, looking up past the warm, strong
> arms of his mother into her eyes, one time sees there a strangeness
> which suddenly reveals to him that she is not him, she is not even
> like him but is another creature of another race, and however much
> this terrible recognition may be obscured by subsequent pats, hugs,
> kisses, coos, years and years of love and encouragement—the ter-
> ror and isolation of that moment, and the fear of it returning, remain
> forever. (*SK*, 37)

In stark contrast to McElroy's representation of "the inchoate," Johnson's
narrator engenders paranoia as the male response to the alien that the
mother represents. Fear of the utter isolation contained in this moment of
rupture between pre-oedipal mother and oedipal son, terror at the thought
of its return, leads to the homogeneous system of suppression that attempts
to border off all of those who recall this differential instant in their lives and
beings by converting them into hysterics and paranoids. Kristeva suggests
that this moment of separation "preconditions the binding of language which

is already syntactical"; therefore, "the common destiny of the two sexes, men and women," is that "certain biofamilial conditions and relationships [i.e., those of the "nuclear family"] cause women (and notably hysterics) to deny this separation and the language which ensues from it, whereas men (notably obsessionals) magnify both and, terrified, attempt to master them."[22] This is precisely the situation in *The Shadow Knows*, where N. attempts to erase the separation between "inside" and "outside" through paranoid confirmations. These confirmations are, in turn, guaranteed by the male system of discipline and control represented by the Famous Inspector, whom society has put in charge of separating good women from bad, hysterics from "normal" women, thus reinstating and mastering the distance between feeling and event that N. attempts to overcome.

Kristeva suggests that to live in this system is to live with the myth of the archaic mother (that woman who existed before the terrifying instant of male recognition and who lives on in alienated versions of femininity). Indeed, the climactic scene of *The Shadow Knows* portrays the huge Osella performing a striptease at a night club while several of the novel's principals, gathered together for the moment of revelation, look on. This, not so fancifully, might be said to be the ambiguous unwritten moment that Oedipa awaits at the end of *The Crying of Lot 49*, or what is portrayed in the secreted films of *Lookout Cartridge* and *Running Dog*, save that, in this scene, the recognition is concretized, disambiguated, and de-mythologized. Johnson portrays what lies behind paranoia in the spectacle of Osella's body: Black, grossly overweight, violent (for it appears to N. that Osella is responsible for Ev's death), Osella is the embodiment of "otherness," brought under control and theatricalized for the consumption of the fascinated audience. As N. remarks, "The naked Osella makes everything clear" (*SK*, 262). In this crucial scene, the moment of separation is reenacted and contained as Osella receives the mythic investment of the archaic mother, but now she is objectified, her bizarreness (in the Club Zanzibar) zoned off and normalized, for she is soon to be a star in Las Vegas:

> The naked Osella, a sight at first so horrifying and then so immensely fascinating that the people watching all drew in their breath. . . . But Osella did nothing at all, merely radiantly stood which was enough, with the light gleaming down on the folds of her body, on her tremendous breasts. She seemed to have been oiled, for she shone so;

22. Kristeva, "Women's Time," 41.

one saw nothing but the gleaming immense breasts lying across her huge belly, breasts astoundingly full and firm like zeppelins overhead. (*SK*, 267)

For Mailer, Pynchon, DeLillo, and McElroy, paranoia is a kind of logical desire: an attempt to make order out of chaos, to make or see connections, and then to resist mimetically the discourse of mastery. In each instance, however, the form resistance takes to the system that represses otherness merely replicates that system. Even more disturbingly, what appear to be resistant *mis*representations of a prevailing linguistic order homologous to the dominant political order—modern/postmodern gestures of hyperrealism, polyglossia, ambiguity, fragmentation, epistemological magnification—are shown to be cooperative resistances that relegate the problem to the realm of hermeneutics. Johnson, too, sees this as the condition of contemporary cultural paranoia, but in *The Shadow Knows* she makes it clear that these forms of verbal resistance or misrepresentation and their entailing of analogous political oppositions are part of a network of sexual and racial differences that the paranoid system always works to erase or contain. For her, paranoia, in addition to being a narratological or epistemological issue—a way of seeing or ambiguating what is seen, a totalized vision or a fragmentation of that vision, a matter of faithfully transcribing the story or disguising one's arrangements—is a political issue, where enforced cultural relations stemming from anxieties about difference and otherness result in specific consequences for women. In *The Shadow Knows*, a novel filled with scenes of violence toward women, a black woman is possibly murdered, and her murder is ignored because N., a paranoid, is the only person who wishes to pursue the issue. Ev's corpse is a stark contrast to Osella's living body, but they are both made objects in the system of terror and domination that passes for middle-class culture in Johnson's novel. For Johnson's protagonist, nameless and lacking identity, paranoia is not so much a matter of seeing—for she sees clearly enough—as it is of surviving warily and invisibly in an unrelentingly threatening environment. N.'s shadowy transformation in the novel's concluding pages is only the obverse of Osella's presence on the stage: Theatricalized or underground, star or paranoid, these strange women are precisely placed. These consequences are not, as the Famous Inspector insists of Ev's murder, in another Dickensian echo reminiscent of another story about a "little" woman (*Little Dorrit*), "nobody's fault." These consequences are, Johnson's novel powerfully argues, no accident.

Techno-euphoria and the Discourse of the American Sublime

Rob Wilson

> War itself, if it is carried on with order and with a sacred respect for the rights of citizens, has something sublime in it, and makes the disposition of the people who carry it on thus only the more sublime, the more numerous are the dangers to which they are exposed and in respect of which they behave with courage.
> —Immanuel Kant, "Analytic of the Sublime"

> The nations are not something eternal. They had their beginnings and they will end.
> —Ernest Renan, "What Is a Nation?"

The emergence of American literature in the first half of the nineteenth century centered around the evocation of a certain kind of representative landscape that, widely circulated as a foundational scene of American appropriation in the paintings of Thomas Cole and Frederic Edwin Church and in the poems of William Cullen Bryant and Walt Whitman, not to mention *Moby-Dick*, for example, had identified and accommodated the emergence of the United States as a geopolitical power of international status. Such representations of the American Sublime that surged into literary dominance during these expansionist decades of manifest destiny (1835–1855) summoned up vast scenes and icons of a national might that had to be tapped into, challenged, and overcome. These landscapes and spectacles of expanding power helped to solidify and to circulate, within the American political imaginary, discourses of national exaltation that allowed this labor of collective appropriation to be hazed over with the light and immensity of divine sanction: "The function of the landscape" served, in the well-known cultural analysis of Leo Marx, "as a master image embodying American hopes."[1]

These hopes for American geopolitical power—displaced unto a manifest landscape that functioned, by such an imaginal consensus, "to ground manifest destiny in the immanence of nature"[2]—were largely liberal, pragmatic, progressive ones, in which even machine technology immediately and increasingly came to be integrated into the scenery "as the fulcrum of national power."[3] "Fear haunts the building railroad," Emerson admitted in his journal in September 1843, "but it will be American power and beauty, when it is done."[4] While fronting this technological emblem of continental expansion and taking a Kantian speculator's delight in the "fifteen or sixteen hours" workday that the Irish railroad workers of Concord were subjected to, Emerson concluded that the railroad was a disciplinary apparatus of pikes and shovels that "is a better police than the sheriff and his deputies to let off the peccant humors" of alienation.[5] Emerson's famous "American Scholar" address of 1837 was not alone in trumpeting a cultural break with the terms and tropes of Great Britain and Europe: "Why cannot our literati comprehend the matchless sublimity of our position amongst the nations of

1. Leo Marx, *The Machine in the Garden: Technology and the Pastoral Ideal in America* (London and New York: Oxford University Press, 1964), 159.
2. Howard Horwitz, "Sublime Possession, American Landscape," in *By the Law of Nature: Form and Value in Nineteenth-Century America* (New York and Oxford: Oxford University Press, 1991), 55. Horwitz argues that Washington Allston's *Lectures on Art*, begun in 1833, and Thomas Cole's *Course of Empire* paintings of 1833–1836 provided "an alternative, evacuative account of sublimity and subjectivity" to the more dominant discourse of manifest destiny, which posited "a nature already possessed, hailing conquest without struggle, transcendence without anxiety or liminality" (37).
3. Marx, *The Machine in the Garden*, 155.
4. Ralph Waldo Emerson, *Selections from Ralph Waldo Emerson*, ed. Stephen E. Whicher (Boston: Houghton Mifflin Co., 1960), 221.
5. Emerson, *Selections*, 221.

the world?" urged John Louis O'Sullivan upon the nationalistic community of Young Americans in the *United States Magazine and Democratic Review*; authors, painters, orators, and historians soon arose to answer this felt need for a cultural sublimity commensurate with the geopolitical power of a fast-industrializing nation.[6] It was during these formative decades of literary nationalism, in fact, that the United States developed, through such sublime self-representations of their own national and global mission, in such works as "Song of Myself," "Self-Reliance," and *Moby-Dick*, into a world leader of spectacle production.

What Leo Marx analyzed as the "rhetoric of the technological sublime" had emerged to displace pastoral images of a receding agricultural community. This rhetoric at once evoked a combination of awe and terror at the power and progress of industrialization and, by means of the idealizing haze of aesthetic ratification, neutralized the dissonance and dissent of political opposition into a massive sublimation: Workers, slaves, and Indians alike were wiped away from such scenes of technological redemption. Any alienation or appropriation laborers suffered, as in Emerson's transcendentalist perspective, built character and ratified progress. This sense of euphoria before the technological sublime, infecting the rhetoric of protectionist Daniel Webster and free marketer Whitman alike, served a hegemonic function: So constructed, icons of the sublime worked to reduce the threat of capitalism to social formations of mass industrialization and to reduce the latter to the terror and wonder aroused by an ever expanding technology seen merely "as the product of inventive [American] genius, and the source of labor-saving machines."[7]

6. On the emergent literary nationalism of "Young America," see Perry Miller, *The Raven and the Whale: The War of Worlds and Wits in the Era of Poe and Melville* (New York: Harcourt, Brace, 1956), 109–15, and Benjamin T. Spencer, *The Quest for Nationality: An American Literary Campaign* (Syracuse: Syracuse University Press, 1957), 102–218. O'Sullivan notoriously coined the phrase *manifest destiny* in 1845 as he urged the annexation of Texas and the settlement of Oregon, though the hegemonic self-representation of America's millennial role in history and corporeal autonomy in space was no novelty: see Ernest Lee Tuveson, *Redeemer Nation: The Idea of America's Millennial Role* (Chicago: University of Chicago Press, 1968), 125–29, and Wai-Chee Dimock, "Nation, Self, Personification," in *Empire for Liberty: Melville and the Poetics of Individualism* (Princeton: Princeton University Press, 1989), 9–14, on Melville's complicity in the discourse of continental appropriation.
7. Carolyn Porter, "Emerson's America," in *Seeing & Being: The Plight of the Participant Observer in Emerson, James, Adams, and Faulkner* (Middletown, Conn.: Wesleyan University Press, 1986), 79. Porter is refiguring Leo Marx's account of "the rhetoric of the technological sublime" in terms of a liberal hegemony over labor and the future.

This discourse of the American sublime materialized national power into credible forms and shared terms that, in effect, conscripted citizens into a dynamic of possessive individualism that insured the industrial incorporation of the country. As a trope of romantic community, the sublime worked for "kindred spirits" within the American political imaginary, not merely as a sentiment to be feigned but as a force to be acted upon, believed in, and enjoyed. Even the skeptical Henry Adams stood in awe of technology with the American inventor Samuel P. Langley as they began "to feel the forty-foot dynamo[s] as a moral force" at the Paris World's Fair on the threshold of the twentieth century: "Before the end," Adams concluded, "one began to pray to it [the sublime dynamo]; inherited instinct taught the national expression of man before silent and infinite force."[8] As a language of democratic longing, the sublime imposed landscapes or technoscapes of national identification and higher force, by means of which puny individuals might identify not so much with the power of the state as with a sublimated spectacle of national empowerment increasingly materialized into a railway train, an electronic dynamo, an airplane, or a bomb. What Adams called this American instinct of credulity before "silent and infinite force" had been long inculcated.

Ratifying aesthetic and technological uses of natural force as equally compelling, however, the ideology of the American Sublime trapped American liberals, such as Whitman and Church, into a contradictory discourse legitimating the expansion of national power. Although in Whitman's New York state, for example, and especially in the Lower Hudson Valley, the doctrine of sublime scenery remained an underlying ideal called upon to justify environmental preservation and was used in the battle to prevent Storm King Mountain from being turned into a Con Edison hydroelectric plant as late as 1980, the equally compelling claim to tap into, command, and develop this natural power was no less rooted in emerging dynamics of the technological sublime.[9] Founded upon a flight from history that sublimated nature and the democratic subject into resources of continental redemption, spectacles of the sublime, such as Church's *Niagara* (1857) and Whitman's "By Blue Ontario's Shore" (1867), disseminated elected spaces of light and

8. Henry Adams, "The Dynamo and the Virgin," in *The Education of Henry Adams: An Autobiography* (Boston: Houghton, Mifflin Co., 1918), 379–81.
9. See Raymond J. O'Brien, *American Sublime: Landscape and Scenery of the Lower Hudson Valley* (New York: Columbia University Press, 1985) for an account of competing aesthetic and technological claims upon the Hudson River, the place that established landscape as the quintessential American genre.

horizons of dematerialized power that valorized American labor and called out for further projects of aesthetic, political, and technological redemption. From the Puritans through the romantics, then, we can now recognize that the American Sublime had evolved into a cultural genre quite capable of sacralizing force, inspiring communal belief, and modulating history to national ends.[10]

Breaking with by now residual discourses linking nature and nation to that powerful complex of ideology Thomas Jefferson called "Nature's Nation," I will claim that this American Sublime will have to be refigured, within a postmodern economy, to imagine forth and represent America as an entity of transnational cyberspace that "knows no national boundaries, feels no geographic constraints."[11] This will increasingly happen, at the superstructural level of cultural production, as transnational corporations emerge, amalgamate, transform, flow, and exchange signs and profits across tired nation-state boundaries and grow oblivious to cultural or ideological distinctions that once inspired allegiance. Passing out of nation-state modernity and Fordist modes of massive industrial accumulation, the United States is fast entering a more fluid world of transnational incorporation. To explain this, Jacques Attali uses a model of totalizing postmodernization that critics as opposed as Fredric Jameson and Walter Benn Michaels might well agree with;[12] he argues, "The world is becoming an ideologically homo-

10. This historical claim is exemplified in Rob Wilson, *American Sublime: The Genealogy of a Poetic Genre* (Madison: University of Wisconsin Press, 1991). The more strictly literary-aesthetic and isolationist claim that the American Sublime is founded upon an Emersonian "refusal of history, particularly literary history" is argued in Harold Bloom, "Emerson and Whitman: The American Sublime," in *Poetry & Repression: Revisionism from Blake to Stevens* (New Haven: Yale University Press, 1976), 254. Bloom has even more solipsistically urged that the American Sublime "is the visual equivalent of what might be called *the* American religion" in which "the American consciousness finds freedom only in solitude, the self-definition only in the Sublime conviction that what is best and oldest in the self is no part of the created world": see Harold Bloom, "The American Sublime: Gregory Botts, the Painting as Icon," *Arts Magazine* 64 (Summer 1990): 37–38. Bloom's increasingly *gnostic* sense of the American Sublime has led him to conclude of George Bush's international politics that "our foreign policy basically amounts to making the world safe for gnosticism": see the interview "The Art of Criticism, I" *Paris Review* 118 (Spring 1991): 227.

11. See Robert B. Reich, "The End of the National Champion," in *The Work of Nations: Preparing Ourselves for 21st Century Capitalism* (New York: Knopf, 1991), 124.

12. Fredric Jameson, "Immanence and Nominalism in Postmodern Theoretical Discourse," in *Postmodernism, or, The Cultural Logic of Late Capitalism* (Durham: Duke University Press, 1991). Jameson provides a homological account of the American

geneous market where life is being organized around common consumer desires, whether or not those desires can be fulfilled."[13] We already inhabit a world system of such unstable reconfiguration that the mighty United States may now be "Japan's granary, like Poland was for Flanders in the seventeenth century."[14] Dependent upon a long-encoded agonistics of power and a dangerously solipsistic sense of natural and technological superiority, this nationalist ideology of the American Sublime will die hard and not without fighting: Indeed, the ongoing abolishment of the United States as an economic superpower, once contingent upon rivalry with the U.S.S.R. for global hegemony and upon proliferating nuclear weapons for the maintenance of sublime terror, may already be a fait accompli within "a world unlocked from its Cold War polarization."[15]

This giddy postmodernization of the nation-state bodes ill for romantic self-conceptions of identity. Like some unimagined poetry of the North American techno-future, William Gibson's cyberpunk science fiction is not alone in mapping the emerging space of this new, postnational, and postnatural immensity: His cybernetic version of the technological sublime registers an intoxicating sense of cybernetic infinitude, as clusters and constellations of data proliferate and collage in the nonspace of the mind. These internal realms of informational immensity and eugenic alteration attract high-tech criminals—"console cowboys" and techno-punks of various classes, and the God-hungry searching for the ultimate Matrix or Code— to appropriate the transnational sublime of this new technoscape. *Cyberspace* is the term Gibson first uses in *Neuromancer* (1984) to imagine forth

---

market as theorized in the antiliberal representations of Walter Benn Michaels "as an asphyxiating total system" determining the desiring subject of postmodernism with an "all-encompassing fatality" (212). Horwitz's term for this New Historicist integration of economic and cultural discourse is "isomorphic" (*By the Law of Nature*, 19).

13. Jacques Attali, "The European Bank for Reconstruction and Development," *Vital Speeches* 57 (1 May 1991): 422.

14. Attali's disparaging comment is quoted in William Pfaff, "Redefining World Power," *Foreign Affairs* 70 (1991): 38.

15. This post–Cold War claim concerning "the abolishment of [American] superpower status itself, which proves to have been the product of superpower rivalry," is developed in William Pfaff, "Redefining World Power," *Foreign Affairs* 70 (1991): 33–43. This is countered, in the same issue, by the more globally interventionist argument that the United States remains a unipolar superpower threatened from within by a waning national consensus, and from without by "Weapon States," like Iraq and North Korea, which can use nuclear and biological weapons to "shrink distance" and "multiply power": see Charles Krauthammer, "The Unipolar Moment," *Foreign Affairs* 70 (1991): 23–33.

this multidimensional matrix of high information, consciousness alteration, and post-Fordist Sense/Net control over a thoroughly introjected medium: "Cyberspace. A consensual hallucination experienced daily by billions of legitimate operators, in every nation, by children being taught mathematical concepts. . . . A graphic representation of data abstracted from the banks of every computer in the human system. Unthinkable complexity." [16] This is how a corporate voice-over too comfortably describes this Cyberspace Matrix as sponsored by the Mitsubishi Bank of America. Such Cyberspace bespeaks, as Gibson urges, "the spiral arms of military systems, forever out of reach." [17]

Flip-flopping at stellar speeds of data-light between financial centers of Tokyo, London, and New York, Gibson's *Mona Lisa Overdrive* (1988) continues to map this neo-transcendental matrix of postmodern space and technological glut with a mingled sense of delight (what I am calling *techno-euphoria*) and paranoia ("universal techno-angst" is what Gibson calls this mood, shared with Katsuhiro Otomo, in "Rocket Radio" [18]): Gibson represents, through compulsive approaches to power of leapfrogging characters, a cybernetic version of this neo-sublime—as space flips over into un-mapped, unlocated immensities of multinational capitalism that recognize no national spaces, abolish regional identities, forge transnational com-munities of telecommunication, and create *awe* (newly found information matrices like God) and *dread* (paranoid conspiracies programmed by some unimaginable nexus of power/Capital with unforeseen complexities and threats of self-sublation). Literary critics might well associate such visions of sublime release with an all but futureless future, a transnational para-

16. William Gibson, *Neuromancer* (New York: Ace Science Fiction, 1984), 51. Related to Gibson's experiments with cyberspace, an even more American-utopic version of "virtual-reality technology" is emerging in multinational America as a ludic enclave of self-transcendence hailing rock fans and computer buffs. I am thinking, for example, of rock guitarist Jerry Garcia's vision of a Grateful Dead concert occurring in cyberspace, 1991: "Wouldn't it be great if we could participate in a concert that doesn't happen in one par-ticular geographical place, and in which we could all contribute something to the mix? The performers and the audience could all put on their 3-D headsets and their body-suits, and wherever they were they could plug in through the telephone network and meet in this computer-created world, this artificial place that is some kind of sum of all their percep-tions. The music and the dancing could all be mixed together, and we could participate in this celebration in pure cybernetic space": see the Grateful Dead as interviewed by Howard Rheingold, *Interview* 21 (July 1991): 73.
17. Gibson, *Neuromancer*, 52.
18. William Gibson, "Rocket Radio," *Rolling Stone*, 15 June 1989, 84–86.

noia and a technophilic disenchantment, as well as the immanence of a degraded bio-future that seems as much a threat to the ancient American landscape as any nuclear annihilation.[19]

••••

Cyberpunk or Language Poetry notwithstanding, residual versions of euphoric nationalism do linger on in American discourse, at least at the level of cultural and political production. What I will want to argue, finally, in a reading of George Bush's Patriot missile speech, is that the "bombs bursting in air" of the recent war in the Persian Gulf gave proof through the postmodern night, to Americans and the First World, that America was still there as an entity/identity of sublime power. But consider, first, a recent ad campaign circulated by the Philip Morris Companies as a post-Fordist instance of such nationalist nostalgia and spectacular sublimity. Superimposed over a color reproduction of Albert Bierstadt's landscape of American wilderness, *Among the Sierra Nevada Mountains, California* (1868), in which a herd of deer and waterfowl, in lieu of displaced Miwok-Paiute Indians, traverse the light- and God-drenched vastness, waterfalls, lakes, and granite of the High Sierras, the Philip Morris Companies blazon the following claims about such representations "equating [American] grandness with largeness"[20]:

A CENTURY AGO THE PAINTINGS OF *ALBERT BIERSTADT* DREW CROWDS. ALL HAD IMAGINED THE AMERICAN FRON-

19. Sublime cyberspace remains the terrain in William Gibson, *Mona Lisa Overdrive* (New York: Bantam Books, 1988). Alan Liu has connected the cybernetic sense of "transcendence" feigned in Gibson's science fiction to the romantic imagination as "source code," as well as to a claustrophobic sense of multinational capitalism simulating and frustrating *sublime release* ("[postmodern] transcendence is a goto routine of the imagination that goes nowhere") in "Local Transcendence: Cultural Criticism, Postmodernism, and the Romanticism of Detail," *Representations* 32 (1990): 75–77. The "technological dystopias" imagined forth in American cyberpunk fiction and cinema are related to the more technophilic origins of American science fiction in Andrew Ross, "Getting Out of the Gernsback Continuum," *Critical Inquiry* 17 (1991): 411–33, and "The Ecology of Images," paper presented at the International Film Festival, East-West Center, Honolulu, Hawaii, 30 Nov. 1990. Also see Pam Rosenthal, "Jacked In: Fordism, Cyberpunk, Marxism," *Socialist Review* 21 (1991): 79–103, on the post-Fordist dynamics of cybernetic subjectivity and socialization.
20. Barbara Novak, "Grand Opera and the Still Small Voice," in *Nature and Culture: American Landscape and Painting, 1825–1875* (New York: Oxford University Press, 1980), 29.

TIER, BUT NOT QUITE LIKE THIS. HERE WERE THE VISIONS
THAT WOULD LURE THEM WEST, AND WHICH REMAIN DEEP IN
THE AMERICAN PSYCHE TO THIS DAY. BEYOND THEIR PURE
DRAMA AND COLOSSAL SCALE, THEY ARE ALSO AMONG THE
MOST ACCOMPLISHED LANDSCAPES EVER PAINTED. PHILIP
MORRIS SALUTES BOTH THE SPIRIT AND THE VIRTUOSITY OF
A MAJOR AMERICAN ARTIST.

Underwriting this re-monumentalization of a Euro-competitive sublime,
Philip Morris announces corporate sponsorship of a nationwide tour entitled
"Albert Bierstadt: Art & Enterprise, A Retrospective," correctly urging the
integration of the aesthetic and the economic within these visions of American cultural capital. As Lee A. Iacocca has proclaimed of such national
landscapes, during Chrysler Corporation's sponsoring of a similar Metropolitan Museum exhibition in 1987 entitled "American Paradise: The World
of the Hudson River School," such paintings "go far beyond celebrating the
beauty of the American landscape in the 1800s; they are a celebration of
America itself."[21] In a world of receding nationalism, furthermore, the motto
Advantage, Chrysler may hinge upon recuperating faith in a new motto:
Advantage, American Sublime.

Through the three-phase dynamic of sublime possession imported
and transformed from northern romanticism, an American emptiness could
be imagined as national ground, anxiety could be overcome as subjective
trauma, and an identification with some vast landscape could function to
sacralize energy for collective appropriation: Fitz Hugh Ludlow wrote of
Bierstadt's first encounter with the Yosemite Valley in 1863, as the Civil War
raged, "We did not so much seem to be seeing from that crag of vision a
new scene on the old familiar globe as a new heaven and a new earth into
which the creative spirit had just been breathed."[22] Bierstadt's metaphor of
American vastness represses such forces of U.S. history as conquistadors,
gold diggers, Union soldiers, laborers, and California railroad barons, not to
mention the native American tribes who had lived along the Merced, Fresno,
and San Joaquin rivers and who had been forcibly removed from aesthetic
contemplation by such tactics as the burning of acorn caches to starve the
Ahwahneechees out of Yosemite Valley (as recently as 1851).[23] This repres-

21. Lee A. Iacocca, "Preface," in *American Paradise: The World of the Hudson River
School*, ed. John K. Howat (New York: H. N. Abrams, 1987), x.
22. Fitz Hugh Ludlow, "Seven Weeks in the Great Yo-Semite," *The Atlantic Monthly* 13
(June 1864): 746.
23. See David Robertson, "First Artists in Yosemite," in *West of Eden: A History of the Art*

sive metaphor has been resurrected from simulacra of postmodern history to disseminate nation-building themes of enterprise, empowerment, and economic appropriation. Such sublime representations were never innocent of imperial ambitions, then or now. As Howard Horwitz describes the dynamic of sublime possession enacted in such paintings as Bierstadt's *Rocky Mountains, Lander's Peak* (1863), which was displayed on a "Great Picture" tour of the northeast along with the painter's collection of Indian artifacts,[24] "In Bierstadt's canvas, the question of rightful proprietorship of western lands, a violent political controversy at the time, is suspended, or rather settled" in favor of the liberal consensus.[25]

Mark Twain trenchantly disagreed with Bierstadt's *Domes of the Yosemite* (1867) when such paintings of the West were being consumed across the country: "It is more the atmosphere of Kingdom-Come than of California."[26] Completed in Rome in 1869, *Among the Sierra Nevada Mountains, California* was never even set in the Sierra Nevada: The foreground deer and ducks appear ten years earlier in *Gosnold at Cuttyhawk*, the massive cliff reconfigures Yosemite's El Capitan from several earlier paintings, and the distant snow peak echoes Mount Lander in *The Rocky Mountains, Lander's Peak*, and Mount Rosalie from *Storm in the Rocky Mountains, Mt. Rosalie*.[27] Bierstadt's painting remains a private composite of the American Sublime, rearranged to serve a vision of national grandeur remarkably reasserting itself during the Civil War trauma as consensus threatened to disintegrate into faction. Such versions of the American Sublime aim less at scenic fidelity than at symbolic typology, churning materials of western U.S. geography into millennial scripture and the violence of history into the un-

---

and *Literature of Yosemite* (California: Yosemite Natural History Association and Wilderness Press, 1984), 1–19.

24. American Adam that he was, Bierstadt named this canvas, which made him Church's sublime rival in national art, *The Rocky Mountains, Lander's Peak* after Colonel Frederick W. Lander, who headed the U.S. government survey expedition that first brought the painter to the West. Similarly, he named another landscape painting *A Storm in the Rocky Mountains—Mount Rosalie* after Rosalie Ludlow, whom he married in 1866. See Gerald L. Carr's commentaries on these paintings in *American Paradise*, 284–93.

25. Horwitz, *By the Law of Nature*, 31–32.

26. See Nancy K. Anderson, " 'Wondrously Full of Invention': The Western Landscapes of Albert Bierstadt," in *Albert Bierstadt: Art & Enterprise* (New York: The Brooklyn Museum, 1990), 91. Twain's comment from August 4, 1867, along with other contemporary responses are discussed in Gordon Hendricks, *Albert Bierstadt: Painter of the American West* (New York: Abrams, 1974), and David Robertson, *West of Eden*, 22–23.

27. Anderson, *Albert Bierstadt: Art & Enterprise*, 93.

examined euphoria of national myth: *Among the Sierra Nevada Mountains, California* envisions the recuperation of a preindustrial Eden, displaying the power of manifest destiny to compel the landscape into enterprise, as well as to ratify the pragmatic spirituality of Adamic capitalists who went on opening the continent to Euramerican designs.[28]

This nationalist ad-poem remains duplicitous, I would add, as befits its postmodern corporation, which, having already become another transnational web transforming Philip Morris U.S.A. into Philip Morris International, will "often cloak [itself] in whatever national garb is most convenient."[29] Circulating tropes of power's sanctification within the American political imaginary, the painting is doing the work of cultural memory, recapitulating a version of literary-aesthetic nationalism that was dying out as Bierstadt painted. America was once a country of abundance and energy: The huge frontier and abundant natural resources stimulated a mobile capitalism in which, in David Potter's analysis of economic abundance as a motivating lure in the 1950s, "the spectacle of vast riches waiting to be grasped [had] inspired men to devise new means for grasping them."[30] Repressing tobacco as it globally diversifies, Philip Morris knows what it is doing with Bierstadt: this company commands the nation's largest advertising budget (it spent $2.07 billion in 1989) and depends on such companies as the Leo Burnett advertising agency of Chicago, which "knows how to touch the heartland of America," to rephrase the American imaginary and summon up a neo-national image worthy of, for example, the Marlboro Man, the Pillsbury Doughboy, the Jolly Green Giant, and the feminist vow of Virginia Slims, "You've Come a Long Way, Baby!"[31] Reeking of postmodern nostalgia, this painting would again resonate as a spectacle of Late Capitalist enterprise

28. Though Bierstadt received $25,000 in 1865 for *The Rocky Mountains, Lander's Peak*, the highest price ever paid for an American painting at that time, *Among the Sierra Nevada Mountains, California* sold at auction in 1892 for a mere $8,000, one-third to one-half of what it would have brought three decades earlier (Kevin J. Avery, "A Historiography of the Hudson River School," in *American Paradise*, 9). That these landscapes of the American Sublime have recovered their cultural capital is indicated by the fact that Church's monumental canvas, *The Icebergs* (1861), sold for $2.5 million in 1979 (Avery, "A Historiography," 17).
29. Reich, "The Global Web," in *The Work of Nations*, 115.
30. David M. Potter, "Abundance and the Frontier Hypothesis," in *People of Plenty: Economic Abundance and the American Character* (Chicago: University of Chicago Press, 1954), 163.
31. See Mark Landler, "Leo Burnett: The Ad Agency Philip Morris Loves to Call For," *Business Week* (15 April 1991): 66.

here deployed along shifting international frontiers: Re-sublimated via Bierstadt and Philip Morris into a "visionary compact" of art/enterprise, the land speaks a comforting brand of literary and economic nationalism.[32]

Such discourses of imaginal vastness presuppose tropes of the American Sublime that, as Philip Morris urges, "remain deep in the American psyche to this day" and would legitimate on some politically preconscious level, as I have suggested, the nineteenth-century project of frontier settlement and technological redemption. Can these "visions that would lure them west" inspire postmodern consensus in American enterprise and lead (as the ad claims) from the symbolic level of cultural symbol ("Art") to economic and technological levels of national action ("Enterprise")? Reconnecting the political to the symbolic, like a semiotic ghost from Frederick Jackson Turner's subconscious, the assumption is that a renewed identification with America's vastness and narratives of strong selfhood will motivate, as they did in the past, faith in American enterprise and lead—guiltlessly, shamelessly—to the sublimation of nature into new projects of national/global domination. No matter that this inalienable wilderness comprises part of the Yosemite concession deal that Universal Studios sold to Matsushita in 1990, provoking another Japan-bashing episode of defensive nationalism, as if this chunk of wilderness vastness somehow was not for sale like everything else under the postmodern sun to the highest, fastest multinational bidder! The frontier still works as an enchanted landscape of genteel self-redemption in Kevin Costner's *Dances With Wolves* (1991), but even the Leo Burnett Company must wonder: What can bind America together anymore if the frontier has vanished and there no longer exists any such entity as a national economy with an expanding GNP to perpetuate a collective misreading of national power based on nineteenth-century vestiges of unified objects and home-based corporations?

Although the nation-state may appear to be over as hegemonic threat, icons of national sublimity are still being summoned to recycle cultural capital and to renew international profits: Recall that Philip Morris recently payed $600,000 to the National Archives for the privilege of adver-

32. On discursive protocols and the expansionist politics of the American Sublime, see Donald Pease, "Sublime Politics," in *The American Sublime*, ed. Mary Arensberg (Albany: SUNY Press, 1986), 46–47, and Donald Pease, *Visionary Compacts: American Renaissance Writings in Cultural Context* (Madison: University of Wisconsin Press, 1987), 223–34, on the dynamics of sublime possession as a visionary compact—that is, "as a cultural reserve, a store of unrealized cultural motives, purposes, and political processes we honor but [seemingly] do not act upon" (48) and that stand in need of renewal.

tising the Bill of Rights in another spectacular project to associate cigarette smoking with certain inalienable American rights like life, liberty, and the pursuit of narcosis. With Asian markets now "Speaking Lark" and still riding "Marlboro Country" to the American Dream, Philip Morris International has managed to keep cigarette consumption rising 4 percent each year, exactly the same rate that U.S. consumption keeps dropping.[33] In an economy of waning nationalism, Morris can, by turns, invoke a symbolic legacy of grand memories and common acts to reclaim what Ernest Renan called the will to perpetuate "the social capital upon which one bases the national idea"[34] or simply bypass such nationalist appeals altogether. Can multinational corporations "make *Made In America* mean something again?" the chairman of Omni Consumer Products asks citizens of a decaying Detroit in *Robocop 2*, as he offers mind-boggling displays of cyborg policemen and a euphoric drug called NUKE.

Bierstadt's homage to the natural sublime must be getting a bad conscience, especially in a Late Capitalist era of ecological deformation and technophilic euphoria. My claim is that this discourse of imaginal vastness resurrected from the past, more than race, religion, geography, military necessity, or ethnic allegiance, may be one of the instruments that hold the *e pluribus unum* heterogeneity of America together. Given that postmodern nation-states are being reconstituted into sites of discursive heteroglossia and disseminated into multicultural histories of plural contention, as well as into post-Fordist cyberscapes of placeless identification, we need to scrutinize the return of what Homi K. Bhabha names "the performativity of language in the narratives of the nation,"[35] which recalls the power of vernacular language and print-capital to forge an "imagined political com-

---

33. Philip Morris has actually expanded its North Carolina cigarette production by $400 million to meet this increasing foreign demand, notwithstanding the rise of "foreign activism": see Laura Bird, "Even Overseas, Tobacco Has Nowhere to Hide," *Adweek's Marketing Week* (1 April 1991): 4–5. Describing the two-hundreth anniversary "Bill of Rights Tour" sponsored by Philip Morris Companies Inc., a red, white, and blue brochure situates this arcane document from Virginia within a high-tech environment of simulated history: "A 5,000-square-foot pavilion has been specially designed to house the exhibit. The architecture of the pavilion is a balanced mix between aerospace-inspired high technology structural systems and traditional gallery-like display space. Upon entering, you will be greeted by a collection of video images and graphic displays providing historical background on the Bill of Rights."
34. Ernest Renan, "Qu'est-ce qu'une nation?" trans. Martin Thom, in Homi K. Bhabha, ed., *Nation and Narration* (London and New York: Routledge, 1990), 19.
35. Bhabha, *Nation and Narration*, 3.

munity" of cultural conviction as portrayed in Benedict Anderson's *Imagined Communities*. To overemphasize, however, that the nation-state is neither biological nor transhistorical but an overdetermined discursive construction can be misleading. Such a textualization of history into discourse must not overlook "the [ideological] role of a remainder of some real, nondiscursive kernel of enjoyment which must be present for the Nation *qua* discursive-entity-effect to achieve its ontological [psychological] consistency."[36] The sublime object, so situated and historicized, answers some imaginary need for national power and motivates the desire, in an American context, for democratic sublimation of subject into nation.

Within a post-Fordist economy, the corporate trope of natural/ national identification remains an uncanny image, encoded with nostalgia and irony.[37] In 1991, a Honda is more likely to be made in America than a Ford or Pontiac, as cars become *signs* of global brands rather than *works* of national origin. How can spectacles of natural/technological sublimity (powers) or discourses of republican principle (rights) resonate in zones of Multinational Capital? Given postmodern reconfiguration, symbolic engineers—advertising executives, politicians, poets, cultural theorists—must wonder: How can images of a national sublime remotivate a consensus of American political superiority and exceptionality amid economic globalization, mass communication, and cybernetic alteration? I will return to this nineteenth-century discourse of the natural sublime as linked, at some deep level of the American psyche reconnecting the political to the symbolic and vice versa, to the ideology of national enterprise and frontier domination, but I want to shift the focus from Californian mountains to Massachusetts

36. On the "fantasy-organization of desire" within the political imaginary of the nation-state sublime, see Slavoj Žižek, "Eastern Europe's Republics of Gilead," *New Left Review* 183 (1990): 53–56, and Slavoj Žižek, "Formal Democracy and Its Discontents," in *Looking Awry: An Introduction to Jacques Lacan through Popular Culture* (Cambridge: MIT Press, 1991), 162–69.

37. Global displacements of national space and cybernetic modes of capital accumulation are discussed in David Harvey, *The Condition of Postmodernity: An Enquiry into the Origins of Cultural Change* (Oxford: Basil Blackwell, 1989): "Arenas of conflict between the nation state and transnational capital have, however, opened up, undermining the easy accommodation between big capital and big government so typical of the Fordist era" (170). Also see David Harvey, "Flexibility: Threat or Opportunity?" in *Socialist Review* 21 (1991): 65–77, a special issue devoted to post-Fordism: "Geographical mobility, for example, permits capitalists to seek out deregulated spaces [outside nation-state boundaries] with more flexible labor markets, allowing them to achieve greater flexibility in production processes" and profit (73).

missiles to scrutinize a contemporary image of the American Sublime that would, in a more postmodern register of cyberspace, re-instantiate American power as a superior force of technological power and global redemption.

• • • •

Working within the everyday discourse of national self-representation, I want to read George Bush's Patriot missile speech, which he gave at the Raytheon Corporation in Andover, Massachusetts, on February 15, 1991, as an uncanny enactment of cultural symbols of power activating a residual language of the American political unconscious. Beyond their material efficacy as "smart weapons" that had emerged as "one of the unexpected heroes of the war,"[38] the Patriot missiles were constructed (misrecognized) as iconic embodiments of the American Sublime. High technology, not nature, was used to instigate the will to global superiority at a moment when transnational reconfiguration and domestic stagnation had left many citizens wondering not only where nature had gone as a ground of value but also what was so superior about American technology or even the American economy itself. The Patriot missiles helped Americans locate one of the ultimate grounds of their own patriotism: belief in the technological sublime as an agent of historical redemption.[39] Beyond their material efficacy, the president used high-tech weapons to re-instantiate and materialize national power—the American Sublime—in a context of post-Fordist globalization and financial insecurity, as well as to regenerate the waning belief system and de-industrializing economy of workers in Massachusetts.

38. As the *Washington Post* described the scene, "The president appeared to be bouyed by the rousing reception given him at the Raytheon plant, where Scudbuster sweatshirts and American flags dominated the scene. Touting the 17-foot missile that has become one of the unexpected heroes of the war, Bush declared, '42 Scuds engaged, 41 intercepted.' The tougher Bush's rhetoric, the louder the roar from workers who chanted 'U-S-A! U-S-A!' when the president took the stage" (*Washington Post*, 16 Feb. 1991, sec. A, p. 12). The *New York Times* observed that Bush "made his remarks flanked by two black, red and white Patriot missiles," while outside the plant, "200 war protesters carried signs reading, 'Negotiate, Don't Obliterate'" (*New York Times*, 16 Feb. 1991, sec. A, p. 6).

39. As David F. Noble has concluded of American social attitudes toward labor and post-war industrial technologies: "Confronted with the unexpected and unaccepted unravelling of their short-lived empire, Americans are now clinging to their epic myths of national identity and destiny, hoping for yet another revival. And central to these myths is a collective fantasy of technological transcendence." See his *Forces of Production: A Social History of Industrial Automation* (New York: Knopf, 1984), xi.

220

To inspire national conviction, Patriot missiles were situated within a long-standing discourse of national empowerment and the moral sacralization of American power that contradicts, if at all examined, the transnational economy of the postmodern nation-state in which these weapons/icons were designed and constructed. The Patriot missile was enlisted to perform, beyond doing battle against Iraq's clumsy, Russian-designed ballistic Scuds, an ideological labor within the discourse of national empowerment and international trade wars. The Patriot missiles, on one level of fetishization, personify American patriotism to American workers, disoriented and de-centered in the postmodern, transnational scene: "Patriot works because of patriots like you," Bush affirms in this region of Lexington-Concord resistance and the New England work ethos.[40] Beyond this democratic identification of national object and national labor and symbolic identification of fathers and fatherland, Bush urges the technological superiority of America as instantiated and materialized in the very sublime of these high-tech weapons: "You see," he explains, "what has taken place here is a triumph of American technology. It's a triumph taking place every day, not just here at Raytheon but in factories and firms all across America, wherever American workers are pushing forward the bound of progress, keeping this country strong, firing the engines of economic growth."[41]

After invoking a frontier of high-tech sublimity in which ordinary Americans at Raytheon "will put unparalleled American technology to use as a tool for change," Bush situates such labor, agonistically, as part of an ongoing global battle against so much more than Iraq and the Third World weapon states: "What happens here is critical, absolutely critical, to our competitiveness now and then into the next century."[42] As Bush remarked to the American Association for the Advancement of Science earlier on the same day, democratically including technicians and workers in the same ideological misrecognition, "Today the spirit of innovation is alive and well in America."[43] Or, as he asserted to the Economic Club of New York on February 6, three weeks into the war, "America is a 'can do' nation. And

40. George Bush, "Remarks to Raytheon Missile Systems Plant Employees in Andover, Massachusetts, February 15, 1991," *Weekly Compilation of Presidential Documents 27*, no. 7 (18 Feb. 1991): 177.
41. Bush, "Remarks to Raytheon," 177–78.
42. Bush, "Remarks to Raytheon," 178.
43. George Bush, "Remarks to the American Association for the Advancement of Science, February 15, 1991," *Weekly Compilation of Presidential Documents 27*, no. 7 (18 Feb. 1991): 174.

America is home to the largest, most productive economy on earth."[44] This sense of technological superiority, ratifying a deeper cultural and moral conviction of political exceptionality at work, underwrites the grander claim of American hegemony that was ultimately propagated through this war in the Persian Gulf that "civilized behavior can begin again."[45] "We can build a better world and a better new world order,"[46] Bush affirmed, with the full conviction of a postmodern American Adam turning the Old World desert into a democratic garden watched over by those machines of loving grace, the Patriot missiles. (It was amid the populist euphoria of the Patriot missile speech that Bush first urged the Iraqi people to "take matters into their own hands and topple Hussein,"[47] leading later to the Kurdish refugee disaster.)

By-products of Cold War terror and cybernetic ingenuity, the Patriot missiles were semiotically enlisted, by President Bush, as connotative agents in the first post–Cold War holy war, in which, with allied support, a New World Order of Pax American sublimity slouched toward Bethlehem to be born. Given the de-centered international web of postmodern production, in which nation-state corporations can barely be located, never mind named as sites of political allegiance, this was a desperate act of national consolidation and corporate identification with an American product, place of production, and brand name. Strictly speaking, in a postmodern economy of instantaneous sign-flow and modular bricolage, there can no longer be any such thing as an "American forklift," nor, for that matter, can there be even an "American Pontiac" or "American Ford" that is *made in America* and that represents, as some fetishized object of national identity, the technological ingenuity, economic might, and cultural superiority of its patriotic makers. Such nationalism works not so much as an economic reality as a social instrument: While marketing research shows that such nationalist cues appeal primarily to consumers over forty-five because they, or their fathers, served in World War II, the Big Three marketers in Detroit, as in Lee Iacocca's rather tiresome "Buy America" pitch, still perpetuate a bunker mentality of competitive nationalism.[48]

44. George Bush, "Remarks and a Question-and-Answer Session at a Meeting of the Economic Club in New York City, February 6, 1991," *Weekly Compilation of Presidential Documents* 27, no. 6 (6 Feb. 1991): 139.
45. Bush, "Economic Club," 139.
46. Bush, "Economic Club," 139.
47. *Washington Post*, 16 Feb. 1991, 1.
48. Reich cites the American forklift example as a multinational product in "The Global Web," in *The Work of Nations*, 115n.: As U.S. Commerce Department officials discov-

By ideological projection, then, the Patriot commodity gave a name and a place to and embodied a materialized focus for national patriotism at an end point in the American century when, as Robert Reich claims, "American capitalism was now [sic] organized relentlessly around profits, not patriotism."[49] Still, romantic nationalism remains a discursive formation subject to public representation and recall. Nations build their communities upon acts of strong forgetting and historical error, as Renan urged, as well as upon sites of everyday enjoyment and empowerment that can still inspire communal conviction.[50] Upon closer examination of this techno-euphoric symbol of American national identity, we might pause to wonder: What's so *American* about the Patriot missile? These smart weapons, as *Business Week* soon pointed out, have foreign brains.[51] Later, James Fallows (known for his Japan-bashing) gleefully observed, lest Americans get complacent in their semiotic battle for global superiority, that "in its coverage of the U.S. victory in the Persian Gulf the Japanese press was much more skeptical about American high-tech mastery than were most American reporters" and that, except for the F-117 Stealth bomber, American "technology was more impressive to the Iraqis than to the Japanese."[52] Indeed, as a point of Japanese pride, semiconductor chips inside the Patriot missile were said to be housed in ceramic packaging made almost exclusively by the Kyocera Company of Kyoto, and even Raytheon's air-to-air Spar-

ered, "strictly speaking, there was no such thing as a U.S. forklift, or a foreign forklift for that matter." On this "marketplace where appeals to nationalism carry much less weight with consumers," see David Kiley, "The End of the 'American' Car," *Adweek's Marketing Week* (4 Mar. 1991): 18–20.

49. Robert B. Reich, "The Coming Irrelevance of Corporate Nationality," in *The Work of Nations*, 140.

50. Renan, "Qu'est-ce qu'une nation?" in *Nation and Narration*, 11. Also see Žižek, "Eastern Europe's Republics of Gilead": "A nation exists only as long as its specific enjoyment continues to be materialized in certain social practices, and transmitted in national myths that structure these practices" (53).

51. See Paul Magnusson, "American Smart Weapons, Foreign Brains," *Business Week* (4 Mar. 1991): 18. Magnusson argues that, despite Vice-President Dan Quayle's boast that laser-guided bombs provide "solid evidence of America's preeminence in technology," the Sparrow air-to-air missile, for example, has "circuits from Japan, a critical memory chip [that] was made in Thailand, and other essential parts [that] bore the West German stamp." The Commerce Department estimates that about 20 percent of American weapons' parts are manufactured abroad, raising the specter of "foreign dependency."

52. James Fallows, "Is Japan the Enemy?" *New York Review of Books* 38 (30 May 1991): 36.

row (now displacing the Patriot as an anti-missile missile in Israel) depends upon high-tech components that must be imported from Japan. Paradoxically, a posture of national autonomy (in Japanese, *Kokusanka*) concerning defense-weapons production has emerged in both countries, despite the postmodernity of the international market that makes such economic defensiveness, as Reich and others have observed, regressively symbolic, if not impossible.[53]

• • • •

As ground or cause, there is no longer any such corporate America that abides and functions, politically or economically, as an entity of economic nationalism. The romantic trope of "corporate nationality," in which champion corporations like GM, National Biscuit, United States Rubber, and US Steel once incarnated the wealth and well-being of the nation in the 1950s, is being deconstructed and de-centered into an international matrix of sign-flow and cash-flow that recognizes no national boundaries nor cultural allegiances beyond increasing profits of mega-capital and the mandates of technological innovation. At the cultural level of racial, ethnic, and regional heteroglossia, moreover, America is being palpably deconstructed into competing traditions and alternative narratives and canons as the controversy over the *Heath Anthology of American Literature* indicates. Nor, for that matter, as I would argue, can there be any such material entity called the American Sublime—unless politically reconstructed with a full, historical understanding of its dangers and damages. As the boundaries and centers of national identity are dissolving into zones of cyberspace and transnational webs of financial interaction, corporate commodities, like Niagara Falls, MGM, Waikiki, or the Empire State Building are being sold away to transnational constructions and cybernetic networks that have no point of origin nor measure of political identity.

Still, as the six-week-long war of American techno-euphoria in the Persian Gulf showed, the Patriot missile was constructed (by President

---

53. Japan, following American Pentagon policy, has taken a defensively nationalist position of "technological autonomy" concerning the manufacture of key defense weapons: see Michael J. Green, *Kokusanka: FSX and Japan's Search for Autonomous Defense Production* (Cambridge: MIT Japan Program, 1991). Since high-tech weapons are designed and fabricated all over the globe, and any firm can be considered American if it is incorporated in the United States, not even "the Pentagon has [any] idea who is making what and where" (see Reich, *The Work of Nations*, 116).

Bush) and misrecognized (by factory workers at Raytheon and the American silent majority) as the by-product of *American* technological superiority manifesting, for all the Old World to see, the faith of the American people in the sacralization of superior force to moral ends. With smart weapons bursting in air over Jerusalem as a sign that the American flag of the brave and free is internationally there, the Patriot missile emerges as a latter-day icon of the American Sublime that embodies and images forth the will to national greatness of the American economy and spiritual grandeur of the hardworking Massachusetts people whose state economy may be failing but whose national sense of mission and God-given errand in the wilderness can still find postmodern ratification in the oil deserts of Kuwait and Saudi Arabia. Raytheon may make Amana microwaves and Speed Queen washers and dryers, but Raytheon's seventeen-foot Patriot missile had captured the national imagination by evoking and reifying this power of the American Sublime. Yes, Raytheon may be the largest user of ozone-depleting chemicals in Massachusetts, and it may have been fined $1 million in March of 1990 for illegally using classified Pentagon budgets and documents to achieve their edge, but Raytheon's Patriot missile, as reimagined by President Bush, helped Americans forget history and remember their own sublimity as displaced into a cybernetic bomb.[54] The Patriot missile helped fuse and socialize ordinary citizens into spectators beholding, in awe and terror, that postmodern hero of the technological sublime—the "cyborg soldier"[55] and his/her weaponry of defense.

Though no poet, Bush euphorically acted the part of the Emersonian poet, reawakening "the power of national emblems," like Niagara Falls, Old Glory, and the Transcontinental Railway, to inspire belief and to tap into the "great public power" of American energy awaiting contemporary use as railways, canals, fisheries, or poems.[56] The American people fancy they hate poetry, but "they are all poets and mystics," Emerson affirmed in "The Poet," citing the power of a flag to motivate a pragmatic array of national enterprises: "Some stars, lilies, leopards, a crescent, a lion, an eagle, or

54. See Diane Dumanoski, "Raytheon Curb on Ozone Threat Brings Praise," *Boston Globe*, 25 Nov. 1990, 59, and John M. Broder, "Raytheon Fined $1 Million in Documents Case," *Los Angeles Times*, 21 Mar. 1990, sec. A, p. 12. Raytheon was one of five major weapons suppliers to admit possessing stolen military documents.
55. See Chris Hables Gray's detailed description, "The Cyborg Soldier: The US Military and the Postmodern Warrior," in *Cyborg Worlds: The Military Information Society*, ed. Les Levidow and Kevin Robins (London: Free Association Books, 1989), 43–71.
56. Ralph Waldo Emerson, "The Poet," in *Selections*, 233.

other figure which came into credit God knows how, shall make the blood tingle under the rudest or the most conventional exterior."[57] Though no poststructuralist, Bush, like the advertising poets of Leo Burnett and Philip Morris, is reconnecting the symbolic to the political.

Constructed out of the sublime poetics of President Bush and his uncanny ghostwriters, the Patriot missile emerges as the latest icon of American techno-euphoria simulating, if not instantiating, the superiority of American technology and corporate ingenuity of Americans at least to themselves. According to Kant's reading of the sublime, the aesthetical judgment must decide for the general over the statesman: General Schwarzkopf is more sublime than President Bush for the dangers he confronts, the violence he enacts and opposes, and the might of nature he engages and masters as dynamical force.[58] Leave it to nay-saying carpers of detail on "60 Minutes" or in *Business Week* to reveal, weeks later, that the Patriot missiles the General commanded were composed of computer components and chip technologies that had been made in Japan, proving the American dependency on Japanese know-how and on the flow of the mighty yen. The American empire may have ended on September 16, 1985, when the United States became a debtor nation and "the money power shifted from New York to Tokyo,"[59] but no one was telling the general, the president, or CNN, who together had produced another spectacle of high technology and patriotic imagery that allowed America to remain the unchallenged world leader of spectacle production. (The inability of a Patriot missile to intercept an Iraqi missile that slammed into a military barracks in Saudi Arabia, killing twenty-eight people, was later blamed on a computer failure in the radar system Raytheon had built.)

The technological sublimity of the Patriot missile as an icon of American invulnerability has been challenged from another quarter. In testimony before the House Armed Services Committee on April 16, 1991, Theodore Postol, a defense analyst at MIT revealed (through examinations of *Ma'ariv*, the Israeli newspaper) that the Scud-busting record of the Patriot was far from sublime: The Patriot's homing device was confused by pieces that

57. Emerson, *Selections*, 228–29.
58. Immanuel Kant, "Analytic of the Sublime," in *Critique of Judgement*, trans. J. H. Bernard (New York: Hafner Pub. Co. 1966), 102.
59. This is the impious claim of Gore Vidal, "The Day the American Empire Ran Out of Gas," in *At Home: Essays, 1982–1988* (New York: Vintage, 1990), 104–7, who argues for the post–Cold War dismantling of what he calls "the National Security State" and the Armageddon mentality still propagated under the Reagan administration.

226

broke away from incoming Scuds, successful hits sprayed lethal Scud fragments over a larger area than would have been affected by the incoming
Scud, and since the Patriots often followed their targets to the ground, they
added their own debris and damage to that of the Scud. Though Bush read
the Patriot record with all the confidence of a football score—"Patriot is
41 for 42—42 Scuds engaged, 41 intercepted"[60]—Postol later revealed a
more dismal tally: Before Patriot was enlisted into the battle, 13 Scuds fell
unopposed near Tel Aviv, killed no one, but wounded 115 people and damaged 2,698 apartments; after the Patriots were used, 11 Scud attacks killed
one person, injured 168, and damaged 7,778 apartments. (Raytheon soon
challenged this assessment, claiming in a FAX news release that Postol's
testimony was based on "unsubstantiated" data.)[61] In "Patriot Failures" (editorial, May 26), the New York Times called on the Pentagon to explain and
defend the actual, as opposed to the cultural, performance of the Patriot
missile as a high-tech weapon.

 The function of ideological construction is to create a misrecognition
a people can believe in and enact into historical fulfillment: to create a sublime object of ideology. The Patriot missile functioned, beyond its military
performance, as a symptom of American desire to install the sublime of
its own geopolitical project in global redemption. There is nothing intrinsi-
cally sublime in a sublime object, which gets enlisted from everyday objects
to embody, temporarily, "the impossible-real object of desire."[62] Simulating

60. Bush, "Remarks to Raytheon," 178.
61. See Eliot Marshall, "Patriot's Scud Busting Record Is Challenged," Science 252
(3 May 1991): 252–53.
62. See Slavoj Žižek, The Sublime Object of Ideology (London and New York: Verso,
1989), 194, for an analysis of the way national ideology interpellates and encodes the
political subject through producing "a sublime object" (which, for him, is anything from
Stalin [see p. 145] to the Titanic [see pp. 69–71] to a Hitchcock movie [see p. 182]), which
here represents lack, or the failure, of desire's representation: "According to Lacan, a sublime object is an ordinary, everyday object which, quite by chance, finds itself occupying
the place of what he calls das Ding, the impossible-real object of desire." The American
Sublime can be distinguished from this more negative Kantian/Hegelian dynamic by its
adherence to a nineteenth-century political imaginary that does not so much refuse as
reify subjective enjoyment into hugely positive spectacles of national empowerment, as
I have claimed. American identification with producing the frontier sublime as a space
of national redemption voided of threats can be contrasted, as cultural ideology, with the
Canadian Sublime, which Margaret Atwood has portrayed as a collective conviction of
"cold empty space" that threatens self/community with hostility, mutilation, failure, exile,
death, and "the ever-present feeling of menace": see Margaret Atwood, Survival: A The-

national grandeur, the Patriot missile had become the sublime object of American political desire. The National Security Council of the United States had recognized since 1987 that chip technologies being produced in Japan posed "a direct threat to the technological superiority deemed essential to U.S. defense systems." [63] The Patriot missile confirmed a shared sense at Raytheon, if not an ideological consensus around the country via CNN, of this "technological superiority" the United States had depended upon to enlist belief and action in the American Sublime during a time of global war.

In the economy of war, national power must be substantiated via a process of outinjuring the opponent, but this material violence gets abstracted and distanced, sublimated, or, in effect, *redescribed:* "The act of injuring, or the tissue that is to be injured, or the weapon that is to accomplish the injury is renamed. The gantry for American missiles is named the 'cherrypicker,' just as American missions entailing the massive dropping of incendiary bombs over North Vietnam were called 'Sherwood Forest' and 'Pink Rose,' " [64] as if war evoked a natural process of blossoming and recreating, say, a "Desert Storm" (sublime nature) or a "Desert Shield" (sublime technology). What Kant called the sublime of war would, in effect, reaffirm the legitimacy and reality of competing cultural constructs: To the victors go the power of world-building and world-destroying. Bodies maimed, injured, and destroyed help to substantiate the military—and moral—superiority of the winning ideology. The individual body of the patriot is enlisted, thereby, into the cause of national substantiation. In Elaine Scarry's uncanny description of war as a formal structure of injury and contest, "When the system of national self-belief is without any compelling source of substantiation other than the material fact of, and intensity of feeling in, the bodies of the believers (patriots) themselves, then war feelings are occasioned. That is, *it is when a country has become to its population a fiction that wars begin,* however intensely beloved by its people that fiction is." [65] Through staging technological spectacles of sublime power in a by now global cyberspace, war had again served to substantiate waning convictions of national superiority, as patriots were reconscripted to believe in, injure, and die

---

matic Guide to Canadian Literature (Toronto: Anansi, 1972), 30–35, 132, and chap. 2, "Nature the Monster."

63. Reich, *The Work of Nations*, 156n.

64. Elaine Scarry, *The Body in Pain: The Making and Unmaking of the World* (New York: Oxford University Press, 1985), 66.

65. Scarry, *The Body in Pain*, 131; Scarry's emphasis.

for techno-euphoric master-narratives of freedom, redemption, sovereignty, and sublimity.

Although as a national rallying cry "America, the Beautiful" portrays panoramas of sublime mountains and sweeping prairies that tap into a long-standing sanctification of the wilderness sublime, this lyric is unlikely to replace "The Star-Spangled Banner" as the national anthem of the United States of America any day soon. The war in the Persian Gulf will prob-ably permanently derail Indiana congressman Andrew Jacobs's 1990 bill to bring about this national anthem shift in the American political imaginary of its innermost purpose, goals, and tools.[66] Whitney Houston's performance of "The Star-Spangled Banner" at Superbowl XXV brought home the oddly poetic, transporting, and profoundly ideological appeal of this song to mil-lions of viewers preoccupied, as they were, with the war in Iraq, which began, as President Bush had promised, shortly after the January 15, 1991, deadline. Since Francis Scott Key had first penned this Anacreontic drink-ing lyric after the British assault on Baltimore in 1814, the "bombs bursting in air" have ratified, celebrated, and consecrated the American project of technological transcendence in ways no political speech can.[67] The war in the Persian Gulf, whatever else it accomplished, gave proof through the long night of postmodernism, that America "was still there."

I think this is so because, beyond legitimating a stance of war-mongering as self-defense, Key's poem circulates images of national en-joyment and social empowerment that presuppose a kind of self-absorbing, spiritualized techno-euphoria: The weapons manifest an American will to maintain international superiority and national distinction. These bombs of reified American intelligence—early "smart weapons" of American origin and end—substantiate the internal dynamics of the American Sublime. If the flag remains an emblem of threatened unity, the bombs better embody a shared conviction of national might and moral legitimacy: They resonate, as do the Patriot missiles, with the terror and wonder of global redemp-tion. These oft-repeated images serve better then body counts or political

66. On this "Star-Spangled Banner" controversy, see Margaret Carlson, "Oh, Say, Can You Sing It?" *Time* (12 Feb. 1990): 27. In a pre–Persian Gulf War CNN poll in January 1990, which presumably would now be higher, 67 percent of Americans preferred that "The Star-Spangled Banner" remain the national anthem.

67. See Robert Ferguson, " 'What Is Enlightenment?' Some American Answers," *Ameri-can Literary History* 1 (1990): 245–72, on material and ideological origins of Key's patriotic ballad, written following the British bombardment of Baltimore's Fort McHenry in 1814. Key's poem was designated the national anthem by an Act of Congress, March 3, 1931.

polemics to substantiate the American construction of itself and its material and spiritual by-products as a blessing to the earth. We are more than prepared to fight a holy war of moral absolutes and sacralized violence—this, as Saddam Hussein failed to realize in his own euphoric counter-rhetoric of Islamic *jihad,* is the only kind of war Americans know. The Patriot weapons helped President Bush convince Americans, within a context of waning national faith and economic dismantlement, that America was still there as a country capable of a national sublime, if only what Kant called the sublime of war. It was Kant, you may recall, who associated the sublime of the North American landscape with a certain kind of primitive mentality and native wildness that could be differentiated from thicker cultures of the European Enlightenment, reckoning in *Observations on the Feeling of the Beautiful and the Sublime* that "among all savages there is no nation that displays so sublime a mental character as those of North America."[68]

68. See Immanuel Kant, *Observations on the Feeling of the Beautiful and the Sublime,* trans. John T. Goodthwait (Berkeley: University of California Press, 1960), 111. My critical assumption has been that, in analyzing these documents of discursive nationalism from domains of literary and everyday culture, as Ariel Dorfman suggests, "there may be no better way for a country to know itself than to examine the myths and popular symbols that it exports to its economic and military dominions": see *The Empire's Old Clothes* (New York: Pantheon Books, 1983), 8. As Terry Eagleton has urged upon literary critics as citizens: "The role of the contemporary critic is to resist that dominance [of market ideology within the mass-mediated public sphere] by re-connecting the symbolic to the political, engaging through both discourse and practice with the process by which repressed needs, interests and desires assume the cultural forms which would weld them into a collective political force": see *The Function of Criticism: From 'the Spectator' to Post-Structuralism* (London: Verso, 1987), 123.

On Becoming Oneself in Frank Lentricchia

Daniel T. O'Hara

il miglior fabbro
—T. S. Eliot, *The Waste Land*

In many ways, Frank Lentricchia is a leading oppositional figure among those who study American literature. Initiated into the profession during the latter days of the New Criticism, schooled in close reading, disciplined by the sublime example of modernist masters, Lentricchia, in his first book on "the radical poetics" of Yeats and Stevens, *The Gaiety of Language* (1968), nevertheless supplements his insightful formalist analyses with a history of nineteenth-century literary appropriations of Kant and post-Kantian philosophical developments. He does so in order to contextualize his chosen poets' collective imaginative and theoretical achievement, which he identifies, hesitantly, as "a poetics of will" that he is uncertain may not really be "a poetics of anti-will."[1] Not only is Lentricchia moving to theory

---

1. Frank Lentricchia, *The Gaiety of Language: An Essay on the Radical Poetics of W. B. Yeats and Wallace Stevens* (Berkeley and Los Angeles: University of California Press, 1968), 6.

prior to its heyday in the early and mid-1970s, he is also going beyond formalism prior to the 1970 publication of Geoffrey Hartman's influential essay collection of that name. Moreover, in raising the question of the individual will and its role in culture, however uncertainly, Lentricchia foregrounds the problems of imaginative and critical agency that preoccupy him, and now us, so urgently.

Similarly, in the mid-1970s, at the height of European theory's major impact, when things American, modern, and subject-centered are generally out, and things continental, (post)romantic, and anonymously textual (or discursive) are generally in, Lentricchia publishes, in 1975, his second book, *Robert Frost: Modern Poetics and the Landscapes of Self*, which relies on a pragmatist understanding of conscious intention.[2] He thereby begins the renovation of modernist studies even as he anticipates the return to the subject of modern American culture and its distinctive historical origins, which seriously begins to occur on a large scale only later in the decade. In his next book, *After the New Criticism* (1980), Lentricchia does double work: He participates significantly in theory's academic institutionalization by writing the first general overview of theory's post–World War II developments; but he also provides, presciently, the first sustained and fully informed critique of theory. Theory has become, as you recall, a new formalism for this historically engaged American critic sympathetic to (albeit sometimes critical of) western Marxism and Foucault's brand of poststructuralism.[3]

Lentricchia comes entirely into his own with *Criticism and Social Change* (1983). He positions himself concretely and personally here by provocatively choosing Kenneth Burke as his American theoretical exemplar, over and against the professional choice of many other critics at the time, Paul de Man. Lentricchia also announces and thematizes the conflict of historical origins and intellectual aspirations—the problematic of American cultural assimilation—which has become so central to the problematics of the New Historicist, postcolonialist (or subaltern studies), and New Americanist projects. In publicly choosing Burke, a maverick American literary intellectual simultaneously of the old Left and one of its most formidable critics, over de Man, Lentricchia chooses the politically committed, yet highly self-conscious, philosopher of the literary symbolic over the ironically self-

---

2. Frank Lentricchia, *Robert Frost: Modern Poetics and the Landscapes of Self* (Durham: Duke University Press, 1975), see especially 145 ff.
3. Frank Lentricchia, *After the New Criticism* (Chicago: University of Chicago Press, 1980), see especially 349–51.

opposing and highly sophisticated (and once so very influential) mandarin of theoretical reflection. Lentricchia justifies this critical choice of Burke, surprisingly, as expressing loyalty to his origins, a choice made in the name of his own and his family's material experiences of class, ethnic, and gender differences, for it is Burke's dramatistic criticism of the socially symbolic action to be discovered in aesthetic encodings of such differences, and not de Man's hieratic deconstruction, that can expose the cultural work literature, in fact, performs. It is these differences, along with those of race, that theory, as de Man practices it, automatically overlooks. Sooner than Lentricchia then thinks, however, such differences come to provide the primary topics of contemporary critical investigation.[4]

Lentricchia thus encapsulates, prefiguratively, the experience of his generation of oppositional literary critics. He goes beyond formalism, turns to theory, historicizes its development, criticizes its emerging professional excesses, and thematizes the minute historical particulars of both imaginative agency and the institutional realities of the proposed American difference in late capitalist culture. From formalism to theory, from theory as a new formalism in disguise to theory as openly postmodern cultural politics—such could be the self-description of Lentricchia's career and that of his generation.

In these ways, we can see that the subject of his criticism, however familiar it finally seems, has always been the fate of the imagination in modern culture. Lentricchia has been concerned about how the imagination has been conceived, practiced, and policed. As one can see, he has discovered and taught, virtually from the beginning of his career, beyond the specifics of such conceptions, practices, and policings, that there is not one imagination, narrowly aesthetic/symbolist derived from Coleridge, Kant, Poe, and his French champions, but there are, in fact, several imaginations, all of them postromantic in the strong sense, yet each significantly different from the other. This is especially true for Lentricchia in the case of the twentieth-century American imagination. Yet, as we shall see, there remains a basic family resemblance among these imaginations.

As I sort out and categorize these imaginations in action (a process based loosely on Hayden White's typology of the historical imagination in *Metahistory*), I discern essentially four types. They can best be characterized by the intellectual movements each has most informed: aestheticism,

4. Frank Lentricchia, *Criticism and Social Change* (Chicago: University of Chicago Press, 1983), see especially 1–20.

totalitarianism, pragmatism, and criticism. Aestheticism, of course, finds its great ancestor in Kant, while totalitarianism follows Hegel, pragmatism revises Emerson, and criticism enshrines Arnold. Lentricchia accepts each of these ancestors as historical points of reference, except Arnold, preferring instead to substitute the actual experiences of difference—economic, social, sexual, and cultural—for some grand literary and/or critical paragon. As we shall see, in writing recently on Pound, Lentricchia does disclose, via his appreciative and critical comments, the profile of his perfect cultural critic.

Another way of characterizing these types of imagination is rhetorically, or figuratively, in terms of what Kenneth Burke calls the master, or ancestral, trope, the performative god-term, especially prized by each of them. Aestheticism is the mode of metaphor, of the desire to be different and to be in a stylish world elsewhere: "I am the king in the palace now." Totalitarianism is the mode of synecdoche, of the desire to subsume all the different parts of a vertiginously multiple life within a totalizing and invariable whole, or system: "I am the State." Pragmatism is the mode of metonymy, of the desire for ever emerging wondrous associations of ever new personal possibilities without end and without definitive consequences: "The crown and scepter, the head and good right arm of the state—c'est moi? Wouldn't it be pretty to think so, or would it?" Criticism, finally, is the mode of irony, of the desire to become and remain flexible and open to the necessities of self-revision within the broadest possible public context: "I am content always to criticize things as they are."

I do not want to multiply complexities in a Shandyean manner, yet I do find in Lentricchia that each of these imaginations may also be self-divided. Aestheticism, as in Pound, may be active and insurrectionary, literally and socially, or it may be, as in early Yeats, far from provocatively innovative, becoming passive and pessimistically escapist. Totalitarianism can take the aristocratic, or vanguard, party form of Fascist authoritarianism or Communist oligarchy; or, antithetically, it can inspire dystopic and paranoid visions, an Orwellian Big Brotherism or a Foucauldian panoptical discipline of power. Pragmatism appears either as the anti-imperialist, barbarically anarchic, and wildly antinomian loose-cannon individualism of the later William James, or as the wishy-washy, Charlie Brownish postmodern bourgeois liberalism of Rorty's contingency theory of private self-creation. Finally, criticism can be, as it usually is in Burke, a consciously complex style of critical engagement, at once imaginatively sympathetic and ironically self-reflective, or, it can regress to its romantic and aesthetic roots in

234

Kant's earlier aestheticism, which anchors his critical philosophy, by adopting the sophisticatedly belated and disillusioned posture, as in de Man, of cloistral retreat. In this complex light, we can see that Lentricchia's project throughout his career, really a historicizing of Frye's *Anatomy of Criticism*, aims at giving a critical anatomy of these imaginations in action as they play crucial roles in the modern world.

Both the popular media, such as the *New York Times Magazine*, and the intellectual media, such as *Critical Inquiry*, now recognize Lentricchia's representative status as an academic oppositional figure. Both kinds of forum generally do so, however, in the most superficial way possible: that of celebrity gossip, thanks (in part) to the notorious photograph on the back of *Criticism and Social Change*, which Lentricchia has recently revealed to be a radically self-parodic spoof of the media's scenes of multiple misrecognition. Just imagine: "The Dirty Harry of critical theory," as the *Village Voice* identifies him on the jacket of *Criticism and Social Change*, the central figure in the current prominence of Duke University's English department, as the *Chronicle of Higher Education* characterizes him, the editor in chief of the critical collective that has revamped *South Atlantic Quarterly* almost overnight into a major journal—these different sides of Frank Lentricchia have a collective sense of humor, and can be ironical at their own expense![5]

More seriously, in the essay "Don DeLillo," Lentricchia focuses on the former's emergence into popular consciousness due to the controversy sparked among influential neoconservative critics like George Will by *Libra*, DeLillo's intentionally "unpatriotic" novel about the Kennedy assassination. In his sustained meditation on the media creation of a Lee Harvey

5. For a sampling of Lentricchia's media exposure, see: the interview with Imre Salusinszky in *Criticism in Society* (New York and London: Methuen, 1987), 176–206; the response to Gilbert and Gubar's counterattack in *Critical Inquiry* 14, no. 2 (Winter 1988): 407–14 (it is here that Lentricchia reveals the self-spoofing nature of the infamous photograph); the interview with David Latane in *Critical Texts* 5, no. 2 (1988): 6–17; the article by Robert Bliwise, entitled "Lentricchia between the Lines: Putting Life into Literature," *Duke: Magazine for Alumni and Friends* 74, no. 4 (May–June 1988): 2–7; and the now famous article by James Atlas, "The Battle of the Books," *New York Times Magazine*, 5 June 1988. The infamous photo in question shows a muscular Lentricchia, looking streetwise and "pumped," wearing a pullover with bold horizontal stripes, and standing up against a graffiti-strewn wall: an image designed both to debunk the stereotype of the shabby-genteel professor and to spoof Lentricchia's own macho reputation among his critics. While clearly succeeding in doing the former, this photo, until recently, anyway, has not been taken in the self-ironical spirit of the latter intention.

Oswald, Lentricchia comments critically on the system of celebrity production and assassination of which he, himself, has recently been a partial and
purely symbolic victim. The brilliance of this performance lies in the ironically allegorical fashion in which Lentricchia theorizes the general situation
of the postmodern subject per se, via his intensely particular reflection on
DeLillo's novel:

> In the radical sense of the word, Lee Harvey Oswald is a contem-
> porary production, a figure who is doubled everywhere in *Libra*,
> even, most harrowingly, in strategic places, in the narrative voice that
> DeLillo invented for this book. . . . The disturbing strength of *Libra*—
> DeLillo gives no quarter on this—is its refusal to offer its readers
> a comfortable place outside of Oswald. DeLillo does not do what
> the media right convicts him of doing—imply that all Americans are
> would-be murderous sociopaths. He has presented a politically far
> more unsettling vision of normalcy, of everyday life so utterly en-
> thralled by the fantasy selves projected in the media as our possible
> third person, and, more insidiously, an everyday life so enthralled by
> the charisma of the media, that it makes little useful sense to speak
> of sociopathology or of a lone gunman. Oswald is ourselves painted
> large, in scary tones, but ourselves.[6]

In what Lentricchia calls "the theater of self" (DD, 14), which the
sociopathology of postmodern America especially encourages, our lives are
like DeLillo's "imagined biography of Oswald, a plotless tale of aimless life
propelled by the agonies of inconsistent and contradictory motivations, a life
without coherent form except for the form implied by the book's [astrological]
title" (DD, 14). We are, like Oswald, negative Librans, barely balancing a
myriad of possibilities, for, as Lentricchia cites the DeLillo narrative voice as
saying, we are " 'somewhat unsteady and impulsive. Easily, easily, easily influenced. Poised to make the dangerous leap' " (DD, 14). Into what? Blindly
into some role or other, in one or another of the coercive, yet captivating,

---

6. Frank Lentricchia, "Don DeLillo," *Raritan* 10, no. 3 (Spring 1989): 16–18; hereafter cited
in my text as DD. See also Frank Lentricchia, "The American Writer as Bad Citizen—
Introducing Don DeLillo," and *"Libra* as Postmodern Critique," in Frank Lentricchia, ed.
"The Fiction of Don DeLillo," a special issue of *South Atlantic Quarterly* 89, no. 2 (Spring
1990): 239–44 and 431–53, respectively. For more of Lentricchia on the subject of post-
modern media and their relation to the American dream, see his "Tales of the Electronic
Tribe," in Frank Lentricchia, ed., *New Essays on White Noise* (New York: Cambridge
University Press, 1991).

236

narratives of our self-alienation already scripted and being revised in and as American cultural history. However much we may deny or critique such narratives, they are still there to ensnare us, most likely when we think we are hatching our most authentic little plots. Following DeLillo's lead (here and in *White Noise*), Lentricchia traces this all-too-probable contemporary fate, a horrific, yet historically specified, marriage of Foucault's discursive nightmares and Lyotard's visions of our postmodern condition, all the way back from DeLillo and Fitzgerald, through Dreiser and Emerson, to the pilgrim fathers and mothers on the Mayflower. Each generation of American dreamers, it seems, is convinced that their given identities, their first persons (or "I's"), are barren, poverty stricken, empty vessels set loose from the ruins of some literal or figurative Europe (or other original homeland), to await, once in America, the sublimely apocalyptic appearance of the fabulous universal third person, the new self-made American identity ex nihilo, standing there and staring back at us from the radiant surface of the latest mirror of our culture: book, newspaper and magazine, film, TV newsreel, video cassette, and so on. In this eery light, the distinction between reality and imagination begins to blur. All the imaginations in action that Lentricchia anatomizes over the course of his career thus lead up to and make possible this historical vision of the saturnalia of contingent masks in postmodern American culture.

Both in *Ariel and the Police* and in his latest book, *American Modernism*, his contribution to the new *Cambridge History of American Literature*, Lentricchia not only explores the historical formation of this postmodern condition but also provides us with an example of a self-critical theoretical practice. His mask play stages an alternative conception of the critic and of criticism's function at the present time. This alternative oppositional criticism can best be elucidated by reading Lentricchia's latest work in terms of the late Foucault's idea of the plural subject and Kristeva's revisionary understanding of imaginary identification.

My own position is close to Lentricchia's as I have, so far, outlined it. (Clearly, he is my Kenneth Burke.) Where it varies is in my reliance on late Foucault and recent Kristeva, neither of whom Lentricchia discusses. I rely on them for, respectively, a historical meditation and a revisionary psychoanalytic treatment of intellectual identity formation. As I read them, and following Lentricchia's lead, critical identity (especially in postmodern America) involves the sublimation of the vulnerable sympathetic reader's initial response (the negative Libran aspect of us all) to an imposing imagination in action. The critic internalizes this sublime wound of aesthetic possibilities as a specular doubling, a spectral scene of instructive mourning for a momentarily usurped, and so somewhat resentful and sharply self-divided, subjectivity. This interpretive process sets up the psychic agency I call "oneself," a radically ambivalent dialectic of self-overcoming identification and critical differentiation, loving transference and defensive distantiation. The source for this internalized agon is the ancient classical model of self-development derived from the complex, ever changing relationship of the pedagogic pair of mentor and student with their (at least) latently erotic bond. Critical identity becomes an internalized economy of such imaginative pairings, a psychic school of formative influence, a continuing mask play of "oneself" in this inescapably plural sense. As such, critical identity is necessarily and radically socialized, indeed, inescapably socialized, if it is internally political, fundamentally dynamic, self-consciously erotic, and so, almost by definition, constitutionally ironic. For me, the ethical aim of such identity formation, when wittingly practiced, comes about in that magnanimous avowal of one's imaginary father(s), which defeats the social pathology of (self-)destructive *ressentiment*. If the material sites of the collective archive of canonical and non-canonical works in our culture are the various institutions and media for the preservation, circulation, and dissemination of knowledge, then what I have just characterized as critical identity formation constitutes both the collective archive's psychosocial site and its changing human face.

I think this agonistic bonding of the pedagogic pair is what informs the historical context of first- and third-person sociopathology that Lentricchia adduces in "Don DeLillo." Male bonding, even across generational, ethnic, and racial lines, is the only thing, in the arena of personal relations, that, traditionally, America likes to think it did even partly well. *Libra* represents in the Oswald-Kennedy bond its demonic postmodern parody: Oswald plays Mordred, and not Percival, to Kennedy's King Arthur. Oswald's fate is representative: He lacks a definite identity; he is all too easily influenced because he is cut off from his historic roots. To be so fated is what it means to be an American—as much as does the dream of impersonating a fabulous figure of one's own creation. In America, perhaps, only the educational institution can provide an important, albeit minimum, basis for collective intergenerational judgment. And we need this basis for judging such wildly self-and-other-destructive dreams of fabulous identity as Thomas Sutpen's doomed dynastic "design" in Faulkner's *Absalom! Absalom!* or as Oswald's pathetic postmodern parody and pastiche of all such imperial designs in DeLillo's *Libra*. The problem with most American appropriations of poststructuralism—New Historicism, New Americanist criticism, neopragmatism—is precisely that whatever they may preach, they nevertheless practice, because of this postmodern American condition, their own belated versions of the sublime dream of the heroically self-made individual: DeLillo's ever aspiring celebrity Oswald from *Libra*, however uncomfortably, may indeed be one of us.

In *Ariel and the Police: Michel Foucault, William James, Wallace Stevens*, Lentricchia takes to task three contemporary critical formations: New Historicism, neopragmatism, and essentialist feminism. He does so because, unlike Michel Foucault, William James, and Wallace Stevens, these critical movements subsume the problematic struggles of such particular (and plural) imaginations in action within the conventional hierarchies of professional discipline. These movements, Lentricchia claims, thereby supervise, homogenize, police, and so make uniform the unique differences of Foucault, James, and Stevens, most often for self-serving careerist purposes. That is, such heterogeneous Ariels become just grist for the mills of professionalism. Filial ingratitude could be the motto of these critical movements, even as saving Ariel (or the particular imagination) certainly is Lentricchia's. Each of these critical positions, after claiming a radically contingent basis, reinscribes the aesthetic dream of the self-made, free-standing, singular subject beyond the reach of history, thereby belying their initial socializing claims. As "Don DeLillo" may already suggest, these critics do so because they are unaware that the postmodern American condition of Oswalds-in-the-making, narrative shards adrift in or bumping wildly about a culture of inherited masterplots, also applies to themselves. Twentieth-century fiction repeatedly traces the evolution of fatal design out of mere chance. As DeLillo dramatizes in *Libra*, once Oswald, the aimless shard, enters the plot of the CIA-Mafia-Cuban-exile conspirators, his own end, like that of his ideal double, Kennedy, is fatally sealed. Similarly, as Lentricchia shows, some theorists of the postmodern end up getting hooked by one or another version of the greatest American grand narrative of them all, that fabulous dream of the self-originating, purely aesthetic subject, the transcendental self that springs full-blown from its own Platonic conception of itself.

In *Ariel and the Police*, Lentricchia traces Stephen Greenblatt's trail of self-contradiction. He starts from Greenblatt's full embrace of the New Historicist nightmare vision from Foucault's *Discipline and Punish*, where history is a totalitarian system of metadiscourses of power supervising and disciplining every molecule of life, with no exit for subjective agency to escape. Lentricchia concludes his hunt with Greenblatt's expressed desire for and fundamental conviction of a "will to play" in the epilogue to his 1980 classic of contemporary criticism, *Renaissance Self-Fashioning*. As Lentricchia points out, Greenblatt ends by contradicting his espousal of New Historicism (really of any historicism), when he claims that "the will to play flaunts society's cherished orthodoxies, embraces what the culture finds loathsome or frightening, transforms the serious into the joke and then unsettles the category of the joke by taking it seriously, courts self-destruction in the interest of the anarchic discharge of its energy. This is play on the brink of an abyss, *absolute* play."[7] Greenblatt, given his New Historicist discursive determinism, has no logical justification for such a vision of the will to play, which is already an absurdity on its face, a subject ripe for radical parody. Where could such a will, particularly in the world of *Discipline and Punish*, whose prototype Greenblatt claims to find emerging in the Renaissance, come from? In any event, this passage echoes, I think, Schiller, from *Letters on Aesthetic Education*, and Nietzsche, from *The Gay Science*.[8] Naturally, the passage also has a then-contemporary resonance in early Derrida and Foucault, particularly their strangely similar remarks on the visions of totally excessive psychic economy and of transgression in Bataille. While such resonances make Greenblatt's illogical position historically understandable, it cannot make it any more logical. Lentricchia's analysis of this passage primarily in terms of Greenblatt's own postmodern American situation of disillusioned liberalism, with its considerable debt to Emersonian transcendentalism, is remarkably perspicacious:

> The personal story that [Greenblatt] tells in the epilogue [of *Renaissance Self-Fashioning*] functions as a cautionary tale of the archetypal political awakening of liberal man to the realities of power. His advice is to imaginatively interiorize the dream of self-fashioning because only by so doing will we keep ourselves from being swept away in history's narrative of repression, in the inevitable movement to the carceral nightmare as the daylight world of everyday life. [Yet]

7. Frank Lentricchia, *Ariel and the Police: Michel Foucault, William James, Wallace Stevens* (Madison: University of Wisconsin Press, 1988), 91–92; hereafter cited in my text as *AP*. See also Stephen Greenblatt, *Renaissance Self-Fashioning* (Chicago: University of Chicago Press, 1980), 220. Lentricchia cites this passage from Greenblatt in *AP*, 100.
8. For a discussion of Schiller's influence on Emerson, Nietzsche, and later cultural criticism, see my "Over Emerson's Body," *The CEA Critic* 49, nos. 2–3 (Winter–Summer 1987): 79–88.

Greenblatt tells us at the end that the human subject which he (and we) wanted to be autonomous and believed to be so "begins to seem remarkably unfree, the ideological project of the relations of power in a particular society." . . . So the Foucauldian new historicist account in its entirety—both what it believes to be the truth and what speaks through and undoes that belief ["the will to play" in Greenblatt]— is the best if unwitting account of new historicism and its political quandary that I know. Hating a world that we never made, wanting to transform it, we settle for a holiday from reality, a safely sealed space reserved for the expression of aesthetic anarchy, a long weekend that defuses the radical implications of our unhappiness. (*AP*, 97 and 101)

Here, Lentricchia exposes how the totalitarian nightmare imagination of Foucault's *Discipline and Punish* effectively inspires the resurrection of the aesthetic imagination's compensatory dream of escape from reality into a sublime vision of the freely self-fashioning dilettante of absolute play. How far the self-made critic of American culture to be found in Emerson has fallen here! Lentricchia thereby reads the critical mask play of these interrelated imaginations from the dramatic intersection of Greenblatt's New Historicist text and his postmodern American context.

Similarly, in his analysis of Steven Knapp and Walter Benn Michaels's controversial 1982 essay "Against Theory," Lentricchia reads the mask play of imaginations in action within their influential brand of neopragmatism, which generally celebrates William James and not C. S. Peirce. Given Knapp and Michaels's ostentatious claims to pragmatist critical pedigree, one might expect that, like the later William James, the antinomian father of pragmatism, they would practice an open-ended metonymic criticism, variously political, aesthetic, historical, and theoretical. Instead, Knapp and Michaels do what all their neopragmatist brethren now also do: They set themselves up, as Lentricchia shows, as synecdochal, or representative, masters of the entire critical field. Knapp and Michaels presume to know, a priori, what counts as theory (namely, strong, foundational, and so self-doomed, attempts to survey and master, systematically from outside and above, the field of critical practice), and what does not count as theory (namely, provisional, improvisatory conceptualizations of practice for getting some critical job of work done). Lentricchia betrays the self-contradiction at the heart of the "Against Theory" project. However much Knapp and Michaels may claim that there is nothing more to theory than practice, professional convention, and social belief, and that theory, therefore, with its presumption to a priori knowledge, can and should simply be dismissed, their own rhetoric nevertheless performs in practice as if they were imperial subjects laying down the law of their neopragmatist vision for everyone and for all time. Lentricchia succinctly puts it this way: "Pragmatism (the vigilante within) is always on the verge of vanquishment, of giving belief over to [such absolutist practice of] theory (the totalitarian within)" (AP, 125). In other words, the mask play of the pragmatist and totalitarian imaginations in action, like that of the aesthetic and totalitarian imaginations in Greenblatt's case, are here dialectically interrelated on the pedagogic model of magisterial presence and prodigal student (Stanley Fish, you recall, became the professional mentor of Michaels), until the supervention of the critical imagination that, as Lentricchia performs it, can read so well the auguries of such far from innocent critical mask plays.

As we will shortly see in his provocative critique of Sandra Gilbert and Susan Gubar's "essentialist feminism," Lentricchia can read such mask plays of imaginations in action performing themselves as the dramatic intersection of text and context, not simply because he draws intellectual sustenance from rough-and-ready Kenneth Burke and his socially symbolic criticism of motives rather than from well-modulated and refined Northrop Frye and his idealist vision of mythic archetypes. It is also because the more than professional circumstances primarily account for Lentricchia's distinctive critical ability. His situation as a second generation Italian-American male—unlike Italian-American women, it has been unusual hitherto for this demographic category, as they say, to make it in significant numbers into the ranks of professional intellectuals—necessarily foregrounds historically specific aspects of class, ethnic, and gender differences. This foregrounding, or underscoring, helps to explain Lentricchia's nearly preternatural sensitivity to differences and nuances of style in the largest sense of the word. I do not mean to imply by making this claim that for a critic to be a self-aware, insightful analyst of style he or she must play the game of moral one-upmanship on the world-historical stage of cultural victimization. Far from it. What I am claiming, instead, is that the power of subjective agency in Lentricchia's representative case, as he himself repeatedly says, is fully historical in nature (and fully historicized in his later criticism). It is never merely a matter of sublime individual genius, whether implicitly his own or ostensibly Burke's (or any other writer's). It is also that this (like any) imaginative agency is necessarily plural, made up of scenes of instruction, in which literary and personal ancestors compete for attention, since imaginative agency, as I have suggested here and argued elsewhere, is grounded in the collective archive and its fostering of critical change by means of its accumulated resources of canonical and non-canonical, positive and negative, exempla. The mask plays of imaginations in action in Lentricchia's work are clearly informed by this collective process of critical identity formation.

Basically, with Gilbert and Gubar, Lentricchia accuses them of what Toril Moi, in *Sexual/Textual Politics*, defines as "essentialist feminism." Lentricchia is referring to the kind of feminist criticism in which a fundamental biological difference in identity along gender lines, which marks women's writing as fundamentally different, is asserted or presumed. The upshot of such criticism is that the patriarchal hierarchy is simply reversed, with women becoming the morally privileged victims in the material history of repression. In such criticism, they are thus always being represented, with distinction, as the moral superiors of imperially empowered males, regardless of all socially specific, historically constructed differences, especially those of class, between people within the same culture, and between people of different cultures. Feminists of the Gilbert and Gubar sort are therefore in danger of erecting into dogma a "Manichean allegory," "a formalism of gender" (*AP*, 179), that is the mirror image of the patriarchy's naturalistic ahistoricism and that would grant to the essentialist feminists in question the rhetorical right to lord it over the entire field of critical and cultural studies as if they were, from Lentricchia's perspective, the self-appointed queens in theory:

> If history, as Gilbert and Gubar argue, is a repetitious sexist drama (not easy to argue otherwise) with men in the plot-controlling role of the oppressor, and women in the role of selfless victim, then history may be in danger of being translated . . . into Manichean allegory, and the very category that Moi and others invoke in order to explain the transformation of biology into history—she calls it, interchangeably, the "social" or the "cultural"—this category will be banished behind the scenes almost as quickly as it is invoked. With the social banished behind the scenes, history begins to look very much again like biology, biology like metaphysics, and the writing of feminist literary criticism like a ritual of scapegoating propelled by paranoia. (*AP*, 179)

From Lentricchia's perspective, their criticism is also propelled by the American dream of sublime self-aggrandizement in one of its more virulent postmodern critical forms. Just as Greenblatt embraces Foucault's totalitarian dystopia of history as all-powerful, suffocating discourses only to retreat into a weak-kneed liberal posture of aesthetic self-fashioning; just as Knapp and Michaels espouse the radical contingency of pragmatism only to re-produce the panoptical desire for total supervision and disciplining of the entire theoretical field at their hands; so, too, Gilbert and Gubar, in the name of the radical ideology of difference, apocalyptically separate all men and women into the very same homogenizing antithetical archetypes of bio-logical determination that the patriarchy loves, and, only in doing so, they simply reverse their evaluations. Ironically enough, the current institutional consequences of such deeply self-conflicted rhetorical strategies are the simultaneous resentful dismissal or confinement of all imaginary fathers and the virtual professional apotheosis of their critical authors.

As his statements in several recent interviews attest, Lentricchia knows from his own and his family's material experiences that class differ-ences, which are not natural but historical, can make as much difference for males from excluded groups as gender differences can for women. Simi-larly, he knows that not all women, until recently, were in the position of homebodies just tending the children and the simulated hearth. His own mother and grandmother had to work to help support the extended family. Such class differences are radically contingent, as Lentricchia reiterates, and, as we will see shortly in more detail, they account for the particu-lar situations of modern American poets and their distinctive achievements more thoroughly than simply the application of one abstract theoretical cate-gory of analysis, whether gender-based or not. In Gilbert and Gubar's case, their conception of poetic vocation derives from the aristocratic model of inherited estates. This model is historically inappropriate for a country in which Wordsworth's democratic dream of the vast majority of its poets (like its citizens) being middle class would indeed become a reality. America's poets rarely experience such inheritance in fact or fancy, are mostly fearful of falling to the lower depths, and are ever conscious, in each generation, of starting over again from next to nothing to make their own new ways in the business of poetry. (By middle class, Lentricchia means neither idly poor nor idly rich; rather, he means working for a more-than-subsistence livelihood.)

In each of these cases—Greenblatt's New Historicism, Knapp and Michaels's neopragmatism, and Gilbert and Gubar's essentialist feminism—Lentricchia reads the mask play of imaginations in action as shaping the criticism in question often to the point of distortion, the self-contradiction of working at cross-purposes with itself. Despite their explicit claims to the contrary, despite the irony that two of these three cases involve pairs of critics, and despite the fact that all three cases represent now widespread critical developments, the formative self-contradiction generally playing itself out is the one Lentricchia discusses memorably in "Don DeLillo": Whatever we may believe and say in theory, our critical practice at any moment may betray us as being Oswald-like narrative fragments awhirl in our postmodern world, chronically in danger of making the dangerous leap and becoming ensnared by some master narrative or other. In our time, of course, this usually means the grand narrative of the American dream's fabulous third person, the heroically self-made universal individual, the Jay Gatsby, Sister Carrie, or Ralph Waldo Emerson, any and all of those figures who change in response to their own words, figures who haunt what Lentricchia dreads may really be our Lee Harvey Oswald–like everyday lives:

> DeLillo writes that Oswald "wanted to carry himself with a clear sense of role." But who is this "he" who wanted a "role," just who is it that stands in the wings waiting for a part in the theater of self? It doesn't much help to say that he is someone named "Oswald" who can get up from a chair where he's been reading a book, calmly walk over to his wife, pummel her with both fists, then return to the chair and resume his reading, quietly. The identity of the negative Libran is an undecidable intention waiting to be decided. And astrology is the metaphor in *Libra* for being trapped in a system whose determinative power is grippingly registered by DeLillo's double narrative of an amorphous existence haphazardly stumbling into the future where a plot awaits to confer upon it the identity of a role fraught with form and purpose. (DD, 14)

For Lentricchia, the feature of Foucault, James, and Stevens that, whatever their limitations, sharply distinguishes them from the American critical formations of New Historicism, neopragmatism, and essentialist feminism that would appropriate and discipline these figures is precisely what DeLillo and Lentricchia also possess: a strongly particular imaginative grasp of their actual historical situations. The problem with contingency theory, therefore, is that it is not really historical enough.

The constructively critical moment in *Ariel and the Police* comes mainly in its second half. It is here that Lentricchia first develops, via his particular readings of his chosen poet, the theoretical-historical perspective of cultural-political analysis that informs his magisterial *Cambridge History* volume. Lentricchia lays out the situation at the turn of the century facing the young man who wants to become a poet. All too briefly, I will summarize his deliberately provocative view of this situation from both books.[9]

Such a young man lives at a time when American imperialism, modern capitalist discipline and commodification, the savvy marketing of sentimentality for insatiable consumption by passive readers, and the feminization of intellectual life—its chronically self-hating and too often self-defined genteel status—combine to enshrine as aesthetic paradigm the belated Fireside poetic of Edmund Clarence Stedman (scholar and anthologist), Ellery Sedgewich (editor of the *Atlantic*), and Jessie Belle Rittenhouse (poet and anthologist). In his chapter on Robert Frost in *American Modernism*, Lentricchia succinctly characterizes, with special panache, the modern poet's antipathy to Belle Rittenhouse and her influence:

> In her various writings and anthologies she could say who was in and who (usually by omission) was out, and though recent historians have not ratified any of her choices and do not know her name, she was a force who represented both in her female person and her taste the aesthetic grain that the emerging modernist male poets worked against: the principle of "the Feminine in literature," as Eliot put it, which he was none too anxious to give space to in *The Egoist*; the "Aunt Hepsy" that Pound saw as typifying poetry's contemporary audience in the United States; one of those—again Pound—who had turned poetry (for serious people) into "balderdash—a sort of embroidery for dilettantes and women." (*AM*, 3)

This poetic, which Palgrave recommends in his statement of principles in *The Golden Treasury*, repeatedly reproduces a watered-down Keatsian or Tennysonian lyric—abstracted from what it sees as the hard grit of life, vaguely pointing out some noble moral—in the Hallmark card style of traditional verse forms and so suitable for immediate framing by pages of advertisements in *Harper's* or the *Atlantic*. This is the world in which Palgrave's *Golden Treasury* is, indeed, king. Lentricchia, with fierce verve, also depicts in his Frost chapter what Palgrave's genteel followers made of this anthology poetic of splendid isolation. *The Golden Treasury* is clearly more various and representative of poetic tradition than this: "No narrative, no description of local, regional cast; no humor (the antithesis of the lyric mode

9. All citations from Frank Lentricchia, *American Modernism*, vol. 4 of *The Cambridge History of American Literature* (New York: Cambridge University Press, forthcoming) come from manuscript copy and will be cited hereafter in my text as *AM*.

according to Palgrave); no intellect at meditation; nothing occasional; nothing dramatic—no textures of blank verse because lyric in its purity excludes the dramatic voice in its speaking cadences; certainly no vernacular. . . . No ironists allowed" (*AM*, 314). Lentricchia's point is not that Palgrave consistently put his principles into practice, only that others did. Confronting such a scene of misrecognition, is it any wonder, Lentricchia asks, that Stevens and Pound, Eliot and Frost, feel not so much the anxiety of influence vis-à-vis their great romantic ancestors (although they surely do) as they feel the anxiety of their imminent emasculations at the dainty hands of cultivated America, or that they, in strategic reaction, celebrate the heroic vitality of business and power, however much they may also come to lament the consequences of these counter-ideals?

Lentricchia's *American Modernism* has three major parts. Part one, in three chapters ("From Gentility to Joyce," "Lyric in the Culture of Capitalism," and "Philosophers of Modernism at Harvard, ca. 1900"), substantiates in greatly effective detail the picture I have just sketched of the poetic situation at the turn of the century.[10] Two things that I must leave out of my present discussion, for reasons of space and appropriateness, are the climactic role of Joyce's *Ulysses* in establishing modernist aesthetics in opposition to the washed-out neurasthenic gentility of conventional culture and the prophetic role such Harvard philosophers as George Santayana, William James, and Josiah Royce played in shaping modernist poetics, particularly the poetic of the image. (This last point is Lentricchia's deliberate effort simultaneously to downplay the traditional role of Bergson and Hulme in the history of modern poetry and to foreground the formative role of mostly American sources). The second part of *American Modernism* interprets the representative careers of Frost, Stevens, Pound, and Eliot as the defining gestures in modern American poetry. Like his elevation of the Harvard philosophers here or, in *Ariel and the Police*, his attacks on three prominent critical formations, this move, too, is intentionally agonistic, indeed provocatively so, especially in light of Gilbert and Gubar's recent multivolume feminist treatment of much of this same material in *No Man's Land: The Place of the Woman Writer in Modern Literature*. Finally, part three of *American Modernism* discusses briefly the complex relations of culture and identity along lines already suggested in *Ariel and the Police*.

10. Two of these chapters have appeared in earlier versions: "Lyric in the Culture of Capitalism," *American Literary History* 1, no. 1 (Spring 1989): 63–88, and "Philosophers of Modernism at Harvard, ca. 1900," *South Atlantic Quarterly* 89, no. 4 (Fall 1990): 787–834.

Although I have elsewhere commented at length on Lentricchia's views of Stevens and so will concentrate on his exemplary reading of Pound in *American Modernism* (it best embodies the spirit of the book), I should say something about the brilliant counterpointing effect of these chapters, which typifies the organization of the whole volume.[11]

Both Stevens and Pound, as Lentricchia rightly sees them, derive primarily from different (if subtly interrelated) aspects of Emerson. Stevens, on the one hand, rehearses Emerson's transcendental desire (from the latter's *Nature*) for an original, vividly transparent relation to nature. He does so by translating it into his late capitalist desire for an original, vividly transparent relation of the connoisseur/gourmand to the rich and strange commodity fetched imperially from around the globe by the new economic world order: the original avant-garde painting from Paris, exotic teas from Ceylon, fresh foot-long bananas from the Philippines. (The greatest danger to this upper middle-class desire, of course, is the democratic proliferation of mass market simulacra and scaled-down or ersatz approximations of such original goods). Such would-be aristocratic commodity desire perfectly characterizes the poetic moment in Stevens as a moment of always anticipated and ever deferred consumption of the ever new and always fresh object of desire: a consumer's paradise of purely acquisitive foreplay. In this ironic fashion of ever postponed climax, Stevens impersonates and updates for the times the very internalized "mask" (*AM*, 4) of the pallid lady poet who consumes emotion for all occasions in her opportunistic verse, which he begins his career by subjecting to abjection. (You recall that Stevens opts, instead, for the Whitmanesque or Lawrentian utopia in the famous seventh stanza of "Sunday Morning," with its ring of naked, well-built men singing their paeons to their masterful lord, the sun). The result of this ironic turnabout in such late lyrics as "The World as Meditation," however, is that, through the ever patient Penelope and related figures, Stevens finally abjures the imperial system of "far-fetchings," that is, the late capitalist world order feeding his narcissistic form of desire with commodities. As he does so, he painfully recognizes the perpetual postponement of any final reunion of imagination and reality, desire and its material object (Penelope and Ulysses), as the sole desire he can ever finally know. As such, the abjected lady poet returns with a vengeance.

11. For my discussion of Lentricchia on Stevens, see "Saving Ariel: Wallace Stevens and the Sexual Poetics of Late Capitalism," *Contemporary Literature* 29, no. 4 (Fall 1988): 624–31.

Pound, on the other hand, as we shall see in some detail, starts from what he plausibly sees as Emerson's vigorous sense of the American psyche (from his essays "History" and "The American Scholar"). Emerson, as Pound understands him, sees the American scholar as the virgin site where, his "History" claims, all "the transmigrations of Proteus," all the self-interpretations of the Sphinx constituting human history, can finally fulfill themselves: What before was merely possible, at last becomes embodied as the American psyche. History, for Emerson (as for Pound and Lentricchia), is the collective archive of imaginative possibilities, at best only half realized or perverted by accident, or mistaken intentions, or human stupidity. These possibilities are to materialize in and as the mask plays of the consummate American virtuoso, the poet, who is therefore "a liberating god," as Emerson declares in "The Poet." "We as we read must become," Emerson counsels (and Pound obviously took him to heart), "Greeks, Romans, Turks, priest and king, martyr and executioner, must fasten these images to some reality in our secret experience, or we shall learn nothing rightly" (from "History"). Given such a poetic figure, Stevens's sexual aesthetics of late capitalist desire can be but one part to improvise. (Pound's conspicuous connection to Browning is his defensive mask for this deeply formative Emersonian influence.)

Lentricchia, in this compelling manner, counterpoints the mask play of Stevens and Pound, significantly opting in his ironic performance for the latter over the former as the more inclusive and worldly imagination. Despite his embrace of fascism, which cannot be redeemed by saying he also writes good poetry, Pound, unlike the schizoid poet/insurance executive, at least knows cultural, social, and economic practices are mutually enmeshed, equally overlapping and reciprocally enveloping each other in diverse ways, not neatly separable (without severe psychic and political consequences) into the routine workweek and the aesthetic holiday weekend. However useful such knowledge was to Pound, it is useful to Lentricchia.

Pound, the youthful dreamy aesthete, the energetic entrepreneur of modernism, the imaginative philologist of the troubadours, the fly-by-the-seat-of-his-pants Chinese scholar, the creative Old English and Latin "translator," the crank economic theorist, the rabid fascist sympathizer, the fierce anti-Semite, the mad bad poet of the Pisan cage, and the bizarrely silent figure in the St. Elizabeth's cell—all these "Pounds," and more besides, begin, for Lentricchia, as any good American does: with no definitive identity he can recognize as his own, but with a host of inherited personae, or masks, to take on and with only the principle of modernization itself (endless change as radical innovation, as poetic metamorphosis) to guide him:

> In the period spanning the many stylistic changes from his earliest poems to his early Cantos, Pound changed not at all on the value of metamorphosis for the sort of writer (himself) who explained the process of writing to himself in his earliest poems as an experience of walking into nonsense—becoming Christ, Villon, or Dante, God or a tree—a writer who would project the psychic value of his own aesthetic experience as the real value of reading his poems. Pound's reader would also be freed from the self of the moment, liberated into some strange and bracing identity, joining the writer in mythic experience in order to take on with Pound what he, like Pound, does not possess. (*AM*, 35–36)

As Lentricchia goes on to say, both Pound and his reader are not versions of everyman but typically American men, in need of "virtù," that is, in need of the virtuoso's liberation from the "fixed and crystallised (*AM*, 36) shell of convention one's latest mask is always liable to become. This is a liberation into perpetual avant-gardism, "the ruling philosophy of everyday life in the land of opportunity and infinite self-development" (*AM*, 36). For Pound, as Lentricchia reads him, this liberating experience of the poet and his reader both parallels the processes of everyday life in America and gives the best "antidefinition of literature as writing without historically prior and persistent identity, writing without a prior 'self' to rely on—a nonidentity of sheerest possibility, an absence of essence" (*AM*, 36). While individual exiles in this or other countries may have experienced a similar "absence of essence," Pound's uniqueness derives from his being born into a country of such essential absence of identity. Such an "absence of essence" defines the contingency theory informing many philosophical movements in the twentieth century, from existentialism through neopragmatism. For Lentricchia, however, this fact of historical contingency and "absence of essence" never licenses the belief that we can simply kick ourselves free of our material origins into purely aesthetic projects of self-creation (as Rorty claims), with no historical or psychic consequences. For example, this "antidefinition of literature" (*AM*, 36) is what Pound describes as "constant transformation" (*AM*, 36) and what Lentricchia portrays as "constant rebirth into a newness of (these are equivalents) an American and a modern literary selfhood" (*AM*, 36). A country of people all out to make it new is the rationale for such equivalency. As Lentricchia sarcastically enjoins us, lest we get too giddy with such pretty prospects: "Never mind that 'constant transformation' also describes the dream of consumer capitalism, [the] avant-garde of capitalist economics" (*AM*, 36). In this passage, as throughout the chapter on Pound and indeed the entire volume, Lentricchia typically reminds us of the imaginative limitations, as well as of the imaginative achievements of his chosen figures, by remarking the material conditions of their lives.

Lentricchia next distinguishes between Pound's American (or Emersonian) sense of metamorphosis and any classical precedent in a fashion that returns us to a main theme of culture and critical identity in America:

> Metamorphosis is the unprecedented master category in Pound's literary theory. In spite of the explicit Ovidian allusion [which earlier poets also invoked], the theory is not Ovidian. Nor does Pound draw upon a notion of biological metamorphosis: the man who comes "before" the glass cannot be traced, not even obscurely, as a surviving form in the new self (hence Pound's [repeatedly] shocked "I"?). But if there is to be metamorphosis in any recognizable sense of the word, there must be a prior something which undergoes transformation. If the prior "something" is, as in Pound, a determinate nothing, a hole needing filling and fulfilling, valuable ("golden") precisely because of its amorphic condition, then Pound, like Emerson, has pressed metamorphosis to the edge of its limiting boundary: [what has become] the classic American dream, self-origination ex nihilo. Pound theorizes metamorphosis, a process of self-emergence, as Emerson had theorized it: on a condition of potential-for-self only, not on the transformation of one self into another; a condition without a memory out of which a self might emerge which is nothing but memory, and so—the irony and paradox of Pound's career—no self at all. (*AM*, 36–37)

This portrait of Pound and his reader is as powerful as it is, I submit, precisely because it is likewise a portrait of Lentricchia and his reader, or, potentially, of any American writer and any American reader, or of any Jay Gatsby and any Nick Carraway. All the masks of imaginations in action from Lentricchia's career begin to resonate through this figure of Pound. Aesthetic, totalitarian, pragmatist, and critical masks appear in a process of surprised mutual recognition. This grand (self-)recognition scene is also a persuasive scene of instruction. It creates a critical portrait of the American: a man without qualities but with a legion of names to come.

Such critical vision does not mean, however, that, like Emerson before him and DeLillo's Oswald after him, Pound, as Lentricchia reads him (and as we read Lentricchia), is simply condemned, in Yeats's haunting refrain, to be only "mad as the mist and snow."[12] What saves Pound in the early Cantos, at least, and, by implication, his critic and his reader, is "the artistic arrangement of the documents" (AM, 68). What finally matters is not the fanciful production of the fabulous third-person dream of self-originating American identity ex nihilo but the careful, patient, actively meditative placement of all the words—historical, philosophical, and poetic—that we can collect from the archive about a subject. (Here, we see the continuing constructive influence of Foucault's practice of critical genealogy.) The oppositional result of such an imaginatively particular "arrangement of the documents"—of such artistry—can be, as here, the dramatic performance of intellectual identity formation in an interpretive moment of some temporal complexity, considerable ethical resonance, and formative cultural influence. Or, the inspiring payoff can be, as it is in the following example from the Stevens chapter, the exemplary imaginative care with which the critic in his style subtly performs his many-faceted judgments: "As a student at Harvard, Stevens learned to distrust (in a thickening fin de siècle atmosphere) overtly moralizing art" (AM, 37). The ironic enactment of the soon-to-be definitively overcome American belatedness vis-à-vis the mother country, England (Stevens leaves that Anglophiliac bastion, Cambridge, for the Big Apple shortly after the turn of the century), the reflexive envelopment of the parenthetical remark, and the pointed positioning of le mot juste—"overtly"—for maximizing the dramatic effect of the negative aesthetic take on "moralizing art": All of these things collectively make the creative performance of this beautiful (because fully animated) sentence's rhetoric a minor example of Lentricchia's major critical art.

Consider, as a final example of what Emerson would call this active soul, Lentricchia on Pound's portrayal of his Renaissance hero, Sigismundo Malatesta, whose "unswerving devotion to the building of the Tempio Malatestiana in Rimini" (AM, 68) here becomes legendary:

> The arrangement of the documents is dramatic: Pound's purpose is to conjure his obscure hero (Canto 8 opens with incantatory rhetoric), show him in the act of emerging from corruption, his voice freeing itself, sailing above, somehow uncontaminated; a voice elegant, dig-

12. "Mad as the Mist and Snow," in Richard J. Finneran, ed., The Poems, vol. 1 of The Collected Works of W. B. Yeats (New York: Macmillan, 1989), 345.

252

nified, gracious, lyrical, and promising violence, a man whose passion rescues him even from the evil that he does. The strength of
Pound's showing lies not in the narrative of Sigismundo—its confu-
sions overwhelm even Pound—but in the rhetorical effects he manages in honor of his hero. Pound loves the man, and his love creates a verbal habitation that insulates him from the garbage of his
circumstances. (*AM*, 68)

As Lentricchia concludes his study of Pound on Malatesta, he focuses on
the sublimely ironic juxtaposition of the "swamp of political confusion" his
beloved hero has faced and the signature statement, as Pound relates it,
on Malatesta's temple of art: " 'He, Sigismundo, templum aedificavit' " (*AM*,
70). Art—Sigismundo's, Pound's, and Lentricchia's—intimately confronts
politics, for like critical identity, it is an imaginative form of politics:

From this swamp of political confusion, this comic litany of the
months and seasons of Byzantine betrayal, spoken, no doubt, in
some smoke-filled backroom, comes a line from another level, ele-
vated in syntax and tone, with a Latin phrase at the end (like an
anchor of final authority) telling us what Malatesta did—the Latin
working for Pound (as languages other than English often did) as
some talismanic discourse, the facilitator of magical transcendence
from politics to the plane of art [and back again]: "He, Sigismundo,
templum aedificavit." "He, Sigismundo"—a phrasing repeated often
in the Malatesta group—not only clarifies just who it is among these
obscure political actors that Pound is talking about, but adds the
sound of awe, like an epitaph which registers the shock of the memo-
rialist, that in the midst of all this, he, Sigismundo, did what he did:
"In the gloom, the gold gathers the light against it." (*AM*, 70)

The complex pedagogic imperative of this sublimely attractive, indeed "talismanic" discourse is that of critical analogy—as Pound may be to Malatesta,
and Lentricchia may be to Pound, so, too, the reader may be to both the
critic and his doubled subject. Unlike the American dream of the singu-
larly self-made, yet impossibly universal, third person, which is something
just too fabulously ideal and individualist to be believed, the "oneself" here
is a historically grounded, socially made (architecture is a public art), and
impersonally plural dialectical subject. This vision is then a sublimely particular, politically positioned, and nobly magnanimous imagination in critical

action.[13] Here the contingent imagination is truly both historical and imaginative.

Pound, whose imagination of the modern has been imprisoned in the obscurity produced by a strange combination of antiquarian commentary and reductive ideological critique, is here seen as an analogy to his chosen hero, a Renaissance man of powerful virtue and savage devotion to art, whom Pound rescues from his captivity in near historical oblivion. Similarly, Lentricchia practices his critical art on Pound's behalf, with the implication that the reader is to go and do likewise for his or her chosen figure. Amidst all the purely professional processes for grinding the particular achievements of writers into grist for the latest mills of careerism, celebrity, and professionalism to no end, I find this truly artistic performance of imaginative generosity that still sees all the historical and political limitations courageous and bracing, an aesthetic use of the collective archive of creative exempla for constructively socializing and humanizing purposes—namely, the anchoring of our culture of critical identity in the authority of "oneself." Pound/ Malatesta, as I see Lentricchia envisioning this relation, perfectly balances his earlier reading of the DeLillo/Oswald relation, as the major parts of his theoretical portrait of the ever elusive American subject: "In the gloom, the gold gathers the light against it" (AM, 70).

This performance thus dramatizes what Kristeva (after Lacan and Freud) analyzes as the imaginary father of individual prehistory. The imaginary father is a supremely social and androgynous figure of primary identification with the symbolic order of culture immediately beyond the mother/ child fusion state. It stands in relation to the oedipal patriarch and the abjected mother, much as Jesus Christ stands in relation to Yahweh and Nature: as an alternative to both repression and abjection, namely, as sublimation—that is, as sacrifice and resurrection. Kristeva reminds us, however, that the imaginary father never makes an appearance as any single figure alone. It is always implied by an entire constellation of figures in a text or over the course of a career. The imaginary father, as Foucault (after Nietzsche and Hegel) also recognizes, embodies the agonistic constitution of the self, that plural subject (or "oneself") that is the historically specific and ironi-

---

13. For further discussion on this topic of the work of critical magnanimity, see both the introduction to my Radical Parody: American Culture and Critical Agency after Foucault (New York: Columbia University Press, 1992) and my Lionel Trilling: The Work of Liberation (Madison: University of Wisconsin Press, 1988).

cally self-overcoming mentor/student bond in its various formal permutations, such as here: Malatesta/Pound, Pound/Lentricchia, critic/reader, and so on. Lentricchia represents a sublimely particular interpretive gathering of dialectically interrelated temporal moments making up the American mask play (modern, Renaissance, postmodern), whose continued imaginative resonance is generously offered for our edification. Such is the genuinely oppositional culture of self-overcoming critical identity. Rather than New Historicism's weakly liberal poetics, neopragmatism's chilling professionalism unbound, or essentialist feminism's apocalyptic separatism—three of the most influential modes of criticism today—here is American critical theory performed as cultural politics radically in and effectively for our time, which moves perpetually into "another intensity."

Melville's *Typee*: U.S. Imperialism at Home and Abroad

John Carlos Rowe

[The Polynesians] have been civilized into draught horses, and evangelized into beasts of burden.
—*Typee*

The ugliest beast on earth is the white man, says Melville.
—Lawrence, *Studies in Classic American Literature* (1923)

Melville's *Typee* is one of the first U.S. literary texts to establish a connection between the institutions of slavery in the United States and the Euroamerican colonialism in Polynesia. Like other travelers to Polynesia in the first half of the nineteenth century, Melville reserves most of his criticism for the British and the French. In at least two significant ways, however, Melville turns the familiar nineteenth-century criticism of the British and the French into a critique more specifically relevant to his white U.S. readers in the 1840s and 1850s. First, his references to Captain David Porter, the U.S. naval commander who claimed the Marquesas for the United States, and his general invocation of this little South Seas' episode of the War of 1812 suggest that Melville wanted to use his experiences in the Marquesas for purposes that went well beyond the merely autobiographical or purely literary. Second, his plotting of his own experience has uncanny resemblances with two important and characteristically American narrative forms in Melville's time: the Puritan captivity narrative and the fugitive slave narrative.

Melville was attempting in *Typee* to explore the relationship between domestic policies of Southern slave-holding and the extraterritorial policies of U.S. colonization that began as early as the War of 1812. By "extraterritorial," I mean "outside the North American continent," and I realize that the term is itself something of a contradiction, since the territory of the North American continent was from the very outset of European exploration and settlement an "extraterritorial" region of European colonization. But this great paradox of United States history remains as difficult to communicate today as it must have been in Melville's nineteenth century. Our revolution against English rule not only deliberately ignored the continuing domestic colonization of African Americans under the perverse laws and practices of North American slavery, but it also led to a series of acts on the part of the new United States by which we consolidated our national identity by exercising political power in a colonial manner. It is customary to associate nineteenth-century U.S. colonialism with Manifest Destiny, westward expansion, and the policies of genocide and removal practiced against native American peoples. Melville argues in *Typee*, however, that the domestic sins of slavery and westward expansion were already finding their equivalents in foreign policies just as insidious.

Two formal ways in which Melville made this connection between domestic and foreign policies are his adaptations in *Typee* of well-established conventions of the Puritan captivity narrative and the fugitive slave narrative. By using the imaginative experience fundamental to the nineteenth-century travel narrative form, Melville put his primarily white readers in the position of the victim in an attempt to transform their affections, as well as their intellectual attitudes with respect to domestic slavery, Euroamerican colonialism in Polynesia, and different cultures in general.

This is an odd thesis to offer in view of the prevailing criticism of Melville's ideological blindnesses, if not complicity in the propagation of the myth of the imperial self. In 1980, Carolyn Karcher argued in *Shadow over the Promised Land: Slavery, Race, and Violence in Melville's America* that Melville was a vigorous critic of slavery but ambivalent about the best political solution: "Melville betrays the same qualms about endorsing violent rebellion in all his works, be the rebels black or white. At the same time, he consistently exhibits tyranny as unbearable and resistance to it as essential if the victim of oppression is to preserve his manhood. The conflict between these two positions . . . is central not only to Melville's art, but to his life as well. By temperament, Melville seems to have been at once a refractory conformist and a reluctant rebel."[1] By the end of the 1980s, Wai-Chee Dimock argued that "Melville dramatizes the very juncture where the logic of freedom dovetails into the logic of empire, or (which is the same thing) where the imperial self of Jacksonian individualism recapitulates the logic of Jacksonian imperialism."[2]

From Karcher's politically conflicted, and thus essentially liberal, Melville to Dimock's Melville, critical judgements have been virtually transformed in the past ten years.[3] We have gained a great deal in the revaluation of U.S. literature by paying more attention to the ideological functions of culture. In our haste to acknowledge aesthetic culture's contributions to ideology, we may also have neglected the ways in which artistic representation can serve emancipatory and progressive purposes. If we are truly interested in *historicizing* the literature we teach, then we must develop subtler means of assessing the historical functions of literature on its own and for our times. At the moment, too many of our interpretations of literature merely judge a text as resistant to or complicit with the dominant ideology. We need subtler, more varied standards of political, and thus aesthetic judgement, if we are to respect the complexity of literature's "action" in an historical moment, especially when such a moment is defined by crisis and conflict.[4]

1. Carolyn Karcher, *Shadow over the Promised Land: Slavery, Race, and Violence in Melville's America* (Baton Rouge: Louisiana State University Press, 1988). 2–3.
2. Wai-Chee Dimock, *Empire for Liberty: Melville and the Poetics of Individualism* (Princeton, N.J.: Princeton University Press, 1989). 10.
3. Michael Paul Rogin's *Subversive Genealogy: The Politics and Art of Herman Melville* (Berkeley: University of California Press, 1985) is a crucial text for understanding the transformation of Karcher's conflicted Melville into the ideologically determined Melville of Dimock's study.
4. During our discussion of early drafts of these essays at the conference on the "Cultures of U.S. Imperialism" at Dartmouth (November 1991), Walter Michaels asked me why it mattered for Melville to be treated as strong critic or subtle advocate of U.S. ideology in the first half of the nineteenth century. It was a good, challenging question that I could not answer adequately at that moment, but which has continued to shape my revisions and thinking about this essay since the conference. What matters, of course, is not the preservation, refunctioning, or political revising of canonical authors. What does matter today is how we can encourage students to find alternatives to the social, political, and economic failures of the democratic promise. Literature has traditionally offered such alternatives— some fantastically utopian and others more relevant to the social and human changes required to turn those failures into successes. In any case, I am grateful to Walter Michaels for his question, which we keep trying to answer in our teaching and writing.

The historical crises and conflicts of the 1840s included not just the issues of domestic slavery but also the widening horizon of European and a burgeoning U.S. colonialism in the Pacific. *Typee* addresses the complication of domestic and foreign policy issues by way of what T. Walter Herbert considers its anthropological dimension: "*Typee* moves along a course that remains perilously close to the brink of sheer confusion. We have found Melville working with contradictory points of view, discontinuous states of mind, resounding moral declarations crosscut by equivocal disclaimers, and moments of hapless incomprehension. It is now time to recognize that Melville's skillful flirting with such vexations has the effect of rendering tolerable the conflicts which it provokes."[5]

Herbert's argument in *Marquesan Encounters: Melville and the Meaning of Civilization*, which appeared in the same year as Karcher's study, suggests that somewhere between literature's contribution to ideology and its contribution to the political transformation of ideology there remains the possibility of literature as the experience of the instability and contradictoriness of ideological categories. Herbert does not conclude that the subversion of nineteenth-century U.S. ideology regarding the Marquesans and, by extension, other "primitive" peoples, is simply the effect of Melville's genius or conscious artistry. Instead, Herbert argues that *Typee* generates out of the "fusion of fact and meaning" a resulting "verbal texture that has a life of its own" (179).

Just what distinguishes this "life of its own" is too often the intrinsic literariness of the text, but in the case of *Typee* this "life" must be understood as the vicarious experience of the reader, who lives through wage-slavery, captivity, colonial subjugation, and several modes of ideological commodification in the course of reading *Typee*. Unlike the nineteenth-century U.S. accounts of the Marquesans discussed by Herbert in *Marquesan Encounters*, ranging from Captain David Porter's plans for a private colony to the proselytizing efforts of the Reverend Charles Stewart (chaplain for the American sloop of war, *Vincennes*) described in his *A Visit to the South Seas* (1831), Melville's anthropological gesture in *Typee* destabilizes our very processes of understanding "other" peoples. In that regard, *Typee* rejects the prevailing ethnographic models of its time and anticipates the more literary anthropologies of our own age.[6]

5. T. Walter Herbert, Jr., *Marquesan Encounters: Melville and the Meaning of Civilization* (Cambridge: Harvard University Press, 1980), 178.
6. By "our age," I mean the understanding of literary texts serving particular anthropological functions, in the manner of Wolfgang Iser's theory of "literary anthropology" as he

Because *Typee* is based so firmly on Melville's experiences on the island of Nukuheva in the summer of 1842, few scholars of the narrative pay much attention to why Melville might have considered the Marquesas to have been the appropriate setting for a critique of burgeoning U.S. imperialism. Ever since Harper and Brothers rejected Melville's manuscript "on the grounds that 'it was impossible that it could be true and therefore was without real value,'" the realism of *Typee* has been a central concern of readers, whether casual or professional. Most arguments supporting Melville's fictional techniques in his first book-length narrative tend to reinforce the assumption that this is a primarily autobiographical account of Melville's youthful experiences. Melville may thus vary narrative perspective by playing upon the "I" recounting his experiences and the more youthful "Tommo" who is the dramatic agent (or character) of those experiences. In a similar manner, Melville may draw upon previously published "accounts by travelers like Langsdorff, Porter and Stewart" either to give his own account greater historical credibility or to trivialize their versions for the sake of his own authority for this "peep" at polynesian life. But in these and other instances of literary liberties taken with these autobiographical materials, Melville is operating very much within the accepted terms of literary autobiography.[7]

The insistence upon *Typee*'s autobiographical realism has caused most literary critics to neglect what most historians of the Marquesas in the nineteenth century have simply taken for granted: that the discovery, exploration, and exploitation of the Marquesas by various European powers and the United States was a microcosm of modern imperialism at its worst. Herbert points out that "the destruction of the Marquesan way of life" was "one of the principal horrors of Pacific history"; the population of the islands declined in the nineteenth century from an estimated 100,000 in the early 1800s to "4,865 in 1882" (*ME* 19). Beyond this depressingly familiar pattern of Euroamerican imperialism eradicating the native population, there is the equally relevant subject of how colonial competition for the Marquesas was a microcosm of the struggle between European and American powers in other areas of the Pacific. The biographer of Commodore Porter, David Long, contends that by the time a Russian expedition "led by Captain Ivan Federovich Krusenstern" visited the Marquesas in 1803, a decade before

---

develops it in *Prospecting: From Reader Response to Literary Anthropology* (Baltimore: Johns Hopkins, 1989), esp. 262–284.

7. Kaori O'Connor, introduction to *Typee: Four Months' Residence in the Marquesas*, by Herman Melville, ed. Kaori O'Connor (London: KPI, 1985), viii.

Captain Porter arrived in Taiohae Bay, "Great Britain, the United States, France, and Russia, the nations which led in opening East Asia and the Pacific to Western influence during the nineteenth century, had presented in this miniscule archipelago a preview of the development of part of a continent and most of an island world."[8]

The preview to which Long refers is the race among these and other European nations and the United States to increase trade with China and Japan by way of sea routes across the Pacific. That which led to John Hay's famous "Open Door Policy" and his apparently democratic call for "free competition," rather than colonial warfare among the European nations vying for influence in the Far East, had its origins in the early part of the nineteenth century as various nations sought to control the Pacific islands that would be virtual stepping stones to the increasingly lucrative trade with Asian markets. As early as Porter's visits to the Marquesas in 1813, it was clear that these and other Pacific islands were of little commercial value in their own rights. As whaling stations, safe harbors, and later in the century as coaling stations, these islands were thought to provide the necessary stages in a commercial bridge between the West and the East.

It is, of course, just this economic imperialism that has characterized U.S. foreign policy from the Revolution to the present, and our conduct in the Marquesas makes this continuity strikingly clear. As many have pointed out, Melville repeatedly criticizes Americans for having failed to complete the revolution by ignoring the issue of slavery and their own colonial policies with respect to native peoples.[9] Whereas Melville endorses the democratic idealism of the Revolution, he understands quite well the economic realities behind our failure to realize such ideals. Irving may have represented the old Dutch patroons of New York as part of a vanishing world, but Melville considers them as mere prototypes of the thinly disguised aristocratic pretensions of the new ruling elite in the United States.

What Melville explores later in *Pierre* and *Benito Cereno* finds an early warrant in the fact that the first modern efforts to colonize the Marque-

---

8. Long, David F. *Nothing too Daring: A Biography of Commodore David Porter, 1780–1843* (Annapolis: U.S. Naval Institute, 1970), 110.

9. See my "Romancing the Stone: Melville's Critique of Ideology in *Pierre*," in *Theorizing American Literature: Hegel, the Sign, and History*. Eds. Bainard Cowan and Joseph G. Kronick (Baton Rouge: Louisiana State University Press, 1991), 195–223, esp. 216–218. There is much in *Typee* that anticipates Melville's arguments regarding the complicity of aristocratic privilege, artistic pretension, and the slave-master's despotism in *Pierre*, confirming I think the degree to which *Typee* should be more integrally treated in Melville's literary career, rather than as an abortive beginning in "travel literature."

sas should have been undertaken by Americans: Captain Joseph Ingraham of Boston in his visit of April to May of 1791 and Captain David Porter in his quixotic plan for a private colony under the sponsorship of the U.S. government in 1813.[10] Ingraham arrived only eight years after the formal end of the Revolutionary War; Porter attempted to annex the Marquesas during his efforts to interrupt British shipping in the Pacific during the War of 1812. In short, while the United States was struggling to establish its own fragile independence in the last decade of the eighteenth and the first decades of the nineteenth century, it was also actively competing for its own colonial territory in the Marquesas.

Until Herbert's *Marquesan Encounters* appeared in 1980, most efforts to link Melville with Captain Porter circled around Melville's explicit denial of any knowledge of Porter's account of his visit to the Marquesas and Melville's apparent reliance on specific details of Porter's published *Journal of the Cruise of the U.S. Frigate Essex*. In *Melville in the South Seas* (1939), Charles Anderson makes a convincing case for Melville's familiarity not only with the history of Porter's visit to the Marquesas but with the actual text of his *Journal* of 1815.[11] But few scholars until Herbert had paid much attention to the fact that Porter's efforts to annex the Marquesas were connected with the earlier visit by Captain Ingraham and thus with what might be termed our first national venture in extraterritorial imperialism.

Anderson does not mention Captain Ingraham in *Melville in the South Seas*, but Melville pays special attention to Ingraham's discovery of the northern islands, in what Ingraham named the "Washington group," including Nukuheva, which: "Although generally called one of the Marquesas, is by some navigators considered as forming one of a distinct cluster, comprising the islands of Ruhooka, Ropo, and Nukuheva; upon which three the appellation of the Washington Group has been bestowed. . . . Their existence was altogether unknown until . . . 1791, when they were discovered by Captain Ingraham, of Boston, Massachusetts, nearly two centuries after the discovery of the islands by the agent of the Spanish Viceroy" (*T*, 11).[12]

10. See Long, *Nothing Too Daring*, 109, for a discussion of the discovery of Marquesas by Alvaro de Mendaña y Castro in 1596, naming the islands for the wife of the Viceroy of Peru, "Las Islas Marquesas de Don Garcia Hurtado de Mendoza de Canate," and the visit by Captain James Cook on 8 April 1774.
11. Charles Roberts Anderson, *Melville in the South Seas* (New York: Dover Publications, 1966), 96–98.
12. Herman Melville, *Typee: A Peep at Polynesian Life*. Eds. Harrison Hayford, Hershel Parker, G. Thomas Tanselle. Northwestern-Newberry Edition, vol. 1 (Evanston, Ill.: Northwestern University Press, 1968). Further references in the text are to this edition.

Although Melville goes on to say that he "shall follow the example of most voyagers, and treat them as forming part and parcel of the Marquesas," he has gone to considerable lengths in the preceding quotation to insist upon their separate discovery by the American captain.[13]

Melville's reference to Captain Ingraham and "the agent of the Spanish Viceroy," Alvaro de Mendaña y Castro, who first discovered and named the southern islands "Marquesas," anticipates in certain ways Melville's doubling of Captain Amasa Delano and Don Benito Cereno in *Benito Cereno* (1855), published less than a decade after *Typee*. In James Kavanagh's reading, *Benito Cereno* explicitly indicts the United States in its colonial and revolutionary origins, as well as nineteenth-century practices, for complicity in the European imperialism in the New World that relied so fundamentally on the economy of slavery.[14] Brook Thomas directly relates *Typee* to Melville's more obvious indictment of New World slavery in *Benito Cereno*: "In *Typee* Melville lays bare the imperialistic motives behind the introduction of Christianity to non-Western cultures, the savagery it causes rather than eliminates. Most important, if opponents of slavery think the eradication of slavery from America's shores will finally make America the land of the free, Melville's works offer example after example demonstrating exploitation in the 'free' states."[15]

Captain Delano orders his men to attack the rebellious slaves on board the *San Dominick* and return the survivors to bondage. Captain Ingraham did not explicitly enslave the native peoples of the Washington group, but he did rename the islands, "commemorating John Adams, Benjamin Lincoln, John Hancock, and Henry Knox by giving their surnames to individual islands. Nukuheva, where Porter later resided, was named 'Federal Island'" (*Nothing Too Daring: A Biography of Commodore David Porter, 1780–1843*, 109). And Ingraham did claim the islands for the United States to the cheers of those on board his small ship, the *Hope*, thus giving Ingraham the dubious claim of being the first agent of U.S. imperialism.

13. Edmund Fanning, who visited the islands in the Spring of 1798, refers to "The Marquesas and Washington Islands" in his *Voyages and Discoveries in the South Seas: 1792–1832* (New York: Dover Publications, 1989), 99.
14. See Kavanagh, "That Hive of Subtlety: 'Benito Cereno' and the Liberal Hero," in *Ideology and Classic American Literature*. Eds. Sacvan Bercovitch and Myra Jehlen (New York: Cambridge University Press, 1986), 352–83.
15. Brook Thomas, *Cross-Examinations of Law and Literature: Cooper, Hawthorne, Stowe, and Melville* (Cambridge: Cambridge University Press, 1987), 137.

Only three weeks after Ingraham sailed from the Washington group, Captain Etienne Marchant in the *Solide* claimed them as part of the "Iles des Marquises" in the name of French colonial power in French Polynesia. But it was Captain (later Commodore) David Porter (1780–1843) whose annexation of the island of Nukuheva on November 19, 1813 was likely to have had the most relevance for Melville and has, according to his biographer, earned him "title as the first American imperialist" (*NTD*, 124). Were it not for Captain Porter's vigorous military campaign against the Taipi during his occupation of Nukuheva, his annexation of the island as U.S. territory would be as nominal as Ingraham's in 1791. Less imaginatively than Ingraham, albeit in a more obvious entrepreneurial spirit, Porter "prepared for his spate of expansionism by providing a brand-new nomenclature: he christened Nukuheva 'Madison's Island,' the American settlement 'Madisonville,' his defensive position there 'Fort Madison,' and, afraid perhaps of too much of a good thing, contented himself with calling Taiohae Bay 'Massachusetts Bay.'" (*NTD*, 124).

Porter had sailed to the Marquesas from the Galapagos, having spent the first year of the War of 1812 interrupting British shipping and whaling in the Pacific. He sailed toward the Washington group for three reasons: to find a safe haven to refurbish his ships, to scout possible British targets in the South Pacific, and to provide his men "relaxation and amusement after being so long at sea," by which he implies sexual intercourse with young Marquesan women, renowned since Mendaña y Castro's visit for both their beauty and avowed sexual compliance.[16] Although Porter immediately notified President Madison of his unauthorized annexation of Nukuheva, neither Madison nor Secretary of State James Monroe even acknowledged Porter's messages and letters. As Long points out, "the main reason for executive inaction was that the intelligence of Nukahiva's entry into the Union arrived just about the time the British were invading Chesapeake Bay, burning public buildings in Washington, and driving the President [Madison] into humiliating flight" (*NTD*, 126).

Such an irony would not have been lost on Melville had he been aware of these consequences of Porter's annexation of the island. The War of 1812 was, after all, ostensibly fought to protect U.S. sailors from impressment by the Royal Navy, although it was more likely fought to protect U.S.

16. Porter, *Journal of a Cruise Made to the Pacific Ocean, in the U.S. Frigate "Essex," in the Years 1812, 1813, and 1814*, 2 vols. (Philadelphia: Bradford & Inskeep, 1815), vol 2, 9–17.

commercial interests and shipping rights during the Napoleonic War. But it was not simply these historical ironies that interested Melville in Porter's annexation of the Marquesas. The portion of *Typee* that Charles Anderson identifies as convincing evidence that Melville not only knew Porter's *Journal* of his visit to the Marquesas but relied on it, "together with Stewart's two volumes," as "the chief source of his information" for his own narrative of Marquesan life is Melville's description in Chapter 4 of "Porter's invasion of Typee Valley" (*Melville in the South Seas*, 96).

In four compact paragraphs, Melville recounts how Porter, having been caught up in the intertribal rivalries on Nukuheva, marched against the Typees with a "considerable detachment of sailors and marines from the frigate Essex, accompanied by at least two thousand warriors of Happar and Nukuheva" (*T*, 26). Although the modern biographer of Porter, David Long, entitles his chapter of Porter's curious annexation of the Marquesas, "Imperialism in the Marquesas, 1813," he sidesteps what Melville makes so explicit about this punitive military expedition against the Typee: "Valiantly, although with much loss, the Typees disputed every inch of ground, and after some hard fighting obliged their assailants to retreat and abandon their design of conquest. The invaders, on their march back to the sea, consoled themselves for their repulse by setting fire to every house and temple in their route; and a long line of smoking ruins defaced the once-smiling bosom of the valley, and proclaimed to its pagan inhabitants the spirit that reigned in the breasts of Christian soldiers. Who can wonder at the deadly hatred of the Typees to all foreigners after such unprovoked atrocities?" (*T*, 26).

We should remember that this description of Porter's "unprovoked atrocities" is occasioned by Melville's recollection of witnessing the French Admiral Dupetit-Thouars's military annexation of the Marquesas in 1842. In fact, as Melville entered Taiohae Bay (which Porter had renamed "Massachusetts Bay"), the French were launching an expedition against the hostile Taoias, as if to repeat the expedition of Porter against the Typee nearly three decades earlier.

Melville's conclusions regarding Porter's imperialist adventure in the Marquesas are interesting for yet another reason. Easy as it would have been for him simply to equate Porter's attack on the Typee with the larger-scale efforts of the French and British to colonize the peoples and islands in the South Pacific, Melville makes the following observation at the end of his indictment of Porter's campaign against the Typee:

> The enormities perpetrated in the South Seas upon some of the in-
> offensive islanders wellnigh pass belief. These things are seldom
> proclaimed at home; they happen at the very ends of the earth; they
> are done in a corner, and there are none to reveal them. But there
> is, nevertheless, many a petty trader that has navigated the Pacific
> whose course from island to island might be traced by a series of
> cold-blooded robberies, kidnappings, and murders, the iniquity of
> which might be considered almost sufficient to sink her guilty timbers
> to the bottom of the sea. (*T*, 26–27)

Of course, French and British navies might be charged with the same
crimes, but it is significant that Melville's account of Porter's actions in the
Marquesas should be concluded with an indictment of secret crimes that
follow from *trade*. What Melville anticipates here and elsewhere in *Typee*
(and thus what makes this text such an interesting one for readers exploring
the origins and history of U.S. imperialism) is the extent to which U.S. imperialism would be predicated on commercial, rather than territorial, control
of other cultures and peoples.

Thus Porter's interest in the Marquesas as islands where he might
find a temporary safe harbor, refit his ships, and entertain himself and his
crew very much fits the pattern of U.S. imperialism in the South Pacific
throughout the rest of the nineteenth century. Captain Ingraham himself
discovered the Washington group while on a voyage from Boston to Canton
like so many other whalers and traders who brought the Marquesas to public attention in the period from 1790 to 1850. Captain Fanning, who visited
the Marquesas in 1798, was also on his way to China. The Marquesas fit
ideally into the navigational plans of ships traveling from the west coast of
South America to China.

Just how much Melville knew of Porter's specific plans to develop the
Marquesas is unknown, but Melville's comment in *Typee* about the sins of
western traders in the region seems to comment directly on Porter's formal
proposal in 1815 to President Madison "that he be placed in charge of a
voyage of exploration into the Pacific," specifically for purposes of commercial and military colonization (*ME*, 82). Herbert summarizes Porter's larger
ambitions in this post–War of 1812 proposal to Madison: "Porter argues that
his voyage might open trade relations with Japan, which was then closed
to all Western nations except the Dutch. He further argues that great improvements could be made in the American relation to China. While the

American national territory extended scarcely west of the Appalachians, in short, Porter had a vision of Pacific empire. He conceived a dominant international position for America as a leader in the advance of civilized achievement." [17]

In this regard, Herbert's interpretation of the larger significance of Porter's otherwise quixotic effort to annex the Marquesas is especially relevant to any rereading of *Typee* as a commentary on the origins of U.S. imperialism:

> Porter's voyage of discovery was never sponsored by the United States government, and his taking possession of the Marquesas Islands was never ratified. But his imperial conception of America has had a long train of successors that have provided a series of corresponding definitions of the meaning of America's relationship to nations conceived not to be civilized. During his stay at the Marquesas he sought to embody his idea of America as a great nation in a form that would bring the blessings of America's superior position to a people he thought well fitted to benefit from them. Porter "took possession" of the Marquesas in the name of the United States because he considered this an appropriate display of the greatness of America; but his definition of civilization also led him to believe that this action was suited to the character of the Marquesans, which he very sincerely admired. (*ME*, 83)

Just how much Porter admired the Marquesans is debatable despite the paternal rhetoric in his *Journal* regarding their social coherence and technical and technological ingenuity. But what Herbert treats at the level of Porter's enlightenment values, I would prefer to understand more practically and materially in terms of those commercial motives that link the southern slave economy with the northern industrial economy and its growing demand in the nineteenth century for global markets. Of course, even Porter's ideas could be read in terms of the paternal rhetoric characteristic not only of the proslavery legitimists in the antebellum period but also more benign proponents of enlightenment notions of "representative man"—that paradigm of a ruling elite that would stake its claim to speaking for (as well as creating jobs for) the rest of society.

17. Herbert, *Marquesan Encounters*, 83. Herbert is quoting from Allan B. Cole's edition of "Captain David Porter's Proposed Expedition to the Pacific and Japan, 1815," *Pacific Historical Review*, 9 (1940), 63 ff.

To be sure, Porter did not enslave the Marquesans; instead, he involved himself from the outset in their intertribal conflicts much in the manner that the United States in the early modern period, in its access to "global power," would offer to negotiate conflicts in Central America and the Caribbean (the Spanish-American War and the Canal treaties), the Philippines (the Spanish-American War), China (the Boxer Rebellion and "Open Door Policy" of John Hay), and the Russo-Japanese War (the Portsmouth Treaty of 1905). His motives prefigure the general U.S. role of global policeman—the legitimation of U.S. authority for the sake of winning hearts and minds, and thus the attainment of both material and immaterial ends. In the former sense, Porter, like U.S. Secretaries of State Hay and Kissinger, wanted to establish trade routes and commercial spheres of influence, recognizing that the future of global domination lay not with forts, settlements, and the exploitation of raw materials, but with markets, trade routes, and commercial opportunities. In the latter sense, he and his more powerful successors in the nineteenth and twentieth centuries recognized that such markets would have to be *made*, in part by converting other peoples not to religious ideals but to the political and social programs of liberal democracy.

What then is Melville's role in the historical narrative of emerging U.S. colonialism and its complicity with domestic slavery? Following Dimock, we might argue that the "author as monarch" which she finds first developed in Melville's *Mardi* has certain affinities with Captain Porter's behavior toward the Marquesans. Interestingly, Dimock excludes *Typee* and *Omoo* from her critical reading of Melville on the grounds that the historical and autobiographical constraints of both works limited Melville from exercising the poetic "freedom and invention" so essential to his "empire for liberty." [18] In this respect, Herbert may be read as extending Dimock's argument to *Typee*, because he finds much in Melville's views of the Typee to compare with the enlightenment thinking of Porter: "Melville enunciates the Romantic moral outlook that governs the second phase of Tommo's sojourn among the Typees; it is an outlook analogous to the view of David Porter, holding that man has an innate knowledge of good and evil" (*ME*, 167). Still ac-

---

18. Dimock, *Empire for Liberty*, 75. It is interesting that Dimock goes to such lengths to exclude *Typee* and *Omoo* from the rest of Melville's literary *oeuvre*, because neither work fits precisely her argument regarding the "poetics of individualism" served so well by Melville's late-romantic concept of literary authority. But read back into his oeuvre, *Typee* certainly challenges the thesis that Melville's individualism is the embodiment of Jacksonian expansionist and colonial policies.

268

knowledging Melville's artistic ability to represent his inner conflicts, Herbert nonetheless concludes that *Typee* typifies the inner contradictoriness of the liberal romantic in this period: "Instead of applying a coherent interpretive framework to Marquesan society, Melville struggles with passionate impulses and moral convictions that refuse to be ordered in a general design. . . . In *Typee* the crisis of meaning is located within Melville himself: he finds his mind radically divided between horror and profound admiration for the islanders, as it is also divided between hatred for civilization and a frantic desire to return to it" (*ME*, 158).[19]

Without wishing to dismiss or resolve entirely the appropriate question of Melville's conflicted identity as a white, male, New England writer in Jacksonian America, I want to propose that his inner contradictoriness does progressive work in the narrative of *Typee* both for the American 1840s and for these 1990s. What is significantly missing from most accounts of Melville as critic of colonialism or as critic of U.S. slavery is the relation between the two practices and their discourses of legitimation. In *Typee*, the narrative enacts an explicit relation from the moment that Toby and Tommo flee the wage slavery on board the *Dolly* to their hysterical efforts to escape what they fear is the cannibalism for which the Typee are preparing them.

There were two popular narrative forms available to Melville as possible models for dramatic situations in which the protagonist's confusion and doubt might advantageously serve the aims of the narrative: the captivity narrative and fugitive slave narrative. Like other literate New Englanders, Melville did know Cotton Mather's *Magnalia Christi Americana*, which includes such famous captivity narratives as "Hannah Dustan." Melville refers to *Magnalia* as a "mouldy book," and Mather's highly conventionalized treatment of colonial captivity as a form of Puritan conversion would not likely have influenced Melville except in a negative manner.[20] But less conventionalized versions, like Mary Rowlandson's *The Sovereignty and Goodness of God, Together with the Faithfulness of His Promises Displayed; Being*

19. Herbert's reading here agrees basically with D. H. Lawrence's judgement more than fifty years earlier in *Studies in Classic American Literature*. (New York: Viking Press, 1923), 141: "In his soul he was proud and savage. But in his mind and will he wanted the perfect fulfillment of love; he wanted the lovey-doveyness of perfect mutual understanding. A proud savage-soul man doesn't really want any perfect lovey-dovey fulfillment in love; no such nonsense. A mountain lion doesn't mate with a Persian cat; and when a grizzly bear roars after a mate, it is a she-grizzly he roars after—not after a silky sheep."
20. Jay Leyda, *The Melville Log: A Documentary Life of Herman Melville: 1819–1891*. 2 vols. (New York: Harcourt, Brace and Co., 1951) vol. 2, 515.

a *Narrative of the Captivity and Restauration of Mrs. Mary Rowlandson* (1682), in which she narrates her captivity by Narragansetts in 1676 during King Philip's War, is full of uncanny moments in which Rowlandson is simply unable to reconcile her admiration for the Narragansetts with what she believes should be her religious and moral contempt for her captors.[21]

In a rather different manner, the fugitive slave narrative (perhaps the most famous example of which is Frederick Douglass' 1845 *Narrative*, published a year before *Typee*) often plays upon the fundamental social and ethical problem that freedom for the fugitive slave means adaptation to a system of laws and culture (especially reading and writing) that has played a central role in the maintenance of the slave system itself.[22] Although the geopolitical distinction between North and South always defines the map of the fugitive slave narrative, many express ambivalence about the otherwise strict boundary of the Mason-Dixon Line—that is, the strict boundary between chattel slavery and freedom. Harriet Jacobs's *Incidents in the Life of a Slave Girl* (1861) was published too late to have any immediate relevance for *Typee*, but Jacobs transforms her own experiences both in the South and the North into the fictional career of Linda Brent, which is distinguished in large part by Brent's discovery of how profoundly racist the nominally free North is, both in terms of the social practices of racial segregation and discrimination and of an urban economy designed to deepen such racial divisions.[23]

21. See Mitchell Breitwieser, *American Puritanism and the Defense of Mourning: Religion, Grief, and Ethnology in Mary White Rowlandson's Captivity Narrative* (Madison: University of Wisconsin Press, 1990).
22. H. Bruce Franklin, "Animal Farm Unbound; Or, What the *Narrative of the Life of Frederick Douglass, An American Slave* Reveals about American Literature," *New Letters*, (Spring 1977): 25–46, concludes by neatly connecting Douglass' 1845 *Narrative* with Melville's *Typee*: "Douglass, writing as a non-white slave in white America, had to veil some of his message in imagery. Melville, writing as a white American who had lived in a non-white society under the shadow of imperialism, spoke more bluntly when he distinguished 'the white civilized man as the most ferocious animal on the face of the earth.' . . . When Melville's *Narrative* was published in America as *Typee*, these words, along with many other crucial passages, were deleted. When Douglass' *Narrative* was published in America, he had to flee his native land." In 1977, such analogies were revelatory, but by the 1990s the tidy equation of Douglass and Melville must be addressed in terms of Melville's rapid transformation in the criticism from vigorous social critic to representative of Jacksonian values.
23. See my "Between Politics and Poetics: Frederick Douglass and Postmodernity," in *Reconstructing American Literary and Historical Studies*, ed. Günter Lenz, (Frankfurt:

A simple allegorization of slavery in *Typee* would, of course, lead us to one of the racialist assumptions so prevalent in the travel writings of nineteenth-century westerners—that peoples of color are related, especially in the imagination of the western and colonial observer. Even an argument working by way of the common fate of enslaved African Americans, displaced and murdered native Americans, and exploited Polynesians risks equating very different peoples, as well as different historical circumstances.

But if we understand the relation of colonialism and slavery in *Typee* to be exemplified by Tommo and Toby, rather than the Typee, then we get some very different results. First, the bond between the commercial working class and subjugated peoples under colonialism and slavery is foregrounded, especially with regard to the issue of who controls the labor power of the body itself. Second, the experience of the commodified subject under chattel slavery is simulated by Tommo and Toby by virtue of the roles they play in the contest between the French and Typee. However well they are treated, they are still hostages held by the Typee most likely for the purposes of commercial or military exchange. Powerless to control their own self-representations for each other, the Typee, or the competing Euroamerican powers, they fall prey to the most fantastic imaginings and paranoia.

Tommo and Toby's flight from the *Dolly* follows the familiar theme in Melville's subsequent works from *Omoo* to *Billy Budd* that life on board a ship is a microcosm of the tyranny exercised in most nineteenth-century societies. It is the brutality of their captain that drives Tommo and Toby into the interior of Nukuheva in the beginning of *Typee*; it is the weakness of the Captain of the *Julia* in *Omoo* that provokes the mutiny. As Carolyn Karcher puts the matter: "Almost equally relevant to the issues raised in these later confrontations is the ambivalent attitude toward authority figures that Melville evinces in *Typee* and *Omoo*, on the one hand through his nostalgic characterizations of the Typee chieftains who befriended him, and on the other hand through his overwhelmingly negative portrayals of the captains whose tyranny and meanness drove him to desertion and mutiny. . . . the gallery of sea captains Melville displays in his subsequent fiction contains a preponderance of petty despots and weaklings . . ." (*Shadow over the Promised Land*, 7).

Tommo and Toby's escape from the *Dolly* and headlong plunge

Campus Verlag, 1989), 192–210, for how this ambivalence between the putatively "slaveholding South" and "free North" also structures Douglass' 1845 *Narrative*.

through the Marquesan wilderness in chapters 5–9 has the most immediate affinities with the fugitive slave narrative. Rather than welcoming and
nurturing Tommo and Toby, the interior of this natural paradise is the site
of psychological terror and genuine physical suffering. Although Melville in
no way condemns Nature in these chapters, he shares the fugitive slave's
sense that Nature can be a very real threat to freedom. Both the fact and
metaphor of Tommo's wounded leg, as well as the general rhetoric of rebirth in these chapters have received considerable comment from previous
critics.[24] But the rhetoric of rebirth, especially as difficult and perilous, is
common to the accounts of flight in slave narratives for reasons that are
perfectly obvious: after all, successful flight was an instance of rebirth from
legally defined "property" to freedom and self-possession.

The rhetoric of the colonial captivity narrative, admittedly without
the Puritan theology, appears primarily in the chapters (10–33) describing
Tommo's acculturation to Typee society. Where both of these conventions
come together is in Tommo's discovery that as a captive he has a distinct
political value for the Typee and that their interests in him are considerably less flattering to his person than he initially suspected. Whether or not
Tommo ever recognizes that he is protected and even pampered primarily
for his future worth in ransom or other forms of political barter, Melville
makes it clear to the reader that Tommo is property both for the captain
of the *Dolly* and for the Typee. Of the two forms of social life he experiences, Tommo clearly would prefer life with the Typee to the drudgery of
the ordinary seaman aboard a ship like the *Dolly*, were it not that Tommo
begins to fear for his life among the Typee. But what becomes Tommo's ob-
session with cannibalism—the common phobia, if not fetish, of New World
imperialists—is for Melville more reasonably to be understood as the commodification of the body by forces over which the subject has little control.

Such an interpretation of Tommo's experience of what amounts to
the subject's schizophrenia under slavery or colonialism—"I am this body
that does not belong to me"—must take into account his daily relations with
Kory-Kory and his family, including Fayaway. To be sure, Kory-Kory's role
as Tommo's savage valet suggests nothing so much as some colonial fan-

24. H. Bruce Franklin in *The Wake of the Gods: Melville's Mythology* (Palo Alto: Stanford
University Press, 1963) and Edgar Dryden in *Melville's Thematics of Form: The Great Art
of Telling the Truth* (Baltimore: Johns Hopkins University Press, 1968), 42, comment on
Tommo's flight and wounded leg in terms of motifs of symbolic castration and the Puritan
felix culpa.

272

tasy of the exotic leisure to be found by westerners in the paradises of the South Seas, most often at the cost of the native's labor. Carrying Tommo about on his back, Kory-Kory enacts daily that grotesque colonial romance, which in the antebellum South had its equivalent in the cliches of the plantation romance. Even the more benign interpretation of Kory-Kory's relation to his nominal master, Tommo, that suggests the mutual dependence of master and servant in the manner of Hegel's romantic paradigm is subject to criticism for its liberal idealization of the otherwise drudging labor of the colonial subject.

In his ultimate escape from the Typee, Tommo narrates how Kory-Kory, his father, Marheyo, and Fayaway mourn his departure and yet facilitate it. But Tommo's perception of Kory-Kory as the faithful servant, who eventually becomes attached by bonds of sentiment to his master, ignores substantial evidence that Kory-Kory acts merely in the interests of the community and in obedience to the order of King Mehevi. Tommo and Toby both imagine that they are being well cared for in anticipation of a cannibal feast, but the more likely explanation is that both have a different potential value for the Typee. Throughout the narrative, Tommo is asked for information about French troop movements (about which he knows nothing), how to repair an old musket (for which he does "not possess the accomplishments of a gunsmith, and was likewise destitute of the necessary tools" [*T*, 185]), and other practical and cultural matters that might be of use in the Typee's military conflicts with the western colonial forces.

Like the vast majority of European colonists taken hostage by American Indians in the seventeenth and eighteenth centuries, Tommo is a hostage worth healing and feeding for his value in future exchanges for goods or prisoners or for the information he has of the enemy. He is an exchangeable commodity for the Typee, rather than a worker to be exploited for his physical labor power. Although it seems typical Melvillean irony for the reader to discover that Tommo has virtually no value other than his physical labor power, it is also one of the serious points of the narrative: that the system of slavery in the so-called civilized West manipulates far more crudely the value of human beings than what the Typee think they see in Tommo and Toby. Observing King Mehevi's disdain after telling the King that he cannot repair the musket, Tommo reflects: "At this unexpected communication Mehevi regarded me, for the moment, as if he half suspected I was some inferior sort of white man, who after all did not know much more than a Typee" (*T*, 185).

Tommo's liaison with Fayaway seems to argue against this interpretation that the Typee merely indulge Tommo's fantasies of leisure-class authority for the sake of maintaining his hostage value. No other parts of the narrative seem so clearly to reveal the contradictoriness of Melville's liberal sympathies with the Marquesans and his longing to preserve the authority of the white, male, New England visitor. Like Captain Porter and his men, Tommo and Toby are familiar with and perfectly willing to exploit the legends of the Marquesan woman's sexual openness. The voyeurism of Tommo's narration is common enough in nineteenth-century travel narratives, especially when nonwestern cultures are described. Prurient interest in the native woman's body is often disguised by romantic sentiments regarding feminine "naturalness," as when Tommo notes the relative lack of feminine tattooing among the Typee. Yet these conventions are often undercut by other analogies that relate Marquesan and western women. In particular, Tommo compares Fayaway's leisure with that of aristocratic western women: "The hands of Fayaway were as soft and delicate as those of any countess; for an entire exemption from rude labour marks the girlhood and even prime of a Typee woman's life. Her feet, though wholly exposed, were as diminutive and fairly shaped as those which peep from beneath the skirts of a Lima lady's dress" (*T*, 86).

Insofar as Fayaway's leisure is analogous to that of women in Euroamerican societies, then it may be said to do ideological work. In effect, this is what Fayaway's relationship with Tommo accomplishes, along with Kory-Kory's work as personal "servant" to him. Only Tommo's naivete prevents him from understanding that the servitude of a native like Kory-Kory or the sexual favors of Fayaway may well be staged in the interests of the community. Such awareness, of course, would require Tommo to acknowledge a bond between himself and Kory-Kory and Fayaway that is based on their shared condition as those required to work for others. It is a connection that Tommo never makes, but that Melville's narrative repeatedly emphasizes.

Typee society is patriarchal in governance, but domestic polygamy seems to grant women special authority as a consequence of the custom that "no man has more than one wife, and no wife of mature years has less than two husbands" (*T*, 191). The practical purpose of such polygamy is to deal with the fact that "males considerably outnumber females" among the Typee, and this anthropological observation gives Tommo the opportunity to suggest various reforms of western monogamy. Yet women do remain subordinate to Typee men, in large part because the women lack the religious and thus social authority displayed by the men in the tattooed bodies that signify specific ranks. The tattooing of women, like the "skirts of a Lima lady's dress," represents quite clearly patriarchal authority. As Tommo learns from Kory-Kory, women are tattooed when married and then not on the faces, as men are, but on "the right hand and the left foot," which are "most elaborately tattooed; while the rest of the body was wholly free from the operation of the art." As if to make the analogy with western marriage practices unavoidable, Tommo adds: "It answers, indeed, the same purpose as the plain gold ring worn by our fairer spouses" (T, 190).[25]

Horrified by the Typee custom of tattooing men's faces, Tommo recognizes a new danger of his captivity: "That in some luckless hour I should be disfigured in such a manner as never more to have the *face* to return to my countrymen" (T, 219). By contrast, the marriage bond is tattooed on the woman's hand and foot, the means but not the objects of self-representation. Indeed, the tattoo artist whose "painter's enthusiasm" Tommo narrowly escapes rejects indignantly Tommo's compromise of his arm (T, 220).

Whatever horror Tommo expresses at having his face tattooed, he knows well enough the custom among seamen to tattoo their torsos and limbs. *Typee* begins with a risqué anecdote of tattooing that equates the subordination of seamen in the western navies with that of women in Marquesan society. Melville tells us that this event occurred "between two and three years after the adventures" of *Typee*, but he chooses it as our passage into Tommo's experiences with another culture. Receiving the King Mowanna and his queen on board an American man-of-war, the U.S. commodore and a French officer representing French colonial authority in the Marquesas witness the King absurdly arrayed "in a magnificent uniform, stiff with gold lace and embroidery," itself the "tattooing" of the French colonial powers. His queen is similarly marked by colonial rule, "habited in a gaudy tissue of scarlet cloth, trimmed with yellow silk, which, descending a little below the knees, exposed to view her bare legs, embellished with spiral tattooing, and somewhat resembling two miniature Trajan's columns" (T, 7–8). There is a continuity in this description that links the "gaudy tissue" of traders' cloth with those tattoos on the legs; it is a rhetorical continuity

25. In " 'Made in the Marquesas': *Typee*, Tatooing and Melville's Critique of the Literary Marketplace," *Arizona Quarterly*, 48 (Winter 1992), 19–45, John Evelev brilliantly connects tatooing in Typee society with the problem of artistic representation for Melville in nineteenth-century America. As Evelev writes: "Tatooing is . . . used by Melville as a tool to critique colonial practices and the binary opposition of 'civilized' and 'savage' " (25). Evelev focuses primarily on Melville's relation to the literary marketplace of the American 1840s, but he connects this topic clearly to Melville's critique of colonialism in *Typee*.

reinforced by the classical analogy Melville makes between her bare legs, their spiral tattoos, and "Trajan's columns."

Like so many of the classical allusions in *Typee*, this reference to Trajan reminds the reader of the colonial origins of Europe and the Americas.[26] Melville does more than simply warn us that we are repeating in the South Seas the colonial projects of the Romans in Europe and Europeans in the Americas. By rhetorical contiguity, Melville dramatizes just who these new colonial subjects are. Mowanna's queen singles out from the ship's company "an old *salt*, whose bare arms and feet, and exposed breast were covered with as many inscriptions in India ink as the lid of an Egyptian sarcophagus. Notwithstanding all the sly hints and remonstrances of the French officers, she immediately approached the man, and pulling further open the bosom of his duck frock, and rolling up the leg of his wide trowsers, she gazed with admiration at the bright blue and vermilion pricking, thus disclosed to view" (*T*, 8). The scene enacts at once the westerner's expectation of the Polynesian woman's licentiousness and *her* recognition that she shares this sailor's "marked" body. In the "India ink" of his tattooed body, he shares with this woman and the New-World slave the "mark" that is variously figured by the colonizer as race, class, and gender.

Amid the bawdy sentiments of the queen rolling up this salt's trousers, "caressing him, and expressing her delight in a variety of wild exclamations and gestures," Melville also dramatizes a serious recognition between these two actors in the drama of colonization. Inverting the classic scene of recognition, Melville concludes by exposing the licentiousness of the colonial imagination, rather than the two figures he has joined in this figurative passage. It is a display that produces an actual retreat, momentary though it may be, of the colonial forces:

> The embarrassment of the polite Gauls at such an unlooked-for occurrence may be easily imagined; but picture their consternation, when all at once the royal lady, eager to display the hieroglyphics on her own sweet form, bent forward for a moment, and turning sharply round, threw up the skirts of her mantle, and revealed a sight from

26. Melville's sardonic comparison of the queen's tattooed legs with Trajan's Column, that venerable tourist destination, recalls the double significance of Trajan for the modern reader of *Typee*. Not only does his column declare his victory over the ancient Dacians, in what is now Germany, and thus the Roman conquest of Europe, but he himself was converted to Christianity and was one of only two pagan emperors admitted to heaven, according to the early Church.

which the aghast Frenchmen retreated precipitately, and tumbling into their boat, fled the scene of so shocking a catastrophe. [*T*, 8]

The last word of this chapter is, of course, a reference to the Fall, and it is for Melville a reenactment of that Original Sin that is underway in the colonial ventures in the South Pacific.

The "hieroglyphics" that must be read are not so much secret signs as the different modes of historical and cultural domination that Melville's anthropology in *Typee* attempts to comprehend. Is it merely the bawdy gesture of the queen that sends the "aghast Frenchmen" into retreat, or is it the exposure of the unconscious of colonial domination that causes them to flee the scene? In his romance with Fayaway, Tommo substitutes his own version of woman, tattooing her hand and foot in this way as decisively as the Marquesan marriage ceremony. When the Typee taboo against women entering boats interferes with Tommo's ludicrous desire to float with Fayaway on the village lake in imitation of some moonstruck youth from an illustrated magazine, Tommo convinces Kory-Kory to argue with the Typee priests for Fayaway's "dispensation from this portion of the taboo" (*T*, 133). Unable to explain his success in achieving Fayaway's emancipation, Tommo nonetheless insists that "for the life of me I could not understand why a woman should not have as much right to enter a canoe as a man" (*T*, 133).

There is a symbiotic relation between the "ludicrous behavior of the queen" revealing her tattoos to the old salt and Tommo's similarly absurd emancipation of Fayaway. Both actions hint at the possible effectiveness of political coalitions among those traditionally exploited, but both episodes end with merely symbolic victories. The retreat of the French is achieved only by indulging the reader's desire to witness savage lewdness, and the emancipation of Fayaway from the unreasonable taboo is achieved only by entertaining Tommo's desire to act out the patriarchal fantasy of romantic courtship.

To be sure, Tommo himself hardly ever recognizes how his own captivity by the Typee parallels the bondage he experienced on board the *Dolly*. By the same token, he never acknowledges the degree to which his own actions among the Typee often reproduce those of the Euroamerican masters he fled and the Typee rulers he soon desires to escape. In this regard, *Typee* refuses the enlightenment of conversion in the captivity narrative and ironizes the emancipation of the fugitive slave narrative. When his opportunity to escape the Typee arrives, Tommo seizes it with all the military zeal of the colonial masters criticized by Melville. The sentimental scene of parting with his adoptive family and lover, Fayaway, is replaced soon enough with Tommo's murder of the pursuing Mow-Mow. Dashing the boat hook at Mow-Mow's throat, Tommo "felt horror at the act" but claims "no time for pity or compunction" (*T*, 252). Even in this unreflective action, however, Melville pauses to comment, because this "strong excitement" causes Tommo to fall "back fainting into the arms of Karakoee," who represents so clearly the colonized Marquesan (*T*, 252).

Tommo's escape, however, is as equivocal as many of the passages of African American slaves to northern freedom, for what he soon discovers is that he has been "saved" by the "captain of an Australian vessel, being in distress for men in these remote seas" (252). There is a special irony in the fact of Tommo's deliverance back into the seaman's servitude by a ship flying the colors of a British colony, but it is an irony lost to Tommo in his transport from strange to familiar captivity. If Tommo has learned relatively little of his own complicity in the colonization of workers, women, and peoples of color, then the narrative of *Typee* has uncovered the shared system of colonial domination in those moments otherwise identified as ludicrous, horrifying, or fantastic.

Melville finds more than an ironic connection between the Marquesan tattoo artist and the Euroamerican portrait artist; both remind him that the body is always framed and thus marked by cultural codes that are the prerequisites for the colonial projects of military conquest and economic exploitation. In *Marvellous Possessions*, Stephen Greenblatt argues that "everything in the European dream of possession rests on witnessing, a witnessing understood as a form of significant and representative seeing. To see is to secure the truth of what might otherwise be deemed incredible."[27] Tommo is the site of just such witnessing in *Typee*, but Melville repeatedly ironizes Tommo's ability to be such a significant representative. Even as he returns to the unfolding narrative of Western colonialism, Tommo has assumed for the other seamen a "strange appearance." In Melville's very literary treatment of his own experiences, he holds before the reader what Greenblatt finds only fleetingly hinted in Renaissance narratives of New World conquest but elaborated and sustained in such literary meditations as Montaigne's "Of Cannibals": "Where we expect to find two terms in Montaigne—subject and object—we find a third: subject, object, and go-between. And if in the history we have been examining the go-between has

27. Greenblatt, *Marvellous Possessions*, 122.

served often as the agent of betrayal, Montaigne's essay suggests that the go-between can also serve as the agent for a marvelous dispossession, a loss of the fiercely intolerant certainty that licensed unbearable cruelty" (*Marvellous Possessions*, 150).

The very act of narrating his experiences in the Marquesas through the character of Tommo seems to be one way Melville performed his own dispossession in *Typee* as a direct response to what he recognized as every human's proclivity for complex modes of domination. Understanding as he does just how deeply entangled the will to possession and the powers to represent are in human beings, Melville may have understandably wondered at the most effective means to defeat the colonial imaginary as it told its story on the bodies of workers, women, and peoples of color. If Dimock is right that Melville's works after *Typee* and *Omoo* enact the narrative of Jacksonian individualism as a prelude to the new empires claimed by the United States in the West and the Pacific, then the dispossession of that authorial self is what distinguishes *Typee* and perhaps sets it apart from Melville's more "literary" productions. On the other hand, it may be that what Dimock uncovers as a "poetics of individualism" is less the territory of Melville and his times than the horizon of our own deep-seated habits of reading, which would account well for our relative neglect of *Typee* as that "autobiographical" narrative from which the more "literate" Melville himself would seek to escape. Like Greenblatt's Montaigne, this Melville peeps at a strange New World only "as a means of articulating the horror at home" (*MP*, 150). The literariness of this gesture is not so much Melville's ability to sustain the manifold cultural contradictions of the colonial experience, but rather his refusal to represent that experience as a simple or singular narrative. The experience *escapes* him, just as we are to be dispossessed in the act of reading, in the hope (desperate though it may be) of offering another way of seeing to that of explorer, conqueror, trader, and teller.

Mass Circulation versus *The Masses*:
Covering the Modern Magazine Scene

Kathryne V. Lindberg

To the east was the final requisite authenticating landmark: "the old building of the American Philosophical Society, founded by Benjamin Franklin." From this outlook on America, came the *Saturday Evening Post*, with the self-imposed mission to "interpret America to itself."
—Jan Cohn, *Creating America: George Horace Lorimer and the "Saturday Evening Post"*

But I submit that in our time, in the Thirties especially, ours [*The New Masses*] was the purest voice in the chorus of American literary journalism. I believe that history will come to us, more than to our contemporaries, to see America as it was then. We had a bead on the time that went to its heart. Most of our readers felt that. I know most of our writers did.
—Joseph North, *The New Masses: An Anthology of the Rebel Thirties*

With the literal and figurative "image" of Benjamin Franklin as icon, George Horace Lorimer, custodian of the Curtis empire, built and headed a publishing enterprise that engaged Americans, from delivery boys who hoped to win prizes and wealth by selling subscriptions and workers in the *Post*'s celebrated building and ultramodern work environment to readers anxious to invest properly and to consume stylishly in the terms of his well-constructed American Dream.[1] Lorimer thoroughly recuperated and further extended Franklin's "self-made" myth by paying boys per paper and with special merit bonuses for distributing the very organ that would invest their identities in the obfuscation and idealization of American individualism and progress. This interpellation of citizens into an American ideology that can cloak imperialism, reactionary politics, and antilabor policies underwrote the *Post*. And, in this fashion, the *Post* came into close relation with Italian fascism, presenting it as a plausible alternative to international socialism and labor activism in general. It was not until ten years after Lorimer's editorship (1898–1936) that the magazine's own employees were provoked into a crippling strike that yielded reflections on the *Post*'s long successful mapping of the mythical route from delivery boy to executive, which ended in the ideal workplace, a skyscraper not only blessed by Franklin but with the latest cafeterias.[2]

Lorimer's imaginary letters, "Letters from a Self-Made Merchant to His Son," present the face of business the *Post* wanted to show, even as they admit a certain philistinism and anti-intellectualism. The magazine had also serialized Frank Norris's *The Pit*, but by far the most popular and characteristic business persona and serial was that of the Franklinian John Graham, "head of the house of Graham & Co., pork packers of Chicago . . . known on the 'Change as 'Old Gorgon' Graham," who offered practical advice to his son, Pierrepont, a Harvard senior, first in his family privileged enough to go to college and in danger of being spoiled by his father's hard-won money and by intellectual "nonsense" itself. Graham promised his son a hard ride to the top, offering *Post* readers an intimate, but quite fantastic, sketch of the proverbial captain of industry as a friend of the worker and

1. Jan Cohn, *Creating America: George Horace Lorimer and the "Saturday Evening Post"* (Pittsburgh, Pa.: University of Pittsburgh Press, 1989), 39–42, 61–63. This work is hereafter cited in my text as *Creating America*.
2. *US, the Members Run this Union!: An Answer to "The Saturday Evening Post"* (New York: United Electrical Radio and Mechanics Union), 1947. Upton Sinclair's participation in a similar strike at the *Los Angeles Times* led to his own arrest and contributed to his loss of the California gubernatorial election of 1934. See Upton Sinclair, *How I Got Licked and Why, by Upton Sinclair, Candidate for California* (London: T. Werner Laurie, 1935); and Greg Mitchell, *The Campaign of the Century: Upton Sinclair's Race for Governor of California and the Birth of Media Politics* (New York: Random House, 1992).

an upholder of common values and good sense. Like Franklin spitting out platitudes, like Polonius suggesting the proper attitude of a princeling to the public, the practical meat-packer says in Letter I:

> I can't hand out any ready-made success to you. . . . There is plenty of room at the top here, but there is no elevator in the building. Starting, as you do with a good education, you should be able to climb quicker than the fellow who hasn't got it, but there's going to be a time when you begin at the factory when you won't be able to lick stamps so fast as the other boys at the desk. *Yet the man who hasn't licked stamps isn't fit to write letters.*[3]

That Polonian rube hardly corresponded to the reality of Lorimer's own more representative rise from Harvard and privilege to editorial prominence. Yet, as a regular editorial feature, *The Letters* indexes Lorimer's personal rise as revisionary image maker along with that of the *Post*. The fiction of merit rewarded and class lines breached by industry and virtue was and is ubiquitous in popular American biographies and ersatz autobiographies of the Captain of Industry—Veblen early on limned this mythological creature or construct:[4] The Captain of Industry sells himself, as *his* publishing empires sell salesmanship.

Addressed more to those who believe that there is indeed room at the top than to the one at the top who knows better than to believe that simple industry put or keeps him there, this is a brilliant filling of the old Franklin mold. Taking the same sort of risks as Franklin, it is ironic, tongue-in-cheek, and self-revelatory of the fiction of autobiography. The reader is made complicit in the construction of the imperfect fiction. Lorimer's project seems properly endorsed by Franklin's face in cameo, which stands as the epigraph or tacit endorsement to every issue of the *Post*; despite all the differences between Lorimer's and today's incarnation of the magazine, Franklin's face is still on the cover. Indeed, Franklin's epitaph, written in 1728, sixty-two years before his demise, endorses, in advance, the use to which Lorimer would put the problematic founding father's reauthorized public image: "The body of B. Franklin, Printer; Like the Cover of an old Book, Its contents torn out, and stript of its Lettering and Gilding, Lies here, Food for Worms. But the Work shall not be wholly lost: for it will, as he

3. George Horace Lorimer, *Letters from a Self-Made Merchant to His Son* (Boston: Small, Maynard & Co., 1902), 4.
4. Max Lerner, ed., *The Portable Veblen* (New York: Penguin, 1958), 377ff.

believ'd, appear once more, In new & more perfect Edition, Corrected and amended By the author. He was born January 6, 1706[.] Died 17__."[5]

Over the years, Franklins and Franklinisms have been revised, not into a book but into fugitive parts of what sometimes seem like spontaneous Americana or typical Americans, not by a godlike author or reader but by the brilliantly elastic construction, by many hands, of an American type, the provincial who imagines himself in a tradition of philosophical and political exceptionalism fully divorced from Continental decadence or sophistication and sometimes, like Rip Van Winkle, gratefully behind the times. If the historical Franklin was industrious, he was anything but frugal, self-effacing, and abstemious; yet, he knew well the utility of such posturing. Of *humility*, a virtue appended to his slate of the tables and precepts that record his moral *"errata"* (yes, printing errors), he at once confessed and flaunted his failures (?): "I cannot boast much Success in acquiring the *Reality* of this Virtue; but I had a good deal with regard to the *Appearance* of it. I made it a Rule to forbear all direct Contradictions to the Sentiments of others, and all positive Assertion of my own. I even forbid myself . . . *certainly, undoubtedly*, etc. and I adopted instead I *conceive*, I *apprehend*, or I *imagine*."[6] A better—or worse?—legacy than Lorimer's stern editorial policy and market sensitive politics Franklin couldn't have fashioned. In short, one should not underestimate the appropriateness of the revisionary logo on the cover and lead (editorial) page of every issue, "Founded AD 1728 by Benjamin Franklin," whose long defunct *Pennsylvania Gazette*, not the *Post*, as such, was founded then. The genealogically conscious and nativist *Saturday Evening Post* began publication as such in 1898 (*Creating America*, 22).

If, as the *Post* audience expanded to include more folks than could possibly identify with Pierrepont Graham, if the narrative of hard work and rewarded merit became increasingly hard to sell to workers and management—during the Great Depression, say—there was, even in the 1902 *Letters,* an explanation in the form of advice left unheeded. Pierrepont and his generation were to fall for intellectualism, foreign and newfangled ideas, socialism and politics as against *common sense*: "I have felt for a long time that when you got a little of the nonsense tried out of you there would be a residue of common sense."[7] Here, a good deal of the political imaginary is

5. J. A. Leo Lemay and P. M. Zall, eds., *Benjamin Franklin's Autobiography: A Norton Critical Edition* (New York: Norton, 1986), 226.
6. Lemay and Zall, *Franklin's Autobiography*, 75.
7. Lorimer, *Letters*, 30.

revealed, even as a more insidious ideological agenda is played out. Such homey sayings were later to manifest themselves in harsher admonitions against modern art, European softness, and international socialism. But the gentler packaging of the American Dream in achievable bourgeois values and rewards was a staple of *Post* serialized fiction and of Lorimer's editorials. With renovations and updates, the image sold magazines, and the magazine sold the accessories and life-style suitable to the rising individuals who could be turned away from class identification. After all, not even the rich and privileged son of the meat-packer was given a free ride, or so goes the story. Finally, the *Post* sold its stories because it could buy and guide a stable of serial writers, punctuated by the occasional rising star who was to become "a serious writer" and who was thus to become incompatible with the *Post*'s overall apolitical politics and anti-style style.

Lorimer set the pattern early on, so that by the thirties, the *Post* seemed America itself: information versus interpretation, clear statement versus foreign theories, common sense versus special interests. These false and weighted dichotomies amounted to Lorimer's editorial policy, nearly stated as such. For instance, a 1904 *Post* editorial on back-to-basics, practical versus genteel education polemically marks the difference between average American (business) interests and the intellectual aristocracy, which is caricatured as foreign and parasitic. While education was more frequently the subtext than the overt topic, the following excerpt from the old curriculum/canon debate might be thought to anticipate tellingly current defensive strategies of such "custodians of culture," if you will, as Allan Bloom and Arthur Schlessinger, Jr. For the emerging manager and his chosen magazine, Lorimer endorsed a four-point curriculum that grounded subsequent *Post* commentaries, as well as fiction and advertisement. The *Post*'s education manifesto admits of a brief summary, even as it promises a transparency it won't deliver:

> Thinking and writing clearly in the English language. A knowledge of the history of democracy of the emancipation of man. A knowledge of taxation—the great fundamental of human society. A knowledge of the mechanism of business—how commodities are produced, distributed and consumed. (*Creating America*, 39)

During Lorimer's years at the *Post*, specific positions were sometimes stunningly changed: Both declared world wars were greeted with isolationism and finally engaged with martial patriotism. This was not whim but the movement of business out of protective into international labor and raw materials markets. The most remarkable change in the *Post* occurred in the twenties, when women consumers were added to the originally targeted readership of men producers. Still, Lorimer, like the public Franklin, stuck to prototypically *American* useful knowledge. Of course, the *Post* never presented the real information about the workings of business and government to an audience increasingly composed of petit bourgeois American dreamers.

The earliest, perhaps the paradigmatic, slide from image-making to direct political manipulation is the career of Senator Albert Jeremiah Beveridge. From 1899 to 1927, he was a close associate of both Teddy Roosevelt and Lorimer, as well as a *Post* staff foreign correspondent and political commentator. This was before and after Beveridge's brief legislative stint as Republican Senator from Indiana (1899–1911), a career that, largely enabled by the *Post*, was notable for his lengthy orations on behalf of child labor laws and, even more, for his saber-rattling nationalism. Moreover, in the following terms, he was advertiser and advertisement for Lorimer's American Dream (or vice versa) of success through rugged individualism and hard work:

> He experienced considerable hardship as a boy, rising at 3:00 A.M. to plow for local farmers and "welcom[ing] rainy days" when he could remain at home reading. . . . From plowboy, Beveridge went on to work as a section hand, a teamster, and a logger until he was finally able to enter high school at the age of sixteen. A fifty-dollar loan enabled him to attend DePauw University . . . where he rose at four in the morning to take a cold bath and exercise, setting to work by six. When he graduated in 1885, he was the top man in his class. In 1887 he entered law in Indianapolis and the same year he married. . . .
> Elected to the Senate in 1899, at the age of thirty-six, Beveridge was youthful, handsome, forceful and idealistic. (*Creating America*, 49)

Throughout his writing and/or political career, Beveridge was a key figure at the *Post*, which, in 1925, serialized his autobiography. If he was useful for his sensational, on-the-spot coverage of the Sino-Soviet War, intimate details of Teddy Roosevelt's political, martial, and hunting adventures, and an insider's view of the Washington beat, sometime-Senator Beveridge was invaluable as the typical "success story." He mapped this territory in advice and personal reminiscence as early as 1905, in *The Young Man and the World*.[8] Following the logic of what should be a familiar symbiotic

8. Albert Beveridge, *The Young Man and the World* (New York: Appleton & Co., 1905).

or convertible legitimation, he was an expert because he was a politician; he was a politician because he was an expert. But something is lost—or gained—in this particular equation, since Beveridge, cast as an apolitical commonsense candidate, was neither politician nor partisan, let alone an intellectual or an academically trained expert.

As early as 1903, through the good offices of Beveridge, Lorimer met Teddy Roosevelt. From this time on, the *Post* was deeply, if covertly, enmeshed in politics and/or public opinion, as well as in the production of consumers. Roosevelt, whose own rough-riding image concealed inherited wealth and position that might otherwise alienate rising dreamers, contributed to the *Post* and was also a favorite subject of commentators. Typically, while ardently supporting the interests of big business, which was then, as now, decidedly Republican—if occasionally tagged "independent" or, historically, "Progressive"—and, as the rhetoric goes, *against* politics and big government, Lorimer's magazine retained the guise of disinterest and advertised the same in its slate of featured writers. Little matter that favorite candidates themselves sometimes wrote for the *Post*, that magazine was open to different opinions, if not other *differences*. On its pages, the two-party system is at once lauded and travestied, even as it is represented by the leading lights:

> By the time of the 1904 election, Lorimer was able to bring a number of authorities and personages to the pages of the *Post* for the purpose of laying out the claims of both parties and both presidential candidates. . . . Grover Cleveland acted as principal spokesman for the "Democracy," as the Democratic party was then termed, with Beveridge, assisted by Alfred Henry Lewis, supporting the Republicans. . . . Then, as if bending over backward to demonstrate his disinterestedness, Lorimer gave space late in the month to William Jennings Bryan for a campaign plea. (*Creating America*, 55)

Lorimer's early public relations successes adumbrate the more strained depression operations of the *Post*, when Lorimer similarly padded his fiction and/or journalistic rolls with ambassadors and other political, and apolitical, supporters of big business.

By 1929, the *Post* enjoyed average weekly direct subscriptions of very nearly 3 million, customarily paid writers $1,500 for fiction and/or news features, and collected from $8,000 to $15,000 for its artful full-page color advertisements (*Creating America*, 165). During the height of the Great Depression, Lorimer was in a position to do forceful political and cultural work; he did so with antilabor, nationalistic, first pro- and then anti-New Deal economic policy, with pro-Mussolini isolationism, and then with antifascist nationalism. The contradictory sources, filiations, and positions that end in a nativist, racist, politically and aesthetically reactionary "typical American" had to be cobbled together in response to ever-new European socialist and other avant-garde imports, some of which were endorsed by competing magazines. It seems that the *Post* contained, or at least revised, it all. Its success depended on the poor long-term memory and self-interests of the readership that it manufactured and modified as it went along.

It is most important to recognize the successful manipulation of all writing within the agencies of official culture by news agencies and mass-circulation magazines, which were rather transparently Big Business—even as media themselves are big business today. These publication empires had considerable influence over public policy and what would become "the military industrial complex." Patriotic and/or everyday magazines such as the *Post*, along with newspapers controlled by other, only apparently alternative, communications empires (Hearst and Chandler, for example) turned the United States away from revolutionary solutions to labor problems and carried on two "just" world wars and several smaller imperialist wars in Latin America, the Middle East, and the Far East. In considering the cultural work literature accomplishes and the cultural workers who produce, distribute, and price it, one must consider the capitalists' as well as the workers'—those who co-opted and those who resisted—official culture. One might compose a pleasant episode or self-reflection out of progressive and energetically revolutionary fragments, but the full story includes the winners of public opinion who were in the employ of profiteers of American cultural—or anticultural—imperialism. *The Masses* and other magazines did battle against the Lorimer and Hearst images and organizations, and lost! There were reasons for this outcome, and, alas, they persist, aided by wishful, if not willful, neglect.[9]

The negotiable borders between the general interests of "cultured" citizens, working men and women, and those of artistic or political coteries were themselves a point of conflict, a pivot of group purpose and identification—even when the group was a whole nation of "average Americans." Moreover, there was no small overlap between the art and mass circula-

---

9. Cary Nelson, *Repression and Recovery: Modern American Poetry and the Politics of Cultural Memory, 1910–1945* (Madison: University of Wisconsin Press, 1989). Nelson, tending to err on the side of aesthetic justification and utopianism, neglects the popular culture giants/villains.

tion markets, as within the latter there were overlaps among advertising, editorial, and *belles lettres*. Novelists and short story writers crossed over from critical acclaim to commercial success or, most often, the other way around. William Faulkner, F. Scott Fitzgerald, and Jack London, for example, enjoyed the *Saturday Evening Post*'s high rates (as high as $1,500 per article in the thirties) and millions in circulation, though largely for their tales of adventure, personal heroism, and macho rectitude, in keeping with the *Post*'s ideological American self. The usual serialized fiction featured such recurring characters as the stereotypically supportive "little woman," the hardworking husband and ideal family, and, Robert Robinson's favorite creation, the wizened old codger who, dressed like Uncle Sam, provided commentary from an earlier generation about which the new self-made men and wives could feel both nostalgic and superior. The fact is that the more original, now more memorable, works of "serious writers" were bought at a high price—high for the writers, that is. Besides, nothing about the occasional stories of more rugged, stylized, and critical individualisms violated the general thrust or raised the eyebrows of the *Post*'s middlebrow readers.

Nonetheless, the *Post* was the target of the oppositional and/or the socialist press. And vice versa. Early exposés of the effect of the new "mass media" upon popular opinion remain marginal, affirming in some sense the pejorative epithet of "muckraking" favored by Lorimer and his ilk. Take, for instance, Upton Sinclair's work. *The Jungle* quite naturally attracted Lorimer's—aka "Meat-Packing Gorgon's"—special editorial ire for exposing industrial abuses of workers and consumers. Earlier and later, Sinclair was even more of a pest for anatomizing the real operations of big business by paid staffers and freelance apologists. Sinclair named Lorimer's *Post*, lynchpin of the Curtis empire, as repeat offender. His *Brass Check* acknowledges successful purchases of writers during the depression, a crucial time for vigilance yet also a buyer's market for the distractions new and better writers could produce:

> From the point of view of the literary business man, these Curtis publications are perfection. They read your manuscripts promptly, and pay the very highest price upon acceptance. So they are the goal of every young writer's ambition, and the most corrupting force in American letters. Their stuff is as standardized as soda crackers; originality is taboo, new ideas are treason, social sympathy a crime.[10]

10. Upton Sinclair, *The Brass Check: A Study of American Journalism* (Pasadena, Calif.: Published by the Author, 1919), 65.

The financial appeal and corruption of the *Post*, among other popular press organs, is a topic to which Sinclair recurred for decades. Though they are, for the most part, dismissed from both literary and historical canons for special pleading and naked political affiliations, his exposés provide running commentaries on the elective co-optation of press and popular magazines as rhetorical tools, American dream fabricators of Big Business and Big Money. Before 1910, numerous mergers of Big Business, publishing monopolies, and politicians worked wonders in defining, and redefining, American race, class, and national interests and identifications. Lorimer and Hearst—that is, the dominant or establishment press in the 1920s and 1930s—marked the rhetorical achievement and propagation of bourgeois individualism and American exceptionalism as subterfuge for economic and cultural hegemony abroad as well as the destruction of class identification and economic struggle at home. Businessmen themselves, wanting to dominate competition in their own market, the print tycoons knew what they were doing. They knew, too, how to absent themselves from the scene. Journalistic or artistic dissent was suppressed and political discourse was marginalized, since these were neither art nor entertainment and certainly not comfortably American.

In *Money Writes* (1927), Sinclair uncovers the work of American proto-fascist journalists in "covering" Mussolini's rise to power and his support by groups such as the American Manufacturers Association.[11] For good reason, then, Sinclair's writings that announced political agendas not only were tagged "muckraking" but also were painted "red" and "un-American"—and he was not alone. Socialism was intellectual and political; idealized America was at once above and beneath such concerns in the innocuous, but insidious, everyday world. The *Post* is but one example of Big Business masquerading and naturalizing itself as the status quo.

The American buzzwords *democracy*, *emancipation*, *individualism*, and *business* were the *Saturday Evening Post*'s stock in trade, but the particular mechanisms of the market were seldom the explicit text of the popular magazine, whose readership was not those capitalists who made "real" the imaginary success story. Instead, as goes the dreary story of ideology—the Siren-like polyphony or "interpellation" (Althusser) of an Ameri-

11. Also see Upton Sinclair, *Mammonart: An Essay in Economic Interpretation* (Pasadena, Calif.: Published by the Author, 1924), and his exposé of specific proto-fascist policies and affiliations of the Merchant and Manufacturers Association and the National Chambers of Commerce, *100%, The Story of a Patriot* (Pasadena, Calif.: Published by the Author, 1920).

Figure 1: Signed and dated (1 January 1928, VI, refers to the sixth year of his dictatorship) photograph of Benito Mussolini, as it appeared on the authenticating inner cover of America's #1 life-style magazine, 5 May 1928.

can *people*—readers were encouraged to look beyond class identifications and to be transformed into individual warriors committed to "making the world safe for democracy." These sacred, nationalistic, hegemonic words were, and are, redefined and redeployed to suit the specific actions they would justify. The *Post*'s success might well be proved by its relative invisibility. Since it dodged politics, responsibility, and critique along with these, the *Post* is largely remembered for Norman Rockwell's nostalgic Americana (Figure 1).

Against this happy picture, touched up by virtually forgotten artisans of the American image, *The Masses* and *The New Masses* arrest attention. *The Masses* consistently exposed various masks of disinterest in the still-controversial attempt to forge political art and artists. An early critique of the "objective" posture of press and publication monopolies was directed at the Associated Press (AP). In the teens, the AP was notorious for its actions against labor and the International Workers of the World (IWW). Of course, the AP remains the source of most newspaper and television news and "info-tainment." If the AP has cleaned up its act, it has also sanitized the muck that its leftist and socialist critics were able to rake up in the opposition press of the 1910s through the 1930s. It did so legally, in the name of objectivity and professionalism. The libel case launched by the growing monopoly against *The Masses* testifies to the deliberately forgotten or, as Cary Nelson rightly notes, the *repressed* critical work of the political Left (not to say that this particular organ, despite its self-consciousness about such processes, hasn't been variously revised and appropriated). In 1913, before it was possible simply to dismiss *The Masses* for promoting organized, foreign, red (Bolshevik) interests (charges that became stereotyped in the McCarthy era), *The Masses* was charged with libel for uncovering the bias of and the money behind the press coverage of the bloody suppression of miners' strikes in Colorado and West Virginia. A "John Doe"/Grand Jury libel suit was brought against Max Eastman and Art Young, unspecified editor and artist, respectively, in response to one paragraph declaring that *The Masses* would "without delicacy" present a few facts about the Associated Press's affiliations with owners who had violently broken strikes. Their cryptic paragraph about AP collusion with mining interests was accompanied by an allegedly libelous cartoon showing an AP officer pouring inky poison into a pool of "News" with cartouches reading "suppressed facts," "lies," "hatred of labor organizations" (Figure 2).

Appropriately, this case was tried in the press. Curtis's *New York Evening Post*, like its weekly cousin the *Post*, depended on the Associated Press's writers and its growing information network. A look at all this makes clear what was at stake in the homogenization of the news: writers' salaries and a steady flow of news among affiliated magazines and papers. The ostensible middle-of-the-road press struck a pose of objectivity against the politically biased socialist and intellectual small magazines. Newspapers adopted a style by which opinion looks like NEWS, which means something like unmediated, or at least *new*, fact (like the new man?). The exchange of insults between the oppositional press and the AP bears directly on the whole popular journalistic scene, where the AP was increasingly construed

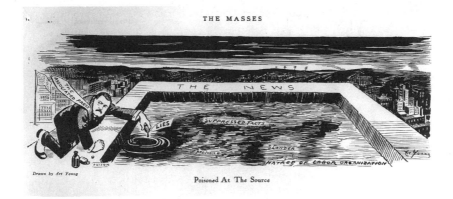

THE MASSES

Drawn by Art Young

Poisoned At The Source

Figure 2: The one of three similar Art Young cartoons about press corruption named in a libel suit against *The Masses*; this appeared in July 1913.

as the source of "objective" reportage. Just so, several *Post* writers doubled salaries and cut travel expenses by also selling stories to the news service. Lacking such resources and cooperation, magazines like *The Masses* were left to comment on this cozy exchange and packaging of information. The indecisive legal case, in which the AP and its supporters accused *The Masses* of libeling, indeed parodying, specific figures in the news monopoly in the interests of pro-labor ideology and propaganda, has wider significance for the deceptive representativeness of mass-circulation organs that claimed impartially to "interpret America to itself." In the face of specious ideals of objectivity and patriotism, which barely concealed media support of strikebreaking, *The Masses* and *The New Masses* proclaimed a commitment to socialism and to the proletariat. Its political and class filiations can be read as easily in its art and poetry as in its editorial statements. Upton Sinclair offers the best summary and ironic rebuttal of the *New York Evening Post*'s defense of the AP and the Curtis empire:

> The personnel of the service is made up as a whole of newspaper men of the finest type; throughout the profession, employment in its service is regarded as evidence of character and reliability. No general policy of suppression or distortion could be carried on without the knowledge, indeed the active connivance, of all these men, stationed at strategic points throughout the world. . . . These members, some nine hundred in number, represent every shade of political and economic opinion, and it is absurd to suppose that a general policy

of distortion or suppression could be carried out without immediate exposure.[12]

Perhaps that seems to affirm the credibility of "objective reportage." After all, some sort of conspiracy theory would be needed to explain the co-optation of so many well-intentioned reporters. That one easily dismisses agency behind networks—*agents* behind agencies—also bespeaks the power and ubiquity of press organizations that even today hold sway over American (and international) public access to news stories and images. The question of objectivity, even of "newspaper men of the finest type," built, for example, by a consensus about some American mission to go beyond class and politics to a better life for all "the People," continues to vex those who would influence public opinion with unpleasant political and economic news.[13] Lorimer was not alone in being aware that politics was motored by the identification of the public with or against class and business interests. As master editor and early advertising genius, he was able to mold American desire through a mixture of the Associated Press and other "objective" news sources as well as through editorial opinion and the presentation of a general success scenario allegedly available to all hard-working Americans. As will become clear, *The Masses* and other avowedly socialist journals could not compete with such organizations, though they were in the business of exposing the political and economic interests that underlay them.

Upton Sinclair gives a full account of how news continued to be "poisoned at the source." For *The Brass Check*, he consulted no less than 4 million words about the libel case. As an indication of the difficulties he encountered in trying to oppose and expose business and/or military interests in suppressing the rise of international labor, Sinclair cites the complex threat represented by *The Masses*. In a sense, given the relative size of the AP and *The Masses*, such confrontations are largely symbolic: Their import lies as much in the slipperiness of the mainstream press as in the persistence of the opposition. *The Masses* continued to support miners' and other strikes, which it connected to resistance to World War I as a colonialist war

12. Sinclair, *Brass Check*, 152.
13. Vide Kenneth Burke's unsuccessful attempt, at the 1935 Writers' Congress in New York, to Americanize party rhetoric, especially from "masses" or "comrades" to "the people." See Matthew Baigell and Julia Williams, eds., *Artists against the War and Fascism: Papers of the First American Writers' Congress* (New Brunswick, N.J.: Rutgers University Press, 1986).

against international labor. Conversely, the AP, the *Post*, and other network affiliates dropped domestic labor issues for a nationalist war to which they had initially objected. Indeed, by the time Sinclair published his account of the affair in book form, Eastman had been forced by the Sedition Act of 1917 to cease publication. The formal criminal charges were "obstructing recruitment" into World War I, a war that, according to Eastman and the IWW, among other socialist and workers' parties, broke international class ties of workers for the profit of military production and under the banner of various nationalisms.[14] Curiously, while the *Post* never encouraged draft dodging, it forsook an ordinarily strictly isolationist, anti-interventionist policy in order to support the war, even more strenuously so after it was declared.

In short, the Big Business view of capitalism was international for management and nationalist for the workers. If big wars seemed like bad business, a militant nationalism could seem the order of the day when market conditions so dictated. Its apolitical posturing, however implausible in the short run, looks brilliantly adaptable over the long haul. While nostalgic accounts and reminiscences of the *Saturday Evening Post* can lament the occasional mistake, even as a fall into politics, they give the nod to America's rising consumerism-as-usual. Wiley old Ben Franklin's signature denomination of sins and vices as errata, marking his profession as editor and his habits as revisionary autobiographer and sinner, might be said to endorse both radical lacunae in *Post* foreign policy specifics and in the general appearance of moderation.

By contrast, facsimiles and histories of *The New Masses*, which resumed publication under that title in 1926, replacing the interim *Liberator*, show that its univocally political and socialist text can sustain any number of interested and legitimizing readings. One recent, nicely reproduced selection from *The Masses* and *The New Masses* announces Irving Howe's nostalgia for pre-Stalinist purity in his introduction of Max Eastman, longest editor of both magazines. Not to let revisionary tangles detain us too long, it is at least noteworthy that Irving Howe, reflecting on his own defection from what he canonizes as the honest, yet naïve, optimism of the early *Masses*, ironically adopts what in the present context might be seen as a version of American exceptionalism. Thoreau, if not Franklin, is his heroic individual pitted against the umbrella of "totalitarianism," which puts communism, fas-

---

14. Joseph North, ed., *The New Masses: An Anthology of the Rebel Thirties*, intro. Maxwell Geismar (New York: International Publishers, 1969), 33. This work is hereafter cited in my text as *New Masses*.

cism, and perhaps a few other foreignisms in the same bag. Of Eastman, and of the "best" of *The Masses'* writers, including those who later wrote for his own chosen magazine, the *Partisan Review*, Howe says:

> They could not anticipate—why should they have?—the traumas of totalitarianism. . . .
>
> For behind them still throbbed the tradition of nineteenth-century American radicalism, the unambiguous nay-saying of Thoreau and the Abolitionists. This tradition implied that the individual person was still able to square off against the authority of the state; it signified a stance—one could not quite speak of it as a politics. . . . They swore by Marx, but behind them could still be heard the voices of Thoreau and Wendell Phillips—and it was a good thing.[15]

If Eastman, too, turned far to the Right after setting the political agenda and oppositional press coverage of his magazine(s) from the teens into the thirties, he was simply too American to do otherwise. Thus, while differently nuanced than, say, the *Post*'s alleged refusal to toe a party line, even Eastman can be enlisted in the anti-Stalinist internecine wars that periodically implode(d) the Left.

The allegedly nonpartisan, if oxymoronically titled, *Partisan Review* version of the fall of the Left is well known. It should suffice here to emphasize *The Masses'* consistent insistence on direct political statement and on uncovering the hidden flirtations of the mainstream press. Joseph North, editor of the late thirties pro-Stalinist weekly version of *New Masses*, assured of his continued political "correctness" and continued commitment to "the cause," suggests something of what remains at stake in the interpretation of the news-art-politics of the polemical little magazines:

> In the Forties they began to rewrite the Thirties, and as so often happens in amending history . . . heroes were reduced. . . . So a new generation was given an image of reality very different from the one we had who lived through it. I still blink when I read Granville Hicks on the Thirties, or any one of the others who were my contemporaries in the days of *New Masses*, and who subsequently decided to follow a different but more orthodox drummer. (*New Masses*, 21)

15. William L. O'Neill, ed., *Echoes of Revolt: The Masses, 1911–1917*, intro. Irving Howe, afterword by Max Eastman (Chicago: Elephant Paperbacks, Ivan R. Dee, 1966), 6–7.

Evaluations of *The Masses*, especially those nostalgic, roughly auto-biographical commentaries on its fall into *The New Masses'* party-line communism of the thirties, confirm the magazine's historical importance as a touchstone for legitimizing and delegitimizing narratives. If the various incarnations, and reincarnations, of *The Masses* still provoke controversy, most would agree that the *Post*, though representative in some ways of the repression of its time, lacks such interest, even as it lacks, for the most part, "literary merit." Yet, its very invisibility testifies to its successful manufacture of America, as a loose confederation of enterprising individuals above politics, suspicious of art, and dedicated to the good life.

Over the years, the *Post* and *The Masses* covered the *same* material, battling ideologically and stylistically on the borders between reportage and the construction of rhetorical/political positions. While strike and war coverage are telling, sports and other heroic stories of typical American boys and the New Man emerging from the masses are more revealing. It is here, over the modeling of personal and national roles and race consciousness, that we can measure the magazines' differential intentions and impact. To stage an exemplary battle, a missed conversation or indirect confrontation, I choose their opposing accounts of Joe Louis. The emergence of Joe Louis as a symbol of Negro power or, in mainstream white publications, as a representative of an emergent race/class identity is no small issue. Not only for black communists and white racists *then* but also for cultural critics and activists *now*—and again.[16] Richard Wright's first piece for *The New Masses*, also his first published essay, is a bristling account of African American reaction to Joe Louis's first great victory. As we shall see, in keeping with that magazine's unabashed political positioning, it is a prose poem to Black Power—not to say a Communist party (CP) rallying call. It marks an attempt, in the contest over "American self," to forge a potent collective force against the bourgeois man.

By contrast, the *Post*'s sports feature writer, Paul Gallico, constructs a persona for Max Schmeling, who, it seems, more than earned his victory over Louis. Wright gives *The Masses* a moving, poetic, mass response to Detroit's "Brown Bomber." Comparison of the Louis coverage cannot be exactly balanced, since two different fights are covered, but the image of black anger against the recuperation of yet another, if foreign and Nazi,

16. See Eldridge Cleaver's differential commentary on Louis and Cassius Clay, "Lazarus Come Forth," in *Soul on Ice* (New York: McGraw Hill, 1968), 85–95.

"White Hope" in the old clothing of the American individualist with professional pugilist's accessories tells a great deal about the two journals. More than the simple appropriation of sports heroes, this case shows that such figures both conceal and embarrassingly reveal the politics coincident with the ideologies of individualism and family values. In 1937, through Schmeling, and that fighter's cultural and racial simpatico, the *Post* quietly endorsed Hitler's use of Aryan athletes. Notwithstanding Jesse Owens's symbolic (much revised) American, democratic challenge to Nazism at the 1936 Munich Olympics, Schmeling looked good to Paul Gallico, the *Post*'s beloved sports commentator. When it came time to praise America's premier black Olympian, Owens's coach ran a series of assisted autobiographies, whose title, "My Boy Jesse," belies its racist paternalism. African Americans, it seemed, posed a greater threat to the *Post*'s staff and readers than did Hitler. Although it was not part of the magazine's style to let money and racism speak themselves as such, it is impossible to miss their gut reaction to Louis—or the even greater threat of a writer such as Wright.

Wright's account is a two-page prose poem/manifesto/report, "Joe Louis Uncovers Dynamite" (*New Masses*, 8 October 1935), about the Baer-Louis fight and ensuing riots of 24 September. Wright is celebratory and unabashedly communist in presenting the revolutionary potential of the coupling of race and class struggle. His prose style mingles dialect and Marxist categories, blurring description and prescription, event and ideal, in a direct call to action against racial and economic oppression:

> "LOUIS! LOUIS! LOUIS!" they yelled and threw their hats away. They snatched newspapers from the stands of astonished Greeks and tore them up, flinging the bits into the air. They wagged their heads. Lawd, they'd never seen or heard the like of it before. . . . It was like a revival. Really, there was a religious feeling in the air. Well, it wasn't exactly a religious feeling, but it was *something*, and you could feel it. It was a feeling of unity, of oneness. (*New Masses*, 176)

Covering the midtown spillovers of enthusiasm into riot, from Harlem to Chicago, upon Louis's capture of the heavyweight title from Max Baer, Wright presents and explains the rioting and looting as the rush of joy into an orthodox proletarian conquest, replete with payback in suddenly inconsequential cash:

> "Who yuh fer—Baer or Louis?"
> A taxicab driver had his cab wrecked when he tried to put up a show

of bravado. In the crush, a pocketbook snapped open and money spilled on the street for eager black fingers.

"They stole it from us, anyhow," they said as they picked it up.

When an elderly Negro admonished them, a fist was shaken in his face. Uncle Tomming, huh?

"Whut in hell yuh gotta do wid it?" they wanted to know. (*New Masses*, 178)

Quite explicitly revising the old figure of the New Negro, as accommodationist, gradualist, bowed, yet upstanding, citizen, Wright turns the generation gap between himself and the writers who played nice to a white audience into the volatile race consciousness and solidarity that threatened readers of such publications as the *Post*, if only by proclaiming its own politics with the CP's masses. Confirming his propagandistic use of literary devices and turning old tropes of difference against themselves, Wright ends with blood, iron, and the promise of "organization, next time," as it were:

Say, Comrade, here's the wild river that's got to be harnessed and directed. Here's that *something*, that pent-up folk consciousness. Here's a fleeting glimpse of the heart of the Negro, the heart that beats and suffers and hopes—for freedom. Here's that fluid something that's like iron. Here's the real dynamite that Joe Louis uncovered! (*New Masses*, 179)

Against this, one might expect Louis and/or his manager to provide one of the celebrity assisted autobiographies in the *Post's* usual manner, but something quite different appeared. Louis's victory over Baer was passed over. A related story, perhaps its ideological sequel, of Louis's defeat by Schmeling was collaboratively written by the German champion and Paul Gallico. The *Post's* intimate account of Schmeling's preparation for and execution of his August 1936 defeat of Louis is longer, calmer, ostensibly more matter-of-fact: more the story of sports hero than of a political event, though, of course, subject to revision for later recruitment of black men into World War II. Deeply ideological and clearly opposed to intervention in the European theater, even as it recognizes Hitler's ascendancy, Gallico's story works on the level of identification. The same *Post* readers who had learned to recognize or misrecognize (as, according to Lacan and Althusser, one actively and appropriately misrecognizes ideology as self-representation) good old American family values are meant to appreciate the intelligence, indeed the industry and upward mobility, of German American dreamers,

Max and his lovely wife. Replete with a few authenticating passages of *Schmeling's* pidgin Anglo-Saxon ("I do not zink so. I tell you somesings, Powl. *Aber*, you write nozzik, yes?"), Gallico's two-piece fluently "average American" lead serial presents "a strange boy. He is unlike any fighter I ever knew. Inside his skull is a brain." [17] Supposedly by his own account, which he asked Gallico to suppress until after the victory, Schmeling traveled to New York months before his own match to supplement his film study of Louis's style by watching Louis knock out Paulino Uzeudun. Schmeling and Gallico appear as focused, apolitical professionals, formalist or New Critical pugilist and sports writer, respectively. [18] The German's preparation, the knowledge that he could train himself to *win*—in short, his "professionalism"—is nearly a refrain. Schmeling testifies, for example:

> I am simply a professional fighter. I have studied my business and tried to learn it. . . . I do not understand . . . why I should be afraid of Joe Louis, or any other man in the ring. I do not understand why any other professional fighter should be afraid of any other fighter. (209: 9, 8)

In an epilogue, Gallico expresses his personal affection for, if not his physical attraction to, Schmeling. The same afterthought displays his reportorial *objectivity* concerning Hitler's challenge when he admits that he, too, is haunted by the "dreadful thing" of Aryan pride. Nevertheless, like Hitler, he is squarely in Schmeling's corner. Hitler is accepted as an enthusiast who wields righteous and exemplary power behind a martial stance and a racial ideology that are only potentially unacceptable:

> After the famous conversation at the Paulino fight, and especially after spending the winter in Germany at the Olympic Games and getting the feel of Nazi Aryan pride—a dreadful thing I have to live with—I sure felt that Schmeling must know he would win. . . . As a personal friend of Hitler and Goebbels, a quick knockout at the hands of the negro would have made them look ridiculous. Germans don't like to look ridiculous. (209: 10, 34)

17. *Saturday Evening Post*, 209: 9. Subsequent references to the *Post* will be cited in my text by volume, issue, and page numbers.
18. "Red" Smith, editor of *The Saturday Evening Post Sports Stories* (New York: A. S. Barnes, 1949), omits Gallico's Louis and Owens stories but says that "Ring Lardner and Paul Gallico could accurately be described as men whose reputations were made as sportswriters for the daily papers." In this way, Gallico is still considered a professional, or "expert" (viii).

Gallico mitigates Hitler's/Germany's threat through Schmeling's positive image, while, along the way, making Louis appear both ridiculous and less than sportsmanlike. Whatever gives Gallico pause, and it seems to be that America is represented by a Negro, he has no difficulty in presenting himself behind the scenes with Hitler's friend, as lunch partner and house guest of Schmeling and his blonde, movie-star wife, Ondra, who "looks enough like June Knight to be her sister or twin" (209: 9, 5). To Gallico's eye, Hitler is just another face in their family picture gallery, there among the favorites in Schmeling's genealogy of champions:

> There is a large signed photograph of Adolph Hitler over the tro-
> phy case, and on the bookshelves stand a large bronze head of
> Schmeling that is not a very good likeness, and a plaster head of
> Dempsey . . . [and] an enormous basket of fast-fading flowers deco-
> rated with red, swastikaed ribbons the gift of Hitler to Frau Schmeling.
> (209: 9, 5)

The Schmelings are a cute couple: imitable stars if only translatable into average Americans. Clean-cut and hospitable, they realize the American dreams of the careerist husband and the tame, yet civilizing, wife. They conform quite readily to the powerful stereotypical American self-image of a Norman Rockwell family rather than to a menacing German/Aryan model. Of the happy couple, one reads that Schmeling

> likes to stay close to her, sits on the arm of her chair, plays with
> her bright hair. . . . At a gay luncheon at which were Schmeling's
> great friend, champion, and trainer, Max Machon, and his pretty wife,
> Rhine wine was served, but Schmeling drank only a bottle of black
> malt beer. He neither drinks nor smokes. (209: 9, 5)

Life-style snapshots of celebrities were requisite in *Post* features, providing easy and deceptive segues from fiction to advertisement to reportage. But there is something more dangerous happening there: The celebrities make real the dreams sold by the stylized drawings of the ads and the overdrawn ladies and adventure scenes of the typical stories. In concert, they sold the attractive, accessible magazine that proffered "American" values.

Two photographs present Schmeling and his wife in rhetorically seductive terms; they are the happy couple upon whom are showered the sorts of gifts advertised in almost every issue of the magazine. There is, for instance, nothing in the text about the Schmelings' wedding, not even a

300

*Story·Book Wedding. A Famous Screen Star and a Nation's Great·
est Gladiator Leave a German Village Church, Bride and Bridegroom*

Figure 3: The perfect couple, the Schmelings, leave the church and pass the Hitler Youth honor guard. *Saturday Evening Post*, 29 August 1936, 209: 9, 7.

vague connection to the fight scenario, but the bride and groom are pictured leaving a country church, passing the badged Hitler youth, accompanied by flower girls. This story fits a template familiar to readers of *Post* stories and advertisements, both of which proffered the stylish bride and the traditional family as rewards to the worker who identified himself as a rising businessman. In keeping with this overall family/success scenario, the caption of the Schmeling wedding proclaims its own instrumental fantasy: "Storybook wedding. A famous screen star and a nation's greatest gladiator leave a German village church, bride and bridegroom" (209: 9, 7) (Figure 3). The deliberately deceptive everydayness of the contradictory construct of Everyman/Hero, or of an *ideal couple* of them, only seems *above* partisanship and politics. Through such happy images, *party* and *politics* were cast as pejoratives that the *Post* and other American life-style magazines hurled at the Left and, less frequently, at the Right.

As for the account of the fight proper, Louis is subjected to all sorts of abusive comparisons that pit "Aryan" brains against "colored" bodies. The blow-by-blow of the twelfth round confirms Schmeling's professionalism. Forget that credibility is at least strained by the fighter's first-person narrative, if not by his persona:

> Funny, how it is I seem to remember every punch. . . . I make Louis miss with a left, and he makes me miss, too, with a left hook. . . . Then he drops his left shoulder and comes in to me with a left hook that is so low that I make no more mistakes about it. I am a fighter and I know how punches are delivered. (209: 10, 32)

Schmeling adds (and, in an author's note, Gallico repeats) the damaging and racist conjecture that Louis, as free of guile as of thought, was simply led by his managers: "Joe Louis is a good boy, and clean, but he does what he is told in his corner. Louis can still save himself and win because of the strange rules which we [sic?] fight in in New York" (209: 10, 32). Schmeling/Gallico positively supports "Nazi Aryan pride" (Schmeling, remember, has "a brain" that makes him both articulate and unusual) by expressing doubts that black athletes can manage themselves, an idea that still enjoys currency in sporting circles. One summary example: "Every man that Joe Louis has met in the last year he has knocked out. He says nothing with his mouth, that colored fellow, he says it with his fists" (209: 9, 6).

Several photographs, reproduced as ringside proofsheets, seem to show Louis delivering low blows, while others simply dish out gratuitous spectatorial violence to the fallen Louis. The only noncombative shot of Louis has him pinned between, virtually dragged by, cop and referee: The original caption reads, "Joe Louis being led to the rubber's table after the twelfth-round knockout" (209: 10, 10) (Figure 4). Only a slice of Louis's profile is visible under a white towel, enough to see his puffy face and downcast eyes. He is out of it, and the readers get to see the process of his being put in his place, as it were. Ten shots of the fight bracket the right and left sides of the page of Schmeling's blow-by-blow; here, captions are extrapolations from the text. Again, there are only those of Louis in bad shape, showing how the "superfighter," according to one of Gallico's interjections, lost "by letting Schmeling cozen him into fighting the way he wanted him to fight" (209: 10, 32). Two captions suggest how far Louis has fallen and with what delight this fall is narrated: "Down goes Louis . . . Just a hurt, bewildered

302

Figure 4: Joe Louis, the loser, is led away by attendants.

boy . . ." (209: 10, 32) (Figures 5a and 5b). The *Post*'s undisguised admiration of Schmeling in American homespun thinly veils the magazine's position in larger political battles and/or class struggle. The very media array of racist, isolationist, and fascist-leaning politics in the metaphorics of sports and the metonymic or representative hero exemplifies, even as it belies, a white American luxury: the *apolitical*. Moreover, many *Post* writers were professional politicians first and contributors later—or vice versa. It is something of a tribute to our national sleight-of-hand "objectivity" that the *Saturday Evening Post* and the likes of the Associated Press, as opposed to, say, *The Masses*, retained the mask—a thin patina—of apolitical objectivity.

It is curious that representatively American national(ist) ideas and habits can be so easily translated and then transported back to the States. Or is it? Nationalism, and a nation's "enemies," can accommodate many interpretations; like Whitman, they can contain great contradictions between real and imaginary conditions and selves. Yet, revisionary evacuations and refillings of symbols happen too fast—or is it too slowly?—to be recognized as such. Franklin = Lorimer = Gorgon Graham = Schmeling. The list of luminaries in Lorimer's pantheon grew and underwent revision over time. In a few years, when the interests behind the *Post* again slid from isolationism into strident nationalism, Joe Louis, standing on Owens's shoulders, was to receive top billing and a representative status radically different from that attempted by Richard Wright. Relying as much on cultural amnesia as on the persistence of American icons, the *Post*'s rhetoric worked, particularly its marshaling of heroes as synecdoches for the American way.

"*. . . I Am Making Him Lead*"

"*I Tease Him a Little . . .*"

"*I Never See So Many Left Hands . . .*"

"*. . . I Have Him in My Pocket*"

"*Down Goes Louis*"

Figure 5a

While the jargon of American cultural and artistic autonomy remained a principle in Lorimer's empire, the *Post* never passed up the opportunity to refill the empty image of the active man. In borrowing from Europe, the *Post* passed over the poets, philosophers, and certainly the avant-gardists in all spheres in favor of a dictator who could be pressed into service as representative—or, in this reading, *simulacrum*—of that strange creature, a fascist bourgeois individual(ist). The *Post* did its cultural work well, even if—*because*—it has disappeared into the "white noise" of yesterday's contemporary, or popular, culture. Soon revised out of the *Post*'s increasingly nationalistic agenda, especially after Italy declared war against the United States, the fascist leader has been made retrospectively to inhabit only the slimiest fringes of American thought. Yet, rather than the exclusive darling of madmen and poets (for example, Ezra Pound), a relatively benign Benito was briefly as familiar as Norman Rockwell.

Indeed, even if it strains credibility, the *Post* tried, in 1928, to dress Benito Mussolini in Franklin's and Whitman's and Teddy Roosevelt's revisionary images. Reviewed from these

September 5, 1936

"*. . . Just a Hurt, Bewildered Boy . . .*"

"*. . . I Got Tired Hitting Him*"

"*He Rolls Over on His Face . . .*"

"*That Means Out!*"

"*. . . So Happy I Have Never Been*"

Figure 5b

later days of media revisionism, the *Post*'s myths and ideology of America might seem silly, but Mussolini's Teddy Roosevelt-like manhood and nearly Yankee inventiveness still shock. With Beveridge and Schmeling as precedent and later incarnation, let us recall a bit—byte?—of forgotten American fascism. In keeping with the *Post*'s use of "experts," no less than a former U.S. ambassador, Richard Washburn Child, would introduce the unlikely Americanized Italian. The place of Mussolini in the very bastion of American nativism (even in verbal slams aimed at Italian, and other, immigrants to America), the appearance of one masterful construct/constructor of the culture industry in the magazine of another, is a notable instance of editing out errata, political appropriation, policy revision, and general mutual legitimation. Mussolini needed American support, and, while usually chary of foreign intellectual trends and fully capable of the nastiest anti-immigrant slams at Italians, Lorimer's organization greeted the centralized power and antilabor doctrines of Italian fascism. Moreover, the flamboyant dictator, a race-car driver and all-around amateur athlete, was a proleptic hedge against the New Deal; even before Franklin D. Roosevelt was in power, the *Post* had begun the virulent probusiness/antilabor campaigns that would be translated into charges of communism—and worse—against the Democratic party.

The details and currency of Mussolini's image, stamped from the Franklinesque mold and Lorimer's-Beveridge's-*undsoweiter*'s success story, was due in large part to a bogus "autobiography," penned by the American ambassador to the Court of Rome from his interviews and manuscripts provided by Arnoldo Mussolini and Margharita Sarfatti, the dictator's brother and mistress, respectively.[19] Mussolini, the athletic man of action pictured on the inside cover of the first segment, was the subject of a ten-part serial feature in 1928. From 5 May 1928 through 27 October 1928, Child's/Mussolini's *Autobiography* appeared with the same titles as the chapters of the book version of the titular autobiography (published in 1928). There are plenty of pictures, *Il Duce* being both photogenic and fond of photo opportunities—even, it seems, as a child and certainly as the founder of his own small socialist, and later fascist, propaganda magazine, *Il Popolo*.

19. Most of the Italian version of Child's edition is in typescript at Harvard's Houghton Library, cataloged as Benito Mussolini, *My Autobiography*. The story of the collaborative authorship of Child, Mussolini's brother, and Mussolini's mistress is summarized in Laura Fermi, *Mussolini* (Chicago: University of Chicago Press, 1961). Her version is different from that of Diggins and others. None of these captures the importance of Child's ideological contributions of Americana and Americanisms.

The photographs are worth examining, especially as they seem consonant with both the sweet and the martial/pugilist images of Schmeling, as well as with Teddy Roosevelt, the generic family man and man of action hybridized into a cuddly roughrider. Lover and auto racer, Child's Mussolini was doubly the updated Progressive Teddy Roosevelt, even as they both indexed other typically American heroes.

Ironies abound in Child's/Mussolini's alleged autobiography as it appeared on the pages of the *Post*. For instance, the authenticating titular claim of autobiography is readily belied by Child, who unabashedly violates the protocols of authorship by a foreword claiming, "For his autobiography I am *responsible*. Lives of Mussolini written by others have interest of sorts." *Responsibility* is a key word in both American ideology and in Mussolini's self-promotion. By such claims, and they are more multivalent than ambiguous, Child puts a paradigmatically American spin on the Italian leader's assertions about being a representative leader as opposed to a partisan or political agitator. Indeed, the autobiographical narrative was so American—or at least so un-Italian—that its version of Mussolini did not appear in Italy until 1971.

Sometime corporate lawyer, sometime novelist and journalist, Child worked for the *Saturday Evening Post* before and after his appointment as American ambassador to Italy (for Harding in 1922 through 1924). By the time of the appearance of the autobiography, he was also a paid publicist for Mussolini.[20] As ambassador, Child paved the way for Mussolini's acceptance into the diplomatic community. He went so far as to advise the Italian about American tastes in (a)politicians. By the time he was writing the autobiography, and was in Mussolini's employ, Child had added a certain rough, yet poetic, flair to his Americanized portrait of the representative Italian. For example, one can hardly fail to hear decidedly Whitmanesque tones in a Mussolini who is both powerful masculine presence and poetic figure on the horizon:

> In terms of fundamental and permanent effect upon the largest number of human beings—whether one approves or detests him—the

20. Upton Sinclair devotes a chapter of *Money Writes* to Child; "The Fascist Career" treats Child's personal finances and/or his loyalties. Far from concealing his connections with Mussolini, Child glories in them throughout *A Diplomat Looks at Europe* (New York: Duffield and Co., 1925). To be sure, Child was something of a loose cannon, and he died in 1932, before canonical delegitimations of Mussolini were in full swing—even in the *Post* of the late thirties and forties.

Duce is now the greatest figure of this sphere and time. One closes the door when one leaves him, feeling, as when Roosevelt was left, that one could squeeze something of him out of one's clothes.

He is a mystic to himself.

I imagine, as he reaches forth to touch reality in himself, he finds that he himself has gone a little forward, isolated, determined, illusive [sic?], untouchable, just out of reach—onward![21]

In this passage, sentiment and language seem to parallel closely an American selfhood familiar from *Song of Myself*. Instance Poem #51, where "The past and present wilt—I have fill'd them, emptied them, / And proceed to fill my next fold of the future.[22] Whitman figured himself as model or manikin for what Gramsci would differently nuance as the "organic intellectual" and as mystical prefiguration of American potential. *Song of Myself*, #52, nearly invited Child's appropriation: "I bequeath myself to the dirt to grow from the grass I love, / If you want me again look for me under your boot-soles. . . . Failing to fetch me at first keep encouraged, / Missing me one place search another, / I stop somewhere waiting for you" (*Complete Poetry*, 247). Kitsch though it might be from Child's pen, it is useful for constructing revolutionary—and counterrevolutionary—heroes.

Child's paean to the Italian dictator, the cross-national, yet nationalistic, ventriloquism by which Mussolini echoes Whitmanian rude eloquence, amounts to a plagiarism of Whitman's representative selfhood. Such ideals and ideologies, however, were made to be reproduced for the masses, even if simulacra are not endorsed by their original author (Whitman?). Subjected to what I confess is a certain (con)textual violence, "Whitman," like "Franklin," is a self-promotional cypher capable of being de-historicized and re-contextualized until it becomes purely formal, simply that which a particular audience wishes, or can be made to identify with. Like Franklin's commonsensical public persona, also an important facet of Child's account of Mussolini's rise, the optative American literatus can be revised for this occasion.[23]

21. Benito Mussolini, *My Autobiography*, foreword by Richard Washburn Child (New York: Scribner's Sons, 1928), xix.

22. Walt Whitman, *Complete Poetry and Selected Prose*, ed. Justin Kaplan (New York: The Library of America, 1982), 246. This work is hereafter cited in my text as *Complete Poetry*.

23. For a most suggestive reading of Whitman's seemingly unlimited ideological appropriations by the Right and the Left, in the specific locus of modern Spanish American writing, see Doris Sommer, "Supplying Demand: Walt Whitman as the Liberal Self," in

Leaving aside partially irresponsible charges of Whitman's proto-fascism, let me suggest that fascism, specifically Mussolini's early revolutionary and internationalist version, is particularly successful at adopting ideological categories from disparate sources. Indeed, as Bataille, more than anyone else, has shown, the true danger of fascism might well lie in its elasticity, not in its authoritarianism or "totalitarianism." Fascism limits individual freedom by creating the arbitrary leader who represents all Freedom. Thus, Mussolini became an abstraction, or blank; in a sense, he became the only free man, or free-floating symbol, in Italy. Not grounded in coherent theory or consistent practice, fascism is improvisational and motivated by *the People*'s—Mussolini edited *Il Popolo d'Italia*, remember—contradictory desire for something like a mass self. For his speeches and scattered writings (mostly magazine pieces and ghostwritten books), Benito Mussolini borrowed what was needed to satisfy—or create—this desire. So, why not Whitman? And why stop there? One might recall Ezra Pound's belated, and rather amateurish, legitimation of the dictator, *Jefferson and/or Mussolini* (1935). The poet, who also mistook Mussolini for a populist, apparently didn't read the *Saturday Evening Post*. While this doubtlessly saved him a lot of bad prose and poetry, it allowed him to persist in the belief that he was defying Big Business and general censorship by introducing *Il Duce* to America for the first time.

Whitmanesque and/or American individualism, self-reliance, nativism, and action as against theory remain potent slogans and ideals for *Americans*—a category elastic enough to include "all nations at any time upon the earth" (*Complete Poetry*, 5). Likewise, Mussolini had his own sense of how to work a crowd, how to be politically and/or poetically embraced by his people. At mass rallies, he enforced the recitative, from dais to groundlings, "tu est Italia."

In addition to demonstrating repressive power through the state police and party thugs, the idealized *Fascisti combattamenti*, Mussolini appropriated and revised successful figures of the state and of the individual. Arguments such as the following, from a 1923 speech of Mussolini's, still prove useful as propaganda against *foreign* theories (Marxist-Leninist) and the class interests that might militate against a certain entrepreneurial and expansionist—or *the* American—myth of "self-reliance":

Reinventing the Americas: Comparative Studies of Literature of the United States and Spanish America, ed. Bell Gale Chevigny and Gari Laguardia (Cambridge: Cambridge University Press, 1986), 68–91.

I do not doubt the good faith of many of those who put forth theories of new arrangements of social, economic, and international struc- ture, but they may all be sure that more important than any of these theories is individual responsibility and the growth and spread of self-reliance in the home and the nation.[24]

That the common rhetoric of (American) romantic individualism was enlisted to describe fascism's practical successes (from vaunted train schedules to violent suppression of trade unionism) against more theoreti- cally based isms, especially Marxism, should come as no surprise. Ameri- can industry was at the same time using these same rhetorical figures and strategies, and Child, calling as well on (American) youth culture, reveal- ingly enthuses about his foreknowledge of Mussolini's March on Rome. The ambassador frankly loved a parade and the fascist anthem *Giovanezza* (youth). Moreover, he authenticates his reminiscence by drawing from that favorite American form, his own journal or fugitive autobiography. Child was undoubtedly revising as he wrote himself simultaneously into high and fascist society:

> Early in the morning J. P. Morgan, who last night dined with us at the meeting of the Harvard Club, came to ask whether it was safe for him to go with Mrs. Morgan on an expedition to the ruins at Ostia. . . . I used this inquiry as an excuse to make new ones of my own of the army corps. Then it was disclosed to us in confidence that the large squadrons of Fascisti were not only following the railway lines but also the seacoast, and were coming up the Valley of the Tiber.[25]

Here, Child treats the violent fascist capture of Rome as a minor interruption of a long—late Jamesian, or at least very aristocratic—Roman holiday. In the speech he made to Mussolini in his official capacity as Ameri- can ambassador, Child goes further. Adopting Mussolini's own revisionary symbology of the *fasces*, which copies or quotes the bound grain, insignia of Roman senators, Child reads fascism as another version of e pluribus unum, an anticipation, too, of Kennedy's mass appeal in "what you can do for your country." Such words as *country*, *you*, *us/U.S.* are remarkably *con- vertible*—in the sense that Whitman used the term for "democracy" and "America" in "Democratic Vistas" (*Complete Poetry*, 930, 981):

24. Barone Bernardo Quaranta San Severino, trans. and ed., *Mussolini as Revealed in His Political Speeches* (London: J. M. Dent & Sons, 1923), 337.
25. Child, *A Diplomat Looks at Europe*, 191.

When one makes the *fasces*, the requirement is to find the individual rods, straight strong and wiry, such as you have found, Mr. President, and so skillfully bound together in the strength of unity. But if they had been rotten sticks you could not have made the *fasces*. Unity in action would have been impossible. . . .

Mr. President, what the world needs is not better theories and dreams, but better men to carry them out.[26]

In Mussolini's case, retrospectively, such figures announce themselves as ideology delivered from above and behind by the State, not arising from the natural ideas of the People. Poets' adaptable ideals work well to conceal the contradictory interests of common man and *dictator*—a title Mussolini adopted as the adequate and etymologically legitimate name for one who rules through powerful speeches and public displays rather than by law or according to political theories and ethical principles as such.

Mussolini's speech writers, among whom Richard Washburn Child can be numbered, were fully aware of the sheer *poetry* that could be discerned in, or alchemized into, the speed, violence, and romantic individualism that were Mussolini's answers to problems of economic and political theory and praxis. One also finds the martial bluster of Italian Futurist manifestos and poetry in the speeches transposed into the autobiography. For example, in "New Paths" (201: 10), one reads again the text(ure) of Mussolini as if it were the Italian State stitched together from the very body parts of the masses:

I am lock-stitched into the fabric. It and myself are woven into one. Other men may find romance in the fluttering leaves on a bough: to me, whatever I might have been, destiny and myself have made me one whose eyes, ears, all senses, all thought, all time, all energy must be directed at the trunk of the tree of public life.

The poetry of my life has become the poetry of construction. The romance of my existence has become the romance of measures, policies, and the future of a State. These, to me, are redolent with drama.[27]

The real attraction Mussolini held for American and international business interests was his rhetorical struggle and police action against class identification and class struggle. The Fascist Corporate State, on paper,

---

26. San Severino, *Mussolini as Revealed in His Political Speeches*, 338.
27. Child, *A Diplomat Looks at Europe*, 223.

if not in increasingly repressive action, promised an alternative to Marxist theory, communism, and other international labor organizations. This utility is not a departure from the highly figurative "rhetoric" of his speeches or the "poetry" of his person but a charged call to nationalistic peace over class warfare. Here, the *Autobiography* slips into third-person clarity in explaining such things:

> Mussolini's plans included the complete end of all class struggle in the interest of the State, brought about by the Corporate Laws which scholars and philosophers of the Fascist revolution were working out under his leadership. Peace was necessary, peace between employers and employees, between landlords and peasants, but not peace by violence or repression, not peace by machine-guns and gendarmes, but through a new conception of social justice. The interest of the State was supreme.[28]

In the *Post*'s coverage of Mussolini, Child and others routinely pitted Marxist intellectualism against the practical accomplishments of *Il Duce*: foreign theories against the universal language of American action and personal industry. The contrasts remain familiar, even in the present Cold War thaw and/or after the death of global theory.

Mussolini was but one of many tools in America's and/or international capital's renewable legitimation game that reached crisis proportion between the world wars and during the depression. There was a good deal of refocusing on the best public image, and I don't intend a sensationalistic guilt by association, but the cultural work—indeed, the "cultural poetics" (a phrase Mussolini suggests in quite different terms before its New Historical coinage)—of the *Post* was varied and stellar. During the time that Mussolini's story was serialized, there appeared stories about Lindbergh, an autobiography by way of anecdote and interview of Eddie Cantor, as well as the patriotic, reactionary editorials and humorous pieces of Will Rogers.

We have seen that Lorimer's general nativist, commonsense pose admitted the likes of the Italian dictator; given the doctrine—or antidoctrine—of action over politics and practice over theory so ingrained in American prejudice, there is no real inconsistency here. It simply is not the case that there is a theory-free praxis any more than an *apolitical* consensus. In this vein, I offer the driving denials of Mussolini, as something of a shocking prose poem consonant with Whitman's stab at philosophical and political

28. Child, *A Diplomat Looks at Europe*, 287.

definition, "very well, I contradict myself" (*Complete Poetry*, 247). If Whitman's contradictions seem to have less theoretical weight and surely less political danger, they nevertheless authorize the action rhetoric of those such as Mussolini:

> Anti-positivistic but positive; neither skeptical nor agnostic; neither pessimistic nor supinely optimistic as are, generally speaking, the doctrines (all negative) which place the center of life outside man; whereas, by the exercise of his free will, man can and must create his own world.
>
> Fascism wants man to be active and to engage in action with all his energies.[29]

In a sense, I have taken the long way around to say that one must negotiate carefully the terrain of poetic and political idealizations; this will always involve a necessary blindness to the scriptive future, not to mention to the past. I have a good deal more to say about the commerce between poetry and politics, between *poetics* (recall that *poeta*, in Latin, means maker—or fabricator) and revisionary or ideological identities. I have also wanted to suggest that as dangerously flexible as the myths of American selfhood can be, they often carry along with themselves a critique. This is to say that Whitman, as much as he might serve as source for fascism's humanistic legitimation, also usefully demarcates the contested, or revisionary, supplement of a peculiarly American "selfhood" faced by Whitman as he walks along the shore: "Death, death, death, death, death"—"Out of the Cradle Endlessly Rocking."

29. Benito Mussolini, *The Doctrine of Fascism* (Firenze: Grafici A. Vallecchi, 1936), 9.

Contributors

Jonathan Arac is professor of English at the University of Pittsburgh. He has completed a contribution to the forthcoming *Cambridge History of American Literature* and is currently working on a book, *"Huckleberry Finn" and the Functions of Criticism*, to which the essay in this issue contributes.

Lauren Berlant is associate professor of English at the University of Chicago and a coeditor of *Critical Inquiry*. She is the author of *The Anatomy of National Fantasy: Hawthorne, Utopia, and Everyday Life* and related essays on the cultural/sexual politics of national identity. Her current project, *The Female Complaint*, engages the sentimental identity politics of American "women's culture" since the 1840s.

Robert J. Corber is assistant professor of English at Chatham College. His essay is part of a book on Hitchcock, tentatively entitled *In the Name of National Security: Hitchcock and the Political Construction of Gender*. In addition to his work on Hitchcock, he has also written about romanticism and homophobia.

Elizabeth Freeman is a graduate student in the Department of English at the University of Chicago.

Kathryne V. Lindberg, currently associate professor at Wayne State University in Detroit, has also taught modern literature, theory, African-American and American culture at Harvard, Columbia, and UCLA. Her writings on American culture, High Modernism, and cultural criticism include *Reading Pound Reading: Modernism after Nietzsche*; and two books in progress—*The Forbidden "Subject" of American Fascism* and a co-edited volume of essays, *America's (Post) Modernisms: Essays Ad-*

dressed to Joseph N. Riddel. The present work on Jean Toomer is part of a larger study of American poetic, racial and national identity crises, *The Ideological "I": Whitmanian Strains in American Poetics*, comprising essays on Whitman, Du Bois, Bob Kaufman, Gwendolyn Brooks, and others.

John T. Matthews is associate professor of English at Boston University. He is the author of *The Play of Faulkner's Language* and *"The Sound and the Fury": Faulkner and the Lost Cause.* He is editor of *The Faulkner Journal* and is currently working on a book about frame narrative in Southern fiction.

Alan Nadel is associate professor in the Department of Language, Literature, and Communication at Rensselaer Polytechnic Institute. He is the author of *Invisible Criticism: Ralph Ellison and the American Canon.* His essay on Alice Walker won the 1988 award for the best essay published in *Modern Fiction Studies*, and his essays on contemporary American literature have appeared in many journals. This essay is part of a book he is completing entitled *Containing History: Narratives of American Culture in the Atomic Age.*

Patrick O'Donnell is the Eberly Family Professor of American Literature at West Virginia University. He is the author of *Echo Chambers: Figuring Voice in Modern Narrative* (forthcoming), *Passionate Doubts: Designs of Interpretation in Contemporary American Fiction*, and *John Hawkes.* He is the editor of *New Essays on "The Crying of Lot 49"* and coeditor of *Intertextuality and Contemporary American Fiction.* He is currently working on a book about cultural paranoia and contemporary fiction.

Daniel T. O'Hara is professor of English at Temple University and the author of three books and the editor or coeditor of two others. He has recently completed a new book entitled *Radical Parody: American Culture and Critical Agency After Foucault*, from which his essay in this issue is taken.

Donald E. Pease is professor of English and holds the Ted and Helen Geisel Third Century Professorship in the Humanities at Dartmouth College. He was a Guggenheim Fellow for 1989–1990. He is the author of two books: *Visionary Compacts: American Renaissance Writings in Cultural Contexts* and *Deterrence Pacts: Formation of the Canon in the Cold War Era.* He is the editor of *American Renaissance Reconsidered* and *New Critical Essays on "The Rise of Silas Lapham."* He is also the editor for the general book series, *New Americanists*, published by Duke University Press.

Ross Posnock is professor of English at the University of Washington. He is the author of *Henry James and the Problem of Robert Browning* and *The Trial of Curiosity: Henry James, William James, and the Challenge of Modernity.*

John Carlos Rowe teaches the literatures and cultures of the United States at the University of California, Irvine, where he is also the director of the Critical Theory Institute. His most recent books include *The Vietnam War and American Culture,*

314

coedited with Rick Berg, and *At Emerson's Tomb: The Politics of Literary Modernism in the United States*.

Rob Wilson, author of *American Sublime: The Genealogy of a Poetic Genre* and *Waking in Seoul*, serves as the general editor for the SUNY Series on the Sublime. He teaches literature, critical theory, and creative writing in the English department at the University of Hawaii at Manoa.

Index

Library of Congress Cataloging-in-Publication Data
National identities and post-Americanist narratives /
Donald E. Pease, editor.
p.   cm. — (New Americanist)
"Text of this book originally published without the
present preface, index, and essays by Lindberg and
Rowe as Vol. 19, No. 1 of boundary 2"—T.p. verso.
Includes index.
ISBN 0-8223-1477-0 (cloth). — ISBN 0-8223-1492-4
(pbk. : alk. paper)
1. American literature—History and criticism.
2. National characteristics, American, in literature.
3. Motion pictures—United States—History and
criticism.   4. National characteristics, American, in
motion pictures.   5. United States—Intellectual life.
6. Minorities in motion pictures.   7. Minorities in
literature.   8. Narration (Rhetoric)   I. Pease,
Donald E.   II. Series.
PS169.N35N37   1994
813.009—dc20   93-49689 CIP